THE ACTS OF THOMAS

SUPPLEMENTS TO
NOVUM TESTAMENTUM

VOLUME CVIII

THE ACTS OF THOMAS

INTRODUCTION, TEXT, AND COMMENTARY

SECOND REVISED EDITION

by

A.F.J. KLIJN

BRILL
LEIDEN · BOSTON
2003

This book is printed on acid-free paper.

First edition: 1962.

Library of Congress Cataloging-in-Publication Data

Acts of Thomas. English.
  The acts of Thomas : introduction, text, and commentary by A.F.J. Klijn. –
2nd rev. ed.
    p. cm. — (Supplements to Novum Testamentum, ISSN 0167-9732 ; v. 108)
  Includes bibliographical references and index.
  ISBN 90-04-12937-5 (alk. paper)
    I. Klijn, Albertus Frederik Johannes. II. Title. II. Series.

BS2880.T4A3 2003
299'.925–dc21

2003052100

ISSN   0167-9732
ISBN   90 04 12937 5

CONTENTS

PREFACE TO SECOND EDITION

This is the second edition of "The Acts of Thomas. Introduction—
Text—Commentary", in: *Supplements to Novum Testamentum* V, Leiden
1992. It was about a century prior to that time that a commentary
had last appeared on this work. For that reason I had to go into a great
variety of subjects.

I am grateful that it is possible to edit a second impression of this
work. The reader will notice that the Commentary can be compared
with that in the first impression. It may be that some of the references
to books and articles are of an early date, but they remind us of a period
during which important subjects were intensively dealt with.

However, it appeared necessary to change the contents of the Introduction extensively. In the earlier text we were supposed to examine
a number of subjects which have since become independent fields of
study.[1] This means that we are not going into the history of the text.
We limit ourselves to the Syriac and Greek versions in so far as it
is necessary to understand the commentary.[2] We have to give up the
idea of going into the beginnings of Christianity in Edessa.[3] In the past

---

[1] See, for example, Fr. Bovon *e.a.*, "Les actes apocryphes des apôtres. Christianisme
et monde païen", in: *Publications de la Faculté de Théologie de l'Université de Genève* 4, Genève
1981; J.H. Charlesworth, *The New Testament Apocrypha and Pseudepigrapha*, Metuchen,
N.J., and London 1987; *Apocrypha*, Revue Internationale des Littératures Apocryphes,
Brepols I 1990 etc.; *Apocryphes*. Collection de poche de l'AELAC, and the Series *Corpus
Christianorum, Series Apocryphorum*, Brepols. The Acts of Thomas were published by
M. Erbetta, *Gli Apocrifi del Nuovo Testamento II: Atti e Leggende*, Torino 1966 313–374;
L. Moraldi, *Apocrifi del Nuovo Testamento II*, Torino 1971, 1125–1350; A.J. Festugière,
Actes Apocryphes de Jean et de Thomas, Genève 1983; H.J.W. Drijvers, "Thomasakten",
in: *Neutestamentliche Apokryphen II*, Tübingen 1989 (5. Auflage), 289–367, cf. The English
Translation of this work by R.Mcl. Wilson Cambridge and Louisville 1991 and 1993, II,
322–411; J.K. Elliott, *The Apocryphal New Testament*, Oxford 1993, 439–511, and F. Bovon
and P. Geoltrain, *Écrits apocryphes chrétiens* I, Paris 1997, 1321–1470.

[2] In the editions of Apocryphal Acts in *Corpus Christianorum, Series Apocryphorum* the
textual history of the various Acts are thoroughly dealt with. We expect the same in the
forthcoming volume about the Acts of Thomas.

[3] Especially I want to refer to the contributions of H.J.W. Drijvers, of which I
mention *East of Antioch*, London 1984 and the articles "Syrian Christianity and Judaism",
in: *The Jews among Pagans and Christians in the Roman empire*, ed. by Judith Lieu *e.a.*,

forty years books and articles have appeared on this subject which have carried the study far beyond the scope of this commentary. It appears that the relationship between Thomas and India is much more part of the study of Church History than of apocryphal literature.[4] Next we decided not to go into the relationship between the Acts of Thomas and the other four ancient Acts. In the first place this would make the study of all these Acts necessary but it would especially call for a discussion of the narrative element which is separately studied in some important books and articles.[5] Finally we refrained from examining the complicated relationship between the contents of the Acts of Thomas and Manichaeism. Also here we can refer to some interesting studies.[6]

Nevertheless the Introduction to the commentary consists of a number of detailed summaries which are meant to elucidate the character of this work. I assume that they, together with the commentary, can be used as the basis of studies on, for example, the christology and liturgy of the Eastern Church.

London and New York 1992, 124–146; "Syriac Culture in Late Antiquity. Hellenism and Local Traditions", in: *Mediterraneo Antico* I 1998, 95–113, and "Thomas, Apostel", in: *Theologische Realenzyklopädie*, Band XIII, 430–433.

[4] L.P. van den Bosch, "India and the Apostolate of St. Thomas", in: *The Apocryphal Acts of Thomas*, ed. by J.N. Bremmer, Leuven 2001, 125–148, gives an extremely well-balanced survey of the research at the moment.

[5] We may refer to L. van Kampen, *Apostelverhalen*, Dissert. Utrecht 1990, and apart from many other publications to W. Rordorf, "*Terra Incognita*. Recent Research on Christian Apocryphal Literature, especially on some Acts of Apostles", in: *Lex Orandi—Lex Credendi*, Freiburg 1993, 432–438, and István Czachesz, "*Apostolic Commission Narratives*", in: the Canonical and Apocryphal Acts of the Apostles, Diss. Utrecht 2002.

[6] See P. Nagel, "Die apocryphen Apostelakten des 2. und 3. Jahrhunderts in der manichäischen Literatur", in: *Gnosis und Neues Testament*, herausgeg. von K.-W. Tröger, Gütersloh 1973, 149–182; J.-D. Kaestli, "L'utilisation des Actes Apocryphes des Apôtres dans le manichéisme", in: *Gnosis and Gnosticism*, in: *Nag Hammadi Studies* VIII, Leiden 1977, 107–116, and P.-H. Poirier, "Les Actes de Thomas et le manichéisme", in: *Apocrypha* 9 1998, 263–287.

ABBREVIATIONS

Achilles Tatius, ed. Gaselee, in: *Loeb Classical Library* 45, London 1917.

Acts of Paul, ed. Schmidt, in: C. Schmidt, *Acta Pauli*, Glückstadt und Hamburg 1936.

Agnad Rosnan, ed. M. Boyce, in: M Boyce, "The Manichaean Hymn–Cycles in Parthian", in: *London Oriental Series* 3, Oxford 1954.

Akhmim-fragment, ed. Dieterich, in: A Dieterich, *Nekyia*, Leipzig–Berlin 1913 (2. Aufl.).

Aphraates, *dem.*, ed. Parisot, in: *Aphraatis Sapientis Persiae Demonstrationes*, ed. I. Parisot, in: *Patrologia Syriaca* I I et II, Parisiis 1894 et 1907.

Arabic. ed. Smith Lewis, in: A. Smith Lewis, *Acta Mythologica Apostolorum*, in: *Horae Semiticae* III and IV 1904.

Badger, *Nestorians*, in: G.P. Badger, *The Nestorians and their Rituals*, London 1852, 2 vols.

Bar Hebr., *Book of the Dove* and *Ethikon*, in: "Bar Hebraeus's Book of the Dove together with some Chapters from his Ethikon" by A.J. Wensinck, in: *De Goeje Fund* IV, Leiden 1919.

W. Bauer, *Leben Jesu*, in: W. Bauer, *Das Leben Jesu im Zeitalter der neutestamentlichen Apokryphen*, Tübingen 1909.

Baur, *Manich. Religionssystem*, in: F.C. Bauer, *Das manichäische Religionssystem nach den Quellen neu untersucht und entwickelt*, Göttingen 1831 (Neudruck 1928).

BKV, in: *Bibliothek der Kirchenväter*, Kempten.

B.L.: British Library, London, with the Syriac manuscript in the Acts of Thomas edited by W. Wright, *Apocryphal Acts of the Apostles*, London–Edinburgh 1871, 2 vols.

Book of the Bee, ed. E.A. Wallis Budge, in: *Anecdota Oxoniensia, Sem. Series* I, Pt. II, Oxford 1886.

Bornkamm, *Mythos*, in: G. Bornkamm, "Mythos und Legende in den apokryphen Thomas–Akten", in: *Forschungen zur Religion und Literatur des Alten und Neues Testaments.* 40, 1933.

Bonsirven, *Le Judaisme*, in: J. Bonsirven, *Le Judaisme Palestinien au Temps de Jésus-Christ*, Paris 1934 and 1935, 2 vols.

Bovon *e.a.*, *Les Actes Apocryphes*, in: "Les Actes Apocryphes", ed. F. Bovon *e.a.*, in: *Publications de La Faculté de Théologie de l'Université de Genève* 4, Genève 1981.

Bultmann, *Kommentar Johannes*, in: R. Bultmann, "Das Evangelium des Johannes", in: *Kritisch-Exegeischer Kommentar über das Neue Tstament*, 2. Abt. Göttingen 1941 etc.

Burkitt, *Evangelium da-Mephrreshe*. in: F.C. Burkitt, *Evangelium da-Mepharreshe*, Cambridge 1904, 2 vols.

Charles II, in: *The Apocrypha and Pseudepigrapha of the Old Testament in English* II: *Pseudepigrapha*, ed. by R.H. Charles, Oxford 1913.

Chronicon Edessenum, ed. Hallier, in: L. Hallier, "Untersuchungen über die Edessenische Chronik", in: *Texte und Untersuchungen zur Geschichte der altchristlichen Literatur* 9.1, Leipzig 1892.

Constitutiones Apostolorum, in: *Didascalia et Constitutiones Apostolorum* ed. F.X. Funk, Paderbornae 1905.

Corpus Hermeticum, in: A.D. Nock and A.J. Festugière, *Corpus Hermeticum*, Paris I and II 1945 and III and IV 1954.

Diodorus of Tarsus, ed. Abramowski, in: R. Abramowski, "Der theologische Nachlass des Diodor von Tarsus", in: *Zeitschrift für die neutestamentliche Wissenschaft und die Kunde der älteren Kirche*. 42 1949, 19–69.

Doctrine of Addai, ed. Phillips, in: G. Phillips, *The Doctrine of Addai*, London 1876.

ed. Becker, in: J. Becker, "Die Testamente der zwölf Patriarchen", in: *Jüdische Schriften aus hellenistisch-römischer Zeit* III 1, Gütersloh 1974.

ed. Böttrich, in: Chr. Böttrich, "Das slavische Henochbuch", in: *Jüdische Schriften aus hellenistisch-römischer Zeit* V 7, Gütersloh 1995.

ed. Brightman, in: F.E. Brightman, *Liturgies Eastern and Western*, vol. I: *Eastern Liturgies*, Oxford 1896.

ed. Burchard, in: Chr. Burchard, "Joseph und Asenath", in: *Jüd. Schr. aus hell.-röm. Zeit* II 4, Gütersloh 1983

ed. Duensing, in: H. Duensing, *Epistula Apostolorum*, in: *Kleine Texte* 152, Bonn 1925.

ed. Elliott, in: J.K. Elliott, *The Apocryphal New Testament*, Oxford 1993.

ed. Gaster, in: M. Gaster, "Hebrew Visions of Hell and Paradise", in: *Journal of the Asiatic Society*. 1893, 571–611.

ed. L. Goldschmidt, in: L. Goldschmidt, *Der Babylonische Talmud*, Berlin 1964–1967, 9 vols.

ed. Goodspeed, in: E.J. Goodspeed, *Die ältesten Apologeten*, Göttingen 1914.

ed. Hammershaimb, in: E. Hammershaimb, "Das Martyrium Jesajas", in: *Jüdische Schriften aus hellenistisch-römischer Zeit* II 1, Gütersloh 1973.

ed. Janssen, in: E. Janssen, "Testament Abrahams", in: *Jüdische Schriften aus hellenistisch-römischer Zeit* III 2, Gütersloh 1975.

ed. Merk und Meiser, in: O. Merk und M. Meiser, "Das Leben Adams und Evas", in: *Jüdische Schriften aus hellenistisch-römischer Zeit* II 5, Gütersloh 1998.

ed. Riessler, in: P. Riessler, *Altjüdische Schrifttum ausserhalb der Bibel*, Darmstadt 1966 (reprint).

ed. Robinson, in: *The Nag Hammadi Library in English*, ed. J.M Robinson, Leiden 1977.

ed. Schmidt–Till, in: *Koptisch-gnostische Schriften* I, herausgeg. von C. Schmidt, 2. Aufl. bearbeitet von W. Till, Berlin 1954.

ed. von Tischendorf, in: K. von Tischendorf, *Apocalypses Apocryphae*, Leipzig 1866 (reprint 1966),

ed. Uhlig, in: "Das Äthiopische Henochbuch", in: *Jüdische Schriften aus hellenistisch-römischer Zeit* V 6, Gütersloh 1984.

ed. Zelzer, in: K. Zelzer, "Die alten Lateinischen Thomasakten", in: *Texte und Untersuchungen zur Geschichte der altchristlichen Literatur* 122, Berlin 1977.

Ephrem, ed. Beck, in: *Corpus Scriptorum Christianorum Orientalium*.

Ephrem, ed. Lamy, in: T.J. Lamy, *Sancti Ephraemi Syri Hymni et sermones*, Mecheliniae I 1882 and IV 1902.

Ephrem, ed. Mitchell, in: *S. Ephraim's Prose Refutations of Mani, Marcion and Bardaisan*, ed. C.W. Mitchell, London–Oxford I 1912 and C.W. Mitchell, A.A. Bevan and F.C. Burkitt II 1921.

Ephrem, *Rede über die Auferweckung des Lazarus*, in: "Des heiligen Ephräm des Syrers ausgewählte Schriften" I, ed. O. Bardenhewer and S. Euringer, in: *Bibliothek der Kirchenväter* 37, Kempten 1919, 165–180.

Erklärung des Evangeliums, ed. Schäfers, in: "Eine altsyrische antimarkionitische Erklärung von Parabeln des Herrn", ed. J.J. Schäfers, in: *Neutestamentliche Abhandlungen*. VI 1–2, Münster 1917.

Excerpta ex Theodoto, in: Clément d'Alexandrie, "Extraits de Théodote", ed. Sagnard, in: *Sources chrétiennes* Paris 1948.

Flügel, *Mani*, in: G. Flügel, *Mani, seine Lehre und seine Schriften—aus dem Fihrist*, Leipzig 1962.

Festugière, in: A.J. Festugière, *La révélation d'Hermès Trismégiste*, Paris 1944–1954, 4 vols.

Gen.R., ed. Freedman, in: *Midrash rabbah* ed. H. Freedman and M. Simon: *Genesis* in two volumes by H. Freedman, London 1939.

Gesch. von Joseph d. Zimmermann, ed. Morenz, in: S. Morenz, "Die Geschichte von Joseph dem Zimmermann", in: *Texte und Untersuche.* 56, 1951.

Ginzberg, *Legends of the Jews,* in: L. Ginzberg, *The Legends of the Jews,* Philadelphia, 7 vols, from 1909 in many impressions.

Ginza, in: M. Lidzbarski, *Ginza,* Göttingen–Leipzig 1925.

Gnost. Adamschr., ed. Preuschen, in: E. Preuschen, *Die apokryphen gnostischen Adamschriften,* Giessen 1900.

Hom. sur la Virginité, ed. Amand–Moons,in: "Homilie sur la Virginité" ed. A. Amand et M. Ch. Moons, in: *Revue Bénédictine* LXIII 1953, 34–69.

Huwidagman, ed.Boyce. See Agnad Rosnan, ed. Boyce.

Irenaeus, *Demonstratio,* ed. Froidevaux, in: "Irénée de Lyon, Démonstration de la Prédication Apostolique", par L.M. Froidevaux, in: *Sources chrétiennes* 62, Paris 1959.

Isaac of Antioch, "Dritte Gedicht über die Menschwerdung des Herrn", in: "Ausgewählte Schriften der syrischen Dichter" ed. P.S. Landersdorfer, in: *Bibliothek der Kirchenväter* 6, Kempten 1912, 139–150.

Isaac of Antioch, "Gedicht über die Busse, in: *BKV,* in: *idem* 155–171,

Isaac of Antioch, "Gedicht über den Teufel", in: *BKV,* in: *idem* 171–187.

Jakob of Serug, "Gedicht über die Decke vor dem Antlitz des Moses", in: *BKV* in: *idem* 344–360.

Johannesbuch, in: M.Lidzbarski, *Das Johannesbuch der Mandäer,* Giessen 1905.

Justi, *Iran. Namenbuch,* in: F. Justi, *Iranisches Namenbuch,* Marburg 1895.

Kephalaia, in: *Manichäische Handschriften der Staatlichen Museen zu Berlin,* Bd I: *Kephalaia,* ed. C. Schmidt–H. Ibscher, Stuttgart 1940.

Kerygma Petri, ed. Preuschen, in: E. Preuschen, *Antilegomena,* Gieszen 195, 88–91 and 192–195.

Krauss, *Talm. Archäol.,* in: S. Krauss, *Talmudische Archäologie,* Leipzig I 1910, II 1911, III 1912.

L.B. in: R.A. Lipsius et M. Bonnet, *Acta Apostolorum Apocrypha* I, II I and II II, Leipzig 1891, 1898 and 1903 (reprint Darmstadt 1959).

Lex. Syr., in: C. Brockelmann, *Lexicon Syiacum,* Halle 1928 (2nd impr.)

Liber Graduum, ed. Kmosko, in: *Liber Graduum,* ed. M. Kmosko, in: *Patrologia Syriaca* I III, Paris 1906.

Liber Legum Regionum, ed. Nau, in: Bardesanes, *Liber Legum Regionum* ed.F. Nau, in: *Patrologia Syriaca* I II, Paris 1907.

Lipsius, *Apokr. Apostelgesch.,* in: R.A. Lipsius, *Die apokryphen Apostelgeschichten,* Braunschweig I 1883, II 1 1887 and II 2 1884, Ergänzungsheft 1890.

Liturg. homilies of Narsai, ed. Connolly, in: "The Liturgical homilies of Narsai" ed. R.H. Connolly, in: *Texts and Studies* VIII 1910.

Mand. Liturg., in: M. Lidzbarski, "Mandäische Liturgien", in: *Abhandlungen der Königlichen Gesellschaft der Wissenschaften zu Göttingen*, phil.-hist. Kl., n.F. Bd XVII 1920.

Manich. Ps., in: *Manichaean Manuscripts in the Chester Beatty Collection*, vol. II: A Manichaean Psalm-Book ed. C.R.C. Allberry, Stuttgart 1938.

Melito, *Passa-Hom*, ed. Lohse, in: B. Lohse, "Die Passa-Homilie des Bischofs Meliton von Sardes", in: *Textus Minores* XXIV, Leiden 1958.

Michael Syrus, ed. Chabot, in: J.B. Chabot, *Chronique de Michel le Syrien*, Bruxelles 1963 (reprint).

Midr. Song of Songs, ed. M. Simon, in: *Midrash Rabba* XI ed. H. Freedman and M. Simon: *Song of Songs* translated by M. Simon, London 1939

Moses bar Kepha, *The Mysteries of Baptism*, ed. Aytoun, in: R.A. Aytoun, "Moses bar Kepha's Explanation of the Mysteries of Baptism", in: *Expositor* 8th Ser., vol. II 1911, 338–358.

R. Murray, *Symbols*, in: R. Murray, *Symbols of Church and Kingdom. A Study in Early Syriac Tradition*, Cambridge 1975.

Narsai, *Memra ü. d. Seele*, ed. Allgeier, in: A. Allgeier, "Ein syrischer Memra über die Seele im religionsgeschichtlichen Rahmen", in: *Archiv f. Religionswissensch.* XXI 1922, 360–390.

Nestorianische Taufliturgie, ed. Diettrich, in: G. Diettrich, *Die nestorianische Taufliturgie*, Giessen 1903.

Odes of Sol., in: J.H. Charlesworth, *The Odes of Solomon*, Oxford 1973.

Orac. Sybill. ed. Kurfess–Gauger, in: A. Kurfess–J.-D. Gauger, *Sibyllinische Weissagungen*, Darmstadt 1998.

Origen, *c. Cels.*, ed. Chadwick, in: H. Chadwick, *Origen, contra Celsum*, Cambridge 1953.

P.G., in: *Patrologia Graeca*, ed. Migne.

Philo, *Quest. on Gen.*, ed. Marcus, in: Philo, *"Questions and Answers on Genesis"*, ed. R. Marcus, in: *Loeb Classical Library*. 380, London 1953.

P.L., in: *Patrologia Latina*, ed. Migne.

Ps.-Clemens, *de virginitate*, ed. Diekamp, in: Th. Diekamp, *Patres Apostolici*, II, Tübingen 1913.

Ps.-Clemens, *homilien*, in: B. Rehm, J. Irmscher, F. Paschke, *Die Pseudoklementinen* I: *Homilien*, Berlin 1969.

Ps.-Clemens, *recognitionen*, in: B. Rehm, F. Paschke, *Die Pseudoklementinen* II: *Recognitionen*, Berlin 1965.

Sachau, The Syriac Text of the Acts of Thomas in: P. Bedjan, *Acta Martyrum et sanctorum* III, Paris 1892.

Sacramentary of Serapion, ed. Brightman, in: F.C. Brightman, "The Sacramentary of Serapion of Thmuis", in: *Journal of Theological Studies* I 1900, 88–113 and 247–277.

Schmidt, *Acta Pauli*, in: C. Schmidt, *Acta Pauli*, Glückstadt und Hamburg 1936.

Sinai, The Syriac Text of the Acts of Thomas in: A. Smith Lewis, *Acta Mythologica Apostolorum*, in: *Horae Semiticae*. III and IV, London 1904.

Strack–Billerbaeck, in: H.J. Strack und P. Billerbeck, *Kommentar zum Neuen Testament aus Talmud und Midrasch*, München 1922–1969 (6 vols).

Syriac, ed. Wright, in: W. Wright, *Apocryphal Acts of the Apostles*, London 1871 (2 vols).

syr c, s and p: The Syriac version of the New Testament according to the Curetonianus, Sinaiticus and the Peshitto.

Testamentum Domini nostri Jesu Christi, ed. Rahmani, in: I.E. Rahmani, *Testamentum Domini nostri Jesu Christi*, Moguntiae 1899.

Theodore of Mopsuestia, ed. Mingana, in: A. Mingana, "Commentary of Theodore of Mopsuestia on the Lord's Prayer", in: *Woodbrooke Studies* VI, Cambridge 1933.

INTRODUCTION

The Text

In this book the commentary on the Acts of Thomas has been based upon the Syriac edition published by William Wright, *Apocryphal Acts of the Apostles*, London 1871 (reprint,ed. Amsterdam 1968), pages ܩܠܒ to ܣܝܚ and its translation on pages 146 to 298.

The choice of this text was made because it is now generally assumed that these Acts were originally written in Syriac and secondly because the text mentioned above is the oldest integral Syriac text of this writing.

Occasionally we were obliged to refer to other Syriac manuscripts of the Acts and various other ancient versions. The following can be said about these texts.

The Syriac text edited by Wright is that of B.L. add. 14. 645 dated to 936 A.D. It is called by Wright "the gem of my small collection". Compared with some of the Greek texts we notice a few corrections but it certainly represents its Eastern origin in an exemplary way. It is important that in the course of its tradition the text of these Acta has not been shortened but, rather, shows a number of additions. This applies, for example, to "The Song of praise of Thomas the Apostle" after ch. 113. We often had to refer to the Greek versions where it obviously displays a text which is supposed to represent an earlier tradition in the textual history.

We had several times to mention other Syriac texts. Of these, that of the palimpsest Sinai 30 is extremely important. In this manuscript a limited number of pages have been used which originally belonged to a text of the Acts of Thomas dated in the 5/6th century. This applies to the following passages according to the text of Wright:

Ch. 17: And the king says—ch. 19: and what I shall send (you).
Ch. 32: I am who stirred up—ch. 34: you have done well to come here.

Ch. 40: the Apostle had said these things—ch. 44: and stood before
   him no one.
Ch. 66: since we too—ch. 70: And the general went, fearing greatly,
   because.
Ch. 83: build for themselves—ch. 85: who are nigh to it.
Ch. 124: never pass away—ch. 127: that is worse than you.
Ch. 128: I will supply—ch. 136: gives life to all those.
Ch. 137: I went and have heard—ch. 139: he will give you. Now tell.
Ch. 140: was enraged—ch. 152: Mazdai, he cut off from me.
Ch. 154: half way—ch. 158: voice was heard, saying.

Its text is about four centuries older than that of Wright. The differences between the two texts are usually of minor importance. However, this cannot be a final conclusion, since Sinai misses a number of
important passages. Nevertheless, we may mention a few characteristic
phenomena.

It is striking that Sinai calls the principal person Judas or the Apostles. in the passages mentioned above the name Thomas is not to be
found.

Secondly the text omits the prayer about free will in ch. 34. This has
to be explained from a tendency in Wright to amplify the text and to
bring it into agreement with ideas current at a later date.

In the third place we notice that in ch. 132 baptism is spoken about
without mentioning the pre-baptismal anointment which also shows
that we have to be aware of a tendency in the text of Wright to bring
the text into agreement with practices in its own time.

Therefore, it appears that the contents of Sinai compared with the
B.L. Manuscript shows an earlier stage of the textual tradition.[1]

Apart from these two texts another three Syriac manuscripts exist of
a much later date. The contents are interesting because they show the
development of textual tradition but they are of minor importance for
our commentary.[2]

---

[1] See A. Smith Lewis, "*Acta Mythologica Apostolorum*", in: *Horae Semiticae* III and IV,
London 1904, and cf. F.C. Burkitt, in: A. Smith Lewis, "Select Narrations of Holy
Women", in: *Studia Semitica* IX, London 1900, 24–77.

[2] Mosul No. 86. Property of the Chaldaean Patriarchate, A.D.1711/12; Sachau
No. 222, Berlin, A.D. 1881, and Cambridge, Add. 2822, A.D. 1883. See A. Baum-
stark, *Geschichte der syrischen Literatur*, Bonn 1922, 14 note 11. See also W. Strothman,

The Greek text can be found in 21 manuscripts but only one represents the complete text.[3] The relation between the Greek and Syriac text is difficult to establish. Generally speaking the Syriac text seems to be original. We are able to point to numerous so-called Syriasms[4] and the passages about Baptism and the Eucharist show an Eastern origin. It is, however, too easy to assume an original Syriac text which has been translated into Greek. We suppose that the Acts were written in a bilingual environment in which both the Syriac and Greek versions originated simultaneously.

The Greek version has been edited by Lipsius and Bonnet. This admirable work shows a complicated textual history. About the various manuscripts the following can be said.

Of the 21 manuscripts mentioned above 15 manuscripts show the text of the chapters 1–29. From chapter 30 until chapter 81 the text is found in about four manuscripts. From chapter 82 until 143 the text is found in two manuscripts, and chapters 108 until 113 in manuscript P only. Chapters 144 to the end are usually represented by about ten manuscripts. In the edition of Lipsius and Bonnet it was sometimes necessary to print two different texts. In a number of manuscripts a much shorter text is found from the end of chapter 5 until chapter 28 and a text with many variant readings from chapter 144 until the end. In addition to this we see that in some manuscripts the passage ch. 144 "My Lord ..." until the end of ch. 148 can be found after ch. 167. We suppose that we are dealing with a rewriter although the relation between the two texts starting from chapter 144 seems to be complicated.[5]

In the text of the manuscript in the B.L. headings are found above chapters 1, 17, 30 and 162, but in our text the other ones in the Greek version have been given between brackets.

"Jakob von Sarug. Drei Gedichte über den Apostel Thomas in Indien", in: *Göttinger Orientforschungen* I. Reihe: *Syriaca*, Band 12, Wiesbaden 1976. About the chapters 1–29, but based upon a text as in Sachan.

[3] See R.A. Lipsius and M. Bonnet, *Acta Apostolorum Apocrypha* II II, Leipzig 1903 (reprint Darmstadt 1959), XV–XXVII. P: *Parisiacum graecum* 1510, *saec. XI aut XII.*

[4] See H.W. Attridge, "The original Language of the Acts of Thomas", in: H.W. Attridge *e.a.*, *Of Scribes and Scrolls.* Presented to J. Strugnell, Lanham, New York, London 1990, 241–250. See also chapters 4, 5, 8, 13 and *passim.*

[5] See also the end of the chapter about "The Syriac and the Greek Version".

The text of the Acts of Thomas is also found in manuscripts with a Latin[6], Armenian[7], Coptic[8], Ethiopic, Arabic[9], Slavonic[10] and Georgian[11] text.[12] Here the text is much shorter than in Syriac and Greek and adapted to the theological taste of a much later generation. For our commentary these versions are of minor importance.

The Contents of the Acts of Thomas

The Acts of Thomas can be divided into a number of "acts" which end with a description of his martyrdom. The contents can be compared with those in the other four ancients Acts, *viz.* those of Paul, John, Peter and Andrew. The Acts of Thomas are striking for their passages with extensive christological remarks, the description of Baptism and Eucharist and two ancient hymns.

The text can be divided into the following parts:

Ch. 1–16: Thomas is sold to Habban, a merchant who comes from king Gudnaphar living in India. On their way they arrive in a town in which the marriage of the king's daughter is celebrated. After Thomas' preaching bride and bridegroom decide to live in purity.

Ch.17–29: King Gundaphorus asks Thomas to build a palace. Thomas gives the money he receives from the king to the poor. He is imprisoned. After the death of Gad, the king's brother, it appears that the king possesses a palace in heaven. Gad returns to earth and asks to buy the palace.

---

[6] We only give the most recent editions in which the earlier ones can be found. See K. Zelzer, "Die alten lateinischen Thomasakten", in: *Texte und Untersuchungen zur Geschichte der altchristlichen Literatur* 122, Berlin 1977.

[7] See L.Leloir, "Écrits Apocryphes sur les Apôtres: traduction de l'édition arménienne de Venise", in: *Corpus Christianorum. Series Apocryphorum* 4, Turnhout 1992, 548–596; 577–591; 597–615 and 622–631.

[8] See R.H. Poirier, "La Version copte de la Prédication et du Martyre du Thomas", in: *Subsidia Hagiographica* 67, Bruxelles 1984.

[9] See M. van Esbroeck, "Les Actes apocryphes de Thomas en version arabe", in: *Parole de l'Orient* 14 1987, 11–77.

[10] See A. de Santos Otero, "Die handschriftliche Überlieferung der altslavischen Apokryphen", in: *Patristische Texte und Studien* 20 and 23, Berlin and New York 1978 and 1981, vol. 1 84–96.

[11] See G. Garite "Le Martyre géorgien de l'apôtre Thomas", in: *Le Muséon* 83 1970, 407–532."

[12] See also Elliott, *o.c.*, 442–443.

Ch. 30–38: Thomas sees the body of a boy killed by a dragon because he fell in love with a girl. The dragon has to suck out the poison and bursts.

Ch. 39–50: Thomas meets a woman who says that she was attacked by a dirty man who does not want to go away. It appears to be a demon who is sent away.

Ch. 51–61: A boy killed his fiancée because he wished to live purely with her but he did not trust her. The girl comes alive and tells of what she experienced in hell.

Ch. 62–67: An officer named Siphorus asks Thomas to go with him to his wife and daughter who are possessed by demons.

Ch. 68–81: Going to the city Thomas asks wild asses to draw the chariot. After arriving the demons are sent away.

Ch. 82–118: Mygdonia, wife of an officer, named Charisius, is listening to Thomas. She wants to live purely with her husband. He goes to the king who puts Thomas in jail.

Ch. 119–133: Thomas is able to leave the prison in order to baptise Mygdonia. Charisius goes to the king and he asks Thomas to persuade Mygdonia to return to her husband.

Ch. 134–138: Misdaeus tells his wife Tertia what happened to Mygdonia. Tertia asks Mygdonia to return to her husband but she also decides to live purely. The king wishes to kill Thomas.

Ch. 139–149: Before the trial Vizan the son of the king speaks with Thomas. Vizan is converted and Thomas is convicted.

Ch. 150–158: In prison Tertia, Vizan and his wife, who is ill, are baptised.

Martyrdom. The apostle is killed by four soldiers and an officer. After this the son of the king falls ill. He asks to take a bone from Thomas' grave. Thomas appears to him, but his body has been brought to the West. With dust taken from the grave the boy is cured. The king also becomes a member of the Christian community.

The Acts of Thomas have ample opportunity to go into the significance of Jesus, Baptism, the Eucharist and hell. It is striking that Thomas' mission is supposed to be a war against the devil. The main emphasis is on living purely.

The Name of Thomas

In the Syriac text in the B.L. the present Acts are called "of Judas Thomas". However the principal person is usually called Judas, sometimes Judas Thomas and often the Apostle.[13] This usage does not agree with the much older Syriac text Sinai where Judas or the Apostle is spoken of. Judas appears to be the original name, because in the B.L. manuscript the name Judas has been systematically corrected into Thomas.

The Greek version of Lipsius–Bonnet uses the name Thomas or Judas Thomas, but gradually only the name Judas is met. It seems that also here we are dealing with a textual tradition according to which Judas has been corrected into Thomas. However, in the overwhelming majority of passages the Apostle is spoken about.

It is interesting to see that, apart from the name Judas Thomas, "Judas, who is also Thomas" is also spoken about. This shows that one is aware that Thomas is not a proper name.

In the other versions the principal person is usually called Thomas and the present work is known as the Acts of Thomas.

A few passages in these Acts ask for our attention. In ch. 1 a list of the Apostles is given in which is spoken of Thomas. This agrees with the text of the New Testament. In this same chapter it is said that India fell by lot and division to Judas Thomas the Apostle and a few lines later that "Judas" did not want to go.

The Greek text also uses the name Thomas in the list but the second time it is said that India fell to Judas Thomas "who is also the Twin". Here the influence of some passages in the Gospel of John can be assumed. Much more important is a remark in ch. 31, where a black snake says to the apostle or Judas as he is called in this chapter: "I know that the ocean flood, ܡܥܡܘܕ, of the Messiah will destroy our nature". This can be explained because the name "Thomas" has been mixed up with ܬܐܘܡܐ. However the Greek texts reads: "I know that you are the twin of the Christ". This must have been the original reading because in ch. 39 it is said in both Greek and Syriac: "Twin of the Messiah and Apostle of the Most High".

---

[13] M. Lipinski, "Konkordanz zu den Thomasakten", in: *Bonner Biblische Beiträge* 67, Frankfurt am Main 1988, appears to be an indispensable tool.

It appears that we are dealing with a tradition according to which the word "thomas" is supposed to mean "twin", that, secondly, the name of this twin is Judas and, finally, that this Judas is the twin of Christ.

It is not clear in which way Judas is supposed to be the twin of Christ. A few passages in the Acts of Thomas seem to be important. In ch. 11 it is said that a bridegroom sees Jesus "in the likeness of Judas". In ch. 34 it is said about Judas that he has "two forms" and in ch. 45 one wonders why Judas is "like unto God". According to ch. 57 and 151 people are astonished that Judas is met in a place where it is physically impossible for him to be.

We are dealing with the idea that Jesus is able to appear in whatever body he likes.[14] He adapts himself to the particular circumstances. Since one of the apostles was named the "Twin" according to an ancient Semitic tradition it was not difficult to consider him the twin of Christ in a special way.[15]

References to the New Testament

In these Acts we notice numerous allusions to passages in the New Testament. Sometimes we are dealing with a few words but often with a whole passage. They are, generally speaking, taken from the Gospels but an occasional reference to Paul and possibly the Gospel of Thomas appears to be present.[16] The references are often part of the text and nothing is said about their origin. However, in ch. 28 it is said: "… and there remains with you (the saying) 'Take no care for the morrow …'", see Matth. 6, 34, followed by: "And bear in mind the other (saying) which is written for you 'Look upon the ravens …'", see Matth. 6,26 and Luke 12, 24–28.[17] The two references are introduced

---

[14] D.R. Cartlidge, "Transfigurations of Metamorphosis Traditions in the Acts of John, Thomas, and Peter", in: *Semeia* 38 1986, 64–76, and R. Kuntzmann, *Le Symbolisme des jumeaux au Proche-Orient ancien*, Paris 1983, esp. 173–182.

[15] See A.F.J. Klijn, "John XIV 22 and the Name Judas Thomas", in: *Studies in John.* Presented to J.N. Sevenster, in: *Supplem. to Nov. Test.* XXIV, Leiden 1970, and J.J. Gunther, "The Meaning and Origin of the Name 'Judas Thomas'", in: *Le Muséon* 93 1980, 113–148.

[16] A very convenient survey of the various references is found in Drijvers' contribution to the English version of Hennecke on 405–411.

[17] Apart from these we may mention a few other obvious quotations: in ch 47 John 21, 3–6; Mark 6, 35–44; John 4, 6 and Mark 6, 45–52; in ch. 48 Matth. 7, 7; in ch. 53 Matth. 7, 7; in ch. 82 Mark 8, 18 and Matth. 11, 28; in ch. 86 Matth. 11, 28–30 and

in the Greek version by the words: "And it remains with you what has been said by the Saviour" and "Remember that word that has been said before".

Apart from the text of the Gospels we meet a few allusions to passages in the Gospel of Thomas but this may be due to the presence of traditions about Thomas which were generally known in the Syriac Church.

The source of the New Testament allusions and possibly quotations is difficult to establish because we are dealing with a text that has often been rewritten. From the commentary we can say that the Greek text shows a tendency of giving a faithful translation of the original Syriac but in explicit quotations the contents have been adapted to the Greek New Testament. This means that we often see that the Byzantine text has been followed. The Syriac text of these passages sometimes agrees with the Peshitto of the New Testament but a number of passages agrees with the Old Syriac. Here ch. 146 is of special importance. The author refers to a number of parables taken from the New Testament. It seems that originally the text of the Diatessaron has been used, which has been changed into that of the four separate Gospels.

Without going into details, we may assume that with regard to the allusions and quotations the Diatessarom has been the basic text which in the course of the tradition has been changed into a text as found in the four separate Gospels and finally into that of the Peshitto.

The Syriac and the Greek Version

The commentary in this book starts from the Syriac version. However, we were obliged to refer to the Greek version continuously, especially because it is supposed to represent an earlier tradition of the contents. In the following we will provide a general impression of the two versions.

The Syriac text clearly shows a theologicval interest. The long doxology after ch. 113 is very important because here the Syriac tradition was able to express ideas which are returning in the present Acts. Also in other passages we notice that the Syriac text appears to be longer than the Greek. This happens, for example, in the chapters 33, 34, 59 and especially 13 and 70.

Matth. 26, 53; in ch. 144 Matth. 6, 9–13 and especially in ch. 146 Luke 19, 16; Luke 7, 41–42; Luke 14, 14–24; Matth. 22, 1–14 and Matth. 25, 1–13.

Apart from numerous passages where we were obliged to show the Greek texts, it was necessary to discuss some others in a more extensive way. This applies to the chapters 25, 26 and 27 about Baptism. It is evident that the course of events during Baptism was different in the Syriac and Greek traditions, which can also be seen in a number of other passages. The same can be said about the Eucharist in, for example, ch. 157, but here we are dealing with the contents of the epiclesis, which appears to be more ancient in the Greek tradition. No less striking is the difference between the two versions in chapters 55, 56 and 57, where a description is given of the punishment in hell. Also here the Greek text appears to represent a more ancient tradition. Finally it appears that the Syriac version is more interested in ethical teaching than the Greek, as can be seen in ch. 85.

Apart from this we notice a few subjects about which the Greek and the Syriac text seem to possess different opinions. Thus, in Hymn I, chapters 6 and 7, the Greek speaks about a female heavenly being and the heavenly world and the Syriac about the Church and the baptistery. Next we see that in the Syriac version a too sharp distinction between body and soul has been avoided (see ch. 30 and 36). From ch. 33 it seems that according to the Greek version the struggle between God or Christ and the devil is still continuing while in the Syriac version the struggle seems to be decided. Next we notice that Syriac does not like to emphasize a too close relationship between God and man (see ch. 34) and a contrast between body and soul (see ch. 36).

If we add to this a passage in ch. 34 about free will in Syriac we may say that the Syriac tradition is trying to avoid unorthodox and possibly Gnostic ideas.

Finally it is interesting that in chapters 144 until 149 according to the Greek version the text differs between that represented by the manuscript U on the one hand, and by P and by three or four other manuscripts on the other hand. In addition to this, the text of P and its allies is found after chapter 167.[18]

---

[18] M.R. James, *The Apocryphal New Testament*, Oxford 1924, 428, and J.K. Elliott, *The Apocryphal New Testament*, Oxford 1993, 505 and 508, are following U.

The Theological Point of View

In this chapter we want to go into some of the theological views of
the author of the Acts of Thomas. We can successively deal with
the matter of corruption—a basic concept in this work—ideas about
Christ and redemption, ideas about some ethical opinions, and, finally,
Baptism and the Eucharist. In this summary we avoid speaking about
the Hymns in chapters 6–7 and 108–113, because they belong to the
sources used by the authors and their contents have been dealt with in
the Commentary.

The contents of the Acts of Thomas are dominated by the struggle
against *corruption*. The Acts have been written to free the reader from
corruption (ch. 15). Especially "filthy intercourse" (cf. 12 and 88) is an
act that represents corruption. However, we see that the Acts are not
always consistent. We can not say that they are rejecting marriage,
although it should not be consummated, which is supposed to be a
"deed of shame" (cf. 14, 54, 55 and 84). It is because of this preaching
that Thomas was finally executed.

A few details ask for our attention. It appears that especially demons
are leading astray and trying to seduce particular persons into having
intercourse (see ch. 43). This means that the struggle against corruption
is a war against the devil in order to be united with Christ, the eternal
Bridegroom (ch. 12 and 14).

Apart from sexual intercourse, eating and drinking is supposed to be
a service to corruption (ch. 20). But it can not be prohibited. It means
that man is paying a necessary debt to the devil or corruption.

We need not say that it is more than once said that Thomas possesses
one garment only (ch. 20) and that he is a stranger and a poor man in
the eyes of those among whom he is living (ch. 107 and 130).

Another element in the Acts of Thomas is that in man himself corruption and purity is present. This means that his body is corruptible
and his soul is basically incorruptible. This does not mean that God
would not be the creator of the body (ch. 34). We also read about
healings of the body, although they have been made of dust and will
become dust again (ch. 78 and 95). Thus we arrive at a remarkable
conclusion: on the one hand the soul is living in pollution (ch. 30), but,
on the other hand, the body can be the dwelling place of the Spirit
(ch. 94).

This does not alter the fact that the body will be dissolved but that
the soul is "not ended in dissolution" (ch. 78 and 93). The soul will be

restored to its own nature (ch. 43 and 148) and returns to God (ch. 22). However, the soul can also be condemned (ch. 55) or even be utterly destroyed (ch. 57). It has to be given "life" (ch. 42 and 156) and healing (ch. 10, 49 and 95). This means that the soul is potentially eternal.

From this point of view we can speak about the *christology* of these Acts and redemption, because speaking about Christ is speaking about corruptibility and incorruptibility. Thomas' preaching is that of Christ who put on a body (ch. 10, 48, 76, 80 and 143). Thus he became poor (ch. 45, 47, 143 and 156), fatigued (ch. 47), despised and humbled (ch. 45, 48, 80, 143 and 159). He received a name (ch. 48), was a slave (ch. 143) and died (ch. 45, 72 and 158).

Because of his body the heavenly Christ was able to approach man and to reveal a path leading to heaven (ch. 10 and 80). Christ possesses "two names" (ch. 10 and 163), the devil did not perceive his godhead. He was a Giver of Life (ch. 45) and therefore both God (ch. 47), walking on the waves of the sea (ch. 47) whose divine form the disciples were not able to bear (ch. 143), and man.

Thus man lives between God and corruption, with a soul that can take part in the heavenly world because this world is revealed to him by Christ who put on the body.

Living with a body and a soul separated from God, man is unable to perceive the heavenly world because he is subjected to the evil ruler of the world. He possesses, however, a free will and he can become mindful of himself and worthy of God.

The way to become worthy of God is found in a particular *ethical teaching*. The most important quality of man is his or her purity. This word is met all over these Acts. It is undeniable that the word has a sexual connotation and it means in the first place that one has to refrain from "filthy intercourse". For the rest we meet a number of elements which can be expected. The poor have to be helped (ch. 26, 56 and 59), one has to fast and to pray (ch. 29) and to show humility. A few times we read that one should avoid theft, fornication and covetousness, which seems to belong to a particular catalogue of vices (see ch. 12, 28, 58, 79, 84 and 126). If one follows this rule and lives in holiness, purity and temperance (ch. 126) one becomes a stranger (ch. 4) and one is despised in this world.[19]

---

[19] It is possible to approach this way of life as being "encratitic", see Y. Tissot, "L'encratisme de Acts des Thomas", in: *ANRW* II 25, Berlin New York 1988, 1415–1430.

Apart from all this, we read about *Baptism and Eucharist* in the Acts of Thomas. Baptism appears to be a prerequisite to participate in God's world. One has to be prepared to receive Baptism, but, if so, one receives divine gifts which do not only make it possible to partake in the Eucharist but also to live as a real Christian.

The following can be said about these two genuine Christian practices. In the first place. the Greek and Syriac versions differ considerably. Next, we notice an agreement with Eastern and, in particular, Syriac Baptismal liturgies. The contents of the epicleses are different.

Here the order of Baptism is given in five passages. Chapters 25, 26 and 27: The Baptism of King Gundaphorus and his brother Gad.[20] Thomas prays that the king may be united to God's fold and may be anointed and purified; that he may be guarded from the wolves and drink from God's fountain and that he may have boldness and be confirmed in God's glorious mysteries. The king asks to receive the sign of Baptism because the sheep are known by the sign. Thomas invites him to partake of the Eucharist.

The bath is closed for seven days. Before Baptism they hear a voice but did not see the form. Thomas pours oil upon their heads. Next follows an epiclesis which ends with the words that the name of the Messiah may communicate with the minds of these youths. They are baptised in the name of the Father, the Son and the Holy Spirit. Finally a youth appears to them.

The Greek version shows some characteristic deviations. In the prayer it is asked that they may be cleansed by Baptism and be anointed by oil. Nothing is said about closing the bath for seven days. Thomas is sealing them. They only heard a voice for they had not yet received "the added sealing of the seal", as it is said in the text. Gundaphorus and Gad are anointed and chrismed and Thomas begins with his epiclesis, ending with: "And seal them in the name of the Father, the Son and the Holy Spirit." Finally, a youth appears to them.

Chapter 49: Baptism of a woman. A woman asks for the seal of her Lord that the enemy may not come again. Thomas baptises her in a river in the name of the Father, the Son and the Holy Spirit. Next follows the Eucharist.

The Greek version generally agrees with the Syriac but omits to say that the Baptism takes place in a river.

---

[20] See also L. Leloir, "Le baptême du roi Gundaphor", in: *Le Muséon* 100 1987, 225–233.

Chapter 121: Baptism of Mygdonia, Thomas casts oil on her head and asks that God's power may come on the oil. Next he asks her nurse to anoint her. Finally Thomas baptises her in the name of the Father, the Son and the Holy Spirit. This is followed by the Eucharist.

In the Greek version it is asked that the power of the oil may rest on Mygdonia. Next Mygdonia is undressed and brought to a spring where Mygdonia is baptised.

Chapter 132: Baptism of Sifur and his family. After a doxology Thomas casts oil upon their heads and they were baptised in a large vat in the name of the Father, the Son and the Holy Spirit.

The Greek version agrees with the Syriac one.

Chapter 157: Baptism in the house of Vizan. Those who are going to be baptised are stripped. It is asked that the Lord abide in this oil which is cast on their heads. Next they are anointed and baptised in the water in the name of the Father, the Son and the Holy Spirit.

The Greek version agrees with the Syriac one.

The order of Baptism in chapters 121, 132 and 157 is generally clear. Thomas casts oil upon the heads of those who are going to be baptised. Next it is said that they are anointed. This obviously applies to the whole body. Finally it is said that Thomas is baptizing in water. In ch. 121 this happens in a spring which seems to agree with ch. 49 where it is said that they go to a river. This means that Baptism took place in moving water.

In the Syriac version of ch. 25, 26 and 27 we recognise the same order of events: Thomas pours oil on their heads and baptizes the believers.

This order of Baptism according to which oil is poured onto the heads before Baptism with water is well known from Syriac and other Eastern sources.[21] It differs from the Western order, according to which we notice a chrism after Baptism with water.

We assume that the influence of the order in the West on the original text is the explanation of the remarkable passage in the Greek version of ch. 25, 27 and 27. Initially here, is spoken of Baptism and anointment which seems to agree with the Western order. Next it is said that Thomas seals them after which they hear a voice only. The reason for not yet being able to see is that they have not yet received "the added sealing of the seal", an expression which can not be found

---

[21] See A.F.J. Klijn, "An ancient Syriac Baptismal Liturgy in the Syriac Acts of John", in: *Novum Testamentum* 6 1963, 216–228.

elsewhere. Next it is said that they are anointed and chrismed. This is
a remarkable order of events which can hardly be understood. Without
going into details we assume that we are dealing with a mixing up of
the Eastern and Western order in which in the Greek version some of
the original elements have been maintained.

To this a few remarks can be added. The pouring of oil on the head
appears to be very important. Here we notice an epiclesis according to
which it is asked that divine gifts are given to the oil or to those to be
baptised. Next is spoken of an anointment of the body which appears
to be a preparation of Baptism with water. This happens in living water
and in the name of the Father, the Son and the Holy Spirit.

Baptism is meant to be a purification but also a protection against
enemies and a "seal" that is recognized by God.

The Eucharist is closely connected with Baptism and it took place
in the early morning. It appears that bread is more important than the
wine. One speaks of "breaking the bread" and sometimes of bread only.

Finally we have to go into the *epiclesis* which is found not only in
passages about baptism in ch. 27, 121 and 157, but also about the
eucharist in ch. 50 and 133. Generally speaking, it can be said that
the Holy Spirit is invited to come into the pre-baptismal oil and the
eucharistic bread. We notice that the words of the various epicleses
are different and that sometimes the emphasis is on the elements but
also on those partaking in Baptism or Eucharist. It is difficult to trace
the background of the various names which are called upon. We are
dealing with very old traditions according to which the Spirit is a
female being and related with Eastern female divine beings.[22]

---

[22] Some recent studies on Baptism and Eucharist: J. Delaunay, "Rite et symbol-
ique en ACTA THOMAE vers. syr. I. 2a et ss.", in: Ph. Gignoux (ed.), *Mémorial
Jean de Menasce*, Teheran 1974, 11–34; G. Winkler, "The original Meaning of the pre-
baptismal Anointing and its Implications", in: *Worship* 52 1978, 24–45; G. Winkler,
"Zur frühchristlichen Tauftradition in Syrien und Armenien unter Einbezug der Taufe
Jesu", in: *Ostkirchliche Studien* 27 1978, 287–306 G. Winkler, "Das Armenische Initiation-
srituale", in: Orientalia Christiana Anelecta 217, Roma 1982 esp. 132 etc.; S. Brock, *The
Holy Spirit in the Syrian Baptismal Tradition*, Bronx NY 1979; L. Leloir, "Symbolisme dans
la liturgie Syriaque primitive. Le symbolisme dans la culte des grandes religions", in:
Homo Religiosus II, Louvain-la Neuve 1985, 247–263; H. Kruse, "Zwei Geist-Epiklesen
der syrischen Thomas-Akten", in: *Oriens Christianus* 69 1985, 33–53; G. Rouwhorst, "La
célébration de l'eucharistie selon les Actes de Thomas", in: Ch. Caspers and H. Schnei-
ders (eds), *Omnes circumstantes. Contributions towards a History of the Role of the People in the
Liturgy*, Kampen 1990, 51–77, and E. Boone, "L'onction prébaptismale: sens et origine.
Un exemple dans les *Actes de Thomas*", in: *Studia Patristica* 30, Leuven 1997, 291–295.

Place and Date

It is generally assumed that the Acts of Thomas have to be dated to the beginning of the third century. The place of origin is more difficult to establish. The city of Edessa is possible, but it is not more than a guess. Here we might say that the work originated in the Syriac speaking Eastern Church.[23]

Conclusion

It can be said that the Acts of Thomas reveal a particular Christian doctrine of which the details are consistent. Nevertheless we notice some influences from outside. This especially applies to the ideas about the Spirit which comes from God and shows the influence of existing ideas about a female divine being. But this is almost totally confined to the baptismal and eucharistic passages.

The ideas in this work can be called orthodox in the sense that man has a free will and that body and soul have been created by God. The emphasis on corruption and a depreciation of the created world is striking.

The commentary shows that the ideas expressed in the Acts of Thomas are the common property of the religious world in the East and were adapted by what is called Gnosticism.

---

[23] See J.N. Bremmer, "The Acts of Thomas: Place, Date and Women", in: *The Apocryphal Acts of Thomas*, edited by J.N. Bremmer, Leuven 2001, 74–90, and J.N. Bremmer, "The Five Major Apocryphal Acts: Authors, Place, Time and Readership", in: *idem* 149–170.

THE ACTS OF JUDAS THOMAS THE APOSTLE

Next the (first) Act of Judas Thomas, the Apostle, when He sold him to the merchant Habban, that he might go down (and) convert India.

I

And when all the Apostles had been **for a time** in Jerusalem,—**Simon Cephas and Andrew, and Jacob (James) and John, and Philip and Bartholomew, and Thomas and Matthew the publican, and Jacob the son of Alphaeus, and Simon the Kananite, and Judas the son of Jacob (James),—they divided the countries among them, in order that each one of them might preach in the region which fell to him and in the place to which his Lord sent him.** And India **fell by lot and division to Judas Thomas the Apostle. And he was not willing to go**, saying: **"I have not strength enough for this, because I am weak. And I am a Hebrew: how can I teach the Indians?"** And whilst Judas was reasoning thus, our Lord **appeared to him in a vision of the night**, and said to him: **"Fear not, Thomas, because my grace is with you."** But he would not be persuaded at all, saying: "Whithersoever you will, our Lord, send me; only to India I will not go.".

Commentary. **Next the (first) Act of Judas Thomas, ...** ܬܘܒ ܦܪܟܣܝܣ. This means that the author of the manuscript begins with a new composition. **all.** In both Syriac and Greek a number of eleven Apostles is mentioned, *viz.* those in the lists of the New Testament, but without Judas Iscariot. **for a time**, ܗܝܕܝܢ and Greek: κατ' ἐκεῖνον τον καιρὸν. This means the time after Pentecost according to Acts 2. **Simon Cephas ... son of Jacob (James).** In the New Testament lists with the names of the Apostles are to be found in Matth. 10,2–3; Mark 3,16–19; Luke 6,13–16 and Acts 1,13. According to Burkitt, *Ev. da-Meph.* II, p. 104: "... the list of Apostles at the beginning of the Acts of Thomas tallies exactly with that of S (*scil.* syr s) in Matt. X 2–4, but with no other authority". The list in the Greek version of these Acts can be compared with that in Matth. 10,2–4. But due to the influence of the underlying Syriac text the name of Thaddaeus or, in other Greek manuscripts of the New Testament, Lebbaeus has been omitted and that of Judas the son of Jacob had been added, a name obviously taken from the lists of Luke and Acts. **they divided ... sent him**. Some manuscripts of the Greek version read "we divided ...". See István Czachesz, *Apostolic Commission Narratives*, diss. Utrecht 2002, esp. 119–135. A partition of the world can be explained from Matth. 28,19 and Acts 1,8. It is also found in Eusebius, *hist. eccles.* III 1, see also Origen, *comment. in Gen.*, t. III, in: *P.G.* 12, c. 92; *Martyrium Andreae* 2, in: L.B. II I, 46,18–47,7; Hist. of Mar Matthew and Mar Andrew, Syriac, ed. Wright, 93 and Preaching of Thomas, Arabic, ed. Smith Lewis,80. See A. von Harnack, *Die Mission und Ausbreitung des Christentums* I, Leipzig 1924, 107–110. **India**. The first witness for relations between the Western world and the Indians is Herodotus, *hist.* IV 44, according to whom Scylax was sent to them by order of Darius, see R. Hennig, *Terrae Incognitae* I, Leiden 1944 (sec. ed.), 116–119. Alexander the Great reached the Hydaspes in the year 324 B.C., see Arrianus, *anabasis* III 30–VI 30. Nearchus sailed from the Euphrates to India, see Arrianus, *anabasis* VII I, 2 and 30 (325–323 B.C.). About the year 100 B.C. Hippalus discovered the use of the monsoon winds to and from India. From that time a regular connection existed between Arabia and Egypt on the one hand and Middle and South India on the other, see Periplus, *maris Erytraei* 37, and Plinius, *natur. hist.* VI 26. Especially North India was thoroughly influenced by the Hellenistic civilisation. This was due to the conquests of the Bactrians, about 250–225 B.C., see W.W. Tarn, *The Greeks in Bactria and India*, Cambridge 1938. For the next period see L.E. van Lohuizen–De Leeuw, *The "Scythian" Period*, Leiden 1949. See E. Heichelheim, *Wirtschaftgeschichte des Altertums*, Leiden 1938, 714–718; *Ancient India*, in: *The Cambridge History of India* 1, ed. E.J. Rapson, Cambridge 1922, 391–426 and especially G. Huxley, "Geography in the *Acts of Thomas*", in: *Greek, Roman and Byzantine Studies* 24 1983, 71–80, and L.P van den Bosch, "India and the Apostolate of St. Thomas", in: *Apocryphal Acts of Thomas*, ed. by J.N. Bremmer, Leuven 2001, 125–148. **fell ... to Judas Thomas the Apostle**. The oldest traditions speak about Thomas as the Apostle of the Parthians, see Origen and Eusebius quoted above; Rufinus, *hist. eccles.* I 9, in: *P.L.* 21, c. 478; Socrates, *hist. eccles.* I 19, in: *P.L.* 67, c. 125 and Ps.-Clemens, *recogn.* IX 29 2, ed. Rehm 312. Influenced by the contents of the present Acts it is said that Thomas visited India, see Hieronymus, *epist.* LIX, in: *P.L.* 22, c. 589; Ambrosius, *in Ps.* 45, in: *P.L.* 14, c. 1145, Gregorius of Naz., *orat.* XXXIII, in: *P.G.* XI, c. 228, and Ephrem, *hymni dispersi* V–VII, in: Lamy IV, c. 693–708; Manich. Ps. 192,15; 194,13 and 193,2, see P.-H. Poirier, "Les Actes de Thomas et le Manichéisme", in: *Apocrypha* 9 1998, 263–289, esp. 270–271, and E. Junod, "Origène, Eusèbe et la tradition sur la répartition des champs de mission des apôtres (Eusèbe, *Histoire ecclésiastique* III, 1, 1–3), in: E. Bovon *e.a.*, *Les actes apocryphes des apôtres*, Genève 1981, 233–248. See for a still wider field of mission F. Haase, "Apostel und Evangelisten in den Orientalischen Überlieferungen", in: *Neutestamentl. Abhandl.* IX. B., 1–3 H., Münster 1922, p. 264–268; Th. Schermann, "Propheten- und Apostellegenden", in: *Texte u. Unters.* 31 1907, p. 272–276 and especially J.-D. Kaestli, "Les scènes d'atribrution des champs de mission et de départ de l'apôtre dans les Actes Apocryphes", in: Bovon, *e.a.*, *Les Actes Apocryphes* 249–264. The Syriac manuscript used by Wright and commented upon here usually speaks about Judas. This agrees with Sinai. This Judas is supposed to be one of a "twin". This "Twin" was mentioned in the New Testament lists of the Apostles under the name "Thomas". Why this "twin" was supposed to be named Judas is not clear. In the same way as the Apostle Judas mentioned in Luke 6, 16/Acts 1, 13 has been chosen to supplement the list at the beginning of this chapter we might assume, however, that the same one was taken to give the "twin" his proper name. In the Greek manuscripts a number of different names are found like ἰούδᾳ Θωμᾷ τῷ καὶ διδύμῳ, which shows the influence of John 11, 16; 20, 24 and 21, 2. In the Greek version the principal person is generally named Judas the Apostle and sometimes Judas Thomas. In the secondary versions Thomas is spoken of. See A.F.J. Klijn, "John XIV 12 and the name Judas Thomas", in: *Studies in John presented to J.N. Sevenster*, in: *Supplem. to Novum Testamentum* XXIV, Leiden 1970, p. 88–96, and J.J. Gunther, "The Meaning and Origin of the Name Judas Thomas", in: *Le Muséon* 93 1980, p. 113–148. **And he was not willing to go**. The rejection of a divine call is often met in the Old Testament, cf. Ex. 3,11 (Moses); Judg. 6,12 (Gideon); Jer. 1,6 and Jon. 1,3. In the secondary Acts an explanation is given why he does not want to go to the Indians, see *De mirac. beati Thomae apost.*, ed. Zelzer 46, 3: *Regio enim illa longinqua et gravis est, incolae quoque loci illius iniqui et ignorantes sunt veritatem*, and Preaching of Thomas, Arabic, ed. Smith Lewis, p. 80: "… for they are hard men, like wild beasts, and it will be difficult for them to receive the hearing of the words of the Gospel". **I have not**

strength ... weak. The Greek version reads: διὰ τὴν ἀσθένειαν τῆς σαρκός, cf. Matth. 26,41: ἡ σὰρξ ἀσθενής. Thomas has to rely upon the strength given to him by his Lord. **And I ... Hebrew**. See Jon. 1,9 and ch. 5. **how can I teach the Indians**. Greek: κηρύξει τὴν ἀλή-θειαν. This can be compared with Acts of John, Syriac ed. Wright: "go forth to proclaim ... the truth", and *Acta Johannis* ch. 109, ed. L.B. II 1, 207. 13–208. 3: δοξάζομεν ... τὸν χαρισάμενον ἡμῖν τὴν ἀλήθειαν. Here the word "truth" stands for the "true doctrine about God". **appeared to him ... night**, ܟܘܐܐ ܕܠܠܝܐ. Greek: διὰ τῆς νυκτός, but manuscripts G H Z: Ἐν ὁράματι, which can be compared with Acts 18,9: Ἐν νυκτὶ δι' ὁράματος and in the Old-Latin manuscript d: *per visum* and in h: *in visum*, syr p: ܟܘܐܐ. **Fear not ... with you**. Cf. Rev. 1,17; Luke 1,13 and 30 etc., and I Cor. 16,23; Philipp. 4,23 etc.

2

And as Judas was reasoning thus, a certain merchant, an Indian, **happened (to come) into the south country from ... (illegible) ...** , whose name was **Habban**; and he was sent by the king **Gudnaphar**, that he might bring him a skilful **carpenter**. And our Lord saw him walking **in the street**, and said to him: "You wish to buy a carpenter?" He says to him: "Yes". Our Lord says to him: "I have a **slave**, a carpenter, whom I will sell to you." And he showed him Thomas at a distance, and bargained with him for **twenty (pieces) of silver** (as) his price, and wrote a **bill of sale** thus: "I, **Jesus, the son of Joseph the carpenter, from the village of Bethlehem**, which is in Judaea, acknowledge that I have sold my slave Judas Thomas to Habban, the merchant of king Gudnaphar." And when they had completed his bill of sale. Jesus took Judas, and went to Habban the merchant. And Habban saw him, and says to him: "**Is this your master?**" Judas says to him: "Yes, he is my master." Habban the merchant said to him: "He has sold you to me outright." And Judas was **silent**.

Commentary. **happened (to come) into the south country from ...** The Syriac text is partially illegible here. Sachau reads "from the south country" and the Greek text "from India". We suppose that the original Syriac text read "from the south country, from India". This might have been already a conflate reading based upon readings like those in Sachau and Greek. This conflate text has been subjected to various corrections. The present reading "into the south country" does not make sense. The word "south country" is known from Gen. 20, 1 and cf. Matt. 12,42/Luke 11,31. **Habban**, ܚܒܢ and Greek: ἀββά-νες. See F.C. Burkitt, "The Name Habban", in: *Journ. of Theol. Studies* 2 1901, 429, who refers to Latin Pap. A.D. 166 in Palaeographical Soc. Facs. Series II, Plate 190, where is spoken of a lieutenant of the imperial fleet on the Tigris who bought *puerum natione transfluminarum nomine Abban quem Eutychem sive quo alio nomine vocatur* for a price of 200 denars. **Gudnaphar**, ܓܘܕܢܦܪ and Greek: γυνδαφόρος is an Iranian name, see Justi, *Iran. Namenbuch* 368–369, *s.v.* Windafarna(h). From coins a king is known with this name who was reigning in North India, see J.T. Reinard, "Mémoire géographique, historique et scientifique sur l'Inde antérieurement au milieu de XIe siècle de l'ère chrétienne", in: *Mémoires de l'Academie des Inscriptions et Belles Lettres* XVIII, 2e partie, Paris 1849, and A. Cunningham, "Coins of Indian Buddhist Satraps with Greek Inscriptions", in: *Journal of the Asiatic Soc. of Bengal* 23 1854, 679–719. See also a coin with Gudnaphar and Guda or Gudana, cf. the name Gad in ch. 21, in: *Cambr. History of India* I, 379 and Plate VII 51, and "Actes de Saint apôtre Thomas" ed. by A.-J. Festugière, *Les Actes Apocryphes de Jean et de Thomas. Traduction Française et Notes Critiques*, Genève 1983, 45, note 1. It is not certain at which time Gudnaphar reigned, but it may be about 30–15 B.C. It seems that the author of these Acts introduced a legendary king who once lived in this area and who also became one of the "three kings" known from Matth. 2,1, see Justi, *Iran. Namenbuch* 369. **carpenter**. See ch. 3 and Act II. **in the street**. Greek adds: περὶ μεσημβρίαν, cf. Acts 8,26 and esp. 22,6. **slave**. The idea that Thomas became a slave and in this way received the same position as his Master is important in these Acts, see also ch. 167. See also M. Pesthy, "Thomas, the Slave of the Lord", in: *The Apocryphal Acts of Thomas* edited by J.N. Bremmer, Leuven 2001, 65–73. **twenty (pieces) of silver**. According to the Syriac version edited by Wright: ܟܤܦܐ ܥܤܪܝܢ, but in Sachau: "thirty ...". In the Greek version we find τριῶν λιτρῶν ἀσήμου, ἀργυρίου λίτρας τρεῖς and ἀργυρίου νομίσματα εἴκοσι. The Greek translation can be explained from the difficulty of rendering the Syriac word ܟܤܦܐ. The same problem is present in Zech. 11, 12, where the Hebrew שְׁלֹשִׁים כָּסֶף has been translated in de Syriac Peshitto by ܬܠܬܝܢ ܕܟܤܦܐ and in the LXX by τριάκοντα ἀργυροῦς. With help of the word ܟܤܦܐ the Syriac tries to say that no particular piece of money was mentioned in the original text. The use of the word "liter" makes the real price of a slave more or less in agreement with the current value. See Krauss, *Talm. Archäol.* II 403, where it is said that a לטרא is 100 denars. In the papyrus mentioned above it is said that Abban was sold for 200 denars and *Papyrus Oxyrhynchus* II CCXIII, 232–234, speaks about a price of 200 denars and IX 1209, 252–254, about a price of 2000 silver drachmae. The price of twenty pieces of silver seems to be original and is also found in Jacob of Serug, in: *Zeitschr. Deutsch. Morgenl. Gesellsch.* XXV 1871, 154, and the Arabic version. This would mean that Thomas is of less value than his master. But the influence of Gen. 37, 28 cannot be excluded according to which Joseph has been sold for twenty pieces of silver. In addition to this Joseph is to be compared with Jesus, see Melito, *Passa-Hom.* 59, ed. Lohse 24: ἀπόβλεψον ... Εἰς τὸν ἰωσὴφ τὸν ὁμοίως πιπρασκόμενον and Aphraates, *dem.* XXI, ed. Parisot c. 953–956. The price of thirty pieces of silver mentioned in some witnesses can be explained from Matth. 26, 15 and parallel passages. **bill of sale**, ܟܬܒܐ and Aramaic: שטר, see Krauss, *Talmud. Archäol.* II, 88–89. The contents are shorter than those known from the papyri. **I, Jesus ... Bethlehem**. See ch. 143; *Acta Petri* XIV, in: L.B. I, 61. 28–29: *et ego te adprobabo in nomine Iudeo et fabri filio credidisse*, and XXIII, in: *idem*, 71, 24–25: *Audaciam habes loqui de Iesu Nazareno, fabri filio et ipsum fabrum cuius genus in Judaeo positum est.* This might be due to the same tradition as met in Matth. 1,16 according to syr s reading: "Joseph, with whom the virgin Mary was betrothed, begot Jesus who is called the Christ". However, this idea also agrees with Syriac christology, see Ephrem, *de fide* XVII 9, ed. Beck, 52–43 (translation) and 69 (Syriac): "Du bist der Sohn des Lebendigen und du bist der Sohn eines sterblichen. Du bist der Sohn unseres Schöpfers ... und ferner bist du auch der Sohn des Joseph, jenes Zimmermann". **Is this your master**. The buyer must be sure to buy a slave and not a free man. **silent**, ܫܠܝ and Greek: ἡσύχαζεν. To be silent under the will of God, cf. Ps. 37,7; 62,6 and Is. 53,7, see also ch. 8.

3

And in the morning he **arose and prayed**, and entreated of his Lord, and said to Him: **See, our Lord, as you will, let your will be (done)**." And he went to Habban the merchant, **without carrying anything with him except that price of his**, for our Lord had given it to him. And Judas went and found Habban the merchant carrying his goods on board the **ship**, and he began to carry (them) on board with him. And when they had gone on board and sat down, Habban the merchant says to Judas: "What is your art which you are skilled in practicing?" Judas says to him: "Carpentry and architecture— the business of the carpenter." Habban the merchant says to him: "What do you know to make in **wood, and what in hewn stone?**" Judas says to him: "In wood I have learned to make **ploughs and yokes and ox-goads** and **oars for ferry-boats, and masts for ships**; and **in stone tombstones and monuments and temples, and palaces for kings**." Habban the merchant says to him: "And I was seeking just such an artificer". And they began to sail, because the breeze was steady; and they were **sailing along gently**, until they put in at the town of **Sandaruk**.

Commentary. **arose and prayed**. Greek adds the word "early", cf. I Sam. 1,9. **See, our Lord ... (done)**. Cf. Matth. 6,10 and 26,2. **without carrying ... price of his**. Greek: "... taking with him nothing at all save only his price. For the Lord had given it to him saying: 'Let your price, τίμηνα, also be with you, together with my grace wherever you go'". The idea is met again in ch. 146: "Your silver, which you gave me, I have cast down upon the table." The word "grace" in Greek may be secondary, although see History of Philip, Syriac ed. Wright, 70: "I go, Lord; but let not your grace be far from me", but the word τιμή which may translated as "dignity" is important, cf. ch. 112; 116; 120 and 165. In secondary Acts it is usually said that the money must be distributed among the poor, see Preaching of Thomas, Arabic, ed. Smith Lewis, 82. **ship**. The author assumes that Thomas goes to India on board ship, but it is not said from where. **wood ... stone**. The carpenter was usually skilled in working with wood and stone, see Bauer, *Wörterbuch* (5. Aufl.), c. 1601, *s.v.* τέκτων, and E. Lombard, "Charpentier ou Maçon", in: *Revue de Théol et de Phil.* 36 1948, p. 161–192. In the Preaching of Thomas, Arabic, ed. Smith Lewis, 82, Thomas is called carpenter, mason and doctor. **ploughs and yokes and ox-goads**. ... ܪܟܘܒܐ, but Greek: ... τρυτάνας, which means "pair of scales". In the secondary Acts a deeper sense was already accepted, see Preaching of Thomas, Arabic, ed. Smith Lewis, 86: "... the ploughs, they are the holy Gospels, which root up all evil from the heart of the believers." In *Acta Petri* XX, in: L.B. I, 68,13, Jesus is called "plough", see also Justin Martyr, *dial. c. Tr.* 88 8: ταῦτα γὰρ τὰ τεκτονικὰ ἔργα εἰργάζετο ἐν ἀνθρώποις ὢν ἄροτρα καὶ ζυγά, διὰ τούτων καὶ τὰ τῆς δικαιοσύνης σύμβολα διδάσκων καὶ ἐνεργῆ βίον. Ephrem, "Rede ü. d. Auferweckung des Lazarus", in: *BKV* 176: "Er (*scil.* Acker Christi) ist mit dem Pfluge des Kreuzes bebaut, und die Dornen sind aus ihm völlig ausgerottet worden ... Der Sohn Gottes verfertigte durch sein Leiden das Werkzeug zu seiner Bearbeitung, um durch das Joch der Kreuzigung das Unkraut aus ihm auszurotten", and Eccles. 12,11: "The sayings of the wise are sharp like goads, LXX: βούκεντρα." **oars ... ships**. Ships and their equipment play an important part in the early Church, see H. Rahner, *Griechische Mythen in christlicher Deutung*, Zürich 1945, 467–486: "Die Seefahrt des Lebens", and 430–444, about the significance of the mast; Justin Martyr, *apol.* I 55 3; Hippolytus, *de antichristo* 59, in: *P.G.* 10, c. 777–780, and Manich. Ps. 63. 17: "I was heading for shipwreck before I found the ship of Truth", and 123. 35: "... the cross was a ship, the souls were passengers". See F.J. Dölger, *Sol Salutis*, in: *Literaturgesch. Forsch.* 4–5, Münster 1920, 207–219; H. Schlier, "Religionsgeschichtliche Untersuchungen zu den Ignatiusbriefen", in: *Beihefte zur Zeitschrrift für die neutestamentlichen Wissenschaft und die Kunde der älteren Kirche.* 8 1929, 199–224; G. Widengren, "Mesopotamian Elements in Manichaeism", in: *Uppsala Universitets Årsskrift.* 1946.3, and R. Schöter, "Gedicht des Jakob von Sarug über den Palast den der Apostel Thomas in Indien baute", in: *Zeitschr. Deutsch. Morgenl. Gesellschaft* 25 1871, 321–377. **in stone ... kings**. Greek reads "pillars", στήλας, see Gal. 2, 9; I Tim. 3, 15 and Apoc. 3, 16, in place of "tombstones and monuments". See Preaching of Thomas, Arabic, ed. Smith Lewis 86: "The temples and fortresses which I have built are the souls which have come; they are the fortresses which I have repaired for the Heavenly King to dwell in", cf. I Cor. 6,10; 3,16.17 and Eph. 2,21. **sailing along gently**. Greek: καταπλέειν. This is a special gift of the gods, see Artemidorus, *oneirokritika* II 23, ed. Hercher, 115–117 and Dio Chrysostemus, *orat.* 63, ed. H.J. Crosby, 35: Τύχης γοῦν ἐν θαλάττῃ γενομένης εὐπλοεῖ ναῦς. See A. Dihle, "Neues zur Thomas Tradition", in: *Jahrb f. Antike und Christentum* 6 1963, p. 54–70. **Sandaruk**, ܢܘܪܝܣܡ, Greek: ἀνδράπολις, ἐναδρωχ, ἐναδόχ and ἐδρον. F.C. Burkitt, "The original Language of the Acts of Thomas", in: *Journ. of Theol. Studies* 1 1900, 280–290, esp. 288, referred to the name ܪܠܘܣܒ ܢܘܪܝܣܡ at the beginning of the Syriac romance of Julianus, see J.G.E. Hoffmann, *Julianus der Abtrünnige*, Leiden 1880, 241,6. A. von Guttschmidt, "Die Königsnamen in den apokryphen Apostelgeschichten", in: *Kleine Texte* II, Leipzig 1890, 332–394, esp. 362–363, supposed a derivation from Andhra, a people in South India, see Plinius, *nat. hist.* VI 19 22 67, and *Ancient India*, in: *The Cambridge History of India* I, ed. E.J. Rapson, Cambridge 1902, 598–601.

4

And when they had disembarked on the land, and were entering and going into the city, they heard the sound of **pipes and organs and much singing**. And Judas was asking and saying: "What is the rejoicing that is in the city?" They say to him: "You too have the gods brought that you may be glad in this city; for the king has an only daughter, and he is **giving her to a man**; and this sound of rejoicing is that of the wedding-feast. **And heralds have been permitted by the king to proclaim that every one should come to the feast, both poor and rich, and slaves and freemen, and strangers and citizens**. And every one who does not come to the feast, is in danger of the **anger of the king**". The merchant Habban says to Judas: "Let us too go, that we may not be spoken ill of, especially as we are strangers". And when they had stopped at an inn and rested a little, they went to attend the feast. And Judas reclined in the middle, and they were all looking upon him as upon a **stranger**, who came from another place. And the merchant Habban, his master, was reclining **in another place**.

Commentary. **pipes and organs, ܩܪܢܬܐ, and much singing**. Greek reads "trumpets" in place of "much singing". See Krauss, *Talmud. Archäol.* III, p. 91–92: "… und es kann sogar erwiesen werden, dass Wasserorgelspieler (אדרכלין= ὑδραῦλαι) und Flötenspieler (כרבלין= χοραῦλαι) gerade zur Hochzeitsfeste aufzuspielen pflegten, so dass die Redensart 'Wasserorgelspieler und Flötenspieler treiben sich in der Stadt herum' so viel hiess, dass jene Stadt *in dulci jubilo* lebe". The waterorgan is described by Vitruvius Pollio V 13, see also J.H. Waszink, *De Anima*, Amsterdam 1947, 216–217. **giving her to a man**, ܘܝܗܒܐ ܠܗ ܓܒܪ and Greek: αὐτὴν ἐκδίδωσεν ἀνδρὶ πρὸς γάμον. The influence of Syriac is evident. **And the heralds … feast**. Cf. Matth. 22,1–14. According to Krauss, *Talm. Arch.* III, 40–41, the whole population of a town was invited to a Jewish wedding by heralds. **both poor … citizens**. Cf. Gal. 3,28. **anger of the king**. Cf. Matth. 22,7. **stranger**. Three times the word "stranger" has been used in this chapter. In the phrase "strangers and citizens" it is the translation of ܢܘܟܪܝ has been used and the other two times the word ܐܟܣܢܝܐ that was used. In the rest of these Acts both words are met. The word ܐܟܣܢܝܐ has been used in ch. 4 (2 x); 33; 61; 72; 98; 100 (2 x); 145 and 154. This has been rendered by ξένος in the Greek version. The word ܢܘܟܪܝ has been used for the adjective "alien" in ch. 4 and 30 in Syriac only and in 38 (2 x); 47; 72 and 93. This word has also been rendered by ξένος. This obviously general usage shows a few deviations. The Greek version reads οὐ ... αὐτοῦ ἐσμεν to render ܐܝܢܣ the first time in ch. 38 and ἀλλότρια the second time. The same word is rendered by ξένον οὐδὲ ἀλλότριον in ch. 47. Finally the Greek version chose the word ξένος in order to translate the Syriac ܐܝܢܣ ܕܒܠܡ ܐܪܝܐ. Apart from this linguistic approach we may say that the word ξένος has been generally speaking applied to Thomas in ch. 4; 61; 98; 100; 145 and 154 or Jesus in ch. 72. In the two passages where ܐܝܢܣ was used we are dealing with "foreigners" in general. This means that we are probably dealing with a technical term in the sense of a "wandering Christian". This agrees with the usage with Ephrem, "Homilie des heiligen Ephram über das Pilgerleben" (ܐܪܟܐܘܡܣܐ ܠܓܠ), ed.A. Haffner, in: *Sitzungsber. der kaiserl. Akademie der Wissensch. Wien*, phil.-hist. Kl. 135 1896 See also Odes of Sal. XVII 6: "And all who saw me were amazed and I seemed to them like a stranger (ܐܪܡܣܘܪ)" and Aphraates, *demonstr.* XXVI 7, ed. Parisot, c. 1003–1004: *veniat mundus iste in contemptionem oculis vestris, quia advenae et peregrini* (ܐܪܡܫܪܐ ... ܐܪܕܐܫ). *) estis in eo.* See also H. von Campenhausen, "Die aszetische Heimatlosigkeit im altkirchlichen und frühmittelalterlichen Mönchtum, in: *Samml. gemeindeverst. Vorträge* 129, Tübingen 1930. **in another place**. Masters and servants are not sitting together, cf. J.H. Petermann, *Reisen im Orient*, Leipzig 1865 (2. Aufl.), 87: "Nach Sitte der Drusen blieb der Wirth in ehrerbietiger Entfernung stehen, und war trotz mehrfacher Aufforderung vom Seiten des Consuls nicht zu bewegen sich neben uns zu setzen".

5

And when they ate and drank, **Judas was tasting nothing at all**. Those who were beside him say to him: "Why have you come hither, since you are not able to eat and drink?" Judas said to them: "For something that is better than eating and drinking, have I come hither; **and for the king's rest**, and that I might accomplish his will; and because the heralds were proclaiming, that he who hears and does not come, **shall receive chastisement."** And when they had eaten and drunk, both **oil and dried fruits** were brought in to them, and they took (thereof). Some were **anointing their faces, others their beards, and others other places; but Judas was praising God, and signing** the middle of his head (with the Cross); and he moistened his nostrils with a little (of the oil), and put (some) in his ears, and made the sign (of the Cross) over his heart; and a **garland of myrtle was placed on his head, and he took a reed branch in his hand**.

Then the flute-girl who was in the middle of the party, was going round to them all; and when she came to Judas, she was standing and playing over him. And the flute-girl was a Hebrew (woman).

Commentary. **Judas was tasting nothing at all**. See John 4,34. **and for the king's rest**. Not in Greek. **shall receive chastisement**, ܢܦܫܗ ܒܪܫܗ ܡܣܒ and Greek: ὑπόδικος ἔσται τῇ τοῦ βασιλέως κρίσει. An obvious Syriasm which can be compared with ch. 21: ܡܐܬܐ ܐܝܟ ܒܪܫܗ and Greek: (καὶ ἐὰν μὴ) ἐπέλθῃς τῇ τιμωρίᾳ κατὰ τῆς κεφαλῆς; ch. 66: ܡܣܒ ܒܪܫܗ ܚܦܨܠܗ and Greek: τιμωρίαν ἀποτίσομεν τῆς ἑαυτῶν κεφαλῆς; ch. 100: ܘܐܡܣܝ ܒܪܫܗ and Greek: ἂν μὴ τὴν ἐκδίκησεν ποιήσῃ μοι διὰ τῆς τοῦ ξένου κεφαλῆς; ch. 101: ܘܡܣܝ ܒܪܫܗܘܢ and Greek: ἐπίθες τῇ κεφαλῇ αὐτῶν and ch. 102: ܘܐܪܥܐ ܐܝܟ ܒܪܫܗ and Greek: ἐκδικήσω σε. See F.C. Burkitt, "The original Language of the Acts of Judas Thomas", in: *Journ. of Theol. Studies* I 1900, p. 280–290, p. 283. **oil and dried fruit**. Greek: "garlands and unguents", see Krauss, *Talmud. Archäol.* III, p. 39: "Für den Nachtisch haben wir anlässlich des *epikomon*, die bestimmte Nachricht, dass es aus Nüssen, Dattlen und Sangen, im allgemeinen also aus Obst und Leckereien bestand". See for Indian meals Philostratos, *Apollonius of Tyana* III XXVII, ed. Conybeare, in: *Loeb Class.Libr.* 290: τραγήματα δὲ καὶ ἄρτοι καὶ λάχανα καὶ τρωκτὰ ὡραῖα, πάντα ἐν κόσμῳ ἐφοίτα διακείμενα ἢ εἰ ὀψοποιοὶ αὐτὰ περισκεύαλον. **anointing**. See Krauss, *Talmud. Archäol.* I, 233: "Man salbte sich insbesondere bei Gastmählern, zu Hochzeiten …" and p. 687, n. 242: "Die Hände werden nach der Mahlzeit mit Öl gereinigt". **Some were anointing … signing**. In Syriac a difference exists between ܡܫܚ, to anoint, and ܚܬܡ to sign (with the Cross). This difference is not present in the Greek version which reads: λαβόντες μύρον ἕκαστος ὃς μὲν τὴν ὄψιν αὐτοῦ κατήλειφεν … ὁ δὲ ἀπόστολος τὴν κορυφὴν ἤλειψεν τῆς ἑαυτοῦ κεφαλῆς. Signing with the cross is known from the History of John, Syriac ed. Wright p. 40: "and took oil in his hand and made him a cross on his forehead and anoited his whole body; *Acta Andraei et Matthaei* ch. 27 in: L.B. II I, 8–10, and Ephrem, *hymni dispersi* ch. VI, ed. Lamy IV, p. 705–706: *Signo crucis et unctione sanabas ut jussus eras.* See for anointing in order to receive strength *acta Archelai* XI, ed. Beesson, p. 19,6–8: ἐὰν παύσησθε (*eclecti*) ἐσθίοντες, εὔχεσθε καὶ βάλλεται ἐπὶ τῆς κεφαλῆς ἔλαιον ἐξωρκισμένον ὀνόματι πολλοῖς, πρὸς στηριγμὸν τῆς

πίστεως ταύτης. **garland of myrtle … reed branch in his hand**.
See Krauss, *Talmud. Archäol.* II, p. 38: "Sein (*scil.* Paranymphios) Abze-
ichen war wohl ein Myrtenzweig (בר של הדם auch שבשא und שושבתא
wovon eben der Paranympios seinen nh. Namen hat), mit dem sich
aber auch sonstige Gefolge, Männer und Frauen, schmückten". It is
possible that this passage is meant to show that Thomas makes his
appearance as a groom. Cf. Philostratus, *Apollonios of Tyana* II XXVII,
ed. Conybeare 189: ὡς, δὲ ἐλούσαντο, ἐβάδιζον ἐς τὸ συσσίτον ἐστε-
φανωμένοί, τουτὶ δὲ νενόμισται ἰνδοῖς ἐπειδὰν ἐν τῷ βασιλέως πινῶσιν,
and XXVIII: τράπεζα δέ ὥσπερ βωμὸς ὕψος ἐς, γόνυ ἀνδρὸς ἐξωκοδόμε-
ται μεσῃ, κύκλον ἐπέχουσα χοροῦ ξύμβεβλημένον ἀνδρῶν τριάκοντα ἐφ᾽
ἧς δαφναι τε διαστρώννυνται καὶ κλῶνες ἕτεροι παραπλήσιοι μὲν τῇ μυρ-
ρίνῃ, φέροντες δὲ ἰνδοῖς μύρον. See also K. Baus, "Der Kranz in Antike
und Christentum", in: *Theophaneia* II, Bonn 1940, 95–96. **flute-girl**.
Flute-girls were generally supposed to be πορνοὶ, cf. Gospel acc. to the
Nazoraeans, in: Eusebius, *theophaneia* IV 22, *P.G.* 24, c. 685–688: … τὸν
μὲν καταφανόντα τῆν ὕπαρξιν τοῦ δεσπότου μέτα πορνῶν καὶ αὐλητρί-
δων. They were rented, as appears from *Pap. Grenf.* II 67 (A.D. 321).
Strabo II 3 4 writes that Eudoxius shipped some flute-girls (μυσικὰ παι-
δισκάρια) to India (end 2nd cent. B.C.). Both the flute-girl and Thomas
are Hebrews and, therefore, strangers from the same country. Thus
they were able to understand each other, see ch. 8.

6 and 7

And when he had stood over him a long time, **Judas did not lift up
his face, but was looking all the time on the ground. And one
of the cupbearers came (and) raised his hand and smote him
on his cheek**. And Judas looked at him and said to him: "**My God
will forgive you this in the world to come, but in this world
He will show His wonders on the hand which smote me, and
I shall see it dragged along by a dog.**" And Judas began to sing
this song:

> "My church is the daughter of light;
> the splendour of kings is hers.
> Charming and winsome is her aspect,
> fair and adorned with every good work.
> 5 Her garments are like unto flowers,
> the smell thereof is fragrant and pleasant.
> On her head dwells the King,

and He feeds those who dwell with him beneath.
Truth is placed on her head,
10 joy moves in her feet.
   Her mouth is open, and it becomes her,
   wherewith she utters all songs of praise.
   The twelve Apostles of the Son,
   and the seventy-two thunder forth in her.
15 Her tongue is the curtain,
   which the priest raises and enters in.
   Her neck is the lofty flight of steps
   which the first architect did build.
   Her hands, both of them,
20 proclaim the place of life;
   and her ten fingers
   have opened the gate of Heaven.
   Her bridal chamber is lighted up,
   and full of sweet odour of salvation.
25 A censer is ready in its midst,
   love and belief and hope,
   gladdening all;
   within truth (dwells) in humility.
   Her gates are adorned with truth.
30 Her groomsmen surround her,
   all whom she has invited
   and her pure bridesmaids (go)
   before her uttering praise.
   The living are in attendance upon her,
35 and they look to their Bridegroom who shall come,
   and they shall shine with his glory,
   and shall be with Him in the kingdom
   which never passes away.
   And they shall be in the glory
40 to which all the just are gathered;
   and they shall be in the joy
   into which some enter;
   and they shall put on shining garments,
   and shall be clothed with the glory of their Lord.
45 And they shall praise the living Father,
   whose majestic light they have received,
   and have been enlightened by the splendour of their Lord,
   of whose food they have received,
   which never has any excrement.
50 and have drunk of the life
   which makes those who drink of it long and thirst (for more);
   and have glorified the Father, the Lord of all,
   and the only-(begotten) Son, who is of Him,
   and have praised the Spirit, His Wisdom.

Commentary. **Judas ... on the ground**. See ch. 8. **And one ... cheek**. Cf. Matth. 26,6; Mark 14,65; John 18,22 and 19,3. **My God ... smote me**. Punishment in this world means expiation in that to come, see J. Bonsirven, *Le Judaisme Palestinien* II, Paris 1935, 96–98, and ch. 147: "Scorn have I received on earth; a recompense do you make me in heaven". Greek: ὀνειδισμὸν ἐδεξάμην ἐπὶ τῆς γῆς, τὴν δὲ ἀμοιβὴν καὶ τὴν ἀντιμισθίαν δίδου μοι ἐν οὐρανοῖς. **and I shall ... dog**. Augustine referred to this passage in order to demonstrate the mentality of the Manichaeans, see *c. Adimantum* XVII 2, *c. Faustum* XXII 79 and *Sermo Domini in Monte* I 20 65. See also R. Söder, "Die apokryphen Apostel-gschichten und die romanhafte Literatur der Antike", in: *Würzb. Stud. z. Altertumswissensch.* III, Stuttgart 1932, 61. **this song**. For hymn-singing during meals, see Ps.-Clemens, *de virginitate* II VI 3–4, ed. Diekamp 38–39: *nec proicimus sanctum canibus nec margaritas ante porcos, sed Dei laudes celebramus cum omnimoda disciplina et cum omni prudentia et cum omni timore Dei atque animi intentione. Cultum sacrum non exercemus ibi, ubi imbriantur Gentiles et verbis impuris in conviviis suis blasphemant in impietate sua. Propterea non psallimus Gentilibus neque Scripturas illis praelegimus, ut ne tibicinibus aut cantoribus aut hariolis similes sumus, sicut multi, qui ita agunt et haec faciunt, ut buccella panis saturent sese, et propter modicum vini erunt et cantica Domini in terra aliena Gentilium faciunt, quod non licet.*

Hymn I *l.* **1. My Church**. The same reading in the Ethiopic and Armenian versions, but Greek: ἡ κόρη. Greek shows the original text, although the relation between the Church and a maiden is fluid. On the Abercius Epitaph the Church is called παρθένος ἁγνός, cf. Justin Martyr, *dial. c. Tryph.* 4; Clement of Alex., *paedag.* I 42 1, where the Church is called μήτηρ and παρθένος, and Eusebius, *hist. eccles.* IV 22 4, who writes that at the time of Hegesippus the Church was still called "virgin". See J. de Zwaan, "Some Remarks on the "Church-idea" in the second Century", in: *Mélanges offerts à Maurice Goguel*, Neuchatêl–Paris 1950, 270–278. But also in Syriac literature the Church is more than once called "daughter of light", see Jacob of Sarug, "Gedicht über die Decke vor dem Antlitz des Moses", in: *BKV* 348: "In einem neuen Mutterschoss führte ihr Verlobter die Tochter des Lichtes", and 356: "... da durchborte man seine Seite, und die Tochter des Lichtes kam aus derselben hervor ...", and Isaac of Antioch, "Dritte Gedicht über die Menschwerdung de Herrn", in: *BKV*, 146: "Der Glaube der Tochter des Lichtes ist ohne jegliche Grübelei". See F.C. Conybeare, "Die Jungfräuliche Kirche", in: *Archiv für Religionswissensch.* 8 1905, 373–389, and 9 1906, 73–86; J.C. Plumpe, "Mater

Ecclesia", in: *Cath. Univ. of America. Studies in Christian Antiquity* 5, Washington 1947, and F. Graffin, "Recherches sur le Thème de l'Église-Épouse dans les Liturgies et la Litérature patristique de langue syrienne", in: *l'Orient syrien* 3 1958, 317–337. In the Greek version of these Acts is spoken of the "daughter of light". This agrees with some passages in the Manichaean literature like *Kephalaia* 35. 15, where she is met together with Jesus Ziwa, and 24. 18–19: "Die Weisheit [ist die] Jungfrau des Lichtes"; Manich. Ps. 116, 5–6: "the Wisdom (σοφία) that looks (?) forth is the Holy Spirit", and *Pistis Sophia*, ed. Schmidt–Till 126. 18 and 138. 26, see W. Bousset, *Hauptprobleme* ... . 63 and H.H. Schaeder, "Urform und Fortbildungen des manichäischen Systems", in: *Vortr. Bibl. Warburg* 1924–25, 65–157, esp. 137–138. We may draw the conclusion that we are dealing with a heavenly figure taken from the surrounding Semitic world showing characteristics related with the Jewish Wisdom.

l. **2. the splendour, ܙܝܘܐ, of kings is hers**. Greek: ... ἀπαύγασμα ... Cf. *Sap. Sal.* 7,25–26: "For she (*scil.* Wisdom) is ... a clear ἀπόρροια of the glory of the Almighty ... an ἀπαύγασμα from an everlasting light", and Hebr. 1,3. Splendour belongs to the heavenly world, cf. ch. 141: "... that I too may receive your splendour, ܙܝܘܐ Greek: φέγγος", and ch. 147: "and worship before your holy splendour, ܙܝܘܐ, Greek: ἀπαύγασμα". The word is important in Manichaeism, see F.C. Burkitt, *The Religion of the Manichees*, Cambridge 1935, 107–111, and H.-C. Puech, *Le Manichéisme*, Paris 1949, 77 and 82.

l. **3.** Wisdom is a source of joy, see Sir. 6,28: "... she shall be turned for you into gladness".

l. **4. fair ... good work**. In the Syriac text edited by Wright we read: ܫܦܝܪ ܥܒܕ, but Sachau: ܫܘܦܪܐ, a word that can be both "beauty" and "good work" which can be compared with Greek:

l. **5–6. flowers the smell thereof ...** Odorous scent belongs to the heavenly world, cf. Ephrem, *de paradiso* 11,9, ed. Beck 44 (translation) and 48 (Syriac): "Dichter und strahlender als die Sterne dieses sichtbaren Himmels (stehen) die Blumen jener Erde, und ein Teil jenes Duftes, der durch die Güte (Gottes) weht, wird ausgesandt als Arzt der Leiden (unserer) Erde des Fluches"; Sir. 24,15: "As cinnamon and asphalthus have I (*scil.* Wisdom) given a scent of perfumes. And as chosen myrrh I spread abroad a pleasant odour", and Manich Ps. 118. 29: "What smell is there in the world (κόσμος) that is like your fragrant smell?" See H. Riesenfeld, "Jésus transfiguré", in: *Acta Sem. Neot. Upsal.* 16, København 1947, 115–129, and E. Lohmeyer, "Vom göttlichen

Wohlgeruch", in: *Sitzungsber. der Heidelb. Akademie der Wissenschaften*, phil.-hist. Kl. 1919.

l. **7.** See tMeg. 15b, ed. L. Goldschmidt, *Der Babylonische Talmud* IV, Berlin 1966, 63: "Ferner sagte R. Eleazer im Namen R. Haninas: Dereinst wird der Heilige, gepriesen sei er, eine Krone auf dem Haupte eines jeden Frommen sein" (follows Is. 28, 5); Odes of Sal. 1. 1: "The Lord is on my head as a crown" and 5. 12: "And as a crown is he on my head".

l. **8.** In the Syriac version of the manuscript B.L. the text reads: ܕܘܬܐ ,ܡܘܝܘܥܠ ܪܝܘ and Greek: τρέφων τῇ ἑαυτοῦ ἀμβροσίᾳ τους ἐπ' αὑτοῦ ἱδρυμένους. Wright's translation does not seem correct because "to dwell with" supposes the Syriac words ܥܡ ܝܕܪ as can be found in John 3, 22 in syr s. Better appears to be a translation like "his dwellers" or "his citizens", cf. Phil. 3, 20 and Eph. 5, 29. The Greek version assumes that "the king" is the foundation which can be compared with 1 Cor. 3, 10–11. Elliott's translation: "... who live under him" seems to be improbable. See also H. Kruse, "Das Brautlied der syrischen Thomas-Akten", in: *Orientalia Christiana Periodica* 50 1984, 291–330, esp. 299–300.

l. **9.** Truth is the dignity of the daughter of light, cf. *l.* 7, and the Odes of Sal. 1. 2: "Plaited for me is the crown of truth", and 9. 8: "An everlasting crown is Truth".

l. **10.** The daughter of light is dancing, see *l.* 32–33.

l. **11–12.** To "open the mouth" in order to praise God, see Sir. 24, 2; Luke 1, 64; Acts 19, 6; Odes of Sal. 8. 4: "You who were in silence, speak, for your mouth has been opened" and Irenaeus, *adv. haer.* I 13 3, about the Marcosians: ἰδοὺ ἡ χάρις κατῆλθεν ἐπὶ σέ. ἄνοιξεν τὸ στόμα σου καὶ προφήτευσιν. Greek reads: τριάκοντα καὶ δυο εἰσὶν οἱ ταύτην ὑμνολογοῦντες, which is not quite clear. Valentinus speaks about thirty aeons with Christ and the Holy Spirit according to Irenaeus, *adv. haer.* I 3 1, cf. also Hippolites, *refut.* VI 31 3: τριάκοντα αἰωνες μετὰ τοῦ χριστοῦ καὶ τοῦ ἁγίου πνευματος. See also *Encyclopaedia Judaica* IX 1932, c. 104–111, esp. c. 105, *s.v.* Jezira, about the 32 ways of wisdom by which God created the world, and Festugière IV 227, n. 4: "Plus difficile est le cas des trente deux ὑμνολογοῦντες (109,8). Lipsius, sans trouver de solution, y voit seulement trente-deux Eons, cf. *Apokr. Apostelgesch.* I, pp. 395s. Faut-il lire τριάκοντα καὶ ἕξ (confusion de l' ἐπίσημον et du βῆτα?): on aurait en ce cas le trente six decans, cf. Asclep. 19 (319, 1) et Stob. Herm VI. See also N. Séd, "Le Memar Samaritain. Le Sefer Yesira et les trente-deux sentiers de la Sagesse", in: *Rev.de l'Hist. des Religions* 170 1966, 159–184.

l. **13–14.** The Syriac text refers to the New Testament, where is spoken of twelve Apostles, see Matth. 10,1 and parallel passages and seventy-two messengers who were sent away to preach the kingdom of God, see Luke 10, 1. A striking parallel is present in Manich. Ps. 22. 23–36: "Victory to our Apostle, our Lord Mani and the Twelve, the seventy-two envoys (πρεσβευτῆς), to every one that sings and praises the ... (defective) ... of wisdom (σοφία) and the soul of Mary".

l. **15–16.** The Syriac version adapted this passage to the liturgy of the Church, where the "curtain" hides the altar, see Litugical Homilies of Narsai, ed. Connolly 11: "As soon as the veil is withdrawn one is allowed to look into heaven"; Liturgy of Jacob, ed. Brightman 401: "they uncover the table and signify the doors of heaven are opened", see also Nestorian Liturgy, ed. Brightman 268. The idea of a veil covering the heavenly mysteries seems aready to have been known in Judaism, cf. E.R. Goodenough, "Jewish Symbols in the Greco-Roman Period", in: *Bollington Series* XXXVII, New York I–IV 1952–1953, esp. I 268 and III, fig. 832. Also in the New Testament is spoken about a veil between heaven and earth, see Hebr. 6, 19–20. See also *Pistis Sophia*, ed. Schmidt–Till, I. 6; 14. 5; 25. 29–30 and *Exc. e Theodoto* 38. 1–2, ed. Sagnard 141: "Et le lieu lui-même est de feu. C'est pour cette raison, dit [Théodote?], qu'il a une voile, afin que les éléments 'pneumatiques' ne soient pas consumés par la vue". The Greek version reads: ἐκτινάσσεται τοῖς εἰσιοῦσιν. The meaning of these words is not quite clear. It is the beginning of the description of the outward appearance of the daughter of light, cf. Song of Songs 5, 10–16.

l. **17–18.** In Greek nothing is said about "the neck". See for the length of the neck Song of Songs 4, 4; 7, 4 and Hos. 10, 11. We cannot agree with Kruse, "Das Brautlied ..." 305–306, saying: "Der Hals ist das unumgängliche Verbindungs- und Vermittlungsstück zwischen dem Haupt (Christus) und dem Rumpf (der Kirche) ... Die Differenzierung der Autoritätsträger in der Kirche ... ist also ... vorausgesetzt." See for the second line Hebr. 11, 10. The addition of the word "first" may try to avoid a possible misunderstanding about the real creator of this world, but see also Is. 44, 6 and 48, 12.

l. **19–20. Place of life.** The same expression in *Liber Graduum* XXI 6, ed. Kmosko c. 461–462, and Ginza L 431,1–2 and 506,33. The Greek version reads: τὸν χορὸν τῶν εὐδαιμόνιων αἰώνων. See *l.* 32–33 about a dance in heaven.

l. **21–22.** For the words **gates of heaven** see Ginza R 212, 2–8: "Als das Mass des Dinanukht voll war und er seinen Körper verliess, führten sie ihn zum Tore des Hauses des Lebens empor. Da sprach Dinanukht: 'Öffnet mir das Tor des Hauses des Lebens'. Da öffneten sie ihm das Tor des Hauses des Lebens und zogen vor ihm den grossen Vorhang der Sicherheit in die Höhe."

l. **23–29.** The Syriac version obviously speaks about the baptistery with a censer and being a place characterized by love, belief and hope, cf. I Cor. 13, 13, and humility. It is not adorned by flowers as we see in the Greek version but by truth. This agrees with a number of passages in which it is said that the adorning of doors has to be rejected, see Tertulian, *de idol.* 15; Ephrem, "Rede auf das Osterfest", in *BKV* 370, and Gregory of Naz., *Oratio in Theoph. Domini* 3, in: *P.G.* 36, c. 316, see K. Baus, "Der Kranz in Antike und Christentum", in: *Theophaneia* II, Bonn 1940, 61–71. The Greek version differs considerably and speaks about the heavenly world: ἧς ὁ παστὸς φωτεινός, ἀποφορὰν ἀπὸ βαλσάμου καὶ παντὸς ἀρώματος διαπνέων, ἀποδιδούς τε ὀσμὴν ἡδεῖαν σμύρνης τε καὶ φύλλου, ὑπέστρωνται δὲ ἐντὸς μυρσίναι καὶ ἄνθέων παμπόλλων ἡδυπνόων, αἱ δὲ κλειστάδες ἐν καλάμοις κεκόσμηνται. Here the word "bridal-chamber" has been avoided. Nevertheless we notice a close relationship between the idea of the baptistery, that of the bridal-chamber and the heavenly world. This can be illustrated with help of some references. In the Liturgical Homilies of Narsai, ed. Connolly 54, it is said: "A beauteous bride-chamber He has fitted on earth for the type of that which is above" and in Cyrillus of Jerusalem, *cat.* III 2, ed. Reischl, 64–65: ἀρξασθε πλῦνειν τὰς στολὰς ὑμῶν διὰ μετανοί ας, ἵνα εἰς τὸν νυμφῶνα καθαραὶ κληθέντες εὑρεθῆτε. At the moment the doors of the baptistery have been opened the doors of heaven are opened, see Nestorianische Taufliturgie, ed. Diettrich 9 and Badger, *Nestorians* II, 275: "Thy church may dwell in this bridal chamber for ever", see also Irenaeus, *adv. haer.* I 33 3, about the Marcosians: καθέδρουν ἐν τῷ νυμφῶνι σου το σπερμα τοῦ φωτός. The bridal-chamber as the heavenly abode is found with Ephrem, ed. Mitchell II, LXXVII and 164: "and that have kept the word of our Lord ... are exalted to the Bridal chamber of Light", and: "For if Lazarus when he died ... has gone to the Bridal Chamber of Light', see also Ephrem, *de fide* 4, 8, ed. Beck 11 (translation) and 55 (Syriac) and 11. 18, 40 (translation) and 55 (Syriac); Isaac of Antioch, "Gedicht über die Busse", in: *BKV* 161: "Den Jungfrauen wird das himmliche Brautgemach zuteil" and Manich. Ps. 62, 13–14; 63, 2; 79, 16 and 102, 31–32. See. W. Bousset. "Hauptprobleme der Gnosis", in: *Forsch. z. Rel. u. Lit. des A. u. N.T.* 13, Göttingen 1921, 76–77; G. Widengren, "Mesopotamian Elements in

Manichaeism", in: *Uppsal. Univ. Årsskr.* 1946. 3, and H. Engberdin, "Die Kirche als Braut in der ostsyrischen Literatur". in: *Or. Christ. Periodica* III 1937, 5–44.

l. **30–31.** This part of the hymn deals with the train of the daughter of light, cf.Prov. 9,4 and *Sap. Sal.* 6,16: "For she goes about seeking them that are worthy of her". In the Greek version it is said that she has chosen "seven" groomsmen, see following lines.

l. **32–33.** In Greek it is said that the number of bridesmaids is again "seven" and that they "dance before her". It seems that the Syriac version wishes to avoid the idea of "dancing", see also *l.* 20. However, we have to take into account that the Greek version speaks about heaven and the Syriac about the baptistery. The situation in heaven explains the number of groomsmen and bridesmaids, cf. Philo, *opif.* 70: ... πλανήτων τε καὶ ἀπλαυῶν χορείαις συμπεριποληθεὶς κατὰ τοὺς μουσικῆς τελείας νόμους, ἐπόμενος ἔρωτα σοφίας ποδηγετοῦντι ... See also Krauss, *Talmud. Archäol.* III, 101: "Die Art eines solches Massentanzes ist ersichtlich aus der mehrfach vorkommenden aggadischen Vorstellung, dass Gott einst den Frommen einen Reigentanz bereiten werde, wo er selbst der Reigenführer (ראש הולה etwa χορηγός), die himmliche Heerscharen die Tanzer das Volk der Frommen, die Zuschauer sein werden ... angeheitert wie sie nun sind, nehmen sie den Vorständer in die Mitte und machen der Reigentanz mit". See also Ignatius, *ad Ephes.* XIX 2; Homilie sur la Virginité III 56, ed. Amans–Moons, p. 49: ... ἔμπροσθεν του χριστοῦ χορεύσαι ἀπὸ ἀγγέλων ἐν εὐφροτύνη τέρψιν γενομένην (virgins in heaven) and *Acta Johannis* 94–97, in: L.B. II I, 197–199.

l. **34.** In this line **the living** are the members of the Church, see Odes of Sol. XLII 1 and II Clem. 3,1. The Greek version reads: δώδεκα δέ εἰσιν τὸν ἀριθμὸν οἱ ἔμπροσθεν αὐτῆς ὑπηρετοῦντες καὶ αὐτῇ ὑποκείμενοι. This corresponds with the number "seven" in *l.* 30. We are dealing with the idea of the seven planets and zodiac. See *Acta Johannis* 95, in: L.B. II I. 19, 4–6: ὀγδοὰς μία ὑμῖν συμψάλλεται. Ἀμήν ὁ δωδέκατος ἀριθμὸς ἄνω χορεύει. The "seven" are mentioned in *Corpus Hermet.* I 26 and XII 15 and the "twelve" in XIII 12, and in Manich. Ps. 203, 33–204,1: "He caught the hand of his seven companions and his twelve helpers (βοηθός)". Striking is the rejection of the "twelve" and the "seven" in Ginza 24. 27: "Lobpreiset nicht die Sieben und Zwölf", and Mand. Liturg. 160: "Deine Gegner waren die Sieben und die Zwölf waren deine Verfolger."

l. **35–38.** This may be compared with Matth. 25,1–13, but we are dealing with the enlightenment, see Greek version: ἵνα διὰ τοῦ θέαματος αὐτοῦ φωτισθῶσαν, which returns in *l.* 45–47. In the New Testament we meet traces of this idea in II Cor. 3, 18 and I John 3, 2, but see Irenaeus, *adv. haer.* IV 29 6: *Homines igitur videbunt Deum ut vivant per visionem immortales facti et pertingentes usque Deum,* and IV 20 7: ... *vita autem hominis visio Dei.* See also Clemens of Alex., *strom.* IV 40 1; *protrept.* 120; Origen, *Comment. Johannis* XXXII 27; *Corpus Hermet.* XIII 18–20 and Ginza R 57, 20–21: "Wir schauten deinen Glanz und erhielten Leben. Wir schauten dein Licht und wurden glaubig". See W. Völter, "Der ware Gnostiker nach Clemens Alexandrinus". in: *Texte u. Unters.* 57 1932, 434: "Vergöttlichung durch Schau—diesen Gedanken hat die östliche Kirche nicht mehr fahren lassen", and Festugière IV, 241–257" "L'Illumination".

l. **39–42. in the glory,** ܪ‍ܘ‍ܒ‍ܚ‍ܐ. G. Hoffmann, "Zwei Hymnen der Thomasakten", in: *Zeitschr. f. d. neutestamentl. Wissensch.* 4 1903, 273–257, proposed to change this word into ܪ‍ܗ‍ܒ‍ܚ‍ܐ, cf. Greek: "... and shall be at the marriage where the princes (μεγιστᾶνες) are gathered together and shall attend at the banquet (τῇ εὐωχίᾳ) whereof the eternal ones are accounted worthy". The Greek version refers to those in heaven. The μεγιστᾶνες mentioned here are also present in biblical texts but usually in an unfavourable sense, see Sir. 4, 7; 10, 24; Mark 6, 21; Rev. 6, 15 and 18, 23. On the other hand we meet in *Sap. Sal.* 6, 21: "Honour wisdom, that you (*scil.* princes of people) may reign for ever"; Manich. Ps. 117, 3: "I am a prince (μεγιστᾶνος) wearing a crown with the kings", and Mand. Liturg. 111: "Ein Brief geschrieben mit Kusta, gesiegelt mit dem Siegelring Grösser". For the idea that man will be king, see ch. 136 and 142.

l. **43–44.** The Greek text reads: "And put on royal garments, and be dressed in splendid robes ...". Both in connection with Baptism and eternal life new clothes are mentioned, cf. Sacramentary of Serapion, ed. Brightman 266; Ephrem, *hymni epiphaniae* VI 9, ed. Lamy I, c. 57–58; Moses bar Kepha, *The Mysteries of Baptism,* ed. Aytoun 256; Theodore of Mopsuestia, ed. Mingana 68, and Nestor. Taufliturgie, ed. Diettrich 44. See also IQS IV 7–8: "... eternal enjoyment with endless life, and a crown of glory with majestic raiment in eternal light"; Rev. 19,6–10; *Kephalaia* 36, 23–25: "Heil, dem welcher sie (*scil.* fünf Väter) erkennt ... denn er wird ... die Licht-gewänder empfangen, die gegeben werden den Gerechten (δίκαιος)"; Huwidagman VI, ed. M. Boyce 101: "Thou shalt put on a radiant garment, and gird on Light; and I shall set on thy head the diadem of sovereignty"; Flügel,

Mani (Fihrist) 100: "Wenn der Tod, lehrt Mani, einem wahrhaftigen naht, sendet der Urmensch einen Lichtgott in der Gestalt des leitenden Weisen und mit ihm drei Götter und zugleich mit diesen das … Kleid, die Kopfbinde, die Krone und den Lichtkranz", and Mand. Liturg. 26–27: "… komme steige zum Jordan hinab, werde getauft, empfange das reine Zeichen, ziehe Gewänder des Glanzes an und richte auf den Haupte prangende Kränze".

l. **45–47.** The Greek text reads τὸν πατέρα τῶν ὅλων in stead of **Living Father** and ἐν τῇ θέᾳ τοῦ δεσπότου αὐτῶν in place of **by the splendour**. See for hymn-singing in heaven Hymn II *l.* 103–104; Rev. 5,9; *Corp. Hermet.* I 26, see Festugière III, 133–137: "Le Chant des Bienheureux"; Manich. Ps. 117. 29–30: "Take me into thy bride-chamber that I may chant with them that sing to thee", and Ginza L. 515. 36–39: "Singet Hymnen und lasset diese Seele vernehmen, dass ihr Mass voll und ihr Gang nach dem Orte des Lebens gerichtet ist". The "enlightenment" is part of the heavenly bliss, see already *l.* 35–38; Odes of Sal. 41. 6: "And let our faces shine in his Light …", and Moses bar Kepha, *The Mysteries of Baptism*, ed. Aytoun, 346: "Again it (*scil.* baptism) is named illumination … Firstly, because from him who is baptized there is expelled the darkness of the ignorance of God … secondly, because he is counted worthy of the light of the kingdom of heaven".

l. **48–51.** The Greek version speaks of τὴν ἀμβροσίαν βρῶσιν, see *l.* 8; ch. 25 and 36; *Sap. Sal.* 19, 21: … ἀμβροσίας τροφῆς, and Philo, *de somn.* II 249: τὸ χαρᾶς τὸ εὐφροσύνης ἀμβρόσιον ἵνα καὶ αὐτοὶ ποιητικοῖς ὀνόμασι χρησωμεθα, φάρμακον. See H. Lewy, "Sobria Ebrietas", in: *Beih. Zeitschr. f.d. neutestamentl. Wissensch.* 9 1929, 91, n. 2; *Theol. Wörterb. z. N.T.* II 35, *s.v.*: δεῖπνον (Behm): "Das Bild des eschatologischen (Freuden- oder Gerichts-) Mahles ist aus israel.-jüd. Eschatologie erwachsen". Cf. Sir. 15, 3: "And she (*scil.* chokma) will feed him with bread of under-standing, and will give him waters of knowledge to drink". Striking is the passage ܐܠ ܚܝܠ ܡܘܠܕ ܡܢ ܐܘܣܝܐܪ in Greek: μηδὲν ὅλως ἀπουσίαν ἔχουσαν. The exact translation is difficult. Both in Syriac and Greek the word ܐܘܣܝܐ—ἀπουσία has been used. The Greek word must be translated into "absence" and Syriac into *dejectio, alvus, interfrimentum, lasanum*, see Brockelmann, *Lexic. Syr.* 22b. One may compare bYoma 75b, ed. Goldschmidt II 1933, about Manna: "… bread that is (wholly) consumed—לחם אב׳ר׳ם". There are examples that Jesus was supposed to consume his food wholly, see Clement of Alex., *strom.* III 59 3 and VI 71 1 (about the Valentinians), and *Book of the Bee*, ed E.A. Wallis Budge, in: *Anecd. Oxon.*, Sem. Series, vol. I Pt. II, Oxford 1886, 101: "Some say that after His resurrection our Lord ate the food unto that which the angels ate in the home of Abraham and that the food was dissipated and consumed by the Divine Power, just as fire licks up oil without any of it entering into its substance". See P.-H. Poirier, "'Απουσια' Note sur un mot des Actes de Thomas", in: *ARAM* 5 1973, 427–435. The reading **drunk of the life** in stead of Greek "of the wine" agrees with a tendency to avoid using wine at the eucharist, see ch. 60.

l. **52–55.** In the Syriac version is spoken of the Father, the Son and the Spirit who is identified with Wisdom, cf. Irenaeus, *demonstr.* 5, ed. Froidevaux 36: "… c'est à bon droit et en toute convenance que le Verbe est appelé Fils, maais 'l'Esprit, Sagesse de Dieu", see note 6. and Theophilus, *ad Autol.* II 9 and 15. The Greek reads: ἐδόξασαν δὲ καὶ ὕμνησαν σὺν τῷ ζῶντι πνεύματι τὸν πατέρα τῆς ἀληθείας καὶ τὴν μητέρα τῆς σοφίας. This passage is not easy to understand because we wonder what is the relation between "the living spirit" and "the mother of wisdom". We might compare ch. 39: δοξάζομεν καὶ ὑμνοῦμεν σὲ καὶ τὸν ἀόρατον σου πατέρα καὶ τὸ ἅγιον σου πνεῦμα καὶ τὴν μητέρα πασῶν κτίσεων. We are also dealing with a doxology. See for the use of the idea "mother" also ch. 27, where she has to be identified with the Spirit. We suppose that the juxtaposition of the figure of the "mother" and the "spirit" shows a stage in which the Semitic mother, see Philo, *de ebrietate* 30, and the Christian Spirit have not yet been wholly identified. See for *Father of truth* II Clem. 3. 1 and 20. 5; Odes of Sal. 41. 9 and *Evang. Veritatis* 16. 33, ed. Robinson 37.

Summarising the contents of the commentary on *Hymn* I we arrive at the following conclusions:

a. The Difference between the Greek and the Syriac Version.
In the Greek version the principal person has been described as a female heavenly person who is living in the company of the King of heaven. Her dwelling place is between heaven and earth. She leads her train into the bridal chamber. The character of this bridal chamber corresponds with the traditional description of heavenly bliss.

In the Syriac version the daughter of light has been identified with the church. It is striking that this was possible with help of a number of minor corrections only.

b. The Background of this Hymn.

The description of the principal person corresponds with that of the well-known Semitic female being in general and that of Jewish wisdom in particular.[1]

c. The Contents of the Hymn.

In *l.* 1–22 a description is given of the outward appearance of the daughter of light. It can generally be explained from biblical sources. The Syriac adaptation was possible with minor corrections only.

In *l.* 23–29 a bridal chamber has been described. It is noteworthy that those entering the bridal chamber do not attend a wedding but are enjoying heavenly bliss. In the Greek version the bridal chamber has been situated in heaven but in the Syriac version it is identified with the baptistery. This was the cause of a number of characteric changes.

In *l.* 30–39 the train of the daughter of light has been described. In this part we see the most important deviations between the Greek and the Syriac versions. In the Greek version the entire heavenly world takes part.

In *l.* 40–51 a description has been given of what happens with those who entered the bridal chamber. We meet remarks about new garments and participation in praising God.

In *l.* 52–55 a doxology has been added. It is difficult to reconstruct the original text because it did not agree with the liturgical development anymore. It appears that especially the original presence of a female being had to be removed.

8

And when he had sung this song, all who were beside him were **looking at him**, and were seeing that **his aspect was changed; but they could not all understand what he was saying, because he was speaking in Hebrew**, and they did not know (it). **But the flute-player heard everthing, because she was a Hebrew (woman) and she was looking at him. And when she left him**

---

[1] In the last decades the number of studies on Wisdom have been increased enormously. Investigation has been stimulated by the emphasis on feminine and sociological studies. See, for example, Rose Horman Arthur, *The Wisdom Goddess. Feminine Motifs in eight Nag Hammdi Documents*, Lanham, New York, London 1984. A special study on the present hymn is found with H. Kruse, "Das Brautlied der syrischen Thomas-Akten", in: *Orientalia Christiana Periodica* 50 1984, 291–330.

**and played to the others, she still kept looking at him, and
loved him, as a countryman of hers**; and in his looks he was **more
beautiful than all** those who were there. And when the flute-player
had finished, she sat down opposite to him and did not turn away her
eyes from him, **but he did not lift up his eyes, and did not look
at any one, but was ever looking upon the ground, (waiting)
till he might arise and depart from the banquet-room. And
the cupbearer had gone down to the fountain to draw water,
and a lion happened to be there, and rent him and tore him
limb from limb. Then the dogs were carrying off his limbs
singly, and a black dog carried off his right hand, which he
had raised against Judas and brought it into the midst of the
banquet-room.**

Commentary. Some Greek manuscripts add καὶ ἡσύχαζεν and other ones
ἡσύχαζον after **looking at him**, see also ch. 2. **his aspect was
changed**. See Matth. 17,2, cf. *Acta Pauli et Theclae* 3, in: L.B. II, 237,
8–9: ποτὲ μέν γὰρ ἐφαίνετο ὡς ἄνθρωπος, ποτὲ δὲ ἀγγέλου πρόσωπον
εἶχεν, and *Acta Philippi* 60, in: L.B. II II 25, 17–18: καὶ ὁ Ἴρεος ἐφο-
βήθη τὸν Φίλιππον, πῶς οὕτως μεταμόρφωσεν ἑαυτόν. Hymn-singing is
a privilege of the inhabitants of heaven, cf. Origen, *in Psalm.* 118, in:
P.G. 12, c. 1628, and Chrysostemus, *Hom. 9 in Coloss.*, in: *P.G.* 62 c. 363:
ψαλμοὶ πάντα ἔχουσιν, οἱ δὲ ὕμνοι πάλιν οὐδὲν ἀνθρώπινον ... αἱ γὰρ
ἄνω δυνάμεις ὑμνῶσιν, οὐ ψάλλουσιν. In the New Testament it is said
that Hymn-singing can only be done in the Spirit, see Eph. 5,18–21.
but they could ... in Hebrew. It is only possible to whom it has
been given to hear his words, see Matth. 4,10–12 and I Cor. 2,11. **But
the flute-player ... Hebrew (woman)**. She is of the same γένος as
Thomas, cf. I Pet. 2,9, an idea expressed in the following way in Syriac:
ܡܝܐܪ ܝܒ ܪܝܠܒܝ ܝܡܝܐ ܐܡܘ ܡܐܝܘܪܐ and Greek: πάνω γὰρ ἠγάπησεν
αὐτὸν ὡς ἄνθρωπον ὁμόεθνον αὐτῆς **and she was looking ... hers**.
A parallel is found in *Acta Pauli et Theclae* 20, in: L.B. I, 249,5: ἡ δὲ
εἱστήκει παύλῳ ἀτενίζουσα followed by 21, in L.B. I, 250,2–4: καὶ εἶ-
πεν (*scil.* Thecla) ὡς ἀνυπομονήτου μου οὔσης ἦλθεν παῦλος, θεάσασθαι
με. Καὶ προσεῖχεν αὐτῇς ἀτενίζουσα· ὁ δὲ εἰς οὐρανοὺς ἀπίει. See also
Ginza L. 441, 8–9: "Sie (*scil.* Hawwa) erblickte den fremden Mann und
gewann ihn lieb". See G. Bornkamm, *Mythos* 72–73, and R. Strelan,
"Strange Stares: ATENIZEIN in Acts", in: *Nov. Test.* 41 1999, 235–255,
esp. 244–247. **beautiful**. This word is often used to describe heavenly beings, see ch. 35; 36; 66; 122; 129; 147; 149 and 160. It is absent

in the New Testament but present in Hellenistic literature, see Plato, *symp.* 210E; Plotinus, *enn.* V 8, ed. P. Henry et H.R. Schwyzer II, 374–409: περὶ τοῦ νοητοῦ κάλλους; *enn.* V 9 2, 412–413, and *Sap. Sal.* 13,3: "And if through delight in their (*scil.* luminaries) beauty they (*scil.* men) took them to be Gods", and Gospel of Peter 13,55: καὶ ὁρῶ-σιν … νεανίσκον … ὡραῖον καὶ περιβεβλημένον; Odes of Sol. VII 23; XII 4 and XVI 5. **more beautiful than all,** ܘܡܢ ܟܠܗܘܢ and Greek: ὡραῖος ὑπὲρ πάντας, which shows the influence of Syriac. **but he did not lift … banquet room.** For a description of an ecstatic experience see Bar Hebraeus, *Ethikon*, ed. Wensinck 109–110: "And while the face of its Lord is detected before it, it becomes stupified and is made radiant by the rays of His beauty. And there takes place transition, which is described by our holy Fathers, so that it is impossible for the soul to return from its delight. And if its Lord loosened it not from union, it would forget its partner the body … And when the mind returns again [to our Lord], the body is almost borne along with it, and the soul can scarcely shake it off when it is elevated … and it forgets not only what is here but also itself. And because of the divine light with which it is clad, it sees itself as the likeness of God", and Isaac of Ninive, *The Perfect Religion*, ed. Bedjan, Paris 1909, 338, quoted by Wensinck, *Book of the Bee*, CVII: "In truth, my brethren, another feature of this state is sometimes, that the mystic does not remember that he himself is clad with a body, and that he does not know that he is in the world". **And the cup-bearer … banquet room.** See ch. 6. **and he tore him limb from limb,** ܘܗܕܡ ܗܕܡ ܦܣܩܗ Greek renders: κατακόψας τὰ μέλη αὐτοῦ and μέλη μέλη κατεκόψεν.

9

And when they all saw it, they were amazed. And when they were all asking which of them was lost, the hand was found to be that of the cupbearer who had smitten Judas. **Then the flute-player broke her flutes,** and came to the feet of the Apostle, (and) sat down, and was saying: "**This man is either God or the Apostle of God**; for I heard him (say) in Hebrew what he said to that cupbearer, and immediately it befell him. For he said to him: 'I shall see a dog dragging the hand that smote me'; and lo, you have seen how the dog dragged it about.'" **And some of them believed the flute-player and some of them did not believe (her).** And the king, when he heard this story, came and said to Judas: "Come with me, and pray for my daughter, because she is my only one, and to-day I am giving her away in marriage". **And he did not wish to go with him, because our Lord had not yet manifested himself to him in that place**. But the king carried him off by force to the bridal chamber.

Commentary. **Then the flute-player ... flutes**. She is stopping with her former way of life, see Acts 19,9. **This man ... God**. Cf. Acts 13,11. **And some of them ... did not believe (her)**. Cf. Acts 28,24. **And he did not wish ... in that place**. Like in ch. 29 and 73 Thomas is guided by his Lord, cf. Acts 16,6 and 9 and 8,26.

10

And he began to pray and to say thus: "**Our Lord,—companion** of his servants and **guide** and **conductor** of those who believe in him, and **refuge** and **repose** of the afflicted, and **hope** of the poor, and **deliverer of the feeble** and **healer of the sick souls, life-giver of the universe, and saviour of (all) creatures,—you know what things are going to happen, and through us you accomplish them, you are the discloser of hidden secrets, and the revealer of mysterious sayings. You are the planter of the good tree**, and through your hands all acts take place. **You are hidden in all your works, and are known in their acts, Jesus, perfect Son of perfect mercy; and you became the Messiah, and did put on the first man, you are the power, and the wisdom, and the knowledge, and the will and the rest of your Father** in whom you are concealed in glory, and **in whom you are revealed in your creative agency; and you are one with two names. And you manifested yourself as a feeble (being), and those who saw you, thought of you, that you were a man who had need of help. And you did show the glory of your godhead in your long-suffering towards our manhood, when you hurled the evil (one) from his power and called with your voice to the dead, and they became alive, and those who were alive and hoping in you, you promised an inheritance in your kingdom. You were the ambassador, and were sent from the supernal heights**, because you are able to do the living and perfect will of your sender. Glorious are you, Lord in your might; and your renovating administration is in all your creatures, and in all the works which your Godhead has established; **and no other is able to annul the will of**

your majesty, nor to stand up against your nature as you are.
And you descended to Sheol, and go to its uttermost end; and opened
its gates, and bring out its prisoners and trod for them the path (leading)
above by the nature of your Godhead. Yes, Lord, I ask of you on behalf
of these young people, that whatever you know to be beneficial for
them, you will do for them". And he laid his hand upon them, and said
to them: "Our Lord be with you", and he left them and went away.

Commentary. **our Lord**. Greek: "Lord and my God", cf. ch. 144 in both
Syriac and Greek, and John 20, 29 and Manich. Ps. 112,26: "Jesus, my
God". See O. Cullmann, *Die Christologie des Neuen Testaments*, Tübingen 1957, 314–324. **companion**. The idea "companion" has been
expressed in various ways and both the Greek version and Wright's
translation do not render the same words each time with the same
English equivalent. In the present passage the word "companion" is the
translation of ܪܒܐ and in Greek: συνοδοιπόρος; in ch. 37: ܪܒܗ and
in Greek: *idem*; in ch. 103: *idem* and in Greek: σύνοδος; in ch. 119: ܪܒܪ
and in Greek; συνοδοιπόρος and in ch. 156: ܪܒܫ and in Greek: έταῖ-
ρος. The word "guide" in the present passage is the translation of ܪܒܗ
and in Greek: ὁδηγῶν; in ch. 37: *idem* and in Greek: συνοδοιπόρος; in
ch. 38: *idem* and in Greek the word has not been translated; in ch. 68:
idem and in Greek: παραπομπὸς; in ch. 103: *idem* and in Greek: σύνοδος;
in ch. 156: *idem* and in Greek: ὁδηγός and in ch. 167: *idem* and in Greek:
ὁδηγός. The word "conductor" in the present passage is the translation
of ܪܒܪܒ and in Greek: εὐθύνων and in ch. 167: ܪܒܠܒ and in Greek:
ὁδηγος. The idea "companion" is not applied to Jesus in the New Testament. See for Jesus who travels with man ch. 1: "My grace is with
you" and *Liturg. Homilies of Narsai*, ed. Connolly 54: "In a new way of
the resurrection of the dead they travel with Him". **guide**. See above.
In the New Testament we find the word ὁδηγήσει in relation with the
Paraclete, see John 16, 13. In the Old Testament, however, God is supposed to be "guide", see Ps. 48, 15; 139, 10; 143, 10 (the Peshitto uses the
word ܒܪ see below). According to *Sap. Sal.* 18. 3 the pillar of fire is leading the people of Israel in the desert, cf. Philo, *vita Mosis* I 178: ἡ γὰρ
ὁδηγός νεφέλη. In *Sap. Sal.* 7, 15 God is a "guide" and in 9, 11 Wisdom,
cf. Irenaeus, *adv. haer.* I 15 1: *facto ducatore ad Patrem veritatis*. The idea is
very often met in Gnostic writings, cf. *Corpus Hermet.* VI I2; XII 2; IX 10
and 21; XI 21; *Evang. Veritatis* 19,17, ed. Robinson 39; *Exc. e Theodoto* 74.2,
ed. Sagnard 198; Manich. Ps. 116,24; *Johannesbuch* 220, 7–9: "Damit sie
Jokabar–Ziwa preisen, den Mann, der [ihnen] ein Führer sei, dass er

[ihnen] ein Führer sei vom Orte der Finsternis zum Orte des Lichts", see *Theol. Wörterb. z. N.T.* V, p. 101–102, *s.v.* ὁδηγός (Michaelis); T. Arvedson, *Das Mysterium Christi*, Uppsala 1937, 224, n. 2; H. Söderberg, *La Religion des Cathares*, Uppsala 1949, 212; Nock–Festugière 78; G. van Moorsel, *The Mysteries of Hermes Trismegistus*, Utrecht 1955 and Bultmann, *Das Evangelium des Johannes* 442, n. 2. **conductor**. See above. In Syriac the words ܕܒܪ and ܗܕܐ are identical. For example, in Luke 6,39 the word ὁδηγέω has been rendered by ܗܕܐ in syr phil and by ܕܒܪ in syr p and s. In Sir 2, 6 and 37, 15 the word εὐθυνειν is applied to God. In the Odes of Sol. we read in 14, 4: "And be me a guide, ܡܕܒܪܢ till the end ..." and in 38, 1: "And the Truth led me, ܡܕܒܪܢ and caused me to come". The *logos* as *paedagogos* is known from Clement of Alex., *protrept.* 6,2, cf. Mand. Liturg. 134–135: "Ein Helfer, Geleiter und Führer warst du den grossen Stamm des Lebens". See W. Völker, "Der wahre Gnostiker nach Clemens Alexandrinus", in: *Texte u. Unters.* 57 1952, 99–100 and 102, n. 5. **refuge**, ܚܣܢ ܓܘܣܐ Greek: καταφυγή, a word very often used in these Acts, see ch. 27; 46; 48; 60; 67; 88; 98; 102; 136 and 156. Also in the Old Testament, see Ps. 46, 2 and other passages and the New Testament Hebr. 6, 18. See also *Acta Petri* VIII, in: L.B. I I, 55,1–2: *viduae omnes sperantes in Christo ad hunc refugium habebant;* Justin, *dial. c. Tr.* CX 2, and Liturg. Homil. of Narsai, ed. Connolly 38: "He names himself ... a fugitive who returned to take refuge with the King of kings". **repose**, ܫܠܝܐ and Greek: ἀνάπαυσις, also in ch. 60 and 154. In biblical literature God or Christ is never called "rest", but see Matt. 11, 28; Hebr. 3, 1.18; 4, 1.3.5.10.11. See J. Helderman, "Die Anapausis im Evangelium Veritatis", in: *Nag Hammadi Studies* XVIII, Leiden 1984. **hope**, ܣܒܪܐ and Greek, ἐλπὶς, also in ch. 144; 156 and 167. See Ps. of Sal. 15, 2: "... for the hope and refuge of the poor are you, o God", and Manich. Ps. 88,23: "O Jesus, the true hope (ἐλπὶς)". **deliverer of the feeble**. The Greek version with αἰχμαλώτων in place of "feeble" seems to be original. For the idea that man is a prisoner cf. Eph. 4, 8 and Hebr. 2, 15. In *Acta Philippi* 110, ed. L.B. II II 42, 18–19, it is said: διὰ τί αἰχμαλωτεύθητε ὑπὸ τοῦ ἐχθροῦ ὑμῶν τοῦ ὄφεως, see also *Acta Andreae* 6, in: L.B. II I, 40,29–31; Ignatius, *ad Ephes.* 17.1; Irenaeus, *demonstr.* 38, ed. Froidevaux 92: "... et [qui] défit les chaînes de [notre] prison. Et sa lumière apparut et fit disparaître les ténèbres de la prison et sanctifia notre naissance et abolit la mort en defaisant ces mêmes liens dans lesquels nous avions été enchaînés".; Odes of Sal. 10. 3; Aphraates, *demonstr.* XXI 10, ed. Parisot c. 957–958: *Iesus omnes gentes a servitio Satanae eripuit*, and Mand. Lit. 39: "... und der Gefangene wird aus

dem Gefängnis befreit". The idea plays an important part in the rest of this chapter. See Murray, *Symbols* 325ff. **healer of the sick souls**. For Christ as healer see ch. 15; 37; 39; 95; 143; 155 and 156. Here the healing of the soul is emphasized which agrees with ch. 141: "… restoring it (*scil.* my soul) to its own nature". See also Clemens of Alex., *paedag.* I 6 1; Origen, *c. Celsum* II 67, and *hom. in Lev.* VIII 1, see also H. Koch, *Pronoia und Paideusis*, Berlin–Leizig 1932, 74–75; Bar Hebraeus, *Book of the Dove*, ed. Wensinck, p. 3: "In the same way as we find, o my brother, in bodily medicine books describing the behaviour of patients not attended by a physician, it is becoming in psychic medicine to give instructions concerning the behaviour of those patients who are without or far from a leader". See Murray, *Symbols*, 200, n. 1. The idea is prominent in Gnostic literature, cf. Book of Jeu, ed. Schmidt–Till 257, 8: "… in der Ankunft des Erlösers (σωτήρ), des Erretters der Seelen (ψυχαί); Manich. Ps. 2, 24: "Jesus the Physician", cf. 152,22; Mand. Liturg. 17: "Ich verehre, verherrliche und preise Manda dHaja, den Herrn der Heilungen, den Mann den das Leben rief und beauftragte der Seelen zu heilen". Also in Hellenistic literature, cf. Jamblichus, *de vita Pythagorica liber* 58: ἀπὸ τούτων ἁπάντων δαιμονίων ἴατο καὶ ἀπεκάθαιρε τὴν ψυχήν, see E. Zeller, *Die Philosophie der Griechen*, Leipzig 1880 (3. aufl.), III I, 232: "Die Affekte sind … Störungen der geistlichen Gesundheit und, wenn sie habituell werden, formliche Seelenkrankheiten". **lifegiver**. ܡܚܝܢܐ, **of the universe, and saviour**, ܦܪܘܩܐ, **of (all) creatures**. Greek: καὶ σωτὴρ πάσης κτίσεως, ὁ δε κόσμον ζωοποιῶν καὶ τὰς ψυχὰς ἐνδυναμῶν. In syr s and c the word ܡܚܝܢܐ is used to render the Greek σωτήρ see A.F.J. Klijn, "The Term 'Life'in Syriac Theology", in: *Scott. Journ. of Theol.* 5 1952, 390–397. Gradually the New Testament word σωτὴρ has been rendered by ܦܪܘܩܐ. However, in these Acts the word ܡܚܝܢܐ has been translated by σωτὴρ, see ch. 39; 42; 47; 97; 136; 143; 149 and 161. In ch. 129 we find the word ζωῆς δοτήρ. In the Syriac version we meet both words which, may be due to the influence of the New Testament known from syr p. In the Odes of Sol. both words are met, see 5. 3 and 11; 8. 24 and 25; 9. 3 and 5; 17. 13; 26. 9; 28. 7 and 9; 31. 6 and 11; 34. 6 and 38. 3 and 11. **you know what things … mysterious sayings**, … ܡܠܐ ܟܣܝܬܐ, Greek: λόγους ἀπορρήτους The revelation of the mysterious sayings is important in these Acts. In ch. 27; 50 and 133 the Holy Spirit reveals mysteries and in ch. 39 Thomas is said to have received mysterious sayings, see also Gospel of Thomas *log.* 1, and in ch. 47 and 79 it is said that Christ revealed the mysteries. Already in Judaism, see Sir. 42, 19: "He (*scil.* God) declares what is in the past and what is in the future and he reveals the profoundest secrets". Especially in the Dead Sea Scrolls the idea "mystery" is important, see, apart from many other passages, F. García Martinez, *The Dead Sea Scrolls Translated*, Leiden–New York–Cologne 1994, 399–401. For the New Testament see Mark 4, 11–12; I Cor 2, 6–7 and II Cor. 12, 4: ... ἄρρητα ῥήματα. According to I Clem. 36. 2 God's revelation is a mystery, but the idea is especially loved in Gnostic literature, see Irenaeus, *adv. haer.* I 25 5, about the Carpocratians: ἐν δὲ τοῖς συγγράμασιν αἰτῶν οὕτως ἀναγέγραπται ... τὸν ἰησοῦν λέγοντες ἐν μυστηρίῳ τοῖς μαθηταῖς, αὐτοῦ καὶ ἀποστόλοις κατ' ἰδίαν λελακηκεναι καὶ αὐτοὺς ἀξιῶσαι τοῖς ἀξίους καὶ τοῖς πειθομένοις ταῦτα παραδιδόναι; Manich. Ps. 3,22–23: "The mysteries that were before the foundation you revealed them to [your] faithful"; *Kephalaia* 167, 10: "Herr, dass du unser Herz aufklärst über das, was alle Menschen verborgen ist", and Ginza R. 404. 3–3: "Er brachte uns geheime Sprüche, damit wir durch sie in dieser Welt aufgeklärt werden". **You are the planter of the good tree**. See for God as planter Jer. 2, 21; 11, 17 and 18, 9. In IQS VIII 5–6 the Council of the Community is called "an everlasting plantation". See also Odes of Sol. 38. 20: "And the Lord alone was glorified in his planting and in his cultivation"; *Kephalaia* 217. 32–218. 1: "Sie (*scil.* die Kirche) gleicht einem guten Baum"; Ginza R. 61. 9: "Euch rufe ich zu, Pflanzer ...", see also 301. 16f; 381. 24f; 409. 9; Ginza L 495. 12, and *Johannesbuch* 219. 3–7: "Ich habe mich in diese Welt begeben um zu pflanzen des Lebens Pflanzung". See H. Schlier, "Religionsgeschichtliche Untersuchungen zu den Ignatiusbriefen" in: *Beih. Zeitschr. f.d. neutestamentl. Wissensch.* 8 1929, 18–54, and Murray, *Symbols* 195ff. **You are hidden in your works and known in their acts**. The passage is not quite clear. It may be possible that we have to read the word "works" as "servants". The idea that God or Christ is hidden in man and that he manifests himself in his action or is seen by faith is well known, see ch. 39; 53; 65 and 143. The Greek version reads: σὺ εἶ κύριε ὁ ἐν πᾶσιν ὢν καὶ διερχόμενος διὰ πάντων καὶ ἐγκείμενος πᾶσι τοῖς ἔργοις σου καὶ διὰ τῆς πάντων ἐνεργείας φανερούμενος. Here the passage begins to state that nothing exists outside God, see *Sap. Sal.* 7,24, which can be compared with *Acta Petri* 39, in: L.B. I I, 99,5–6: *et omnia in te, et quidquid tu, et non est alius nisi tu*; Hermas, *mandata* I 1: (God) καὶ πάντα χωρῶν μόνος δὲ ἀχώρητος ὤν; *Oxyrh. Pap.* I V: ἐγει[ρ]ον τὸν λίθο[ν] κάκεὶ εὑρήσεις με, σχίσον τὸ ξύλον, κάγω ἐκεῖ εἰμι; *Kerygma Petri*, ed. Preuschen, *Antilegomena* 83,3: [ὅ] ἀχώρητος, ὁ τὰ πάντα χωρεῖ; *Evang. Veritatis* 22,25–27, ed. Robinson 40: "... the one who encircles all spaces while there is none that encircles him"; *Corpus Hermet.* V 9: οὐδὲν γὰρ ἔστιν ἐν παιτὶ ἐκείνῳ ὅ οὐκ ἔστιν αὐτός; Manich. Ps. 54,25: "I am in everything, I bear the skies, I am the foundation" and 155, 34–37: "Thou art within, thou art without. Thou art above, thou art below, that art near and far, that art hidden and revealed". See J. Geffcken, *Zwei griechische Apologeten*, Leipzig–Berlin 1907, 35–36. In the Greek version Christ passes everything in order to show his power, cf. Hebr. 4,14; Severus of Antioch V VII, ed. *Patrol. Orient.* VI 145: "The host of heaven shook with amazement when they saw that … Christ … had in his body lifted into the heights … and had passed through all the heavens" and Gespräche Jesu, ed. Duensing 11: "Ich durchschnitt sie (*scil.* Herrschaften und Gewalten)". In Gnostic literature we find Irenaeus, *adv. haer.* I 30 12, about the Ophites: *Descendisse autem eum per septem coelos … dicunt* and Mand. Liturg. 77: "Er drang durch die Welten, kam erwaltete das Firmament und offenbarte sich". See for the idea *Corp. Hermet.* XIII 6: τὸ μὴ διαδυόμενον τὸ μόνον δυνάμει, καὶ ἐνεργείᾳ νοούμενον … **Jesus, perfect Son of perfect mercy**. The Greek version seems to paraphrase: ἰησοῦ χριστέ, ὁ τῆς εὐσπλαγχνίας υἱὸς καὶ τέλειος σωτήρ, χριστὲ υἱὲ τοῦ θεοῦ τοῦ ζῶντος. This agrees with other passages in which the expression has been found, cf. the Syriac version in ch. 39: "Son of perfect mercy" and Greek: "understandest the perfect mercy"; in ch. 48, Syriac and Greek: "Jesus exalted voice that arose from perfect mercy"; in ch. 50, Syriac and Greek: "Come perfect marcy"; in ch. 122, Syriac: "Glory to the mercy which was sent by the mercy" and Greek: "Glory to the compassion that was sent forth of his heart", and ch. 156, Syriac: "Son of perfect mercy" and Greek: "Son of mercy". The expression may go back to Luke 2, 30: ὅτι εἶδον οἱ ὀφθαλμοί μον τὸ σωτηρίον σου, in which syr s and p use the word ܪܚܡܐ, cf. Ephrem, *sermo de dom. nostro*, 48, ed. Lamy I, c. 259–260: *recte Simeon Miseratoris (ܪܚܡܐ) nomine appelavit Dominum qui illius misertus est, qui eum solvit ab illecebris huius mundi ut pergeret ad delicias paradisi*, and Liturg. Hom. of Narsai, ed. Connolly 14: "Simeon bore Him upon his arms, as a man, and he named Him 'the Mercy'". In the Syriac version the word ܪܚܡܬܐ has been used but this has the same meaning as ܪܚܡܐ as appears from the translation of ἔλεος in Luke 1, 50 where syr phil uses ܪܚܡܬܐ and syr s and p the word ܪܚܡܐ. **and you became … first man**. This passage is not found in the Greek version. It is the typical way in which Syriac theology speaks about the incarnation, cf. ch. 48 and 72: "and did put on the body" and Burkitt, *Ev. da-Meph.* II 144: "… the word made flesh, a phrase which (so far as I know) never occurs in Syriac literature before the

5th century". The idea is often found in the Testaments of the Twelve Patriarchs, see Test. of Sim. VI 7; of Zeb. IX 8 and of Benj. X 7 and 8. See also Acts of John, Syriac, ed. Wright 6; "and you appeared to the world in the body from Adam"; Aphraates, *demonstr.* XXII 4, ed. Parisot c. 995–996: *quando autem advenit Iesus, interfector mortis, corpusque induit de semine Adam*; Ephrem, *adv. haer.* XXIV 1, ed. Beck 97 (translation) and 106 (Syriac): "Er legte den Körper an, der von Adam und auch von David stammte"; *Sermo de Dom. nostro* 9, in: Lamy I, c. 165–166, and *de paradiso*, ed. Beck 47 (translation) and 51 (Syriac); Isaac of Antioch, in: *BKV* 116: "Deine Natur hat sich in unserm Staub gehüllt. Dein Glanz hat sich mit unserem Leib bekleidet"; Nestor. Taufliturgie, ed. Diettrich 17: "und in seiner Leibe unseren Leib anzog ...", *Testamentum Domini*, I 28, ed, Rahmani 59 I: *Ipse est, qui Adam iam mortuum induit, eumque vivicavit ...* , but also *Kephalaia* 94,2–4: "Jesus ... legte Eva an (φορεῖν)". From this conception the differences summed up in ch. 47 and 80 between Jesus' manhood and godhead can be explained. From here the Syriac and Greek text differ considerably. First the Syriac text will be commented upon. **you are the power ... Father**. Christ as power and wisdom, see I Cor. 1,24, as knowledge, see Col. 2,3, as will, cf. John 6,38–39, and as rest, cf. Matt. 11,29. **in whom ... agency**, ܒܐܝܕܘܗܝ. For Christ partaking in the glory of the Father, see John 17,22. This glory is shown by his works, see John 2,11, cf. ch. 30: "O hidden rest, that is manifested by your working". **and you are one with two names**. These two names are his human and his divine name, of which his divine name is the real one, see ch. 163: "You can not hear his true name at this time". The "name" is the way in which God reveals himself, see Ephrem, *de fide* XXXI 1–2, ed. Beck 85–86 (translation) and 105–106 (Syriac): "Lasst uns danken dem, der in die Namen von Gliedern sich kleidete, ... hätte er sich nicht gekleidet in die Namen der Dinge, dann hätte er nicht reden können mit uns Menschen" and also XL, 118 (translation) and 141 (Syriac): "Denn er hat Namen, vollkommene und genaue. Er hat Namen, entliehene und vorübergehende". In Gnostic literature the hidden name is important, see Irenaeus, *adv. haer.* I32 1 about the Marcosians: *Nomen quod absconditum est a universa deitate et domitione et veritate, quod induit Iesus Nazarenus in zonis luminis*, and Mand. Liturg. 35: "... Öl ... über das ich diesen verborgenen Namen gesprochen habe ...". **And you ... help**. Cf ch. 47: "Jesus, that was in need like [a poor man]", see Is. 53,1–3. **And you did ... alive**. A contrast with the sentence above. This one speaks about the resurrection of the dead during the life of Christ on earth, cf. John 11, 41: ... φωνῇ μεγαλῃ ἐϰϱαύγαζεν Δάζαϱε ... and John 5,28. **and those ... king-dom**. See Matth. 25,34 and Matth. 19,20. **You were ... heights**. The use of the word "ambassador", ܐܪ ܠܐܪ, agrees with Johannine chris-tology, see C.K. Barrett, *The Gospel according to St. John*, London 1956, 473–474: "The Hellenistic world was not unfamiliar with the thought of a man who was sent from God, and inspired and enpowered for his mission." See for numerous parallels E. Percy, *Untersuchungen über den Ursprung der johanneischen Theologie*, Lund 1939; E. Käsemann, "Das wandernde Gottesvolk", in: *Forsch. z. Rel. u. Lit. des A. u. N.T.* 55, 1939, 95–98; G. Widengren, "Mesopotamian Elements in Manichaeism", in: *Uppsala Univ. Årsskrift* 1946,3, 167–175; R. Bultmann, "Die Bedeutung der neuerschlossenen mandäischen und manichäischen Quellen für das Verständnis des Johannes-evangelium", in: *Zeitschr. f.d. neutestamentl. Wissensch.* 24 1925, 100–146, esp. 105–106; W. Staerk, *Erlösererwartung in den östlichen Religionen*, Stuttgart–Berlin 1938, 83–84, and Murray *Smbols* 171–176. **and no other ... art**. In Syriac we find ܠܐ ܩܘܡ which has been translated by "to stand up against", but the translation "to understand" seems to be preferred. This agrees with, for example, Ephrem, *de fide* XXVI 4–5, ed. Beck 72 (translation) and 89–90 (Syriac): "Grenzenlos verborgen ist daher der Unsichtbare und zu tief ist seine Erforschung für Schwachen ... denn seine Natur ist zu mächtig für jenen Mund". In this passage the word "nature" has been used, a word often met in both Syriac and Greek. It is used in the following passages: Christ destroyed the nature of the devil in ch. 29; 31; 33 (Syriac only) and 75 (Syriac only). The expression "nature of the devil" is more or less the same as "the devil", but his power is emphasized. In other pas-sages the devil is showing his "nature", see ch. 29; 32; 33; 47 and 74. In relation with God the word is met in ch. 10; 78 and 153. Here the words speaks of God's healing activity. The word is also found in rela-tion to man or his soul, see ch. 34 (Syriac only); 43; 141 and 148. These passages deal with the particular condition of man. Next the word is used in relation with various things, see ch. 34 (Syriac only); 37 (Greek only); 61 (Greek only) and 70 (Greek only). Here the translation "char-acter" is possible. In a few passages the word circumscribes the "created things", see ch. 70 (Syriac only) and 143 (Greek only). We meet pas-sages like in ch. 48: the evil overthrown in his own nature and Christ gathering his own nature (Greek only). In ch. 62 is said that man and woman love each other as nature teaches. Finally it is said in ch. 141 that Christ is asked to "bind this nature". The word "nature" shows the particular activity of God, man and other creatures. It is from his, her or its nature that a phenomenon is known. See also A.F.J.Klijn, "The word kejan in Aphraates", in: *Vig. Christian.* 12 1958, 57–66. **And you descended … Godhead**. The expression "doors of sheol" has been taken from Ps. 9,14: ὁ ὑψῶν με ἐκ τῶν πυλῶν τοῦ θανάτου, see also Ps. 116, 16 (LXX). The *descensus ad inferos* is part of Syriac theology, see Testament of Levi 4,1: καὶ τοῦ ἄδου σκυλευομένου; Odes of Sol. 17,9 and 10: "And from there He gave me the way of his steps, and opened the doors which were closed. And I shattered the bars of iron, for my own shackle(s) had grown hot and melted before me"; Manich. Ps. 106,15–16: "He opened the doors … The doors and bars (μοχλός) of the men of Hades he broke"; Ginza L 549,14–15: "Ich rufe dem Gefangenenaufseher zu: 'Öffne den Seelen das Tor'", cf. Ginza L 586, 10–11. Christ who leads the way of those liberated from sheol, see ch. 80 and 156; Odes of Sol. 22. 7: "And Thy hand levelled the way for those who believe in Thee", see also 39. 13; Aphraates, *demonstr.* XII 6, ed. Parisot c. 523–534: … *nos ducem et Salvatorem habemus … Salvator noster apparuit infernum, portas eius confregit, quando ad interiora eius penetrans illas aperuit, et viam ante omnes qui in eum essent credituri calcavit;* Ephrem, *Sermo de Dom. nostro,* ed. Lamy I, c. 147–148: *Ab inferis etiam ascendit et in regno coelesti commoratus est, ut appireret viam ex inferis ubi omnes opprimuntur, ad regnum coeleste ubi omnes retribuntur,* and *Testamentum Domini* I XXIII, ed. Rahmani 41: *Qui … mentem Patris perficeret, inferos calcaret, viam vitae appiret, justos lumen versus dirigere … .* The contents of this passage about Jesus are closely related to the sermon of Thaddeus to Abgar according to Eusebius, *hist. eccles.* I XIII 19–20., see also Doctrine of Addai, ed. Phillips 8–9. In the Greek version we find from the passage "You are the power …" the following: "The undaunted power that has overthrown the enemy, and the voice that was heard of the rulers (ἄρχουσιν), and made all their powers to quake (σαλεύσασα), the ambassador that was sent from the height and came down even unto hell, who didst open the doors and bring up thence them that for many ages were shut up in the treasury of darkness, and showed them the way that leads up unto the height". In this version Jesus is called **voice** which is also found in ch. 48 and the Syriac version of ch. 56, but especially in Gnostic literature, see Hippolytus, *refut.* V 14 1 about the Perates: ἐγὼ φωνὴ ἐξυπνισμοῦ ἐν τῷ αἰῶνι τῆς νυκτός and Ginza L 485, 3–6: "Höre auf den Ruf, den wir dir zurufen, zu ihm habe ich Vertrauen", see H. Odeberg, *The Fourth Gospel,* Uppsala–Stockholm 1929, 194–195 and 207–208. In the Greek version no sharp distinction has been made between Christ descending to earth and to sheol, which is already found in *Sap. Sal.* 1,14; Philo, *de congr.* 57;

de somn. I 151; Ephrem, *adv. haer.* XXII 7, ed. Beck, 97 (translation) and 106 (Syriac): "In einem Kerker gebar Eva". This means that redemption is described in a way which can be compared with the liberation from sheol, see Ephrem, *adv. haer.* XXV 2, ed. Beck 92 (translation) and 99 (Syriac): "Er vollendete den Weg der Propheten und bahnte hinwieder den Weg für seine Apostel. Lasst uns alle auf den Weg des Sohnes eilen damit wir (aus dem Leben) scheidend die Herrlichkeit des Vaters sehen"; Liturg. Hom. of Narsai, ed. Connolly 63: "A new path He shewed them that they might travel towards Him"; Severus of Antioch 16 II VIII,in: *Patrol. Orient.* 58: "... he wished by his baptism to open before us an ascent leading up to heaven"; Ps. Clemens, *recogn.* I 16 1, ed. Rehm 65: *... illum esse dicimus, qui appellatur verus propheta, qui solus inluminare animas hominum potest, ita ut oculis suis viam salutis evidenter inspiciant;* Manich. Ps. 41, 22–23: "Open to us the passage of the vaults (ἀψίς) of the skies and [walk] before us to the joy of thy kingdom, o glorious one", and Manich. Liturg. 38: "Du zeigtest uns den Weg, auf dem du aus dem Hause des Lebens gekommen bist." See for **rulers** being "evil powers" Eph. 2, 2 and ch. 118. The expression **treasury of darkness** is based upon Prov. 7,27: ὁδοὶ ᾅδου ὁ οἶκος αὐτῆς, κατάγουσαι εἰς τὰ ταμεῖα τοῦ θανάτου, cf. Odes of Sol. 16,15: "The reservoir of light is the sun, and the reservoir of darkness is the night", and Manich. Ps. 129,16–16: ... (defective) ... in their abyss, in the five storehouses (ταμεῖον) and *Kephalaia* 28, 7–8.

11

And the king requested the groomsmen to go out of the bridal chamber. And when all the people had gone out, and the door of the bridal chamber was closed, **the bridegroom raised up the curtain, that he might bring the bride to himself. And he saw our Lord in the likeness of Judas**, who was standing and talking with the bride. And the bridegroom said to him: "Lo, you went out first; how are you still here?" Our Lord said to him: "I am not Judas, **but I am the brother of Judas**". And our Lord sat down on the bed, and let the young people sit down on the chairs, and began to say to them:

Commentary. **the bridegroom raised up ... himself**. It seems that the bride is inside the bridal chamer and the bridegroom outside. This appears to agree with a wedding with the Mandaeans, see H. Petermann, *Reisen im Orient*, Leizig 1865, 117–118, where it is said that in the house of the bridegroom a bridal chamber was made in which the bride dwelled with her train. The men were standing outside and during the ceremony the two groups were standing each on one side of the curtain. After that the bridegroom entered the bridal chamber. See for a Jewish bridal chamber, Krauss, *Talmud. Archäol.* II, 42–43. **And he saw … of Judas**. The same is found in History of Thecla, Syriac, ed. Wright, 128: "… she saw the Lord Jesus the Messiah, who was sitting beside her in the likeness of Paul", cf. *Acta Pauli et Theclae* 21, ed. L.B. I I, 250. 1–2, and History of Mar Matthew and Mar Andrew, Syriac ed. Wright 97: "… but our Lord concealed the might and power of his godhead, and appeared like a steersman". Christ is able to appear in various forms and was, therefore, called πολύμορφος, see ch. 48 in Greek and ch. 153 in Syriac and Greek. This idea is often met in early Christian literature, cf. Justin Martyr, *dial. c. Tr.* LVI 1, where it is said that Christ appears to Abraham at Mamre, and LVIII, where Christ is supposed to have been wrestling with Jacob, see also Irenaeus, *adv. haer.* I X 3: ἐφάνη τοῖς προφήτοις ὁ θεός οὐκ ἐν μιᾷ ἀλλὰ ἄλλως ἄλλοις. Christ adapts himself to human perception, see Irenaeus, *adv. haer.* II XXII 4: *Ideo (Christus) per omnem venit aetatem, et infantibus infans … in parvulis parvulus.* This is easily explained by a christology according to which is spoken of Christ putting on human flesh, see ch. 10 and Ephrem, *adv. haer.* XXXVI 5, ed. Beck 130 (translation) and 144–145 (Syriac): "Gott also, der niemals kleiner noch grösser wurde, hat das Lob verschmäht und den Tadel verachtet, und hat sich in alle Bilder gekleidet (ܠܟܠ ܨܠܡܐ ܕܝܠܢ) and *de fide* XI 9, ed. Beck 38 (translation) and 54 (Syriac): "Er is der Gütige: wie er sich in alle Gestalten gekleidet hat (ܕܐܝܟ ܕܠܒܫ ܠܟܠ ܕܝܠܢ) für unsern Blick, so hat er sich (auch) in alle Stimmen gekleidet für unsere Belehrung". **but I am the brother of Judas**. This passage has to be read in the light of ch. 31 in Greek and 39 in Greek and Syriac, where Thomas is called the twin of Jesus. With regard to ch. 1 we already mentioned the influence of the name Thomas = twin upon various speculations about his name.

12

"Remember, my children, what my brother spoke with you, and know to whom he committed you; and know that **as soon as you preserve yourselves from this filthy intercourse, you become pure temples**, and are saved from afflictions manifest and hidden, **and from the heavy care of childen, the end of whom is bitter sorrow.**

And if you have children, for their sakes you will become **oppressors and robbers and smiters of orphans and wrongers of widows, and you will be grievously tortured for their injuries.** For the greatest part of children are the cause of many pains; for either the king falls upon them, or a demon lays hold of them, or paralysis befalls them. And if they be healthy, they come to ill either by adultery or theft, or fornication, or covetousness, or vain-glory; and through their wickedness you will be tortured by them. But if you will be persuaded by me, **and keep yourselves purely** to God, **you shall have living children,** to whom not one of these blemishes and hurts comes near; and you shall be without care and without grief and without sorrow; **and you shall be hoping (for the time) when you shall see the true weddingfeast; and you shall be in it praisers (of God), and shall be numbered with those who enter into the bridal chamber**".

Commentary. **as soon ... filthy intercourse.** This idea plays an important part in these Acts, see ch. 51; 84; 88 and 144. The same applies to other apocryphal Acts, cf. *Acta Pauli et Theclae* 5–7, in: L.B. II, 240–241; *Acta Johannis* 63, in: L.B. I I, 181–182, and *Acta Philippi* 114, in: L.B. II II, 45, see M. Blumenthal, "Formen und Motive in den apokryphen Apostelgeschichten", in: *Texte u. Unters.* 41 1937, 157f. This agrees with, for example, Philo, *de vita contempl.* 68: γηραιαί παρθέναι ... διαφυλάξασαι ... διὰ ζῆλον καὶ πόθον σοφίας ... οὐ θνη τῶν ἐκγόνων ἀλλ' ἀθανάτων ὀρεχθεῖσαι ... σπείραντος εἰς αὐτὴν (ψυχὴν) ἀκτῖνας νοητὰς τοῦ πατρός; I Cor. 7, 8; Ignatius, *ad Polycarpum* 5.2; II Clement 8. 4 and 6, and Aphraates, *demonstr.* XVIII 10, ed. Parisot c. 839–840: *Homo donec uxorum non duxit, diligit et colit Deum, patrem suum, et Spiritum Sanctum, matrem suam; neque ullum alium habet amorem. Ut autem homo uxorum accepit, patrem et matrem relinquit eos scilicet quos superius signavi; mens eius saeculo isto decipitur ...* . See also W. Völker, "Der wahre Gnostiker nach Clemens Alexandrinus", in: *Texte u. Unters.* 57 1952, 1899–200, and W. Völker, "Das Vollkommenheitsideal des Origenes", in: *Beitr. z. hist. Theologie* 7 1931, 44–50. The present Acts, however, speak about virginity as a condition to be kept. This agrees with Gnosticism, see K. Müller, "Die Forderung der Ehelosigkeit aller Getauften in der alten Kirche", in: *Samml. gemeinverst. Vorträge ...* . 126, Tübingen 1927, and A. Vööbus, "A Requirement for Admission to Baptism in the early Syriac Church", in: *Papers Eston. Theol. Soc. in Exile* I, Stockholm 1951, but see also A.F.J. Klijn, "Doop en ongehuwde Staat in Aphraates", in: *Ned. Theol. Tijdschr.* 14 1959, 29–37. The idea of virginity is connected with that of the originally incorruptible way of life of Adam in paradise, see ch. 15. This is a Jewish idea, see Ginzberg, *Legends of the Jews* V 134, cf. Gnostische Adamsschr., ed. Preuschen 41: "Als Adam dies alles verloren hatte ... [und es kam] zu Adam der Erzengel Gebriel und er sagte zu ihm, dass er sich Eva nahen sollte, um Sohne zu erzeugen". Here Matth. 22, 30 seems to be important. However, in later Syriac literature these strict ideas have been rejected, see Ephrem, *adv. haer.* XL 6, ed. Beck p. 153 (translation) and 179 (Syriac): "Wer die Ehe lästert, ist eine verfluchte Frucht, die ihre Wurzel verfluchte". The same is found in Ginza R 23, 26–27: "Zeuget und bekommet Kinder". In Ps. Clemens, *homiliae* and *recognitiones* a development can be noticed. In the "Grundschrift" marriage seems to be accepted, see *Epistula Clementis* 7. 1, ed. Rehm 10, but in the *Kerygma Petri* a more encratitic way of life appears to be propagated, see *homil.* III 26 4, ed. Rehm 66, and in younger parts marriage is to be rejected, see *homil.* III 27 2, ed. Rehm 66, see G. Strecker, "Das Judenchristentum in den Pseudoklementinen", in: *Texte u. Unters.* 70 1958, 140 and 199. **you become pure temples**, ܩܕ̈ܫܐ ܕܟ̈ܝܐ and in Greek: ναοὶ ἅγιοι. In this chapter it is also said: **keep yourselves purely**, ܕܟܝܐܝܬ and Greek: τὰς ψυχὰς ὑμων ἁγνάς. A number of words have been used to express the same idea, *viz.* the verbs ܕܟܐ, to be pure; ܩܕܫ, to be holy, and ܢܟܦ to be chaste. The Greek version does not always show the same equivalent. We meet the words ἁγιάζω, καθαρίζω, ἁγνίζω. In the New Testament the word ἁγιάζω has been translated by ܩܕܫ, καθαρίζω by ܕܟܐ and σωφρονέω by ܢܟܦ. See also ch. 51; 52; 85; 97; 104; 126; 131; 139; and 156. The destination of men is to be a temple of Christ, see ch. 76; 87; 94; and 156. The idea is found with Philo, *quest. on Gen.* IV 8, ed. Marcus 282: "O thrice happy and thrice fortunate soul, in which God has not disdained to dwell ... and to make it his palace". See H. Lewy, "Sobria Ebrietas", in: *Beih. Zeitschr. f.d. neutest. Wissensch.* 9 1929, 55–56. See for the New Testament I Cor 6, 19 and the early christian literature: Ignatius, *ad Ephes.* 9. 2; 15.2; *ad Magn.* 12. 1; II Clement 9. 3; Hermas, *mand.* III 1; Tatianus, *orat. ad Graecos* XV 2, ed. Goodspeed 282; Clemens of Alex., *strom.* VII 82 2–3; VII 29 5, and *paed.* III 33; Aphraates, *demonstr.* VI 10, ed. Parisot c. 281–282: *Christus enim ad dexteram Patris sui sedens, in hominibus simul habitat; Constit. Apost.* VIII VI 6: βεβαιώσῃ δὲ αὐτοὺς ἐν τῇ εὐσεβείᾳ ἑνώσῃ καὶ ἐγκαταριθμήσῃ αὐτοὺς τῷ ἁγίῳ αὐτοῦ ποιμνίῳ, καταξιώσας, αὐτοὺς τοῦ λουτροῦ τῆς παλιγγενεσίας, τοῦ ἐνδύματος τῆς

ἀφθαρσίας τῆς ὄντως ζωῆς ... ἐνοικήσῃ τε ἐν αὐτοῖς καὶ ἐμπεριπατή-
σῃ; *Kephalaia* 166. 13: "Der grosse Herrliche wohnt in ihnen allen" and
Ginza L 461. 16–18: "Du (Helfer) sollst mit mir wohnen, und in deinem
Herzen werden wir Platz nehmen". See Festugière IV 12: "Cette image
de l'âme 'maison' ou 'temple' de Dieu est sans doute commune dans
la mystique hellénistique, juive, chrétienne, et paienne. On la rencon-
tre chez Philon, chez saint Paul et jusque dans une texte alchémique".
and from heavy care ... will be tortured by them. The Greek
version omitted the passage "for either the king ... will be tortured by
them", probably at the time of the Byzantine empire. The same idea is
found in ch. 126: "... and should be free from the heavy burden of sons
and daughters", and *Acta Johannis* ch. 34, ed. L.B. II I 168, 24–25: μηδὲ
ἡγεῖσθε παίδων ὑμῖν συγγινομένων αὐτοῖς ἀναπεπαῦθαι. Children being
a burden can be found in early christian literature, see Justin Martyr,
apol. II 4 3; Clemens of Alex., *strom.* III 22; Aphraates, *demonstr.* XVIII
2–4, ed. Parisot c. 819–826, esp. 823–826: *Sed virginitatem et sanctitatem tibi
ostendam in populo illo coram Deo placuisse, et magis excelluise in populo illo pri-
ori quam multorum liberorum generatio, quae nihil profuit*; Gregorius of Nyssa,
de virginitate III, ed. Jaeger 258–259: εἰ γὰρ ἦν δονατὸν πρὸ τῆς πείρας
τὰ τῶν πεπειραμένων μαθεῖν! εἰ γὰρ ἐξῆν δι᾽ ἄλλης τινὸς ἐπινοίας ἐντὸς
τοῦ βίου γενόμενον ἐποπτεῦσαι τὰ πράγματα, πόσος ἂν ἦν ὁ δρόμος τῶν
αὐτομολούντων πρὸς τὴν παρθενίαν ἀπὸ τοῦ γάμου! and Homilie sur
la Virginité III 50, ed. Amand–Moons 47: μέμφεται ἑαυτήν (married
women) ὅταν ἡ θύγατηρ ἀποθάνῃ καὶ ὁ υἱὸς νοσῇ, ὅταν τῷ προσηγησα-
μένῳ πένθει αὐτῆς ἕτερον πένθος, ἀπειλῇ καὶ τὸν στεναγμὸν αὐτῆς στε-
ναγμος διαδέξηται. Also in the Hellenistic world see Festugière IV 224.
adultery ... vainglory. See ch. 28. **you shall have living children**.
Cf. i Tim. 1, 1; Tit. 1, 4; Philem. 10 and also in *Corp. Hermet.* XIII, see
Nock–Festugière II 210, n. 22 and Festugière IV 224. **and you shall be
hoping ... bridal chamber**. In the Greek version: "looking to receive
that incorruptible and true marriage and you shall be therein groomsmen entering into the bridal-chamber which is full of immortality and
light". See Hymn I *l.* 23–29. It is not clear whether the heavenly bridal
chamber is meant or the baptistery. In the Syriac version is spoken of
the marriage only. Here we may refer to Ps. Clemens, *recognit.* IV 35 5,
ed. Rehm 129: *Interim nos iussit exire ad praedicandum et invitare vos ad coenam
regis coelestis, quam praeparavit pater in nuptiis filii sui, et ut demus vobis indu-
menta nuptalia quod est gratia baptismi*. For the Greek version we may refer
to Ephrem, *hymni dispersi* V, ed. Lamy IV c. 701–702: *Beatus es, quem misit
rex supremus ut Indiam desponsares Unigenito suo*.

13

And the young people were persuaded by our Lord, and gave themselves to him, and were preserved from filthy lust, **and passed the night in their places**. And our Lord went forth from beside them, and said to them: **"May the grace of your Lord be with you"**. And in the morning, when it was dawn, the king had the table furnished early, and brought in before the bridegroom and bride. And he found them sitting the one opposite the other, **and the face of the bride uncovered and she was sitting, and the bridegroom was very cheerful. The mother of the bride said to her: "Why are you sitting thus, and are you not ashamed, but (are) as if, lo, you were (married) a long time and for many days?" And her father too said: "Because of your great love for your husband do you not even veil yourself?"**

Commentary. **and passed the night in their places**, ‏ـܐܢ ܟܝܢܐܢ ܠܢ‎ ‏ܐܢܠܟ‎ Greek: καὶ ἔμειναν οὕτως ἐν τῷ τόπῳ διανυκτερεύοντες and in other Greek manuscripts: ἔμειναν ἅπασαν τὴν νύκτα ἐν ἀγρυπνίᾳ διάγοντες καὶ σωφιροσύνῃ καὶ ἔμειναν οὕτως. Syriac seems to translate the expression καὶ ἔμειναν οὕτως which is used to circumscribe the unmarried state, see John 21, 22 in manuscript D; I Cor. 7, 26, and *Acta Pauli* 11, in: L.B. I 243, 11: ἵνα γάμοι μὴ γίνωνται ἀλλὰ οὕτως μένωσιν. The Greek version, on the other hand, shows the influence of the Syriac text. **May the grace ... with you**. See ch. 1. Syriac reads: ‏ܪܐܠܚܕܢ ܚܘܐܪ ܠܢܘ‎ and Greek: τὴν ὄψιν ἀσκέπαστον or in other manuscripts: ἐν πολλῇ παρρησίᾳ. From ch. 14 it appears that being uncovered has a deeper sense because if one is righteous before God one does not need to be covered, see Is. 25, 7; Joseph and Asenath 15. 1, ed. Chr.Burchard 674–675: "Dann geht sie zu dem Gottesführer, vor ihn tretend. Da spricht zu ihr des Herrn Engel: 'Entfern von deinem Haupt den Schleier, weil eine reine Jungfrau du heut bist; es gleicht dein Haupt dem eines Jünglings'"; II Cor 3, 7–18; Jacob of Serug, "Gedicht über die Decke vor dem Antlitz des Moses", in: *BKV* 355: "Alle Worte der Weissagung waren wie Bräute und durch Schleier vor den Beschauern verhüllt. Als aber der Bräutigam kam enthüllte er ihre Angesichter und liess sie deutlich erkannt werden, weil die Verhüllung für die Bräute nicht mehr notwendig war. Beim Hochzeitsfest trat die Braut in das Gemach ein, und hinfort war zwischen ihr und dem Bräutigam kein Schleier mehr erforderlch"; Severus of Antioch 115 I

V, in: *Patrol. Orient.* VI, ed. E.W. Brooks, Paris 1911, 155: "But the holy church, clearly beholding and seeing with open face, ܣܒܪ̈ܝܐ ܠܢ, the glory of the new life that is to come; Theodore of Mops., ed. Mingana 47 and 178 (translation): "… to possess so much confidence with God that we look at Him with an open face, ܕܒܐܪ̈ܐ ܠܝܗ; Bar Hebraeus, *Book of the Dove*, ed. Wensinck 79–80: "When the sun of the Beloved rises for the lover … while she shows herself to him without a cover … she will inform the beloved concerning all things …", and Nestor. Taufliturgie, ed. Dietterich 21: "… und mogen sie würdig werden mit offenem Angesichte zu unserem Herrn zu sagen …". See W.C. van Unnik, "'With unveiled Face'. An Exegesis of 2 Corinthians iii 12–18", in: *Sparsa Collecta* I, in: *Supplem. to Novum Testamentum* XXIX, Leiden 1973, 194–210.

14

And the bride answered and said to her: "Truly, my mother, I am in great love, and I am praying to my Lord that I may continue in this love which I have experienced this night, **and may call for the incorruptible Bridegroom** who has revealed himself to me this night. And that I am not veiled, (is) because the veil of corruption is taken away from me; and that I am not ashamed, (is) because the **deed of shame** has been removed far from me, **and that I am not repentant, (is) because the repentance which restores to life, abides in me**. And that I am cheerful and gay, (is) because in the day of this transitory joy, I am not agitated by it; and that the **deed of corruption** is despised by me, and the spoils of this wedding-feast that passes away, (is) because I am invited to the true wedding-feast; and that I have not had intercourse with a husband, the end whereof is bitter repentance, (is) because I am betrothed to the true **Husband**".

Commentary. **and may call … Bridegroom,** ܐ ܐܬܠܐ ܐܪܥܝܐܘ ܠܚܬܘܒܐ which is not quite clear. The verb ܐܝ ܠ has to be translated by "to call to", cf. Mark 9,35 in syr p. Greek reads: καὶ αἰτήσομαι τούτων τὸν ἄνδρα οὗ ἠσθόμην σήμερον. It obviously means that the bride desired to be with Jesus. In this chapter is spoken about the theme **corruption** and **incorruption**. This idea plays an important part in these Acts, see ch. 15; 36; 37 and 78. That which belong to earth is corrupted and has to be rejected. This idea is not wholly absent from the New Testament, see Mark 6, 24; Luke 12, 13–21; Matth. 19,

16–30; I Cor. 15, 42 and 15, 54. In these Acts the starting point of the message of redemption is the corruption to which everyone on earth is subjected to. In early christian literature we find similar ideas with Ignatius, *ad Eph.* 17. 1; 20. 2; *ad Magn.* 6. 2; *ad Philipp.* 8. 2; *ad Polyc.* 2. 3, and Aphraates, *demonstr.* XXII 6–11, ed. Parisot c. 999–1014. **deed of shame**, ܕܐܒܗܬܐ ܕܚܙܐ also in ch. 55 and 84. The Greek translation τὸ ἔργον τῆς αἰσχύνης is supposed to be a Syriasm, see F.C. Burkitt, "The original Language of the Acts of Thomas", in: *Journ. of Theol. Studies* I 1900, 280–290, esp. 284. This applies to sexual intercourse. **and that I am not repentant, (is) because ... abides in me**, ܪܐܬܒܠܗ ܕܐܝܢܐ ܐܝܟ and Greek: καὶ ὅτι οὐκ ἐκπλήσσομαι ἐπειδὴ ἡ ἔκπληξις ἐμοὶ οὐ παρέμεινεν, probably because Greek reading ܪܚܡܐ ܗܘܐ ܕܡܚܒܠܬܐ, see Burkitt, *The Original Language* 284. **deed of corruption**, ܠܚܒܠܬܐܝܢ ܠ ܥܒܕܐ ܗܘ ܕܚܒܠܐ and Greek: καὶ ὅτι ἐξουθένισα τὸν ἄνδρα τοῦτον. The Greek version obviously reads ܥܒܠ in place of ܚܒܠ. Sexual intercourse being corruption, see Tatian in Hieronymus, *Comment. in ep. ad Gal.* III VI, *P.L.* 26, c. 431: *qui putativam Christi carnem introducens, omnem conjunctionem masculi ad feminam immundam arbritatur, Encratitarum vel accerrimus haeresiarches, tali adversum nos sub occasione praesentis testimonii usus est argumento: Si quis seminat in carne, de carne metet corruptionem: in carne autem seminat, qui mulieri jungitur; ergo et qui uxor utitur, et seminat in carne eius, de carne metet corruptionem.* See also Clemens of Alex, *strom.* III 81. For Marcion, see Hippolytus, *refut.* X 19 4: γάμον δὲ φθορὰν εἶναι λέγων. Cf. Homilie sur la Virginité II 13, ed. Amand–Moons 38. **Husband**. Here is spoken of a wedding between Christ and man, see also ch. 12 and Athenagoras 33, ed. Goodspeed 354: εὕροις δ᾽ ἂν πολλοὺς ... καταγηράσκοντας ἀγάμσος ἐλπίδι τοῦ μᾶλλον συνέσεσθαι τῷ θεῷ ... About virgins being brides of Christ, see Tertullian, *de orat.* 22.

15

And many things which were like unto these was she saying. Then too the bridegroom answered and said: "**I praise you, new God, who by means of a stranger has come hither. I glorify you God, who has been preached by means of a Hebrew man; who has removed me from corruption, and has sown life in me**; who has delivered me from the **disease** that was abiding in me for ever; **who has revealed to us yourself, and I have perceived in what (state) I am**; who has saved me from falling and has led me on to a better state; **who has rescued me from these transitory things,**

**and has deemed me worthy of those that are not transitory;
who has let yourself down even to my littleness, that you
might bring me to your greatness**; who did not withhold your
mercy from me who was lost, **but did show me (how) to seek for
myself and to put away from me the things that are not mine;
who, when I did not know you, has sought me yourself; who,
whom I did not perceive you, has come to me; whom I have
not perceived, and am not able to say anything which I do not
know; against whom I cannot consent that I should say aught
with boldness, for it is because of your love that I am bold**".

Commentary. **stranger.** See ch. 4. **I praise you ... life in me.** Greek:
εὐχαριστῶ σοι κύριε διὰ τοῦ ξένου ἀνδρὸς κηρυχθεὶς καὶ ἐν ἡμῖν εὑρε-
σθείς. The Greek version is not easy to understand. It might be possible that ܡܙܪܥ was read as ܡܙܪܥ and that the rest of the sentence has
been omitted. **sown life in me.** See also ch. 34; 93; 94 and 144.
For sowing of the word see Mark 4, 14; John 4, 36 and I Cor 9,11
and also *Corpus Hermet.* I 29: καὶ ἔσπειρε αὐτοῖς τοὺς τῆς σοφίας λόγους **disease.** See ch. 10, where Christ is called "physician"; ch. 143:
"Believe in the healer of all pains hidden and manifest; ch. 155: Have
you come my healer from sore disease", and Odes of Sol. XXV 9:
"Because your hand ... caused sickness to pass from me". **who has
revealed ... (state) I am.** See end of this chapter. **who has rescued ... transitory.** Redemption means to be saved from transitory
things which is the same as to be saved from "corruption", see ch. 14.
See for the word **worthy** ch. 24. **who has led ... greatness.** Christ
adapts himself to the perception of man, see ch. 11. This is also the
cause of his incarnation, see ch. 80 and 123. This idea is very often
found in early Christian literature, see Odes of Sol. VII 6: "Like my
nature He became, that I might understand Him. And like my form,
that I might not turn away from Him"; Ephrem, *Sermo de Dom. nostro* 46, ed. Lamy I, 253–254: *Gloria autem abscondito illi, qui aspectabilem
induit formam ut possent peccatores ad ipsum accedere;* Ephrem, *de fide* XI 1,
ed. Beck 38 (translation) and 54 (Syriac): "Er ist der Gütige, wie er sich
(auch) in alle Gestalten gekleidet hat für unsere Blick, so hat er sich
(auch) in alle Stimmen gekleidet für unsere Belehrung", and XXXV 6,
p. 95 (translation) and 116 (Syriac): "Die Natur wurde niedrig wegen
Adam und Christus wurde klein wegen des Köpers". The Greek version adds the words "and unite me to yourself", ἵνα ... ἐνώσῃς σεαυτῷ,
cf. Odes of Sol. III 8: "Indeed he who is joined to Him who is immor-

tal, truly shall be immortal", where the word ܢܣܩ has been used which renders κολλᾶσθαι in Mark 10,7 in syr p. Liturgical Homilies of Narsai, ed. Connolly 17: "... and did join me to you". See also Rom. 12, 4–5. **but did show me ... sought me yourself**. The Greek version which is probably the original one, reads: "but has shown me how to seek myself and know who I was, and in what manner I now am, that I may again become that which I was; whom I knew not, but you yourself did seek me out; of whom I was not aware, but you yourself have taken me to you.". Here man has been shown in which state he is in order to bring him to a better one. This idea is often met in early Christian literature, see ch. 34 (Syriac) and 43 and *Acta Andraei* 6, in: L.B. II I 40, 25–26: εὖ γε ψυχὴ ... ἐπανιοῦσα ἐφ' ἑαυτὴν and 9, in L.B. II I 42, 3: βοήθησον καὶ ἐμοί, ἵνα γνωρίσῃς τὴν ἀληθῆ σου φύσιν; *Constit. Apost.* VII XXXIII 4: ἐξ ὑπαρχῆς γὰρ τοῦ προπάτορος, ἡμῶν ἀβραὰμ μεταπολουμένου τὴν ὁδὸν τῆς ἀληθείας ὁραματισμῷ ὡδήγησας διδάξας, ὅτι ποτέ ἐστιν ὁ αἰὼν οὗτος· καὶ τῆς μὲν γνώσεως αὐτοῦ προώδευσεν ἡ πίστις, τῆς δὲ πίστεως ἀκόλουθος ἦν ἡ συνθήκη and VII XXXIX 2: ὁ μέλλων τοίνυν κατηχεῖσθαι τὸν λόγον τῆς εὐσεβείας παιδευέσθω πρὸ τοῦ βαπτίσματος τὴν περὶ θεοῦ τοῦ ἀγεννήτου γνῶσιν ... ἐπιγινωσκέτω τὴν ἑαυτοῦ φύσιν, οἷα τις ὑπάρχει; Gregorius of Nyssa, *de prof. christ.* in: *P.G.* 46, c. 243: καὶ ἡ τοῦ χριστιανισμοῦ ἐπαγγελία ἐσεὶ τὸ εἰς τὴν ἀρχαίαν εὐκληρίαν ἐπαναχθῆναι τὸν ἄνθρωπον; Origen, *Comment. Cant.* II 143 11, cf. J. Daniélou, *Origène*, Paris 1948, 290: "le principe de la vie spirituelle sera pour l'âme de connaître sa dignité d'image de Dieu, de comprendre que le monde réel est le monde inférieure", and W. Völker, "Das Vollkommenheitsideal des Origenes", in: *Beitr. z. hist. Theol.* 7 1932, 23. It is important to notice that in early Christian literature the Gnostic idea of knowing oneself being the same as knowing God is not to be found. See for the Gnostic idea Irenaeus about the Marcosians, *adv. haer.* I 21 5; *Exc. e Theodoto* 78 2, ed. Sagnard 202; *Corp. Hermet.* I 18 and X 8; Gospel of Thomas *l.* 3, and Huwidagman VIII 2, ed. Boyce 109: "I shall take you up and show (you) (your) own origin". See E. Norden, *Agnostos Theos*, Leipzig–Berlin 1913, 193; G.P. Wetter, "Ein gnostischer Formel im 4. Evangelium", in: *Zeitschr. f.d. neutest. Wissensch.* 18 1917/18 49–63; H. Söderberg, *La Religion des Cathares*, Uppsala 1940, 38, n. 3; Polotzky, "Manichäismus", in: Pauly–Wissowa, Supplementband VI 1935, c. 240–271, esp. 257; J. Dupont, *Gnosis*, Bruges 303–305; A.D. Nock, "Sarcophagi and Symbolism", in: *Amer. Journal of Archeol.* 50 1946, 140–170, esp. 156, and G. Quispel, *Gnosis als Weltreligion*, Zürich

1951, 18. **who, whom ... am bold**. The passage is not quite clear but it is said that true knowledge about Christ has not yet come. See for **boldness** ch 13.

16

And when the king heard these things from the bridegroom and from the bride, he rent his garments, and said to those who were by him: "Go forth in haste through the whole city, and go about, (and) bring me that **sorcerer**, whom I introduced with my own hands into my house, and bade him to pray over my unlucky daughter. To the man who shall find him and bring him to me, I will give whatever he shall ask". And they went (and) were going about looking for him, and did not find him because he had set out. And they went to the inn where he stayed, and found the flute-girl sitting and weeping, because he had not taken her with him. And when they told her what had happened, she was glad and said: "I have found rest here". And she arose (and) went to the young people, and was dwelling with them a long time. And they taught the king too, and collected a number of brothers, until news was heard of the Apostle (being) **in the realm of India**; and they went to him and were united unto him.

Here ends the first act.

Commentary. **sorcerer**. Thomas is called "sorcerer" very often, see ch. 21; 89; 96; 98; 99 etc. The name was also applied to Jesus in Jewish sources, cf. Sanh. 7. 4 and see E. Stauffer, "Antike Jesustradition und Jesuspolemik im mittelalterischen Orient", in: *Zeitschr. f.d. neutestamentl. Wissensch.* 46 1955, 1–30, esp. 8. Also in the History of Phillip, Syriac, ed. Wright 81, and *Acta Pauli et Theclae* 20 in: L.B. I I 249. **in the realm of India**, ܡܕܝܢܬ ܗܝܢܕܘ, Greek: ἐν ταῖς πόλεσιν τῆς ἰνδίας or ἐν ἰνδίᾳ which shows the influence of the ambiguous word ܡܕܝܢܬ.

The second Act, when Thomas the Apostle entered into India,
and built a palace for the King in Heaven

17

And when Judas had entered **into the realm of India** with the merchant Habban, Habban went to salute Gundaphar, the king of India, and he told him of the artificer whom he had brought for him. And the king was very glad, and ordered Judas to come into his presence. And the king says to him: "What art do you know to practice?" Judas says to him: "I am a carpenter, the servant of a carpenter and architect". He says to him: "What do you know to make?" Judas said to him: "In wood I know (how) to make **yokes and ploughs and ox-goads, and oars for barges and ferryboats, and masts for ships**; and in hewn stone, tombstones and monuments and palaces for kings". **The king says to Judas: "And I want such an artificer"**. The king says to him: "Will you build me a palace?" Judas says to him: "I will build it and finish it, for I have come to work at building and carpentry".

Commentary. **into the realm of India**. Greek: "into the cities of India", but Sachau: ⲁⲩⲟⲗ, cf. manuscripts B H and Z: ἐν τῇ ἰνδίᾳ, see ch. 16. Sinai is present from "And the king says ..." until ch. 19: "and what I shall send (you)". **yokes ... ships**. Greek: ἐν μὲν ξύλοις ἄροτρα ζυγοὺς τρυτάνας τροχιλέας καὶ πλοῖα καὶ κώπας καὶ ἱστούς see ch. 3. **The king says ... artificer**. This passage is present in the Greek manuscripts B H and Z only.

18

And he took him and went outside the gate of the city, and was **talking** with him about the construction of the palace, and about its foundations, how they should be laid. And when he had reached the place where the king wished him to build a palace for him, he said to Judas: "Here I wish you to build for me a palace". Judas says to him: "(Yes), for this is a place which is suitable for it". Now it was of his sort; it was a meadow, and there was **plenty of water** near it. The king says to him: "Begin to build here". Judas says to him: "Now I cannot build, at this time". The king says to him: "And at what time will you be able to build?" Judas says to him: "**I will begin in Teshri, and I will finish in Nisan**". **The king says to him: "All buildings are built in summer, and you build in winter**". Judas says to him: "Thus (only) is it possible for the palace to be built". The king says to him: "**Well then, trace it out for me that I may see it, because after a long time I shall come hither**". And Judas came and took a cane, and began to measure; and he left doors towards the east **for light**; and windows towards the west for air, and (he made) the bake-house to the south, and the water-pipes for the service (of the house) to the north. The king says to him: "Verily, you are a good artificer, and are worthy to serve a king"; and he left **with him** a large sum of money, and departed from him.

Commentary. **talking**. Apart from the Greek manuscripts S H and Z the words "on the way" have been added. See for the following story A. Hilhorst, "The Heavenly Palace in the *Acts of Thomas*", in: J.N. Bremmer (ed.), *The Apocryphal Acts of Thomas*, in: *St. in early Chr. Apocrypha*, Leuven 2001,53–64. **plenty of water**. See Krauss, *Talmud. Archeol.* I 22: "In Babylonien baute man mit Vorliebe am Wasser". **I will begin in Teshri ... winter**. The Greek manuscripts B H Z read ὑπερβερεταίον in place of Teshri, but the other ones διόυ. The word Nisan has been rendered ξανθικῷ in the Greek manuscripts. According to *Chronicon Edessenum*, ed. Hallier 87, winter falls from Tishri to Nisan. Building is supposed to be reprehensible in winter, see Erklärung des Evangeliums, ed. Schäfers 7–8: "Und z.B. die, denen Gebäude gehören, beeilen sich die ganze Zeit des Sommers um zu bauen und zu vollenden (cf. the end of ch. 17!), dass sie unter Obdach sind und ruhen in den Tagen des Winters, denn die Tage des Sommers gehören den Bauten". Jacob of Serug gives the following explanation of Thomas' suggestion in: *Zeitschr. Deutschen Morgenl. Gesellsch.* 25 1871, 356: "Im Winter möge der König bauen ... denn gut wird der Bau und Arbeiter findet man", which is probably wrong. Thomas decided to "build" during winter because at that time many people were in need of support, see ch. 19. Winter as the time during which one prepared oneself for baptism, see ch. 14–27, seems to be far-fetched, but cf. Ephrem, *de virginitate*, quoted in E. Beck, "Le Baptême chez Saint Éphrem", in: *l'Orient Syrien* I 1956, 113–136, esp. 125: *(Mensis) October recreat fatigatos a pulvere et sordibus aestatis, pluvia eius lavat, et res eius ungit arbores et fructus earum. Aprilis recreat* *ieiunantes, ungit baptizat et dealbat; abluit sordes peccati ab animis nostris*, and Cyril of Jerusalem, *procat.* 11: νομισόν μοι οἰκοδομὴν εἶναι τὴν καθήχησιν. See also Ph. Vielhauer, *Oikodome*, Heidelberg 1939, esp. 52–53. **Well, then, trace ... hither**. Thomas obviously traced an example in the sand, cf. Krauss, *Talmud. Archäol.* I 21: "Ein gröserer Bau, z.B. ein Palast, konnte nur auf grund von Bauplänen, die der Architekt auf Pergament oder auf Schreibtaflen entwierf, mitunter wohl auch in den Sand zeichnete (חרט) unter genauer Angabe von Räumlichkeiten, Türen, Fenstern u.s.w. aufgeführt werden". **for light**. Greek: "towards the sun rising to look towards the sun", but B H and Z: πρὸς τὸ φῶς. **with him**. The Greek manuscripts B and H add these words *in the margin* and they are omitted by Sinai.

19

And he was sending silver and gold from time to time. But Judas was going about in the villages and cities, **and was ministering to the poor**, and was making the afflicted comfortable, and was saying: **"What is the king's shall be given to the king, and many shall have rest"**. And after a long time, the king despatched messengers to Judas, and **sent** (a message) to him thus: "Send me (word) what you have done, and what I shall send you". And Judas sent him (word): "The palace is built, but its roof is wanting". Then the king sent to Judas silver and gold, and sent him (word): "Let the palace be roofed". And the Apostle was glorifying our Lord and saying: "I thank you, Lord who died that you might give me life, **and who sold me that I might be a liberator of many**". And he did not cease to teach, and to relieve those who were afflicted, saying: "May your Lord give you rest, to whom alone is the glory; **for he is the nourisher of the orphans and the provider of the widows, and he ministers unto all those who are afflicted**".

Commentary. **and was ministering to the poor**. Also in ch. 26 and 59, see also Matth. 6,1–4. Very important in Syriac christianity, see A. Vööbus, "Einiges über die karitative Tätigkeit des syrischen Mönchtums", in: *Contrib. of Baltic Univers.* 51 1947. *Kephalaia* 192. 30 mentions: "... Fasten, Beten und Almosen geben", cf. 216. 31–218. 32, and Ginza L 525. 4–6: "... meine Hände geben Almosen, Almosen geben meine Hände und sie reichen Kusta". **What is the king's ... rest**. Greek: "The king knows how to obtain recompense fit for kings, but at this time it is needful that the poor should have refreshment", but the manuscripts B H and Z: τὰ τοῦ βασιλεώς τῷ βασιλεῖ δοθήσεται καὶ ἦν ἄνεσις τότε τοῖς πτωχοῖς. The Syriac text reminds us of Matth. 22, 21. The meaning probably is hat the king's money has to be given to Christ, the King, cf. Matth. 25, 35–37 and 40. **sent**. Both Greek and Sachau read: "wrote". **and who sold ... of many**. See ch. 2. **to whom ... glory**. Greek: "and he gives every man his food", but the manuscripts B H and Z: αὐτοῦ γὰρ πόνον ἐστὶν ἡ ἔντιμος. **for he is the nourisher ... widows**. Cf. Ps. 68,6. **and he ministers ... afflicted**. Greek: "and to all that are afflicted he is a relief and rest", but B H and Z: καὶ τοῖς ἐν θλίψει αὐτὸς γένετου ἀντιλήπτωρ, which especially agrees with Sachau: ܘܠܟܠܗܘܢ ܐܠܝܨ ܕܐܝܬ ܗܘ ܗܘܐ ܠܗܘܢ.

20

And when the king came to the city, he was asking every one of his friends about the palace which Judas had built for him; but they say to him: "There is no palace built, nor has he done anything **else**, but he was going about the cities and villages, and giving to the poor, and teaching them the new God and also healing the sick, and driving out demons, and doing many things; and we think that he is a **sorcerer**; but his compassion and his healing, which was done without recompense, and his **ascetism**, and his **piety**, make (us) think of him either that he is a magus, or an Apostle of the new God; for **he fasts much and prays much, and eats bread and salt and drinks water, and wears one garment**, and takes nothing from any man for himself; and whatever he has he gives to others". And when the king heard these things, he smote his face with his hands, and was shaking his head.

Commentary. **else**. Greek adds: "of that he promised to perform" which has been omitted by the manuscripts B H and Z. **sorcerer**, ܚܪܫܐ, see ch. 16, Greek: "righteous man", but manuscript Z: μάγος, and Sachau: "a God who has come from heaven". **ascetism**, ܡܟܝܟܘܬܐ, derived from ܡܟܝܟ, being *humilis*, Greek: ἁπλοῦς, see also ch. 80 and 85. **piety**, ܕܚܠܬܐ better: *timor*, Greek: ἐπιεικής. **he fasts ... water**. See for fasting and praying Luke 2, 37; Matth. 17, 21 in the New Testament manuscripts K C and D and Acts 14, 23. Bread, water and salt are also mentioned in ch. 29; 104 and 130. Food of this kind is also mentioned in History of John, Syriac ed. Wright 8: "bread and herbs with a mess of boiled lentils". Drinking water only is already known in Judaism, cf. *Pirke Aboth* VI 4: "This is the way of the Torah: A morsel with salt you shall eat, and you shall drink water by measure; *Martyrium Jesajas* 2. 11, ed. Hammershaimb 27: "Sie hatten nichts zu essen ausser Wüstenpflanzen"; Philo, *de vita contemplativa* 37, about the Therapeutes who use bread, salt and water only. See also *Liber Graduum* V 17, ed. Kmosko c. 129–130: ... *apostoli carnes non manducabant, sed usque ad horam nonam ieiunabant et panem et sel et herbas et fructus olivae manducabant*, and see for Manichaeism the *oris signaculum* in Baur, *Manich. Religionssystem* 249–252. **wears one garment**. Cf. Matth. 10,9.

21

And he sent (and) called Judas and the merchant who had brought him, and said to him: "Have you built me the palace?" Judas says to him: "I have built you the palace". The king says to him: "In what time can we go (and) look at it?" Judas says to him: "**You can not see it now, but when you have departed from this world**". Then the king became very furious in his anger, and commanded that Thomas and the merchant who had brought him, being bound, should go to prison, till he could question him about what he had done—to whom he had given it—and then destroy him. But Judas went **rejoicing**, and said to the merchant: "**Fear not, but only believe**, and you shall be **freed from this world**, and shall receive everlasting life in the world to come". And the king was considering by what death he should kill Judas and the merchant; and he took the resolution that he would burn him, after being **flayed**, with the merchant his companion. And in that very night the brother of the king whose name was **Gad**, was taken ill through grief and through the imposition which had been practiced upon the king. And he sent (and) called the king, and said to him: "My brother, I commend to you my house and my children, for I am grieved and I am dying because of the imposition that has been practiced upon you. If you do not **punish** that **sorcerer**, you will not let my soul be at peace in Sheol". The king says to him: "The whole night I have been considering, how I should kill him and I have resolved to burn him with fire after he has been flayed". **Then the brother of the king said to him: "And if there be anything else that is worse than this, do (it) to him; and I give you charge of my house and my children**".

Commentary. **You cannot see … world**. For a treasure in heaven
cf. Matth. 6, 19–20; Luke 18, 22. Also in Judaism, cf. IV Ezra 7, 77
and II Bar. 14,12, see Strack–Billerbeck I 429–431. In Syriac Literature:
Aphraates, *demonstr.* VI, ed. Parisot c. 249–250: *Qui domum amat quae in
caelis est, in habitatione lutea et caduca ne laboret*; Erklärung des Evangeliums,
ed. Schäfers 6: "Denn, wenn sie, die irdische Häuser bauen, sich selbst
der Arbeit hingeben, dass sie sich kurze Zeit dauernde Wohnungen
machen, wir aber das Lager der Ewigkeit für unsere Seelen bauen
und das Haus der Herrlichkeit in Himmel, um wie viel mehr geziemt
es sich für uns besorgt zu sein und zu arbeiten", and Ephrem, *hymni
dispersi*, ed. Lamy IV c. 705–706: … *Thomas, apostolus, Filii, qui, dum
in terra degeret domos mensuras, supra aedificaret in coelis? Aut quis sapiens in
terra per suam sapientiam aedificium construxit quod in caelo coronari praeciperet?*
See H. Riesenfeld, "Jésus transfiguré", in: *Acta Semin. Neotestament. Upsal.*
16, København 1949. **rejoicing**. Greek: "went into prison rejoicing",
but manuscripts B H and C: "went rejoicing". **Fear not, but only
believe**. Greek adds: "the God that is preached by me", but this has
been omitted by the manuscripts B H and Z. Cf. Luke 8, 50. **freed
from this world**. Greek: "setting free fom the body". Cf. IV Ezra VII
88: "When they shall be separated from the vessel of mortality", and
Geschichte von Joseph dem Zimmermann XIII 4, ed. Morenz 5: "Jedes
Geschöpf unter dem Himmel, in dem eine lebendige Seele ist, Leid und
Betrübnis bedeutet es, bis seine Seele sich von seinem Leibe trennt".
But see also Rom. 7,24 and II Cor. 5,4. **flayed**. According to the
Preaching of Thomas, Arabic, ed. Smith Lewis 87, Thomas has been
flayed and a considerable part of this work is dealing with the miracles
done with his skin. **Gad**, ܓܵܕ and Greek: γάδ. It might be the same
word as Gudana, see ch. 2. **sorcerer**. See ch. 16. **punish**. See ch. 5.
Then the brother … my children. This passage has been omitted
in Greek.

22

And when he he had said these things, **his soul left him**. And the
king was grieved for his brother, because he loved him much, and he
wished to bury him in a splendid sepulchre. But when the soul of Gad,
the brother of the king, had left him, **angels took it and bore it up
to heaven**; and they were showing it **each place in succession**, (and
asking) in which of them it wished to be. Then, when they came to the
palace which Judas had built for the king, his brother saw it, and said

to the angels: "**I beg of you, my lords, let me dwell in one of the lower chambers of this palace**". The angels say to him: "**You can not dwell in this palace**". He says to them: "**Wherefore?**" They say to him: "**This palace is the one which the christian has built for your brother**". Then he said to them: "I beg you, my lords, let me go, that I may go to my brother and buy this palace from him; for my brother has not seen it and will sell it to me".

Commentary. **his soul left him**. The idea that the soul leaves the body is not known in the New Testament, but cf. Rev. 6, 9. See for Jewish writings IV Ezra 7, 75; Eth. Hen. 9, 10, ed. Ublig 526 and 22, 3, ed. Ublig 556. See also ch. 30. **angels took ... heaven**. Cf. Test Asser 6.6, ed. J Becker 116; Test. Abraham XX, ed. Enno Janssen 253; Targum Hohelied 4. 12, see Strack–Billerbeck II 225: "... der Garten Eden, den niemand betreten darf ausser den Gerechten, deren Seelen durch die Engel hineingebracht werden"; Gedulah Mosheh, ed. M. Gaster, "Hebrew Visions of Hell and Paradise", in: *Journ. Royal Asiatic Soc.* 1893, 571–611, esp. 577: "And Moses asked Metatron: 'Who is this?' He answered: 'This is the angel of death, who takes the souls of men'"; *Orac. Sibyll.* II 314–316, ed. Kurfess–Gauger 56–59, and in Gnosticism Geschichte von Jospeh dem Zimmermann XXII, ed. Morenz, 18, and Manich. Psalms 52. 1–2: "He gave me victoriously into the hands of the angels (?) and they escorted me to the kingdom". **each place in succession**, ܪܐܘܬܪܐ ܬܘ ܬܘܐ The same word as in John 14, 2 in syr s: ܪܐܘܬܪܐ ܪܟܝܠܣ. The word "place" being heaven also in Tob. 3, 6; I Clement 5. 4; II Clement 1. 2 and Pol. 9,2. **I beg you, my lords ... brother**. See Luke 16, 27–28.

23

Then the angels let go the soul of Gad. And as they were enshrouding him, his soul came into him, and he said to those who were standing before him: "Call my brother to me that I may make one request". Then they sent word to the king: "Your brother has come to life". And the king sprang up from his place, and went into the house of his brother with a number of people. And when he had gone in beside the bed, he was astounded and was unable to speak with him. His brother says to him: "I know, my brother, that **if a man had asked you for the half of your kingdom**, you would have given it to me. And now I beg of you that you would sell me that at which you have laboured". The king says to him: "Tell me, what shall I sell you?" He says to him: "Swear to me". And he swore to him that he would grant him whatever he asked of all that he had. He says to him: "Sell me that palace which you have in heaven". The king says to him: "Who has given me a palace in heaven?" His brother says to him: "**(It) is that which the christian has built for you**".

Commentary. **if a man had asked … kingdom**. A biblical expression, see Esther 5, 3.6 and 7, 2 (LXX) and Mark, 6, 23. **(It) is that … you**. Greek: "Even that which that christian built for you who is now in prison, whom the merchant brought to you, having purchased him from one Jesus. I mean that Hebrew slave whom you desired to punish as having suffered deceit at his hand, whereat I was grieved and died and am now revived", and the manuscripts B H and Z: ὁ ᾠκοδόμησέν σοι ἐν ἀληθείᾳ ὁ θωμᾶς (B: ὁ χριστιανὸς ἐκεινός).

24

The king says to him: "That I cannot sell to you; but I pray and beg of God that I may enter into it and receive it, and may be worthy to be among its inhabitants. And you, if you really wish to buy yourself a palace, this architect will build (one) for you which will be better than that of mine". And he sent (and) brought out Judas and the merchant who was imprisoned with him and said to him: "I beg of you, as a man who begs of a minister of God, that you would pray for me, and beg for me from the God whom you worship, that he would forgive me what I have done you; and that he would make me **worthy** to enter into the palace which you have built for me; and that I may become a worshipper of this God whom you preach". And his brother came and fell down before the feet of the Apostle, and said to him: "I beg of you—I too supplicate before your God that I may become worthy to be a worshipper of His, and may also receive what He has shown me by the hand of the angels".

Commentary. **The king says to him**. Greek: "Then the king considering the matter understood it of those eternal benefits which should come to him and which concerned him, and said", but the manuscripts B H and Z: τότε ὁ βασιλεὺς περιχαρὴς γενόμενος λέγει. **worthy**. The word is often used in these Acts. Man can be worthy to be servants of Christ: ch. 24; 72 and 159; worthy to inherit heavenly glory: ch. 15; 24;

139 and 146; worthy to partake in the mysteries: ch. 49; 88 and 136; worthy to receive the Holy Spirit of Christ: ch. 76 and 94; worthy of the wealth: ch. 145, and worthy of God: ch. 160. See Festugière III 110: "Dieu appelle tout le gendre humain: ὅπως τὸ γένος τῆς ἀνθρωπότη-τος ... σωθῇ (I 26, p. 16, 14), *omnibus se libenter ostendit* (Ascl. 29, p. 336, 4). Il vaut donc mieux comprendre dignes parce que leur dispositions morales les rendent dignes (capables) de prêter attention à la Parole. Or précisément ἄξιος en ce sens est presque technique dans les milieux spirituels et les confrères de mystères sous l'Empire". Also in Judaiism, cf. *Sap. Sal.* 6, 16: "For she (*scil.* Wisdom) goes about, seeking them that are worthy of her". The preparation for being worthy is found in *Sap. Sal.* 6, 15, but especially in Philo, see W. Völker, "Fortschritt und Vollendung bei Philo von Alexandrien", in: *Texte u. Unters.* 49 1938, 204: "Erst muss der Mensch von sich aus etwas getan haben, eine Leistung aufweisen können, ehe Gott ihm hilft (*Somn.* I 149f), ja die Ausschüttung des göttlichen Gaben wird zuweilen von der Würdigkeit des Empfängers abhängig gemacht (*spec.* I 43, *immut.* 105, 106)". This agrees with ch. 136: "But at first a man cannot near Him, when he is unclean and when his works are evil"; Theophilus, *ad Autolycum* I 2: τοῖς γὰρ ταῦτα πράσσουσιν ὁ θεὸς οὐκ ἐμφανίζεται, ἐὰν μὴ πρῶτον ἑαυτοὺς καθαρίσωσιν and Manich. Ps. 151. 29: "Perhaps I too am worthy to [hear] the divine call" and 150. 14: "The soul that is free from stain is able to come to God".

25

Judas says: "I Praise you, our Lord Jesus the Messiah, who is alone the God of truth, and there is no other, **and you know whatever man does not know**. You, whose mercy is upon man, whom you have willed and made—and they have forgotten you, but you have not neglected them—receive the king and his brother, **and unite them to your fold, and anoint them, and purify them from their uncleanness, and guard them from the wolves, and feed them in your meadows, and let them drink of your fountain, which is never turbid and the stream thereof never fails; for, lo, they beg of you and supplicate, and wish to become servants of you, and to be persecuted by your enemy, and to be hated for your sake. Let them therefore have boldness in you, and be confirmed by your glorious mysteries, and receive of the gifts of your gifts**".

Commentary. In this and the next chapter the Greek and Syriac versions differ considerably. Greek reads: "And the Apostle filled with joy, said: 'I praise you, o Lord Jesus, that you have revealed your truth in these men; for you alone are the God of truth, and none other, and you are the one who knows all things that are unknown to the most; you are the one that in all things shows compassion and spares men. For men by reason of the error that is in them have overlooked you, but you have not overlooked them. And now at my supplication and request receive the king and his brother and join them into your fold, cleansing them with your washing and anointing them with your oil from the error that encompasses them; keep them also from the wolves, bearing them into your meadows. And give them drink out of your immortal (ἀμβροσιώ-δους) fountain which neither fouled nor dries up; for they entreat and supplicate you and desire to become your servants and ministers, and for this they are content even to be persecuted of your enemies, and for your sake to be hated of them and to be mocked and to die, like as you for our sake suffered all these things, that you might preserve us, you that are Lord and verily the good shepherd. And grant them to have confidence (παρρησίαν) in you alone, and the succour that comes of you, and the hope of their salvation which they look for from you alone, and that they may be grounded (βεβαιωθῶσιν) in your mysteries and receive the perfect goods of your graces and gifts, and flourish in your ministry and come to perfection in your Father'". In the Greek version we notice a distinction between **truth** and **error**. The word "error" is often found in these Acts, see ch. 37: "this land of error"; ch. 38: "evil things ... done in error" (2x); ch. 39: "you have come to men that were in error" (Greek: "straying from God)"; ch. 48 (Greek) and 67: "redeemed your own from error"; ch. 98 (Greek): "Save them that are held in error"; ch. 80: "destroyer of error"; ch. 122: "who has delivered his universe from misery and error", and ch. 156: "guide ... in the path of error". This means that as long as man lives on earth he is in error. The idea is not unknown in the LXX and the New Testament, see *Theol. Wörterbuch z. N.T.* VI 230–254, *s.v.* πλανάω (Braun), but it does not play an important part. In Syriac literature the word is frequently met, cf.Odes of Sol. 15.6: "I repudiated the way of error ...", J.H. Charlesworth, *The Odes of Solomon*, Oxford 1973, 68, n. 5; Ephrem, *hymni epiphan.* XV 2, ed. Lamy I c. 129–130: ... *expulsae sunt ab eo tenebrae erroris et illuminati sunt fines orbis*; Ephrem, *hymni disp.* V, ed. Lamy IV c 701–702: *Beatus es, qui fiduciam habes in sponsa a te ex ethnicismo abducta, quam daemones induxerant in errorem et servam effeceunt sacrificiorum; tu eam deal-*

basti lavacro benedicto, quae sole nigra affecta erat fulgentem reddidisti; Liturgical Homiles of Narsai, ed. Connolly 36: "the darkness of error which blinded them from understanding", and *Constit. Apost.* VII XXXVIII 7: πεπλανημέης ἀγνοίας ἠλευθέρωσας, cf. VIII X 17. Later the word "error" shows a tendency to become the equivalent of "sect", see *Kephalaia* 30. 2–5; 224. 22; 225. 8 and 232. 11, but also Ephrem, *adv. haer.*. ed. Beck, and Gregorius of Nyssa, *orat. catech.*, prologue. See for Mandaeism E. Percy, *Untersuchungen über den Ursprung der johanneischen Theologie*, Lund 1939, 84–105. The idea that "truth" is the contrast of "error", see *Testam. Juda* 20.1, ed. Becker: "... zwei Geister ... der der Wahrheit und der der Verirrung"; *Constit. Apost.* VII XXXIX 3: ἀλλ' ἀπὸ πλάνης καὶ ματαιότητος εἰς ἐπίγνωσιν ἀληθείας ἐκάλει. Nestorian. Taufliturgie, ed. Diettrich 14: "Zum Zeichen derer, die von dem Irrtum [der Finsternis] zum Erkenntnis der Wahrheit sich bekehren"; Badger, *Nestorians* II 221: "... glory be to Thee, o Thou who restores those who err to a knowledge of truth, and Aristides, *apol.* 12. **and you know ... not know**. Greek: τὰ τοῖς πολλοῖς ἄγνωστα, which wishes to say that Thomas and those with him possess knowledge. **unite them ... wolves**. The passage speaks about baptism. According to the Syriac version the anointing is followed by a baptism with water and according to the Greek version baptism with water is followed by the anointing. The difference has to be explained by the baptismal practice in the Western and Eastern church, see ch. 27. To be united to the fold is also met in ch. 26; 39; 59; 67; 131 and 156. The idea that Israel and the church is compared with a fold can be found in biblical literature, see Ps. 77, 21; 78, 52; Is. 40, 11; Jer. 13, 17; Zech. 10, 3; John 10, 16; Acts 20, 28 and I Pet. 5, 2. In this connection it is important "to be known", see John 10, because one was sealed, see ch. 26 and 131. This means protection, see ch. 26 and 49. The word "purity", see also ch. 12, in Greek καθαρίσας shows agreement with Eph. 5, 26: καθαρίσας τῷ λουτρῷ τοῦ ὕδατος ἐν ῥήματι and καὶ καθαρίσας αὐτοὺς τῷ σῷ λουτρῷ. This means that here is spoken of baptism with water, see also *Theol. Wörterbuch z. N.T.* IV, *s.v.* λούω (Oepke), 297–309. The expression "to guard from the wolves" alludes to John 10, 12–13, see also ch. 49. **and feed ... meadows**. This again can be compared with John 10, 9, cf. Ps. 23, 2. **and let them drink ... fails**. As in ch. 39, but the influence of Ps. 23, 2 is obvious. The presence of the fountain is empasized, cf. Greek: ἀπὸ τῆς ἀμβροσιώδους σου πηγῆς, which reminds us of Hymn I *l.* 8. The idea is known from biblical literature, cf. Ps. 87, 7; Is. 12, 3; Joel 3, 18 and Zech. 13, 1: "a fountain ... to cleanse them from sins and uncleanness"; John 4, 14; Apoc, 7, 17 and 21, 6. The fountain being a gift of God is a favourite idea, see Eth. Hen. 96, 6; 22,9; Sir. 15, 1–3; Philo, *de ebriet*. 112, see Strack–Billerbeck II 436. Drinking out of the fountain means life, cf. Odes of Sol. 6. 11–12: "Then all the thirsty upon the earth drank ... For from the Most High the drink was given ... 18: And lived by the living water of eternity" and 30. 1. "Living Water" can be the equivalent of the Spirit, cf. Barn. 1. 3, or baptism, cf. Ephrem, *hymni epiphan*. XII 5, ed. Lamy I c. 109–110: *Baptismus fons est vitae quem apparuit, cum in vivis esset Filius Dei*; Liturg. Hom. of Narsai, ed. Connolly 46: "Our Lord had opened up for us the sweet spring of Baptism, and has given our race to drink of the sweetness of life immortal". In gnosticism a tendency seems to exist to identify baptism with drinking, cf. Hippolytus, *refut.* V 27 2, referring to the Book of Baruch: καὶ πίνει ἀπὸ τοῦ ζῶντος ὕδατος ὅπερ ἐστὶ λουτρὸν αὐτοῖς; and V 19 21 about the Sethians: καὶ ἔπιε τὸ ποτήριον ζῶντος ὕδατος Mand. Liturg. 27: "Gieb ihnen drei Handvoll Wasser zu trinken und sprich zu Ihnen: 'Trinke, finde Heilung und Bestand, der Name des Lebens und der Name des Manda dHaije ist über dich ausgesprochen" and Gospel of Thomas XIII. **and wish ... for your sake**. Cf. Matth. 10, 22 and John 17, 14–18. **Let them therefore ... gifts**. In the Greek version Thomas asks for confidence, παρρησία, succour, βοήθεια, hope ἐλπίς, that they may be grounded in your mysteries ἵνά βεβαιωθῶσιν εἰς τὰ σὰ μυστήρια, for the perfect goods and your graces and gifts, τῶν σῶν χαρισμάτων καὶ δομάτων τὰ τελεια ἀγαθά, that they may flourish in your ministry, ἀνθήσουσιν ἐν τῇ σῇ διακονίᾳ, and come to perfection in your father, τελεσφορήσιν ἐν τῷ πασρί σου. The Syriac only reads: "Boldness, ܪܘܿܐܝܣ that they may be confirmed, ܢܐܝܚܡܙ, in your glorious mysteries, and receive the gifts of the gifts, ܝܕܡܡܥܙܪ ܪܟܫܙ ܡܢ ܢܩܡܙܘ". These last words are apparently returning in Greek: τῶν σῶν χαρισμάτων καὶ δομάτων. The word ܪܟܡܡܥ is also present in John 4, 10, being a translation of δωρέα, the gift of God. See also ch. 27. First of all is asked for παρρησία, which agrees with ch. 13 and 14. In ch. 61 we read alongside: "perfect you ... that we may have boldness". See also Hebr. 4, 16 and 10, 19. In the second passage we find the words παρρησίαν ... ἐν τῷ ἅιματι, where the word ἐν is the equivalent of the Syriac ܒ in the expression "boldness in you". In these Acts the word "boldness" has been used in ch. 15: "that I should say aught with boldness"; ch. 61: "and give us boldness that is in you"; ch. 78: "for the Lord encourages you and engenders boldness", Greek: ὁ γὰρ σὸς δεσπότης προτρέπεται σε θάρσος σοι ἐγγεννῶν; ch. 81: "Giver of freedom of speech"; ch. 103: "and will give you a sovereignty, παρρησία, that does not pass away and does not change". Boldness appears to be a gift of God to those who belong to Him. It is often connected with baptism. It makes it possible that man is able to go to God without shame and to say whatever he likes. The "glorious mysteries" are the sacraments, see also *Theolog. Wörterbuch z. N.T.* IV 809–834, *s.v.* μυστή-ριον (Bornkamm). See for a different meaning ch. 10 and 27. The Syriac word ,ܝܙ has been used to render the idea "to confirm", Greek βεβαι-όω in Mark 16, 20 according to syr p, but also in order to translate the word στηρίζω in Luke 22, 32 according to syr p s c and phil. The parallel in Rom. 16, 25: τῷ δὲ δυναμένῳ ὑμᾶς στηρίξαι is important, cf. I Pet. 5, 10 and Ignatius, *ad Ephes.* 12. 1: ἐγὼ ὑπὸ κίνδυνον, ὑμεῖς ἐστη-ριγμένοι. In the New Testament is spoken of being confirmed in the faith, see Coloss. 2, 7. and in Ignatius, *ad Magnes.* 13. 1 in the doctrine. See also Irenaeus, *adv. haer.* I 21 3, about the Marcosians: ἐστήριγμαι καὶ λελύτρωμαι; Ginza R II. 37–38: "Sie wachsen in jeglichem Wachs-tum, leben und stehen fest an ihrem Orte; *Evangelium Veritatis* 19, 30–32, ed. Robinson 39: "Having been strengthened, they learned about the impressions of the Father". The idea of giving gifts can be explained by passages like John 4, 10 and Eph. 4, 8. "Coming to perfection" accord-ing to the Greek version can be compared with ch. 26: καὶ τελειωθῆναι ἐν αὐτῇ (*scil.* eucharist) and ch. 54: ἵνα τελειωθῇ (Syriac adds: "in her love by faith", cf. Did. X 4). The word τελεσφορέω is only found in Luke 8, 14 in the New Testament but with a different meaning. The idea of "coming to perfection" which has to be related with baptism seems to be of Hellenistic origin, see G. Anrich, *Das antike Mysteriemwesen in seinem Einfluss auf das Christentum*, Göttingen 1894, 160–161. The word, however is often used in early christian literature, see Philipp. 3, 12 and 15; Coloss. 2, 8; Clemens of Alex., *paedag.* I 26: βαπτιζόμενοι φωτιζό-μεθα φωτισόμενοι υἱοποιούμεθα, υἱοποιούμενοι τελειούμεθα, τελειούμενοι ἀπαθανατιζόμεθα; Aphraates, *demonstr.* XXIII 3, ed. Parisot II c. 9–10: *illuxit lumen intellectus, et fructus germinarunt olivae splendidae, in qua signum est sacramenti vitae, quo perficiuntur christiani et sacerdotes et reges et prophetae*; Ephrem, *hymni epiphan.* III 17, ed. Lamy I c. 37–38: *Ecce oleo obsignamini; in baptismo perficimini; gregi Christi commiscemini eius corpore nutrimini*; Nestor. Taufliturgie, ed.Diettrich 48: "Er ward getauft und vollendet N.N. im Namen des Vaters ..."; Moses bar Kepha, *The Mysteries of Baptism*, ed. Aytoun 357: "The reception of these holy mysteries shows first that he is fully initiated and perfected in gifts", and Irenaeus, *adv. haer.* I 21 2 about the Marcosians: τὸ μὲν γὰρ βάπτισμα τοῦ φαινομένου ἰησοῦ ἀφέσεως ἁμαρτιῶν, τὴν δε ἀπολύτρωσιν τοῦ ἐν αὐτῷ χριστοῦ κατελθόντος εἰς τελειώσιν. See also F. Sagnard, *La Gnose valentienne et le Témoignage de S. Irénée*, Paris 1947, 403.

26

And they were rejoicing with holy hymns, and were cleaving to the apostle and not parting from him; **and every one who was needy, was receiving and being relieved. And they begged of him that they might receive the sign of baptism, saying: "For we have heard that all the sheep of that God, whom you preach are known to him by the sign".** Judas says to them: **"I too rejoice, and ask of you to partake of the eucharist and the blessing of the Messiah whom I preach". And the king gave orders that the bath should be closed for seven days** and that no man should bathe in it. And when the seven days were done, on the eighth day they three entered into the bath by night that Judas might baptise them. **And many lamps were lighted in the bath**.

Commentary. The Greek version reads: "Being therefore wholly set upon the apostle both the king Gundaphoros and Gad his brother followed him and departed not from him at all, and they also relieved them that had need, giving unto all and refreshing all. And they besought him that they also might henceforth receive the seal of the word, saying unto him: Seeing that our souls are at leisure and eager toward God, give you us the seal for we have heard from you that the God whom you preach knows his own sheep by his seal. And the Apostle said to them: I also rejoice and entreat you to receive this seal, and to partake with me in this eucharist and blessing of the Lord, and to be made perfect therein. For this is the Lord and God of all, even Jesus Christ whom I preach, and he is the father of truth, in whom I have taught you to believe. And he commanded them to bring oil, that they might receive the seal by the oil. They brought the oil therefore, and lighted many lamps for it was night." See for the composition of chapters 26, 27 and 28 Y. Tissot, "Les Actes de Thomas. Exemple de Recueil Composite", in: Bovon e.a. *Les Actes Apocryphes*, 223–232. **and every … relieved**. Cf. Ps. Clemens, *homil.* VIII 23 1, ed. Rehm 130–131: ἔνδυμα οὖν εἰ βούλεσθε γενέσθαι θείου πνεύματος σπουδάσατε πρῶτον ἐκδύσασθαι τὸ ῥυπαρὸν ὑμῶν προκάλυμα (ὅπερ ἐστιν ἀκάθαρτον πνεῦμα). **sign**, ܪܘܫܡܐ and Greek: τὴν σφραγῖδα τοῦ λόγου, but in manuscript C: … τοῦ λουτροῦ, cf. Hermas, *simil.* IX 16 5: τὴν σφραγῖδα τοῦ κηρύγματός. The passage Eph. 5,26: καθαρίσας τῷ λουτρῷ τοῦ ὕδατος ἐν ῥήματι may have been of influence, cf. Liturg. Homilies of Narsai, ed. Connolly 36: "Lo, the sheep are gathered together, and the lambs and the ewes, and he sets upon the stamp of life of the word of his Lord". **Our souls … sign**. Greek: σχολαζουσῶν τῶν ψυχῶν ἡμῶν καὶ προθύμων ἡμῶν ὄντων περὶ τὸν θεόν. This is obviously the same idea as in Matth. 12, 43–45. Man has to make room in order to receive God, cf. *Corpus Hermet.* XIII 1: ἕτοιμος ἐγενόμην καὶ ἀπηνδρείωσα τὸ ἐν ἐμοὶ φρόνημα ἀπὸ τῆς τοῦ κόσμου ἀπάτης. **for we have heard … sign**. Also in ch. 25 is spoken about the seal by which man is known by God. See also Odes of Sol. 8. 13: "I recognized them and imprinted a seal on their faces" and 4.7: "Because Thy seal is known and thy creatures are known to it"; Cyril of Jerusalem, *catech.* I 2, ed. Reichl 30; Theodore of Mopsuestia, ed. Mingana 46: "The sign with which you are signed means that you have been stamped as a lamb of Christ", and Badger, *Nestorians* II 196: "Gather us, o Lord, unto Thyself, and make us to enter into Thy fold, and seal us with Thy sign". **I too rejoice … preach**. See for "perfect therein" ch. 25. **And the king … seven days**. A parallel is present in *De mirac. beati Thomae apostoli*, ed. Zelzer 42. 11–13: … *et flagitabat (Gundaphorus) signaculum beatae crucis accipere et credere deo illius. Beatus vero apostolus indicens eis jejunium per septem dies praedicavit verbum dei. Et die septima baptizavit regem et fratrem eius* … . For fasting before baptism see Justin Martyr, *apol.* I 61 2; Tertullian, *de bapt.* 20, and *Constit. Apost.* VII 22 5. See also Th. Schermann, "Frühchristliche Vorbereitungsgebete zur Taufe", in: *Münch. Beitr. z. Papyrusforschung* 3 1917, 22–23. **And he commanded by the oil**. In Greek only. It is obvious that the anointing has been emphasized, cf. ἵνα διὰ τοῦ ἐλαίου δέξωνται τὴν σφραγῖδα. **And many lamps … bath**. Baptism takes place during the night, see also ch. 27; Gregory of Nyssa, *orat. IV in sanct. pasch.*, in: *P.G.* 46, c. 681; Gregorius of Nyssa, *orat. 45. 2 in sanct. pasch*, in: *P.G.* 36, c. 623 and *orat.* 44. 5, in: *P.G..* 36, c. 611. See also G. Quispel, "De besterde Hemel in de christelijke Baptisteria", in: *Ned. Theol. Tijdschr.* 3 1948, 355–358. The eucharist was celebrated after baptism in the early morning, see ch. 29.

27

And when they had entered into the bath-house, Judas went in before them. And our Lord appeared to them, and said to them: "Peace be with you, my brothers". And they heard the

voice only, but the form they did not see, whose it was, for till now they had not been baptized. And Judas went up and stood upon the edge of the cistern, and poured oil upon their heads, and said: "**Come, holy name of the Messiah; come, power of grace, which is from on high; come, perfect mercy; come, exalted gift; come, sharer of the blessing; come, revealer of hidden mysteries; come, mother of the seven houses, whose rest was in the eighth house; come, messenger of reconciliation; and communicate with the minds of these youths; come, Spirit of holiness, and purify their reins and hearts**". **And he baptized them in the name of the Father and the Son and of the Spirit of holiness. And when they had come up out of the water, a youth appeared to them, and he was holding a lighted taper**; and the light of the lamps became pale through its light. And when they had gone forth, he becaeme invisible to them; and the Apostle said: "**We were not even able to bear your light, because it is too great for our vision**". **And when it dawned and was morning, he broke the Eucharist** and let them partake of the table of the Messiah and they were glad and rejoicing. **And when many were added** and were coming to the **refuge** of the Messiah, Judas did not cease to preach and says to them:

Commentary. In Greek this chapter reads: "And the apostle arose and sealed them. And the Lord was revealed to them by a voice saying: 'Peace be to you, brothers.' And they heard his voice only, but his likeness they did not see, for they had not yet received the added sealing of the seal. And the Apostle took the oil and poured it upon their heads and anointed and chrismed them, and began to say: 'Come, you holy name of the Christ that is above every name. Come, you power of the Most High, and the compassion that is perfect. Come, gift of the Most High. Come, compassionate mother. Come, communion of the male. Come, she that reveals the hidden mysteries. Come, mother of the seven houses, that your rest may be in the eighth house. Come, elder of the five members, mind, thought, reflection, consideration, reason; communicate with these young men. Come, holy spirit, and cleanse their reins and their heart, and give them the added seal, in the name of the Father and Son and Holy Spirit'. And when they were sealed, there appeared to them a youth holdng a lighted torch, so that their lamps became dim at the approach of the light thereof. And he went forth and was no more seen of them. And the apostle said to the Lord:

'Your light, o Lord, is not to be contained by us, and we are not able to bear it, for it is too great for our sight'. And when the dawn came and it was morning, he broke bread and made them partakers of the eucharist of the Christ. And they were glad and rejoiced. And many others also believing were added to them, and came into the refuge of the Saviour." **And when they had ... my brothers**. In ch. 121 a voice is heard after baptism and in ch. 158 after eucharist. Apart from this a difference exists between the Syriac and the Greek version. In Greek this voice is heard after having received the (first) seal. This has to to with the different order of baptism in Syriac and Greek. In Syriac we find the anointing before baptism with water. In Greek the words spoken during baptism with water: "And he baptises them in the name ...", are part of the epiclesis which begins with the words: "come, you holy name ...". The Syriac version is the original one although the Greek version also shows two different rituals. This was possible by adding another act before the anointing also mentioned in Syriac but now called "added sealing of the seal". The act which precedes this "added sealing of the seal" has been rendered by the words at the beginning of this chapter: "And the apostle arose and sealed them". The contents of this "sealing" are not clear. It might be baptism with water, but see also ch. 56–57. **And they heard the voice ... baptised**. Those who are not yet baptised, but in Greek not yet anointed, were able to hear the voice but were not able to see. We may compare Cyril of Jerusalem, *procat.* 9: τῶν δὲ ὀφθαλμῶν ἐσκεπασμένων, οὐκ ἐμποδίζεται τὰ ὦτα δέξασθαι τὸ σωτήριον. Although Acts 9,7 is a parallel passage, but see also Acts 22,9, it does not explain the present passage. Here we are dealing with the liturgical practice in the early church where the relation between baptism and the possibility to "see" is important, see Clemens of Alex., *paedag.* I 28 1: οἱ βαπτιζόμενοι ... φωτεινὸν ὄμμα τοῦ πνεύματος ἴσχομεν, ᾧ δὴ μόνῳ τὸ θεῖον ἐποπτεύομεν; Ephrem, *hymni epiphan.* VIII 22, ed. Lamy I c. 89–90: *Estis omnes illo igne per oleum uncti, per aquam induti* (note the order!), *per panem refecti, per vinum potati, voce illum audistis, mentis oculo illum contemplati estis.* We may also refer to passages in which is spoken of a difference between those who are able to hear and those that are able to see, see Liturg. Homilies of Narsai, ed. Connolly 3: "After these the proclamation concerning the hearers (catechumenens) is made, that they should go ... 'Go, ye hearers'", and p. 39: "and lo, he entreats to enter (and) see the face of the king'; Nestorian. Taufliturgie, ed. Diettrich 29: "Geht ihr hörenden, und beachtet die Thüren". Also in Judaism the gift of seeing is supposed to be the most important one, cf. Ex.R 41. 3, ed. Lehrmann 471: "Two things did Israel ask of God—see his likeness (דמוחו) and to hear from His own mouth the Decalogue"; Philo, *de confus. ling.* 146: ὁ ὁρῶν Ἰσραήλ, cf. *Constit. Apost.* VII XXXVI 2: δι' αὐτοῦ γὰρ προσηγάγου τὰ ἔθνη ἑαυτῷ εἰς λαὸν περιούσιον τὸν ἀληθινὸν ἰσραήλ τὸν θεοφιλῆ τὸν ὁρῶντα θεόν. See Pacher, H ΒΑΣΙΛΙΚΗ ΟΔΟΣ, Paderborn 1931, in: *Stud. z. Gesch. u. Kult. des Altert.* XVII 1931, 175 and W. Völker, "Fortschritt und Vollendung bei Philo von Alexandrien", in: *Texte u. Unters.* 49 1938, 283. In Gnostic literature, see *Exc. e Theodoto* 63–65, ed. Sagnard 184–189, where it is said that the *pneumatici* are going to the Pleroma, but the *psychici* are standing in front of the bride-chamber hearing the voice of the bridegroom only; Hippolytus, *refut.* V 8 14 about the Naassenes: τοῦτ' ἔστι, φησί, τὸ εἰρημένον φωνὴν μὲν αὐτοῦ ἠκούσαμεν, εἶδος δέ αὐτοῦ οὐχ ἑωράκαμεν and Ginza L 471. 25–36: "Wenn es dir beliebt, werde ich kommen, und deine Gestalt schauen". **added sealing of the seal**. Greek: ἐπισφράγισμα τῆς σφραγῖδος. The word is unknown in christian literature. It is apparently chosen by the Greek translator of these Acts because in the passage an earlier sealing had already taken place. **Come, holy name of the Messiah**. This epiclesis shows striking agreement with the one found in ch. 50. Here the Greek version adds some words taken from Philipp. 2,9. The independent use of the Name is also present in ch. 132; 133 and 157, but is already to be found in the New Testament, see Acts 5, 28 and II John 7, see *Theol. Wörterbuch z. N,T*, V 269–281, *s.v.* ὄνομα (Bietenhardt); Did IX: οἱ βαπτισθέντες εἰς ὄνομα κυρίου and Hermas, *simil.* IX 16: καὶ τὰ πνεύματα τῶν παρθένων μετὰ τοῦ ὀνόματος ἐφόρεσαν. We also find an epiclesis of the name in *Acta Petri* XIX, ed. L.B. I I 7–8: *accepit enim aquam et invocans nomen Iesu Christi sanctum*. See E. Lohmeyer, "Kyrios Jesus", in: *Sitzungsber. der Heidelb. Akad. der Wissensch.*, phil.-hist. Kl. XVIII 1927/8, 54: "Der Name trägt den gleichen Sinn wie etwa 'das Wort' oder 'der Geist' oder 'die Weisheit' oder 'die Schechina'"; W. Heitmüller, "Im Namen Jesu", in: *Forsch. z. Rel. u. Lit. des A. u. N.T.* I 1903, and C.H. Dodd, *The Interpretation of the Fourth Gospel*, Cambridge 1955, 93–96. The descent of the name causes a union of man and Christ, see Odes of Sol. 8. 19: "And they shall not be deprived of my name for it is with them"; 15. 8 and 39. 8: "Therefore, put on the name of the Most High and know him ...", and Isaac of Antioch, in: *BKV* 128: "Gelobt sei dein Name, welcher unseren Namen angezogen hat". In Irenaeus, *adv. haer.* I 21 3, about the Marcosiams we find a prayer for the ὄνομα τὸ ἀποκεκρυμμένον, see F. Sagnard, "Extraits de Théodote. Clément d'Alexandrie", in: *Sources Chrétiennes*, Paris 217–219:

"Doctrine de Marc de Mage sur le Baptême de Jésus et le NOM (Ir., *Adv. Haer.* I, 14–16)"; *Exc. e Theodoto* 217–219 and K. Müller, "Beiträge zum Verständnis der Valentian. Gnosis", in: *Nachr. kön. Gesellsch. der Wissenschaften*, Göttingen, phil.-hist. Kl. 1920, 179–242, esp. 186ff; Mand. Liturg. 35: "Einem jedem, der mit diesem Öl bestreicht, über das ich den Namen des gewaltigen fremden Lebens, über das ich diesen verborgenen Namen gesprochen habe, wird Heilung dem Körper zuteil werden". **Come, power of the grace ... high**. In the Syriac version "power" is not personified. but the request for "power" is often found in these Acts, see ch. 52; 81; 121; 132; and 157, cf. Odes of Sol. 32. 3: "Because he has been strengthened by the holy power of the Most High". "Power" is the same as the Holy Spirit, see Luke 24, 49 and Acts 8, 10.9, or even Christ, see I Cor. 1, 24. The idea is sometimes related with baptism or eucharist, see Ephrem, *hymni epiphan.* IX 5, ed. Lamy I 91–92: *Jesus virtutem suam aquis inmiscuit*, and Liturg. Homilies of Narsai, ed. Connolly 20: "The Spirit descends upon the oblation ... and causes the power of his godhead to dwell in the bread and wine". Very often in Gnostic literature: Irenaeus, *adv. haer.* I 30 about the Ophites: *Non autem oblitum suum Christus, sed missus desuper virtutem in eum* and I 31 2 about the Cainites: *o tu angele, abutor opere suo; o tu potestas, perficio tuam operationem; Exc. e Theodoto* 77. 2, ed. Sagnard 200: ἡ δύναμις δὲ τῆς μεταβολῆς τοῦ βαπτισθέντος, cf. 82.1, 206, and *Corp. Herm.* I 27: ... ὑπ᾽ αὐτοῦ (πατὴρ) δυναμωθεὶς καὶ διδαχθεὶς, see Nock–Festugière 25, n. 68 and Festugière IV 249; C.F.G. Heinrici, *Hermes–Mystik und das Neue Testament*, Leipzig 1918, 34–36, and *Theol. Wörterbuch z. N.T.* II, 286–318, *s.v.* δύναμις (Grundmann). **Come, perfect mercy**, ܪ̈ܚܡܐ ܓܡܝܪ̈ܐ, and Greek: ἡ εὐσπλαχνία ἡ τελεία. In ch. 10 it was shown that "mercy" can be identified with Christ. **Come, exalted gift**, ܡܘܗܒܬܐ ܡܪܝܡܬܐ and Greek: τὸ χάρισμα τὸ ὕψιστον. In syr p the word χάρισμα has been rendered by ܡܘܗܒܬܐ. In the New Testament the word χάρισμα is closely related with the Holy Spirit, see G.P. Wetter, *Charis*, Leipzig 1913, 168–187. **Come, compassionate mother**. In Greek only: ἐλθὲ ἡ μήτηρ ἡ εὔσπλαγχνος.The word "mother" has been avoided in Hymn I *l.* 52–54; ch. 39 and 132, although in this chapter is spoken of the "mother of the seven houses". See also Aphraates, *demonstr.* XVIII 10, ed. Parisot c. 839–840: *Homo ... diligit et colit Deum, patrem suum, et Spiritum sanctum matrem suam*. The idea of a "mother" is often met in Gnostic literature, cf. Hippolytus, *refutat.* IX 13 3, about the Elchesaites; Irenaeus, *adv. haer.* I 5 2, about the Valentinians; Origen, *c. Cels.* VI 3 and Epiphanius, *pan.* XXXVIII 4 2, about the Ophites; Epiphanius, *pan.* XXXIX 2 3, about the Sethians and *pan. XL 2 3*, about the Archontici. See S. Hirsch, *Die Vorstellung von einem weiblichen πνεῦμα ἅγιον im Neuen Testament und in der ältesten christlichen Literatur*, Berlin 1936, and W. Bousset, "Hauptprobleme der Gnosis", in: *Forsch. z. Rel. u. Lit des A. u. N.T.* 10, Göttingen 1907, 66–68. **Come, sharer of the blessing,** ܟܘܢܝܐ ܕܡܒܪܟܬܐ and Greek: ἡ κοινωνία τοῦ ἄρρενος. Syriac appears to be secondary. See F.C. Burkitt, "The Original Language of the Acts of Thomas", in: *Journ. of Theol. Studies* I 1900, 280–290, esp. 289, supposed an original ܒܪܗ ܕܓܒܪܐ being the same as ܒܪܗ ܕܐܢܫܐ, cf. Mark 7, 38 in syr s. Here it is said that the Spirit is united wth Christ, see ch. 10 and Hermas, *simil.* V VI 5: πνεῦμα τὸ ἅγιον τὸ προόν τὸ κτίσαν πᾶσαν τὴν κτίσιν κατῴκισεν ὁ θεὸς εἰς σάρκα ἣν ἠβούλετο and *Epistula Apost.*13, ed. Duensing 11, where it is said that Christ puts on the Wisdom of the Father. The idea of a σύζυγος is known from the Valentinians, see Irenaeus, *adv. haer.* I 21 3: εἰς ὄνομα ἀγνώστον πατρὸς τῶν ὅλων εἰς ἀλήθειαν μητέρα πάντων, εἰς τὸν κατελθόντα εἰς ἰησοῦν and *Sophia Jesu Christi* 101. 16–17, ed. Robinson 214: "And his consort is the great Sophia", cf. 102. 14, ed. Robinson 215: "… and the tri-male spirit, which is that of Sophia his consort". The opposite is found in ch. 46, where it is said that the devil who dwells in a woman speaks about τὴν καλλιστὴν μου σύζυγον. **Come, revealer of the hidden mysteries**. In ch. 10 it is said that Christ reveals the mysteries and according to ch. 121, a passage which can be compared with the present one, mysteries are revealed by the holy oil. In *Sap. Sal.* 8, 4 wisdom is revealing mysteries, cf. IQS IV 21–22: "He will sprinkle over him the spirit of truth like lustral water (in order to cleanse him) … In this way the upright will understand knowledge of the Most High and the wisdom of the sons of heaven will teach those of perfect behaviour". see F. Nötscher, "Zur theologischen Terminologie der Qumran–Texte", in: *Bonner Bibl. Beitr.* 10, Bonn 1956, 71–77, esp. 73: "Tatsächlich aber belehrt השכיל nun Gott den ihm wohlgefälligen. Frommen in seine wunderbaren Geheimnisse (1 QH 11. 10) öffnet ihm dafür das Ohr (1 QH 1. 21) durch seinen 'Heiligen Geist' und erschliesst seinen Inneres die Kenntnisse seiner geheimnisvollen Weisheit (1 QH 12. 12f) דעת ברו שכלכה". **Come, mother of the seven … house**. The Greek and the Syriac version are slightly different. According to the the Syriac version the mother lives in the eighth house, ἀνάπαισις σου εἰς τὸν ὄγδοον οἶκον γένηται. In Greek Thomas asks whether the brothers may live in the eighth house: ܕܢܫܒܬܐ ܕܐܚܝܢ ܗܘܐ ܒܣܒܥ The idea, however, to which the passage goes back is clear. The seven houses are the seven planets, cf. Prov. 9,1 and W. Staerk,

"Die sieben Säulen der Welt und des Hauses der Weisheit", in: *Zeitschr. f.d. neutestamentl. Wissensch.* 35 1936, 232–261. The eighth house is the place above the planets, where God is living, cf. Clement of Alex., *strom.* VII 57 1: εἰς τὴν πατρῶαν αὐλὴν ἐπὶ τὴν κυριακὴν ὄντως διὰ τῆς ἁγίας ἑβδομάδος. Dwelling in the eighth house is the same as being perfect, an idea reflected in the octagonal baptistery, see F.J. Dölger, "Zur Symbolik des altchristlichen Taufhauses", in: *Antike und Christentum* IV 1934, 153–187. For the Mother dwelling in the eighth house, see Epiphanius, *pan.* XXV 22, about the Nicolaites: βαβηλω ... δοξάζουσιν, ἣν ἄνω φάσκουσιν εἶναι ἐν ὀγδόῳ οὐρανῷ; *pan.* XL 2 3, about the Archontici: καὶ τὴν μητέρα τὴν φωτεινὴν ἀνωτάτω ἐν τῷ ὀγδόῳ εἶναι; Irenaeus, *adv. haer.* I 30 4, about the Ophites; *Exc. e Theodoto* 63.1, ed. Sagnard 184: ἐν ὀγδοάδι ... παρὰ τῇ μητρί and Johannesb. 95.1–2: "In Kleidern der Acht ging ich in der Welt, ich ging im Gewande des Lebens und kam in die Welt". See also *Corp. Hermet.* I 26, Nock–Festugière 25, n. 64 and XIII 15, 215–216, n. 65 and 66. For the gift of "rest" see ch. 35 and Matth. 11,27, but esp. Hebr. 4,6.8 and 9, see E. Käsemann, "Das wandernde Gottesvolk", in: *Forsch. z. Rel. u. Lit. des A. u. N.T.* 55 1939, 44. **Come, messenger ... youths**. Greek: ἐλθὲ ὁ πρεσβύτερος τῶν πέντε μελῶν νοός ἐννοιάς φρονήσεως ἐνθυμήσεως λογισμοῦ, κοινώνησον μετὰ τούτων τῶν νεωτέρων. Syriac is secondary, but it helps to show that the word πρεσβύτερος has to be read as πρεσβευτής, cf. ܐܝܙܓܕܐ. See for the word "messenger" ch. 10. The five members are also found in *Kephalaia* 29. 13–14,; *Acta Archelai* X, ed. Beessson 15,11, see H. Pognon, *Inscriptions Mandaïtes des Coupes de Khouabir*, Paris 1896, 184 (translation) and 127. This does not mean that we are dealing with a direct relation, cf. W. Bousset, "Mandäisches in den Thomasakten", in: *Zeitschr. f.d. neutestamentl. Wissensch.* 18 1917/18, 1–19, esp. 5: "Ich deute nur die Vermutung an, dass die manichäische Lehre und jene schon der griechischen Welt bekannte seltsame, scheinbar psychologische Spekulation auf eine orientalische Hypostasenspekulation zurückgehen wird". There are a great number of more or less identical lists, cf. bHag. II 12a, ed. L.Goldschmidt III: "Durch zehn Dinge wurde die Welt geschaffen, durch Weisheit, durch Einsicht, durch Erkenntnis, durch Kraft, durch Anschreien, durch Stärke, durch Gerechtigkeit, durch Recht, durch Gnade und durch Barmherzigkeit", see H. Grätz, *Gnostizismus und Judentum*, Krotschien 1846, 36–40. This obviously goes back to the Old Testament, cf. Ex. 35, 31; Deut. 4, 6; Eccles. 1, 17; Job 21, 22; 22, 2; Sir. 1, 19 and Is, 11, 2. But also in Barnabas 2. 3: σοφία—σύνεσις—ἐπιστήμη—γνώσεως—λόγισμος—ἐνθύμησις; Hippolytus, *refut.* VI 12 2 about Simon Magus: νοῦς—ἐπίνοια—φωνή—ὄνομα—λόγισμος—ἐνθυμη-σις; Irenaeus, *adv. haer.* I 24 3 about Basilides: νοῦς—λόγος—φρόνησις—σοφία—δύναμις *Sophia Jesu Christi* 96. 4–7, ed. Robinson 210: "For he is all mind. And he is thought, and thinking, and reflecting, and rational-ity, and power" and 102. 20–103. 1, ed. Robinson 215: "First Man has his unique mind within, and thought, which is like it, reflecting, think-ing, rationality, power" and Aristotle, *ethic. Nicom.* I 13: σοφίαν μὲν καὶ σύνεσιν καὶ φρόνησιν διανοητικάς (*scil.* ἀρετὰς λεγομεν). See F.C. Burkitt, *The Religion of the Manichees*, Cambridge 1925, 72, and E. Käsemann, "Leib und Leib Christi", in: *Beitr. z. hist. Theol.*, Tübingen 1933, 61–63, with Indian parallels. **Come, spirit ... hearts**. Greek: ἐλθὲ τὸ ἅγιον πνεῦμα καὶ καθάρισον τοὺς νεφροὺς καὶ τὴν καρδίαν, cf. Luke 11,2 according to the manuscripts 162 and 700 reads: ἐλθέτω τὸ πνεῦμα σου τὸ ἅγιον ἐφ᾽ ἡμας καὶ καθαρισάτω ἡμᾶς, which may be a liturgical for-mula, see R. Leaney, "The Lucan Text of the Lord's Prayer (Lk. XI 2–4), in: *Nov. Test.* I 1951, 103–111, See for "reins and hearts" Ps 26 (25) 2. **And he baptised ... holiness**. For reasons given above, the Greek version differs considerably. **And when they had come out of the water**. Greek: "and when they were sealed". The anointing took place while those being baptised were standing in the water. There-fore it is said that Judas stands upon the edge of the cistern. **a youth appeared ... taper**. Here is spoken about the appearance of Christ, cf. *Apocr. Johannis* 1.31–2.4, ed. Robinson: "Straightaway ... behold the [heavens opened and the whole] creation ... shone ... [... and behold I] saw in that light [a youth ...]" Christ in the form of a child is often met, cf. History of Mar Matthew and Mar Andrew, Syriac ed. Wright 99; *Acta Petri* V, in: L.B. I I 50, 35–51, 21: *factum est autem ubi Theon baptizatus est, in eodem loco apparuit iuvenis decore splendidus*, and *Acts Pauli*, ed. Schmidt 3, 13–14: εἰσῆλθεν παῖς λείαν εὐειδὴς ἐν χάριτι καὶ ἔλυσεν τὰ δεσμὰ παύλου. In III Henoch III 2 and IV 1 Metatron is called "youth", see H. Odeberg, *3 Henoch*, Cambridge 1928, 7 and 8. The rela-tion between "light" and baptism is often met, cf. Eph. 5,14, where the influence of Ps. 112, 4 and 97, 11 seems to be present, but especially Matth. 3,15 in the Old-Latin manuscript a: *et cum baptizaretur (Jesus) lumen ingens circumfulsit de aqua ita ut timerent omnes qui advenerant*, and paral-lel texts mentioned in H.J.W. Drijvers–G.J. Reinink, "Taufe und Licht. Tatian, Ebionäerevangelium und Thomasakten", in: *Text and Testimony.* Essays ... in honour of A.F.J.Klijn, Kampen 1988, 91–110; Tertullian, *De Anima* 41. 4: *Proinde cum ad fidem pervenit reformata per secundam nativi-tatem ex aqua et superna virtute, detracto coruptionis pristinae aulaeo totam lucem* *suam conspicit*, see J.H. Waszink, *De Anima*, Amsterdam 1947, 456; Moses bar Kepha, ed. Aytoun 356–357: "The lights which are before him signify that he has removed from the darkness of ignorance and sin to the light of the knowledge of God … that he is prepared for the heavenly light"; Odes of Sol. 25.7, and Mand. Liturg. 14: "Ohne Sünde, vergehen … sollen diese Seelen, die zum Jordan hinabsteigen und die Taufe empfangen, emporsteigen und den grossen Ort des Lichtes und die lichte Wohnung schauen". **We were … vision**. It is impossible to see Christ with bodily eyes, cf. ch. 36; 53; 143; *Acta Petri* XXI, in: L.B. I, 68, 32–69, 2: *sed nec tale lumen … quod enarrare nemo hominum possit, tale lumen, quod non inluminavit usque adeo ut exentiaremur aboratione*; Philo, *de opif. mundi* 69: ἀόρατός τε γὰρ ἐστιν οὗτος τὰ πάντα ὁρῶν. and Gedulah Mosheh, ed. Gaster 573. 3: "And Metatron answered and said: 'O Lord of the universe, Mosis is not able to come up and see the angels, for there are angels who are of fire and he is only flesh and blood', 4. God said: 'Go and change his flesh into fire'". The invisibility of God is well known, cf. Theophilus, *ad Autol*. I 7; Origenes, *comment. in Joh*. XX 7; Ps.-Clemens, *recogn*. III 30 1, ed. Rehm 118; Cyril of Jerusalem, *catech*. IX 1, ed. Reichl 237 and X 7, 268, and Bar Hebraeus, *ethikon*, ed. Wensinck 93. **And when it dawned … eucharist**. See ch. 26 about eucharist in the morning. Syriac speaks about "breaking eucharist", ܐ̈ܝܪܣܛܘܪܐ ܡܝܪ. The same is found in ch. 29; 121 and 158. In Greek we read καὶ εὐχαριστίαν κλάσας in this chapter and ch. 29 and 158. In ch. 169 the word ܩܘܡ has been used. The expression is well known, cf. Luke 24, 30; Acts 2,46. In Ps.-Clemens, *homil*. XI 36, ed Rehm 172, we find the same as in Syriac: καὶ εὐχαριστίαν κλάσας **and they were glad and rejoicing**, ܘܐ̈ܝܕܚܘ ܘܘܗ ܢܝܕܚܡܘ and Greek: ἔχαιρον δὲ καὶ ἠγαλλιῶντο, cf. Matth. 5,12: χαίρετε καὶ ἀγαλλιᾶσθε, but in Syriac syr s c p: ܘܐ̈ܝܕܚ ܘܘܗ **many were added**. Cf. Acts 11,24. **refuge**. See ch. 10.

28

"Men and women and children, youths and **maidens, shun fornication and covetousness and the service of demons**; for under these three heads comes all wickedness. For fornication blinds the intellect, and darkens the **eyes of the soul**; it confuses the **steps** of the body, and changes its complexion, and makes it sick. And covetousness puts the soul in agitation in the midst of the body, that it takes what does not belong to it, and is afraid lest, when it returns the thing to its owners, it should be put to shame. And the service of the belly makes the soul dwell in care and sorrow, fearing lest it should come to want, and grasp at things that are far from it. For since you have been delivered from there, you have become without care and without grief; and there remains with you (the saying): '**Take no care** for the morrow, because the morrow will take care of itself'. And bear in mind the other (saying) which is written for you: '**Look upon the ravens**, and consider the fowl of heaven which sow not nor reap, and God feeds them; how much more will he have care for you, you who are lacking of faith?' But expect the **coming of Jesus, and hope in him, and believe in his name, because he is the judge** of the dead and the quick, and he shall recompense every man, according to his works at his last coming. For it will be no excuse for one to say: 'We did not know'. His heralds are proclaiming in the four quarters of the world: 'Repent and believe in the new preaching and receive the **pleasant yoke and the light burden**, and live and die not. Gain (these) and perish not. **Come forth from the darkness, and the light will receive you**. Come to the Good, and receive for yourselves grace, and plant the cross in uour souls".

Commentary. **maidens**. Greek adds: "strong men and aged, whether bound or free", but omitted by the manuscripts C and D. **shun fornication … demons**. Greek reads τῆς ἐργασίας τῆς γαστρός in place of "service of the demons", see later. This list can be compared with some other ones in this work, see ch. 12: adultery—theft—fornication—covetousness—vainglory, in Greek: adultery—murder—theft—fornication; ch. 58: lying—oppression—drunkenness—slander, in Greek: covetousness—lying—oppression—drunkenness—slander; ch. 79: adultery—theft—oppression—greed, Greek: fornication—theft—covetousness; ch. 84: fornication—murder—theft—gluttony—covetousness—vainglory—slander—evil actions—deeds of shame—hateful intercourse—unclean connexion, Greek: adultery—theft—covetousness—vainglory—foul deeds of the belly, and ch. 126: adultery (Greek adds: prodigality)—theft—drunkenness—lavishness (Greek omits)—service of the belly—deeds of shame—odious actions (Greek omits). We may assume that these lists are related with each other. It is important that sexual intercourse itself is not mentioned. Lists of this sort are popular in both Judaism and christianity, cf. IQS IV 9–10: "However, to the spirit of deceit belong greed, frailty of hands in the service of justice, irreverence, deceit, pride and haughtines of heart, dishonesty, trickery, cruelty, much insincerity, impatience, much insanity etc.";

Testam. Simeon 5.3, ed. Becker 43: "Hütet euch nun zu huren, denn die Hurerei ist die Mutter aller Übel ..."; Matth. 15, 19; Mark 7, 21–22; Gal. 5, 19–21; Did. X 1; Barnabas 20. 1 and Hermas, *mand.* VIII 3 5. See Ph. Carrington, *The primitive christian Catechism*, Cambridge 1940, 19, and S. Wibbing, "Die Tugend- und Laterkataloge im Neuen Testament", in: *Beih. Zeitschr. f.d. neutestamentl. Wissensch.* 25 1959. Also in *Kephalaia* 190. 14–15: "Vier grosse [Werke] gibt es in der Welt, auf (Grund) deren alle Menschen [der Erde sich] gegenseitig [töten]: [Das erste] Werk is [die Sorge?] des Menschen, damit sie essen [behufs Wachstum] ihres Körpers. Das zweite is [der Geschlechts-] verkehr (συνουσία) ... (defective) ... Hurerei (πορνεία). Das dritte Werk is das [Vermogen (χρῆμα) und] der unnütze Reichtum ... Das vierte ist der Krieg und die [Streitigkeiten (φιλονικιά)]", and Augustine, *de moral. Manich.* II 19: *tria ... signacula ... oris certe et manuum et sinus*, cf. Baur, *Manich. Religionssystem* 248–267. **eyes of the soul**. See ch. 65. **steps**, ܗ̈ܘܠܟܬܗ and Greek: πολιτείας. This treatment of virtues is well known in Hellenistic popular literature about ethics, cf. Achilles Tatius II 29, ed. Gaselee, in: *Loeb Class. Libr.*: "Shame, grief and anger may be compared to three billows which dash against the soul; shame enters through the eyes and takes away their freedom; grief diffuses itself about the breast and tends to extinguish the lively flame of the soul; while anger, roaring round the heart overwhelms the reasoning power with its foam of madness". We may also refer to Augustine, *c. Faustum* V, in which Faustus especially emphasizes the way in which the Manichees keep the commandments. **Take no ...** , ܕܠܐ ܬܐܨܦܘܢ ܕܡܚܪ܆ ܡܛܠ ܕܗܘ ܡܚܪ ܕܝܠܗ ܢܐܨܦ, cf. Matth 6,34 in a free rendering. Greek: μὴ μεριμνήσητε εἰς τὴν αὔριον, ἡ γὰρ ἄυριον μεριμνήσει ἑαυτῆς. **look upon the ravens ...** , ܕܚܘܪܘ ܒܥܘܪ̈ܒܐ ܘܐܬܚܙܘ ܒܥܘܦܐ ܕܫܡܝܐ ܕܠܐ ܙܪܥܝܢ ܘܠܐ ܚܨܕܝܢ ܘܐܠܗܐ ܡܬܪܣܐ ܠܗܘܢ. ܟܡܐ ܗܟܝܠ ܠܟܘܢ ܢܬܒܛܠ ܠܗ ܚܣܝܪ̈ܝ ܗܝܡܢܘܬܐ. Greek: ἐμβλέψατε εἰς τοὺς κόρακες καὶ ἄφιδετε εἰς τὰ πετεινὰ τοῦ οὐρανοῦ ὅτι οὔτε σπείρει οὔτε θερίλει οὔτε συνάγει εἰς τὰς ἀποθηκας, καὶ ὁ θεὸς οἰκονομεῖ αὐτά. Πόσῳ μᾶλλον ὑμᾶς ὀλιγόπιστοι. The present quotation in the Syriac version combines both Matth. 6,26 and Luke 12, 24 and 28. This has been taken over by the Greek text which adds, however, οὔτε συνάγει εἰς τὰς ἀποθήκας, see Matth. 6, 26. **Coming of Jesus ... Judge**. Jesus being judge also in ch. 30 according to the Greek text and ch. 130. See for the New Testament Matth. 16, 22; 25, 31–46 and Acts 10, 42, but also in *Kephalaia* 234.10–11: "Wenn er sich in seinem Katechumenat festige, empfängt er Vergeltung für seine Guttaten (ἀγαθόν)" and 14: "Das Gericht, das seine Sünden verurteil wird über ihn ausgesprochen", and

Ginza L 544. 29–31: "Der Richter fragt sie aus nach ihren Sünden und Verfehlungen: 'Was für Werke hast du, Seele, getan in der Welt der Täuschung in der du weiltest?'" **pleasant yoke and light burden**, ܪܘܠܝܠܐ ܡܫܒܐܘ ܟܘܡܣ ܐܝܘ which agrees with Matth. 11, 29 in syr s c p. Greek: ζυγὸν πραότητος καὶ φορτίον ἐλαφρόν. This agrees with the text of the New Testament but here the word πραότητος has been chosen in place of χρηστος. **Come forth ... receive you.** Also in ch. 119 and 153 is spoken about the contrast between light and darkness. This is very important in Judaism, see S. Aalen, "Die Begriffe "Licht" und "Finsternis" im Alten Testament", in: *Skriften utgitt av det Norske Videnskaps-Akad. Oslo*, hist.-fil. Kl. 1951, but also in the New Testament, see Eph. 5, 8 and I Pet. 2, 8. See for early christian literature Hist. of Phillip, Syriac ed. Wright 80: "Flee from the darkness and come to the celestial light"; I Clement 59. 2; Theophilus, *ad Autol.* II 36: καὶ λίπετε σκοτίην νυκτός, φωτὸς δε λάβεσθε; very often in the Odes of Sol, cf. 7. 4; 8. 2; 10. 6; 25. 7; 32. 1; 36. 3 and 41. 6; Ephrem, *hymni epiphan.* VII 22, ed. Lamy I c. 71–72, and esp. *Epist. Apost.* 21, ed. Duensing 19: "Wahrlich ich sage euch, dass ich alle Gewalt von meinem Vater empfangen habe, damit ich die in der Finsternis Befindlichen ins Licht zurückführe und die in der Vergänglichkeit Befindlichen in die Unvergänglichkeit und die im Irrtum Befindlichen in die Gerechtigkeit und die im Tode Befindlichen entfesselt werden ..." See for Gnostic literature Hippolytus, *refutat.* V 19 2 about the Sethians: αἱ δὲ τῶν ἀρχῶν, φησι, οὐσίαι φῶς καὶ σκότος; *Acta Archel.* c. 67, ed. Beesson 96.27–29 about Basilides: *Quidam enim horum dixerunt initia omnia duo esse ... id est in principüs lucem fuisse et tenebras.* See for Bardaisan H.H. Schaeder, "Bardesanes von Edessa in der Überlieferung der griechischen und der syrischen Kirche", in: *Zeitschr. f. Kirchengesch.* 51 1932, 21–72, esp. 52–53 and H.J.W. Drijvers, *Bardaisan of Edessa*, Assen 1966, Index of Subjects; *Pistis Sophia*, ed Schmidt–Till 50. 36–39, and 98. 1–7; *Kephalaia* 164. 5–8: "Heil dem, der ... unterscheiden wird (διακρίνειν) die beiden Wesen (οὐσιά) des Lichts und der Finsternis, die nicht auseinander hervorgegangen sind, denn er wird das ewige Leben ererben (κληρονομεῖν)", and Johannesbuch 54. 28–29: "Werdet nicht Anteil der Finsternis, sondern richtet eure Blick zum Orte des Lichtes empor". See H. Jonas, *Gnosis und spätantiker Geist* I, Göttingen 1934, 103–104, and H. Odeberg, *The Fourth Gospel*, Uppsala–Stockholm 1929, 286–296. **cross**, ܨܠܝܒ, but this may also be "sign", Greek: σημεῖον, although the sign of the cross is probably meant, see ch. 5.

29

And when the Apostle had said these things, some of them said to him: **"It is time for the debtor to be paid"**. He says to them: **"The creditor always seeks more, but let us give him as much as is proper"**. And he spoke a blessing over the **bread and the olives**, and gave to them. **And he himself ate, because the Sunday was dawning**. And when the Apostle was asleep in the night, our Lord came and stood over him and said to him: "Thomas, rise, go away in the morning after the **service**, and go along the eastern road about two miles, and **I will show you my glory**; for because of this, on account of which you go out, many shall come to my refuge and shall live, and you shall reprove the power and the **nature** of the enemy". And when he awoke from his sleep, he said to the brothers who were beside him: "My children, our Lord will do to-day whatsoever he will; but let us pray and beg of him that there be to us no hindrance towards him, but, just as at all times when he wishes to show his power in us, (so) now too let his will be accomplished". And when he had spoken thus, he laid his hand upon them, and **broke the Eucharist** and gave to all of them, and said to them: **"Let this Eucharist be to you for grace and mercy, and not for judgment and vengeance"**. And they said: "Amen".

Here ends the second act

Commentary. **It is time ... proper**. Eating is service to corruptibility. This agrees with Origen, *Comment. in Matth.* XVII 27, where it is said that eating has to be identified with paying taxes to the body. **bread and olives**. Greek: ἄρτον καὶ ἔλαιον καὶ λάχανον καὶ ἅλας, see also ch. 20. **And he himself ate ... dawning**. Greek: αὐτὸς δὲ παρέμεινεν τῇ ἑαυτοῦ νηστείᾳ ... There is a difference between the Syriac and the Greek version. According to the Syriac Thomas is eating because it will be Sunday. This agrees with orthodox practice in Judaism and christianity, cf. Jubil. 50, 12; Sadok. fr. XIII 12, see Charles II 827, n. 13; Tertullian, *de cor.* 3; *Constit. Apost.* V 20 19: ἔνοχος γὰρ ἁμαρτίας ἔσται ὁ τὴν κυριακὴν νηστεύων. Bar Hebraeus, Book of the Dove, ed. Wensinck 28, and *Kephalaia* 191. 31–192. 1: "Die, welche keine Kraft haben täglich [zu fasten] auch sie fasten [am] Herrentag (κυριακή)", cf. 192. 32–33. See also H.-C. Puech, "Liturgie et pratiques rituelles dans le manichéisme [1959–1960]", in: *Sur le manichéisme et autres essais,*

Paris 1979, 275–187. **service**, ܬܫܡܫܬܐ and Greek: μετὰ τὴν εὐχὴν καὶ διακονίαν. In *Liber Graduum*, ed. Kmosko c. 797–798, the word is met in the same sense: *omnino simile est ministerium (ܬܫܡܫܬܐ) terrestre ministerio caelesti*. The word is usually used in the sense of service in the world or to God, cf. Aphraates, *dem.* I, ed. Parisot c. 4, 11–12: ... *ita et homo qui domus fit et domicilium habitationis Christi videat quid prosit ad ministerium (ܬܫܡܫܬܐ) Christi habitationis in se*. In the New Testament the Syriac word has been used to render λατρεία in John 16, 2, ἱερατεία in Luke 1, 9 and λειτουργία in Luke 1,23; II Cor 9,12; Philipp. 2, 17 and 30 and Hebr. 8, 6 and 9, 21. **I will show you my glory**. Cf, John 2, 11. **nature**. See ch. 10. **broke the Eucharist**. See ch. 27. It seems that here a proper meal ends with the Eucharist. **Let this Eucharist ... vengeance**. The same is found in ch. 50 and 158. It is a liturgical formula also found in the Liturgy of Serapion, ed. Brightman 106: καὶ ποιήσον πάντες ... φάρμακον ζωῆς λαβεῖν ... μὴ εἰς κατάκρισιν ... μηδὲ εἰς ... ὄνειδος and *Testamentum Domini* I XXIII, ed. Rahmani 43: ... *fac ut nobis sint non in judicium, neque in ignominiam vel in perditionem, sed in sanationem et in robur spiritus nostri*.

30

And the Apostle went forth to go whither our Lord had told him. And when he reached (the distance of) two miles, he turned aside from the road a little, and saw lying there a corpse of **a handsome youth**. and said: "Was it for this trial you brought me out hither, our Lord? **Let it be as you will**". And he began praying and saying: "Our Lord, **Lord of the dead and the quick**—of the quick, who, lo, **are standing**, and of the dead, who, lo, are lying,—**O Lord, Lord of the souls which abide in the body, and Father of all the souls which have gone out of the body,—come, Lord, at this moment, for the sake of the dust which your holy hands have fashioned**, and look down from heaven for I call upon you and **show your glory** in this (man) who is lying here". And he said again: "This deed has not taken place without the instigation of the enemy, who does these things; **but the enemy, who does these things, has not dared (to attempt it) through one who is alien to him, but (through one) who is subject to his will**".

Commentary. **a handsome youth**. Cf. ch. 31: a woman fair; ch. 42: a beautiful woman and ch. 53: a comely girl. The evil one is especially attracted by beautiful men and women, see ch. 44: "O hideous (one) who strives with the comely". **Let it be ... will**. Cf. Luke 1, 38. **Lord of the dead and of the quick**. Cf. Matth. 22, 32 and Rom. 14,9. Greek: "O Lord, the judge of ...", see ch. 28. **are standing**, ܩܝܡܝܢ and Greek: παρεστώτων. The Syriac verb ܩܐܡ probably speaks about those who are living. **Lord ... fashioned**. God being creator of man, see Gen. 2,7. See for the expression "fashioned" ch. 34. The Greek version reads: "and master and father of all things; and father not (only) of the souls that are in the bodies, but of them that have gone forth (of them); for of the souls (also) that are in pollutions (ἐν μιάσμασιν) you are lord and judge". Here the distinction of body and soul has been emphasized. In ch. 22 we were able to draw the conclusion that the soul is going to God only. The following references are showing the way in which is spoken about the body: ch. 39 alien bodies (Greek); ch. 78:

His bodily healings (which are) ended by dissolutions (Syriac, cf. 95) and ch. 147: The bound (body) -the unbound (soul). It appears that the body is the corruptible part of man. This distinction is not generally accepted in early Syriac literature, cf. Ephrem, *adv. haer.* 19. 1, ed. Beck 65 (translation) and 67 (Syriac): "Den Körper nannten die Irrlehrer verwerflichen Schmutz … schmutzig sind die Teufel und Dämonen". Nevertheless the idea that the body is of less value than the soul is already well known in Judaism, cf. *Sap. Sal.* 9, 15 and 11, 17; Mekh. Ex. 15. 1: "Ehe du mich wegen des Leibes, der Unrein ist, fragst, frage mich wegen der Seele, die rein ist"; Narsai, Memra über die Seele, ed. Allgeier 367: "Dass sie (*scil.* die Seele) lebe und den toten Körper, in dem sie wohnt, belebe". In ch. 158 is even spoken of the renewing of both body and soul. The idea of the identity of devil and body is known in Gnosticism only, see Ephrem, *adv. haer.* 17. 2, ed. Beck 59 (translation) and 60 (Syriac): "Die Finsternis und der böse haben ein und die selbe Natur, und der Körper und die Schlange haben die gleiche Natur" and 4: Der Körper ist (völlig) getrennt von der Seele; denn nicht kann eine tote Natur leben durch ein andres Lebewesen", and Ginza L 430. 33–34: "Steh auf, steh auf Adam, leg ab deinen stinkenden Körper, den Lehmrock, in dem du weiltest … und schlag es den Sieben und den Zwölf, den Männer, die es geschaffen, um den Kopf". **show your glory**. Cf. ch. 29. **but the enemy … his will**. For the word "alien" see ch. 4. To be safe in the power of Christ, see ch. 25.

31

And when he had said these things, **a black snake** came forth from a fissure, and was shaking his head violently, and beating his tail on the ground. And with a loud voice he said to the Apostle: "I will say before you on what account I slew this youth. There was **a woman fair of face in this village which is over against you and she passed by me, I saw her and loved her**; and I went after her, and saw the youth kissing her, and he also slept with her, and did other things with her which are unseemly,—easy for me (to say), but to you I do not dare to utter them, because I know that the **ocean-flood** of the Messiah will destroy our **nature**. And in order that I might not alarm her, I did not kill him at that time, **but I watched him, and in the evening, when he passed by me**, I struck him, **and killed him, and especially because he had dared to do this thing on the Sunday**". Judas says to him: "**Of what seed are you?**"

Commentary. **a black snake**. Greek: a great serpent. For the devil being a snake see ch. 44, and being black, see ch. 55 and 64. The devil as snake see Theophilus, *ad Autolicum* II 28: δαίμων δὲ καὶ δράκων καλεῖται διὰ τὸ ἀποδεδακέναι αὐτὸν ἀπὸ τοῦ θεοῦ and *Theol. Wörterbuch z. N.T.* II 284–286, *s.v.* δράκων (Foerster). For the idea "black" see Barnabas 4.10; *Acta Petri* XXII, in: L.B. I I 70. 8–10, and VIII, p. 56. 14–15; Ketzer-Katalog des B. Maruta, ed. A. Harnack, "Der Ketzer-Katalog des Bishofs Maruta von Maipherkat", in: *Texte u. Unters.* XIX 1890, 11: "Häresie (der Daizaniten) ... Sie tragen und hüllen sich in weisse Kleider, weil sie sagen, wer weisse Kleider trägt sei von der Partei des Guten, wer schwarze trägt, von der Partei des Bosen", and Mand. Liturg. 491. 34–35: "Finster ist ihre Gestalt und ihr Ansehen ist dunkel", 492. 2–4: "Sie wurden schwarz und nahmen Schwärze an, alle sind hässlich und schwarz, flüsternd stehen all da". See F.J. Dölger, *Die Sonne der Gerechtigkeit und der Schwarze*, Münster 1919 and T. Adamik, "The Serpent in the *Acts of Thomas*", in: J.N. Bremmer, *The Apocryphal Acts of Thomas*, Leuven 2001, 115–124. For the Greeks India was famous for its snakes, see Strabo XV I 45, and Philostratus, *Apollonius of Tyana* III VI, ed. Conybeare 242. **a woman fair ... loved her**. See also ch. 30. Especially women and virgins were in danger of the devil, see Ephrem, *On Virginity*, ed. Mitchell II, LXXX–XC and 170–189; Methodius, *Convivium X virginum* VI 1, in: *P.G.* 18, c. 113, and Manich. Ps. 60. 18: "The murderous snake, the enemy of virginity (παρθένια). **ocean-flood**, ܡܒܘܥܐ, and Greek: διδύμον. Syriac is secondary, cf. *Onomastica Vaticana* 174. 85, 175. 15–16 and 191. 71–72, ed. Paul de Lagarde, *Onomastica Sacra*, Hildesheim 1966 (Nachdruck Göttingen 1887): θωμᾶς ἄβυσσος ἢ δίδυμος. **nature**. See ch. 29. **but I watched ... passed by me**. See Cyril of Jerusalem, *procat.* 16: ἀλλὰ δράκων παρὰ τὴν ὁδὸν τηρεῖ τοὺς περιπατοῦντες βλέπει μὴ δάκῃ τῇ ἀπιστίᾳ. **and killed him ... Sunday**. Cf. Bornkamm, *Mythos* 24: "Der Drache übernimmt also die ihm slecht stehende Rolle des Sittenhüters". **Of what seed are you**. Greek: ποίας σπορᾶς καὶ ποίου γένους ὑπάρχεις, see also ch. 74. The words γένος and σπορά are identical, cf. *Corpus Hermet.* XIII 1: ἀγνοῶ, ὦ τρισμέγιστε, ἐξ οἴας μήτρας ἄνθρωπος ἐγενείθη, σπορας δε ποίας.

32

The snake says to him: **I am** a reptile, **the son of reptile**, and **harmer**, the son of harmer: **I am the son of him, to whom power was given over (all) creatures, and he troubled them. I am the** son of him, who makes himself like to God to those who obey him, that they may do his will. I am the son of him, who is ruler over everything that is created under heaven. I am the son of him, who is outside of the ocean, and whose mouth is closed. I am the kinsman of him, who spoke with Eve, and through her made Adam transgress the commandment of God. And I am he who incited Cain to slay his brother. And on my account,—because of this I was created,—the earth was cursed and thorns grew up in it. I am he who dared, and cast down the just from their height, and corrupted them through the lust of women; and they begat some large of body, and I worked in them my will. And I am he who hardened the heart of Pharaoh, that he might slay the children of Israel, and keep them down in hard slavery. I am he who led the people astray in the desert, when I subdued them so that they made for themselves the calf. **I am he who stirred up Caiaphas and Herod by slander against the righteous Judge. I am he who caused Judas to take the bribe, when he was made subject to me, that he might deliver up the Messiah to death.** I am he to whom the power of this world was given, and the **son of Mary** has seized me by force and taken **what was his** from me. I am the kinsman of him, who is to come from the **east**, to whom the power is given.

Commentary. **I am …** See E. Schweizer, "Ego Eimi", in: *Forsch. z. Rel. u. Lit. des A. u. N.T.* 56 1936, and H. Becker, "Die Reden des Johannesevangeliums …", in: *Forsch. z. Rel. u. Lit. des A. u. N.T.* 50 1956. **the son of a reptile**. Greek: "of the reptile nature", see ch. 29. **harmer**, ܟܝܣܐ. The word is only found in the Gospels in Matth. 16, 18. **the son of him … his will.** Greek: υἱὸς εἰμι ἐκείνου τοῦ βλάψαυτος καὶ πληξάντος τοὺς τέσσερα ἀδελφοὺς τοὺς ἐστῶτας. See for the word βλάπτειν in relation with the devil Luke 4, 35. The Syriac version is secondary but the Greek is not clear. The "four standing brothers" are not supposed to be the four elements as it was suggested by R.A. Lipsius, *Apokr. Apostelgesch.* I 323, and James, *Apocryphal New Testament* 379. The influence of a Jewish idea can not be rejected, see D.S. Margoliuth, "Some Problems in the 'Acta Thomae'", in: *Essays in Hon. of G. Murray*, London 1936, 249–259, esp. 251–252, who referred to Shabbath 55a, ed. Goldschmidt I 1933, 445: "Vier sind durch die Verleidung der Schlange gestorben …", also in Baba Bathra 17a, idem VI 989. The word "standing" in the sense of "righteous", see Margoliouth 252. **I am the son**

of him who is ruler ... heaven. The devil as ruler of the world, see *Ascensio Isaiae* I 3; II 4 and X 29; John 12, 31; 14, 30; 16, 11; II Cor. 4, 4; Eph. 2, 2; 6, 12; Ignatius, *ad Eph.* XVII 1; XIX 1; *ad Magn.* I 13; *ad Trall.* IV 2; Barnabas 2. 1 and 18. 2; Freer Logion added to Mark 16, 15 in manuscript W. Greek adds: "that receives back his own from them that borrow". In ch. 29 the name "debtor" was met in relation wth the devil. In both passages it is said that things borrowed from the devil have to be given back again. In the meantime man is supposed to be the property of the devil. **I am the son of him who is outside ... closed**. Greek: συγγενὴς δὲ εἰμι ἐκείνου τοῦ ἔξωθεν τοῦ ὠκεανοῦ ὄντος οὗ ἡ οὐρὰ ἔγκειται τῷ ἰδίῳ στόματι. The Syriac version with the words "mouth is closed" seems to be secondary. On the other hand, the idea of the devil surrounding the earth is known in Judaism and christianity, see Chagiga 11b, ed. Goldschmidt III 817: "Die Oede (Tohu) ist ein grüner Streifen, der die ganze Welt umgibt, und von dem die Finsternis ausgeht"; Origen, *c. Celsum* VI 25, about the Ophites, see ed. Chadwick 340, n. 2 with references. *Pistis Sophia*, ed. Schmidt–Till 207. 6–9: "Die äussere Finternis ist ein grosser Drache (δράκων), dessen Schwanz in seinem Munde"; and Ginza L 430. 20–21: "... dem Drachen, der die Welt umkreist ..." The influence of originally Jewish ideas here and in the following is striking, see H. Gressmann, "Das Gebet des Kyriakos", in: *Zeitschr. f. d. neutestamentl. Wissensch.* 20 1921, 23–25, ch. 8, and also *Acta Petri* VIII, in: L.B. I 55. 23–56. 18. **I am the kinsman ... commandment of God**. Greek: "I am he that entered through the barrier (διὰ τοῦ φραγμοῦ) into paradise and spoke with Eve the things which my father bade me to speak to her". For the idea that paradise was surrounded by a wall, see Gnost. Adamschriften, ed. Preuschen 12: "Und sogleich hängte sich die Schlange herab und liess sich auf die Umfriedigung des Garten fallen"; Apocalypse of Moses 17, ed. von Tischendorf 9: "Die Schlange hing sich alsbald an die Paradiesmauer", and Revelation of Joshua b. Levi, ed. Gaster 591: "So they went together till they reached the wall of Paradise", see Lipsius, *Apokr. Apostelgesch.* I 342; L. Troje, "ΑΔΑΜ ΖΩΗ", in: *Sitzungsberichte der Heidelb. Akad. der Wissensch.*, phil.-hist. Kl. VII 1916; H. Schlier, "Christus und die Kirche", in: *Beitr. z. hist. Theol.* 6 1930, 18–26, and H. Schlier, "Religionsgeschichtliche Untersuchungn zu den Ignatiusbriefen", in: *Beih. Zeitschr. f. d. neutestamentl. Wissensch.* 8 1929, 21. **I am he who incited Cain ... grew up in it**. See about Cain Gen. 4, 16. It is striking that after this an allusion follows about the thorns, taken from Gen. 3, 18. **because of this I was created**. This has been omitted by the Greek version, see ch. 34 and Adamantius, *de recta in Deum fidei*, ed. van de Sande Bakhuyzen 116, about Marinus: τρία δὲ ἔστιν ἐν οἷς οὐ συμφωνοῦμεν τῇ καθολικῇ ἐκκλησίᾳ ... τὸν διάβολον οὐχ ὑπὸ θεοῦ λέγομεν ἔκτίσασθαι, **I am who dared ... my will**. Greek adds after the word "height": καὶ ἐν ταῖς ἐπιθυμίαις τῶν γυναικῶν αὐτοὺς καταδήσας ἵνα γηγενεῖς παῖδες ἐξ αὐτῶν γένωνται. Burkitt, *The Original Language* ... , 284, supposed that the word ܕܝܘܐ was read as ܐܣܪ = καταδήσας. The expression γηγενεῖς παῖδες is striking which is also found in *Sapientia Salomonis* VII 1: εἰμὶ μὲν κἀγὼ θνητὸς ἴσος ἅπασι, καὶ γηγενοῦς ἀπόγενος πρωτοπλάστου. It expresses the idea of weakness and corruptibility. It appears that the contents of this passage combined with the omission of Adam's sin shows a parallel with the contents of the Pseudo-Clementines according to which the fall of mankind began with Gen. 6, see O. Cullmann, *Die Christologie des Neuen Testaments*, Tübingen 1957, 145–148. Other Jewish-Christian ideas are found in ch. 82 and 88. **And I am he who hardened ... slavery**. Cf. Ex. 7, 3; 10, 27 and 11, 10. **I am he who led ... calf**. Cf. Ex. 32, 1ff **I am he who stirred ... Judas**. The Syriac manuscript of Sinai is present until ch. 34: "you have done well to come here". The Greek version reads: "I am he that inflamed Herod and enkindled Caiaphas unto false accusations of a lie before Pilate". This agrees with the tendency to put the guilt of Jesus' death on Herod, see Tertullian, *de resurr. carnis* 20; *Acta Andreae et Matthiae* 26, in: L.B. II I 105. 2–3: καὶ ἀποκτενοῦμέν σε ὡς καὶ τὸν διδάσκαλον σου τὸν λεγόμενον ἰησοῦν ὃν ἀπέκτεινεν ἡρῴδης, and Luke 23, 8–12. **I am he who caused ... death**. Cf. ch. 84, where it is said that theft was the cause of Judas' act. See also Matth. 26, 14–16 and par. passages; John 13, 27, and Tertullian, *de anima* 11. 15, see ed. Waszink 199. **Son of Mary**. Greek: "Son of God", see ch. 143. **what was his**. Here can be referred to ch. 33: "who struggled ... for his human beings" (Syriac, but Greek: "... his own"); ch. 38: "we do not dare to say that we are his, because our works are alien from him"; ch. 39: "who became bereaved, that by the power of your Lord you might deprive the enemy of many" (Syriac, but Greek: "that has condemned the enemy and redeemed his own"); ch. 44: "O lying slanderer, who strives with those that are not yours" (Syriac, but Greek: "that are alien to him"); ch. 45: "You have power over them that obey you, and we have power over them that are subject to us" (Syriac, but Greek: "your own ... ours") ch. 48: "You who rescued from deceit your human beings" (Syriac, but Greek: "your own from error"); ch. 58: "and you shall become servants of him" (Syriac, but Greek: "that you may become his own"); ch. 67: that delivers from error your human beings" (Syriac, but Greek: "men that are your own"); ch. 76: "and you receive your reward, and I mine" (Syriac, but Greek: "your own and I mine"), and ch. 144: "You, who has made me know that I am yours". It appears that the Syriac version avoids the use of the expression "his own", which seems to imply a particular way of living, because according to ch. 38 and 58 it is possible to become "his own" if one does the will of God. **east**. The devil is coming from the east, see F.J. Dölger, "Sol Salutis", in: *Liturgiegeschichtl. Forsch.* 4/5, Münster 1920, 165: "Ganz entsprechend (*scil.* das Wiederkommen Jesu vom Osthimmel) sollte auch der Antichrist vom Osten kommen", and *Theol. Wörterbuch z. N.T.* I, 354–355, *s.v.* ἀνατολή (Schlier).

33

And when the snake had said these things, because Judas having asked of our Lord that speech was given to him, he was compelled to speak about his nature. And when he had finished, the multitude was hearing all these things; and fear with belief settled on all those who were there, when they saw and heard these wonders. And they were crying out alike with one voice: "One is the God of this man, who has informed us concerning his God, and by his word has commanded this fearful beast, and it has disclosed its nature". And they were begging of him that, as he had commanded it by his word to speak like a man, so too by his word he would kill it. Then Judas made a sign to them with his hand, and raised his voice and said: "You are audacious, though your nature is laid bare, and you shall be slain. And your insolence, which has gone so far, ought not have been (such) that you should tell those things which were done by those who were subject to you; and you have not feared that your end has come. But to you I say, in the name of our Lord Jesus who struggled against your nature **even to the end** and **for his human beings, that you suck out the poison** which you have cast into this youth; because my God has sent me to kill you and to raise him up alive before this multitude that they may believe in him, that he is the true God and that there is no other". And the snake said to him: "Our destruction is not yet come, as you have said. Why do you compel me to take (back) what I have put into this youth? For were even my father to suck out and take (back) what he has cast into creation, it would be his destruction". The Apostle says to him: "Show, then, the **nature** of the father". And the snake came and put his mouth upon the wound of the youth, and was sucking the poison from it, and by little by little, as the poison was drawn out the colour of the youth, which had become like purple, became white, and the snake was swelling. And when he had drawn out the whole of the poison from the youth, he sprang upright, and ran to the feet of the Apostle, and fell down and worshipped him. Then the snake **burst**, according to the word of Judas; and a great pit was made in the place where the poison of the snake fell. And Judas commanded the king and his brother to fill up that place, and lay foundations and made in it **houses (as) places of entertainment for strangers**.

Commentary. **And when the snake had said ... end was come**. Greek: "And when that serpent had spoken these things in the hearing of all the people, the apostle lifted up his voice on high and said: 'Cease henceforth, o most shameful one, and be put to confusion and die wholly, for the end of your destruction has come; and dare not to tell what you have done by them that have become subject to you'". **because Judas ... to him**. Probably an addition, cf. ch. 39. **nature**. See ch. 29. **even to the end**. Greek and Sinai add: "until now". According to the Greek version the struggle between Christ and the devil is continuing, cf. the Greek version in this chapter: "and die before our time" after: "I have put into this youth". The same difference is present in ch. 47, where the Syriac version reads: "he was being consumed" and the Greek: "he shall be consumed". We assume that Syriac is secondary, because it is said in the present chapter: "Our destruction is not yet come, as you have said", which agrees with ch. 45 in the Syriac version: "Why do you wish to destroy us, when our time has not yet come", cf. ch. 73: "... ere the time of the consummation comes and you are going to your own pit", and ch. 75: "And as I see, you do not wish to let us remain on earth; but you are not able at this time to do this to us". **for his human beings**. Greek: διὰ τοὺς ἰδίους ἀνθρώπους, see ch. 32. **that you suck out the poison**. See for the idea that the serpent injects poison into creation, the *Apocalypse of Moses* 19, ed. von Tischendorf 11; Odes of Sol. XXII 7: "Your right hand destroyed his evil venom"; Ephrem, *adv. haer.* I 2, ed. Beck 2 (translation) and 1 (Syriac): "Der Neid wütete gar sehr und biss die Menschen. Sein Gift treibt ihn an und er verwundet jeden, den er antrifft ... sein Quell und sein Wurzel ist von Gift", and Manich. Ps. 149. 12–13: "The poison of the serpent spreads out ... I became an enchanter until I had extracted (?) his poison". **nature.** See ch. 29. **burst,** ܚܣܡ and Greek: ἐλάκησεν, cf. Acts I, 18, see F.J. Foakes Jackson–K. Lake, *The Beginnings of Christianity* I, vol. V, London 1933, 22–30, sp. 28–29. **houses (as) places of entertainment for stangers,** ܒܬܐ ܥܒܕ ܚܝܬ ܠܚܬܐ ܐܪܟ and Greek: καὶ οἴκους οἰκοδομήσατε ἐπάνω, ἵνα οἴκησις γένηται τοῖς ξένοις, cf. Matth. 27,7.

34

And the youth was glorifying God, through whose grace he had come to life by the hand of the Apostle Judas, and had been rescued from all his former deeds. And he begged of the Apostle that he would aid him in prayer to our Lord, being upbraided by his own conscience, and was saying: "To you be glory, merciful and great and glorious God, maker and founder of all created things. You have set a limit and a measure to all your creatures whom you have created and have appointed to them changes that are beneficial to their natures, you are he who made man, as your godhead wanted, with the fashioning of your hands that he might be ruler above; and created for him another creation, that he might strive against it with the free will which you gave him. But the free nature of man went astray, and he became subject of his fellow, and that (fellow) became an enemy of him; because he found that he had been unmindful of his free-will. And the enemy rejoiced that he had found an entrance into his fellow, and he thought that he would be master over all the slaves; but you, o Merciful, through your great mercy, spread over us your goodness, and sent to our human race your word, the disposer of all created things, through your glorious Son. And he, through his free-will, which you gave him,—your goodness aiding him,—came and found us in those works which our human race did from the first day. And you did not enter into reckoning with us for our sins, but brought me to life through your goodness and showed me my remissness and sowed in me your heavenly love, and opened my mouth, which was shut, that I might speak of my enslaver and your abundant grace, which is not angry with me for what I say concerning it, about whose great love I am speaking". And Judas stretched out his hand to him, and raised him, and embraced him, and said to him: "The grace of our Lord be with you and with all those who believe in him". And the youth said: "Glory to you, o God,—who did not withhold his mercy from me, who was lost, but showed me (how) to seek my own soul and informed me concerning you, that you are his Apostle, and said to you: "I have many things to show through you, and you have many works to accomplish through me, for which you shall receive their reward; and you shall give life to many, and they shall become on high, in the light, sons of God. Do you, therefore, bring to life this youth, who was smitten by the enemy, **because you at all times behold your Lord? Yes, my Lord, Apostle of God, you have done well to come hither, and you have drawn many unto Him, and he will not fail you. And I am without care and without suffering, because of his grace which has come upon me through you, and (because) his gift has been poured out abundantly upon my weakness.** And I have been freed from evil cares and from deeds of **corruption**, and have been delivered from him, who was alluring me and inciting me to do things in which you found me, and have understood him who was saying to me the opposite of them. And I have destroyed him, who through **darkness, his kinsman, made me stumble by his works; and I have found the light, the Lord of the day, who had not been seen by me, and I have seen him.** I have destroyed him, who was darkening and obscuring all those who cleave unto him and obey him, so that they cannot see what they are doing, and be ashamed of their deeds and desist from them, and his work (thereby) come to an end, **and I have found him, whose doing this is, that those who do his will should never repent. I have been delivered from him, whom fraud supports, and before whom goes a veil (of darkness) and after whom comes shame, and she daring in impudence. And I have found Him who clears away evils, the Lord of peace and the confirmer of truth, who makes the enemy pass away from those who turn repenting to him, and heals afflictions, and destroys their dis-turber. But I beg of you Apostle of God, sow in me your word of life, so that I may again hear perfectly the voice of him, who delivered me to you and said to you: 'This is (one) of those who shall live through you, and henceforth let him be with you'"**.

Commentary. **And the youth was glorifying ... and inform me concerning you, that you are his Apostle and said to you**. Most of this passage about God who created man has been added by a Syriac rewriter. Greek reads: "But the youth said to the Apostle with many tears: 'Wherein have I sinned against you for you are a man that has two forms, and whatsoever you wish (there) you are found and are restrained of no man, as I behold. For I saw that man that stood by you and said to you'". Sinai is corrupt and reads: "and the youth was sorrowful, and wept [and said with] his [many] tears [to the Apostle: 'What] wrong have I done [to you, o man] in whom are [two] likenesses?' And as you wish ... to him according as I see. For I have said to this [man] ... that is his Apostle, and say to you.'". **two forms**. The same idea is found in ch. 57; 118; 151 and 156. Thomas appears to be πολύμυρφος like Christ, see ch. 48. In ch. 11 it is said that Christ and Thomas are identical which will be repeated in ch. 45: "Why are you like to God your Lord". It it not uncommon that those who have been baptized have been identified with Christ because of their gift of the Spirit, cf. Aphraates, *demonstr.* VI 18, ed. Parisot, c. 307–308: *qui igitur Spiritu Christi receperint similitudinem habebunt Adae coelestis, qui est Vivificator Dominus noster Iesus Chrstus*; also Tertullian, *de bapt.* 7, writes that those who have been anointed become *Christi*. **with the fashioning of your hands**. See also ch. 30. In the passage added in the Syriac version the idea that God created man has been emphasized. See I Clement 32.4, and also T. Jansma, "L'Hexaméron de Jacques de Serug", in: *L'Orient Syrien* 4 1959, 2–42 and 129–162, esp. 33: "En précisant: 'Faisons l'homme', il estime digne de lui travailler de ses propres mains à la stature", and see the references on 134, n. 105. **changes**. I Clement 20 goes into the order which is part of God's creation. It is important to notice that the devil belongs to the creation, cf. ch. 32: "because of this I (*scil.* the devil) was created". **free will**. The free will of man has been very much emphasized in orthodox circles against Gnosticism, see Ephrem, *adv. haer.* 11.3, ed. Beck 41 (translation) and 40 (Syriac): "Die Leugner und Chaldäer heben in ihrer Freiheit die Freiheit auf", and 21. 7, ed. Beck 75 (translation) and 75 (Syriac): "Adam und Satan haben durch ihre Freiheit das Böse, das aus dem Willen stammt, eingeführt"; Isaac of Antioch, "Gedicht über den Teufel", in: *BKV* 181: "Die Willensfreiheit des Menschen ist eine Vollständige"; Severus of Antioch, in: *Patr. Orient.* VI, ed. E.W. Brooks 101–102, speaks about Judas Iscariot and his free will, and in 59 II II, in: *Patrol. Orient.* 102–103, about Adam and his free will, but see also Justin

Martyr, *apol.* I 43; Theophilus, *ad Autolycum* II 27; Ireneus, *adv. haer.* IV 4 3; Clemens Alex., *strom.* VI 96 2; Origen, *Comment. in Matth.* X 11, and *c. Cels.* IV 65. See W. Völker, "Der wahre Gnostiker nach Clemens Alexandrinus", in: *Texte u. Unters.* 57 1952, 115–117 and W. Völker, "Das Vollkommenheitsideal des Origenes", in: *Beitr. hist. Theol.* 7 1931, 27–31. **but showed me (how) to seek my own soul**. See ch. 15. **because you at all times behold your Lord**, ܗܠ ܐܢܬ ܗܘ ܚܙܐ̈ܬ̣.ܒܟܠ ܠܗ̇ ܥܕ̈ܢܝܢ but Greek: καὶ ἐν παντί καιρῷ ἔφορος αὐτοῦ γενοῦ, which is probably due to a misunderstanding of the Syriac, see ch. 88. **Yes, my Lord ... fail you**. Greek: "Well, therefore, are you come hither, and well shall you depart again to him, and yet he never shall leave you at any time". It is striking that here again the Greek text only slightly differs from the Syriac version. Are we to assume that the Greek translator used a somewhat corrupt Syriac text? **grace ... gift**. See ch. 27. **and (because) of his ... weakness**. Greek: and has enlightened me from care of the night and I am at rest from the toil of the day. **deeds of corruption**. This obviously means sexual intercourse. **darkness, his kinsman ... seen him**. See ch. 43. The Greek writes that he has found the Light "being my kinsman (ὄντα μου συγγενῆ)". It seems that the Syriac version avoids to speak about the kinship between Christ and man. This may be compared with ch. 39 in Greek: "You (*scil.* Thomas) kinsman of the great race", but Syriac: "son of a great family"; ch. 43 in Greek: "and receive the grace that has been given to your kindred", but Syriac: "... given to the penitent"; ch. 143 in Greek only: "... that I may come and be with their kindred", but in ch. 61 it is said in both Syriac and Greek: "... that we might be joined to your kinship" (Greek: συγγενεία and Syriac: ܠܟܢܫܘܬܟ). From this last passage it appears that one may be joined to the kinship of Christ as soon as the earthly possessions have been left. See for other passages speaking about this subject Erklärung des Evangeliums, ed. Schäfers 60: "Und wie der Bräutigam der Jungfrau nicht fremd ist, die ihm anverlobt ist, weil sie von einer Natur sind, und ein Gott sie erschaffem hat, und sie gemäss dem Willen ihres Schöpfers miteinander verbunden sind, so auch sind wir unserem Herrn nicht fremd ..."; Odes of Sol. 41. 8: "All those who see me will be amazed, because I am from another race" (ܐܢܐ ܐܚܪܢܐ ܡܢܓܢܣܐ ܕܡܢ); Ephrem, ed. Lamy I c. 43–44: *Descendite, fratres, obsignati, induimini Dominum nostrum, eius prosopiae commiscemini* (ܐܬܚܠܛܘ ܒܨܘܪܬܗ); Clemens of Alex., *strom.* VII 68 5: "The τέλειος comes πρὸς τὸ συγγενές" and VII 57 1: "Hence, too, it (*scil.* γνῶσις) easily transplants a man to that divine and holy state which is akin to the soul (εἰς τὸ συγγενὲς τῆς ψυχῆς θεῖον)". **Sowing in me the word of life.** See ch. 15. **And I have found ... with you.** Greek: "And I have found him that shows me fair things that I may take hold on them, even the Son of truth that is akin to concord, who scatters away the mist and enlightens his own creation, and heals the wounds thereof and overthrows the enemies thereof. But I beseech you, o man of God, cause me to behold him again, and to see him that is now become hidden from me, that I may also hear his voice whereof I am not able to express the wonder for it belongs not to the nature of this bodily organ". See for "seeing" and "hearing" ch. 27. **who scatters away ... creation.** See Ps.-Clement, *recogn.* I 15 3, ed. Rehm 15: *... primo error, inde contemptus ... velut fumus quidam inmensus, universam mundi huius domum replevit*, and Clemens of Alex. *paedag.* I 28, cf. Is. 44,22.

35

Judas says to him: "**If you will be delivered from these things which you have learned, as you have said, from the doer of evils,** and **will listen to him, whom in the fervour of your love you now seek, you shall see him,** and shall be with him for ever, **and shall rest with him in his grace,** and shall be with him in his **joy.** But if you are negligent of him, and come to those, your former deeds, and insult him, whom because of (his) **beauty** and because of **the aspect of his light** you now eagerly desire, you shall not only be deprived of that life which you have seen, but you shall also lose that in which you are abiding".

Commentary. **If you will be delivered ... evils.** See ch. 24. **listen to him ... see him.** See ch. 27 about "hearing" and "seeing". The passage may be a liturgical formula, cf. Greek: καὶ μάθῃς, καὶ κατήκο-ος ... καὶ ὄψῃ. **and shall rest ... grace.** Greek: ἐν τῇ ἀναπαύσει αὐτοῦ ἀναπάησῃ. Cf. ch. 27 and 142: "My giver of rest", and ch. 169: "He will soon prepare for you your rest"; Sirach 24,7: μετὰ τούτων πάντων ἀνάπαυσιν ἐζήτησα; Philo, *de post. Caini* 28: σὺ δὲ αὐτοῦ στῆθι μετ' ἐμοῦ (Deut. 5, 31): ἐξ οὗ δύο περίσιαται, ἐν μὲν ὅτι τὸ ὂν τὸ τὰ ἄλλα κινοῦν καὶ τρέπον ἀκίνητόν τε καὶ ἄτρεπτον, ἕτερον δ' ὅτι τῆς ἑαυτοῦ φύσεως. ἠρε-μίας τῷ σπουδαίῳ μεταδίδωσιν. Odes of Sol. 3. 5: "And where his rest is, there also am I"; *Evangelium Veritatis* 42. 19–22, ed. Robinson 48: "... nor have they envy nor groaning nor death wihin them, but they rest in him who is at rest", and *Kephalaia* 234. 5–8: "Und er wird gereinigt ... Dann wird er … umher gezogen und erreicht das Land der Ruhe". **joy**. See Hymne I *l.* 45–47. **beauty**. See ch. 8. **the aspect of his light**. See Hymne I *l.* 45–47.

36

And Judas came to the city, and took the hand of the youth, and said to him: "My son, these things which you have seen are a few out of the many that belong to our God; for he does not send us tidings concerning these things that are seen, but promises us better things; **for as long as we are in the world, we are unable to speak about that which all the believers in God are going to receive**. For if we say that he has given us light, we mention something which we have seen; and if we say that he has given us wealth, we mention something that is in the world; and if we speak of (fine) clothing, we mention something that nobles wear; and if we speak of dainty meats, we mention something against which we are warned; and if we speak of (this) temporary rest, a chastisement is appointed for it. But we speak of God and our Lord Jesus, and of the angels and the guardian spirits and the saints, and of the new world; and of the **incorruptible food of the tree of life**, and of the draught (of the water) of life; **of what eye has not seen nor ear heard nor has it entered into the heart of man (to conceive),—what God has prepared from old for those who love him**. Of this we speak, and of this we preach. Believe in him, therefore, my son, that you may live, and trust in him, that you may not die; for he will not take a bribe, that you should offer (it) to him, nor is he pleased with a sacrifice, that you should sacrifice it (to him). Look at him, and he will not neglect you, and turn to him, and he will not forsake you; for **his beauty** will incite you to love him, and he will not suffer you to turn away from him".

Commentary. **for as long as we are in the world … receive**. In the Greek version it said "for as long as we are in this body". The Syriac appears to avoid a contrast between body and soul, see ch. 30. Also in ch. 14; 37; 88; 117 and 135 is spoken about the contrast between the things on earth and in heaven, cf. Odes of Sol. 34.5: "For everything is from above and from below is nothing"; Decease of Saint John, Syriac ed. Wright 66: "who delivered me from temporal show and preserved me for that which produces fruit always"; Aphraates, *demonstr.* VI 7, ed. Parisot c. 269–270: *Habent Hevae filiae ornamenta lanea, marcida*

et corruptibilia; illarum autem vestimenta non veterascent; Ps-Clemens, *homil.*
XV 7, ed. Rehm 215; Origen, *Comment. in Ps.* 38, 6, in: *P.G.* c. 1389:
τὰ σωματικὰ πάντα ματαιότη ἐστὶν, ἡ γὰρ ἀσώματος φύσις κατ' εἰκόνα
γεγένηται θεοῦ and Ps.-Clemens, *de virgin.* I V 3, ed. Diekamp 8: *vince
vanas istas praesentis saeculi res, quae transeunt et alteruntur et corrupuntur et finem
habent.* The Greek version adds a number of references to the New
Testament, *viz.* Matth. 19, 13 after the word "wealth"; Matth. 11, 28
after "clothing" and Luke 21, 34 and Matth. 6, 25 after "dainty meats".
The texts of these passages do not show a relationship with the Syriac
version of the New Testament and seems to be added in the Greek
tradition. **incorruptible food ... of life**. See Hymne I *l.* 48–51. For
eating from the tree of life see Rev. 3,7 and 22,2. Greek reads: "But
we speak ... περὶ τῆς ἀμβροσιώδος τροφῆς", see Hymne I *l.* 48–51,
and drink τῆς ἀμπέλου τῆς ἀληθινῆς, cf. John 15,1. **of raiment that
endures and does not grow old**. See Hymn I *l.* 43–44; Manich.
Ps. 155. 10: "I have received my washed clothes, my robes (στολή) that
grow not old", and Huwidagman I 18, ed. Boyce 69: [The clothes
which they wear none] has made by hand. [They are ever clean and
bright and] no ants (?) are in them". **of what eye ... love him**. See I
Cor. 2,9. The text agrees with that of syr p. Also *Acta Petri* XXXIX, in:
L.B. I 99. 8–10: ... *quae neque oculis vidit, nequ[e auris] audivit, neque in cor
hominis pecca[toris] ascendit* ... . It is striking that also in the Greek version
is spoken of ἁμαρτωλῶν, which is not found in the Greek text of the
New Testament, but which is found in the Gospel of Thomas XVII.
his beauty. See ch. 8.

37

And when Judas had said these things to the youth, great multitudes
joined (them). And the Apostle lifted up his eyes, and saw people raised
upon one another that they might see him, and going up to lofty
places. And the Apostle says to them: "You men who are come to the
assembly of the Messiah, men who wish to believe in Jesus, take to
yourselves an example from this, that if you do not raise yourselves up,
you can not see me who am little. Me, who am like yourselves, you
are unable to see; **he who is on high and is found in the depths,
how shall you be able to see, unless you raise yourselves
above your former works**, and above the deeds that profit not,
and the pleasures that abide not, **and the corruptible wealth** that
remains here; and above riches and possessions that perish on the earth,

and above garments that decay and above beauty that becomes old and is disfigured, and above the body, in which all these are included, and which becomes **dust**, and which all these support? But believe, and trust in our Lord Jesus the Messiah, him whom we preach, in order that your hope may be in him, and that in him you may live for ever and ever, and that he may be to you **a guide in the land of error**, and may be to you a fountain of living water in the region of thirst and may be to you **a haven in the sea of trouble**, and may be to you a full basket in the place of hunger, and may be a rest to your souls and a **healer and giver of life to your bodies**".

Commentary. **assembly,** ܟܢܘܫܬܐ and Greek: συνέδριον. The same word is found in ch. 48 in the Syriac version and ch. 102. **you cannot ... little**. It seems that Thomas is supposed to be small. For the traditions about Jesus' statue see J.R. Harris, "On the Stature of our Lord", in: *Bull. of the John Ryland's Libr.* 10 1926, 112–126, and Bauer, *Das Leben Jesu* 31–32. **he who ... former works**. See also ch. 24. For the expression "raising up" see also ch. 119 and cf. Philo, *Mosis* II 68; Clemens of Alex., *strom.* IV 53 1; Origen, *comment. in Joh.* XXXII 27; *c. Celsum* I 19, *hom. in Gen.* 17,9, *hom. in Matth.* XXII IX 146; *Kephalaia* 24. 10–12: "Nicht wandelt (πολιτεύεσθαι) in ihnen (*scil.* Dienst ihrer fünf Körper), auf dass ihr entgeht ihrer Fessel und ihrer Strafe (κόλασις) ewiglich", and 106. 8–11: "... festigt euch in diesen Geboten, die ich euch gegeben habe, damit ihr entrinnt jenem zweiten Tode und entkommt dieser letzten Fessel, in der es keine Lebenshoffnung (-ἐλπίς) gibt". **and the corruptible wealth.**. See ch. 36. **dust**. Greek adds: "returning to its own nature", see ch. 29. Also Ephrem, *de fide*, XLVI 7, ed. Beck 124 (translation) and 147 (Syriac), considers the body to belong to the corruptible nature: "... er zeigte, dass aus dem Staub die Natur des Menschen stamme". **a guide in the land of error**. See for "guide" ch. 10 end for error ch. 25. **a haven,** ܠܡܐܢܐ, **in the sea of trouble**. Cf. Ps. 107, 30, but see also Odes of Sol. 38. 3: "And became for me a haven of salvation": Ignatius, *ad Smyrn.* 11.3: καὶ ὅτι λιμένος ἤδη ἔτυχεν ἐν τῇ προσευχῇ; Aphraates, *demonstr.* XIV 30, ed. Parisot 683–684: *insistamus vestigiis eius, ut ad portam perveniamus;* Liturgical Homil. of Narsai, ed. Connolly 65: "As a guide he (*scil.* the priest) shows the way before travellers ... and makes straight their course to the harbour of life that is hidden in the height", and *Corpus Hermet.* VII 2: οἱ δυνάμενοι λαβέσθαι τοῦ τῆς σωτηρίας λιμένος. **a healer ... bodies**. See ch. 39 in the Syriac version; ch. 42 in both Syriac and Greek;

ch. 78 in Syriac and Greek; ch. 117 in Syriac and Greek; ch. 156 in Syriac and Greek and ch. 158 in Syriac. These Acts speak about both the healing of bodies and souls and that of the bodies is meant to show that one is not allowed to disdain the body, cf. Clement of Alex., *stromat.* III 104 4: οὐχὶ ὁ σωτὴρ ὥσπερ τὴν ψυχήν, οὕτω δὲ καὶ τὸ σῶμα ἰᾶτο τῶν παθῶν; Ephrem, *adv. haer.* 43. 10, ed. Beck 153 (translation) and 172 (Syriac): "'Tadelnswert ist der erste, der den Körper erschuf'. (Dann) auch sein Arzt ... Unser Herr fand einen blinden Körper und gab ihm das Licht", but cf. also Mand. Liturg. 45: "Fortführen und wegeilen sollen von ihnen alle hässlichen Krankheiten und bösen Verwünschungen des Körpers".

38

Then the multitudes were crying out: "Apostle of the living God, and **guide** in the path of life, and **revealer of the mystery of truth**, many are the things that have been done for us, **who are aliens from the glorious God whom you preach, and until now we do not dare to say that we are his, because our words are alien from him and hateful before him**, But if he will have compassion upon us, and deliver us from our former deeds, and from the evil things that were done by us in error, and will not enter into reckoning with us nor remember against us our former sins, we will become servants of his and accomplish his will". Judas says to them: "He will not reckon against you your sins which you did in error, but he will pardon you your iniquities, those former ones which you did **without knowledge.**"

Here ends the third Act

Commentary. **guide**. See ch. 10. **revealer of the ... truth**. See ch. 1. **who are aliens ... hateful before him**. See ch. 32. **without knowledge**, The ἄγνοια appears to be the source of sin. See also ch. 58 in Syriac and Greek; ch. 59 in Syriac and Greek and ch. 98 in Greek. Cf. Luke 22, 34; Acts 17, 30 and also Eph. 4, 18 and I Pet. 1, 14. The idea is often found in early Christian literature, cf. Ignatius, *ad Ephes.* 19. 3; Aristides, *apol.* 1 and 17; Justin Martyr, *apol.* I 61 10; Ireneus, *adv. haer.* II 30 3; Clement of Alex., *stromat.* VII 16 2, and Ps.-Clement, *homil.* XI 11 4, ed. Rehm 159 and X 12 2, ed. Rehm 146. Very often in Gnostic literature, cf. *Evang. Veritatis* 17. 9–11, ed. Robinson 38; Irenaeus, *adv.*

haer. I 21 4, about the Marcosians; *Apocr. Johannis* 61.6–7: "Beide (*scil.* Adam und Eva) hatten (den) Makel (πτῶμα) der Unwissenheit"; Ginza R 58. 36–37: "Als wir ohne Kenntniss waren trieben wir Ehebruch …", see also 59. 13–14; 30–31; 37–38, and *Corpus Hermet.* I 27 and VII 1.1.

39

And whilst the Apostle was standing in his place on the road, and speaking with those multitudes concerning the kingdom of God, and concerning their conversion and repentance to our Lord,—whilst the Apostle was standing on the road, and speaking with those multitudes, an ass's colt came and stood before him. **And Judas said: "It is not without the direction of God that this colt has come hither. But to you I say, o colt, that, by the grace of our Lord, there shall be given to you speech before these multitudes who are standing here; and do you say whatsoever you wish that they may believe in the God of truth, whom we preach".** And the mouth of the colt was opened, and it spoke like a man by the power of our Lord, and said to him: "**Twin of the Messiah** and Apostle of the Most High, and **sharer in the hidden word of the Life-giver, and receiver of the secret mysteries of the Son of God; freeborn, who became a slave, to bring many to freedom by your obedience; son of a great family, who became bereaved, that by the power of your Lord, you might deprive the enemy of many**, so that you might become the cause of life to the country of the Indians; (**you**) **who came against your will to men who were straying from God**, and, lo, by the sight of you and by your godly words they are turned to life; **mount (and) ride on me, and rest until you enter the city**". And Judas lifted up his voice and said: "O Jesus, **Son of perfect mercy, o you quiet and silent (one)**, who speaks by animals that have no speech; **o hidden (one), that is seen in your works; our nourisher and guardian; the giver of life to our bodies and the giver of life to our souls; sweet spring that never fails, and clear fountain that is never polluted; you are a help to your servants in the contest, and crushes the enemy before them; you who stand up in contest for us, and make us victorious in them all; our true athlete, who cannot be hurt, and our holy general, who cannot be conquered**; you who give to your own joy that does not pass away, and rest in which there is no more affliction; **you good shepherd that gives his life for his** flock, who has overcome the wolf and rescued his lambs; we glorify you and we exalt through you your exalted Father, who is not seen, and the Holy Spirit that broods over all created things".

Commentary. **And Judas said ... whom we preach**. This has been omitted in the Greek version. **without direction**. See ch. 9. **speech**. See ch. 33 in Syriac. This is a well-known theme in Apocryphal Acts, cf. *Acta Pauli*, ed. Schmidt 51. 4–5, about a speaking lion; *Acta Philippi* 96, ed. L.B. II II 37.28–30: λεόπαρδης ἐξηλθέν ... καὶ φωνῇ ἀνθρωπινῃ ἐλάλησε πρὸς αὐτούς; Philaster, *haer.* 88, ed. Marx 48: *in quibus* (*scil.* Apocr. Acts) *quia signa fecerunt* (*scil.* the Apostles) *magna et prodigia, ut et pecudes et canes et bestiae loquerentur, etiam et animas hominum tales velut canum et pecudum similes imputaverunt esse haeretici perditi.* See M. Blumenthal, "Formen und Motive in den apokryphen Apostelgeschichten", in: *Texte u. Unters.* 48 1937, 151–152. **Twin of the Messiah**. See ch. 1; 11 and 31. **sharer in the hidden word of the Life-giver**, ܪܚܡܐ ܪܐܠܐ ܝܘܗ ܪܚܘܫܕܐ and Greek: συμμύστης ... See Gospel of Thomas, Prologue, and Clement of Alex., *strom.* VII 4 2, about the gnostics: παραδίδοναι δύνασθε θεοπρεπῶς τὰ παρὰ τῇ ἀληθεῖα ἐπικεκρυμμένα. The word συμμύστης was taken from the environment of the mystery-religions, see G. Anrich, *Das antike Mysterienwesen in seinem Einfluss auf das Christentum*, Göttingen 1894, but also Gregorius of Nyssa, *in diem lum.*, in: *P.G.* 46, c. 580; Isidorus Pelus., *epist.* IV 162, in: *P.G.* 78, c. 1248; Chrysostemus, *ad I Tim. hom.*, in: *P.G.* 62, c. 530, and *in Joh. hom.*, in: *P.G.* 59, c. 100. **and receiver of the secret mysteries**, ܚܒܐ, ܝܐܘܪܐ, **of the Son of God**. Greek: ἀπόκρυφα λόγια It is possible that the present Acts refer to the Gospel of Thomas. The Syriac text speaks about the revelation only, but Greek adds the word ὁ συνεργὸς cf. I Cor 3,9 and Coloss. 4,11. **free-born ... obedience**. See ch. 2. An allusion to Philipp. 2,8. **son of a great family**, ܪܪܚܝܡ ܪܚܘܡܐܠ and Greek: ὁ συγγενὴς τοῦ μεγάλου γένους, see ch. 34. **who became ... enemy of many**. Greek reads: "that has condemned the enemy and redeemed his own", see ch. 32. **(you) who came ... from God**. See ch. 1. Greek: "that were in error", see ch. 25. **mount (and) ride ... city**. The influence of Mark 11, 7 and parallel passages seems to be evident. The story appears to have a deeper sense. This already appears from ch. 41, where it is said that the ass dies and is not raised from the dead. Bornkamm, *Mythos und Legende* 37, supposed that the ass is the body. This is doubtful because of the important part it plays in ch. 41, although parallels are present, see Bar Hebraeus, *Book of the Dove*, ed. Wensinck 73, where it is said that the body is the riding animal of the rational soul. In the present passage the ass wishes to give rest and to receive "its part". It seems that the ass stands for mankind, cf. Severus of Antioch 52 II IV, in: *Patrol. Orient.* VI 95: "When I see the ass's colt, I understand the people taken from among the peoples, Lord, whom you released from the bonds of error and upon whom you spiritually sat and rested, as upon the back of the holy cherubim". This also makes clear the contents of ch. 40. **Son of perfect mercy**. See ch. 10. **o, you quiet and silent (one)**, ܪܘܳܐ ܕܶܐܬ ܕܰܠܐ and Greek: ὦ ἡ ἡσυχία καὶ ἡ ἠρεμία. The same words are found in I Tim. 2,1. God is silent, see Rom. 16, 15; Ignatius, *ad Magn.* VII 2; *Apocryphon Johannis* 4. 10–12, ed. Robinson 100: "His aeon is ... at rest and being in [silence ...]" and Mand. Liturg. 9: "Über den vier Ecken des Hauses und über die sieben Seiten des Firmamentes lagert Schweigen, Ruhe und Glanz". See also H.-W. Bartsch, "Gnostisches Gut und Gemeindetradition bei Ignatius von Antiochien", in: *Beitr z. Förderung d. Theol.* 44 1940, 53–61: "Die Bezeichnung des Wesen Gottes als Ruhe", and J. Pacher, *Η ΒΑΣΙΛΙΚΗ ΟΔΟΣ*, Paderborn 1931, 228–230. **o hidden (one) ... works**. See ch. 10. **our nourisher ... life to our souls**. Greek: "Saviour of us and nourisher, keeping us and resting in alien bodies". Here the word ܣܘܳܣ has been translated by σωτήρ—Saviour, see ch. 10. According to the Syriac version Christ is supposed to be Saviour of both body and soul, but in Greek it is said that Christ is found in the soul of man. See also ch. 30 and 41 about the idea "strange". **sweet spring ... polluted**. See ch. 25. **you are ... conquered**. God or Christ being a "help" is not found in the New Testament, but see Hebr. 13,6, although frequent in the Odes of Sol., see 7.3; 8.6; 21.2 and 25.2, see also I Clement 59.3; Manich. Ps. 94.1 and *Kephalaia* 11.11. See about life being a struggle Eph. 6,10–20; Odes of Sol. 9.9. 12 and 29.9. Christ being an athlete see ch. 50 and Liturg. Homilies of Narsai, ed. Connolly 53: "As an athlete he went down to the contest on behalf of his people; Ephrem, *de parad.* XII 6, ed. Beck 47 (translation) and 51 (Syriac): "Er kam aber der Athlet der andere, der nicht unterliegt ...", and *de fide* XXIV 1, ed. Beck 66 (translation) and 83 (Syriac): "In der Waffenrüstung der unterliegenden Athleten siegte unser Herr". Christ's work is compared with a contest in Odes of Sol. 8.7: "And peace was prepared for you before what may be your war"; Irenaeus, *adv. haer.* III 18: *Luctatus est enim et vicit; erat enim homo pro partibus certans; Exc. e Theodoto* 72. 1–2, and Manich Ps. 59.21–24: "You received the victory (?) in the fourth war (πόλεμος). **you good shep-**

herd … lambs. See ch. 24. **Father, who is not seen**. See ch. 27 and 33, cf. *Apost. Constit*. VIII XV 7, about God: ὁ τῇ φύσει ἀόρατος, and Cyril of Jerusalem, *cat*. IX 1, ed. Reichl 238: σαρκὸς μὲν ὀφθαλμοῖς θεωρῆται τὸν θεὸν ἀδύνατον. **we glorify … created things**. Greek reads: "… and praise you and your invisible Father and your Holy Spirit and the mother of all creation". The Syriac version alludes to Gen. 1,1 and see for the Greek version Hymn I *l*. 52–55.

<h3 style="text-align:center">40</h3>

And when the Apostle has said these things, all the multitudes that were assembled there were looking to see what answer he was about to give to the colt. And after the Apostle had stood a long time wondering and looking up to heaven, he said to the colt: "Who are you? And what is your errand that by your mouth wonders are uttered and great things that are more than many?" The colt says to him: "**I am of that stock that served Balaam the prophet, and God your Lord rode upon my kin; and I am sent to you to give you rest, and that thereby the faith of these might be confirmed, and that that other portion might be added to me, which I have got today in order to serve you and which will be taken away from me when I have served you**". Thomas says to him: "God who has given you this gift now, is to be relied on to give it hereafter too in full to you and your kindred, for I am too little and weak for this mystery". And he would not ride upon it. And the colt was begging of him and supplicating him that it might be blessed by his riding (upon it). And he mounted and rode upon it. And the people were going after and before the Apostle, and were running to see what would happen to him, and how he would let the colt go.

Commentary. The manuscript Sinai is present from: "… the Apostle had said these things" until ch. 44: "and stood before him no-one". **I am … my kin**. Cf. Pirke de Rabbi Eliezer XXXI, ed. G. Friedlander, New York 1970 (repr. London 1916) 224–5: "And Abraham rose up early in the morning, and he saddled his ass … The same ass was also ridden upon by Moses … The same ass will be ridden upon in the future by the Son of David …" **and I am sent … served you**. In the Greek version: "… and (that) I may receive faith". This seems to be better since the ass has to be identified with the people of God on which Christ is riding. See ch. 39.

41

And when he reached the gate of the city, he dismounted from it, and said to it: "Go, be preserved as you have been". **And at that moment the colt fell down and died. And all who were there were very sorry for it, and were saying to the Apostle: "Bring it to life again". The Apostle says to them: "It is not because I am unable to bring this colt to life, that I do not bring it to life, for he who gave it speech was able to make it not die; but this is a benefit to it".** And the Apostle commanded those who were with him to dig a place and bury its body; and they did as he commanded them.

Here ends the fourth Act

Commentary. **And at that moment ... benefit to it**. See ch. 147: "The dead I have not brought to life ..." Death must be preferred to life see ch. 21 and also *Acta Petri* XII, in: L.B. I I 60. 11–12: *Et cum dixisset canis haec verba, discessit*, and the Coptic fragment of the Acts of Peter in: C. Schmidt, "Die alten Petrusakten", in: *Texte u. Unters.* 23 1903, 8.

The fifth Act, concerning the Devil
that took up his abode in the Woman

42

And the Apostle went into the city, the multitudes accompanying him; and he was thinking of going to the house of the family of the youth whom he had brought to life, because he had begged this earnestly of him. And **a fair woman** cried with a loud voice and said to him: "Apostle of the new God, who has come to India, servant of the holy God, who by you is proclaimed both the **Giver of life to the souls of those that come to him, and the healer of the bodies** of those who are tortured by the enemy; (you) who are the cause of life to the whole people of India; permit them to bring me before you, that I may tell you what has befallen me, so that perchance I may get hope from you, and these who are standing by may be greatly strengthened in the God who is proclaimed by you. And I tell you that I am not slightly tormented by the enemy, lo, for the space of five years. For I was sitting in ease, and peace was around me on all sides, and I had no concern about anything, because I knew no care.

Commentary. **a fair woman**. See ch. 30. **Giver of life**. Greek: "Saviour", see ch. 10. **souls ... bodies**. See ch. 37.

43

And it happened **one day**, as I was coming out of the bath, a man met me, who seemed troubled in his aspect, (and) his voice **and speech was very weak**. And he said to me: 'I and you shall be in one love, and you have intercourse with me as a man and a woman have intercourse'. I said to him: 'I did not yield myself to my betrothed, because I cannot bear a man, and to you, who wish to have adulterous intercourse with me, how can I give myself to you?' And I said to the maiden who was with me: 'See the impudence of this young man, (who goes) so far as to talk licentiously to me'. And he said to me: 'I saw an old man who was talking to you'. And when I had gone home and supped, my heart made me afraid of him, because he appeared to me in **two forms**; and I went to sleep thinking of him. And he came in the night and had filthy intercourse with me, and by day too I saw him and fled from him; **but by night he used to come in a terrible form**, and torture me. And, lo, up to the present, as you see me, lo, for five years he has not left me alone. But because I know and believe that both devils and spirits and demons are subject to you and dread your prayer, I beg of you, my lord, that you would pray over me, and ask of God, and drive away from me this affliction, **and (that), for me the time that is appointed to me, I may be free and may be united to my former nature, and receive the gift that is given to the penitent**".

Commentary. **One day**, ܚܕ ܡܢ ܝܘܡܬܐ, cf. Greek: ἐν μιᾷ τῶν ἡμερῶν. **and speech was very weak**. Cf. Mand. Liturg. 492. 2–4: "… alle sind hässlich und schwarz. Flüsternd stehen sie allen da". **two forms**. Both Christ and the devil is able to appear in more than one form, ch. 8, 34 and 44, cf. *Acta Johannis* ch. 70, in: L.B. II I 185. 9–10: … ἐπιθυμίᾳ καὶ ἐνεργείᾳ τοῦ πολυμόρφου σατανᾶ; Firmicus Maternus, *de errore prof*. 21, ed. Ziegler 68. 4–6: *Deus iste vester non biformis est, sed multiformis: in multas enim species venenati oris forma mutatur*, and 26, 75. 35: *ideo se (serpentem) per omnes formas multiplici diversitate convertit*. **but by night he used to come in a terrible form**, ܒܠܠܝܐ ܕܝܢ ܒܕܡܘܬܐ ܕܚܝܠܬܐ ܗܘܐ ܐܬܐ ܠܝ and Greek: ἐν δὲ τῇ συγγενίδι αὐτοῦ νυκτί ἐρχόμενος, but the manuscript Sinai reads: ܒܠܠܝܐ ܕܝܢ xx ܠܓܢܣܗ ܐܝܟ ܗܘܐ which has been translated by Smith–Lewis 226: "in the night he used to come (in the shape) of his race". It is, however possible to read: … ܒܪ(ܐ) ܠܓ, which agrees with the Greek version and may be compared with ch. 34: ܘܐܒܕܬ ܠܗܕܐ ܕܒܚܫܘܟܐ ܒܪ ܓܢܣܗ. This results in the translation: "I have destroyed him, who through darkness, his kinsman …". See Rom. 13, 12; I Thessal. 5, 5 and *Liber Graduum*, ed. Kmosko 627–628: *Satanas … filius tenebrarum*. **and may be united**, ܘܐܬܚܝܕ and Greek: συναθροισθῶ, see ch. 48. **to my former nature**. Cf. ch. 29 and 141: "restoring it (*scil*. my soul) to its own nature", and Ephrem, *adv. haer*., ed. Beck 70 (translation) and 71 (Syriac): "Und wie er erden Körper (nur) heilte und seine Natur (nur) zurückgab … so hat er auch der Seele (nur) die Gesundheit zurückgegeben, die sie verloren hatte …" **(that) for me the time … penitent**. According to the Greek version: καὶ δέξωμαι τὸ χάρισμα τὸ τοῖς συγγενεῦσι μου δεδωρημένον. Also in ch. 15 we noticed that according to the present Acts the main purpose of salvation is the restoration of man to his original situation. It is noteworthy to see that the words τοῖς συγγενεῦσιν in Greek have been avoided, see also ch. 34.

44

Then the Apostle when he saw the instigation of the enemy, lifted up his voice and said: "**O evil that cannot be repressed! O enemy that is never at rest! O envious one who is never quiet! O hideous (one) who strives with the comely, that you may subdue them under you! O (you) who has many hideous shapes and appears as you wish, but your black colour never changes, because it is your nature! O crafty (one) and disturber of good works! O bitter tree, the fruits of which are like unto it!. O lying slanderer, who strives with those that are not yours!** O deceit which coiled up upon itself, rears itself with impudence and dares to assail those who are better than itself! O wickedness that creeps like a serpent and crawls, and enters in, and aims at virtue! **But how long do I say these things! (Keep me not waiting) but show yourself quickly, you enemy of the servants of the Messiah, that these multitudes may see that we call them to the true God**". And when the Apostle had said these things the enemy came and stood before him, no one seeing him except the Apostle and the woman, and cried with a loud voice, whilst all those who were there heard him.

Commentary. **O evil that cannot … are never at rest,** ܠܡܣ ܪܕܝ, … **are never quiet,** ܪܕܠܡ ܡܠ ܕܘܠܝ. Greek: "O shamelessness of the enemy. O envious one that is never at rest, ἠρεμῶν". The world of the devil is the opposite of the world of God in which rest and quietness is found, cf. Gregorius of Nyssa, *orat. cat.* XXXIX 2: διχῇ τοίνον τῶν ὄντων μεμερισμένων εἰς τὸ κτιστὸν καὶ τὸ ἄκτιστον, καὶ τῆς μὲν ἀκτίστου φύσεως τὸ ἄτρεπτον τε καὶ ἀμετάθετον ἐν ἑαυτῇ κειμένης, τῆς δὲ κτίσεως πρὸς τροπὴν ἀλλοιουμένης … See also Theodore of Mopsuestia, ed. Mingana 10: "our mortal and changeable nature"; Severus of Antioch 13 XIII VII, in: *Patrol. Orient.* VI 56: "… the Word … brought himself down, the invariable to the variable", and *Evang. Veritatis* 29. 1–5, ed. Robinson 43: "Since it was terror and disturbance and instability and doubt and division …" The idea that the devil is envious has to do with its envy of Adam, cf. History of John, Syriac ed. Wright 13: "And when the Satan came with his envy, and counselled Eve"; *Sap. Sal.* 2,24; Gnost. Adamschr., ed. Preuschen 27 and cf. 12, 2–6, and *Vita Adae et Evae* XII 1, ed. Merk und Meiser 795. Contrary to God, cf. Odes of Sol. III 6: "Because there is no jealousy with the Lord Most High and Merciful", and *Acta Johannis* ch. 55, ed. L.B. II I 178.17–179.1:

ἀκούομεν ὃν κηρύσσεις θεὸν ἄφθονός ἐστι. See H.J.W. Drijvers, "Die Oden Salomos und die Polemik mit den Markioniten im syrischen Christentum", in: *Symposion Syriacum. Orient. Christ. Analecta* 205, Rom 1978, 39–55. **O hideous ... you**. See ch. 30. **O (you) who has ... is your name**. For "black" see ch. 31; for "nature" ch. 29 and "many forms" ch. 43. **O crafty (one) ... works**. This has been omitted by the manuscript Sinai. **O bitter tree ... unto it**. See ch. 10 and 148; *Acta Petri* VIII, in: L.B. I I, 55. 29–30: *tu es fructus arboris amaritudinis totus amarissimus*; *Acta Johannis* ch. 84, in: L.B. I II 192. 19–21; Odes of Sol. XI 21: "For they turned away from themselves the bitterness of the trees", and Gospel of the Egyptians, according to Clemens of Alex., *strom*. III 66 2. **O lying slanderer ... are not yours**. Man belongs to God, see ch. 4. **serpent**. See ch. 31. **But how long ... the true God**. This passage has been omitted in Greek and the manuscript Sinai.

45

"**What have we to do with you**, Apostle of the Most High? What have we to do with you, servant of Jesus the Messiah? What have we to do with you, you **sharer in the holy mysteries** of God? Why do you wish to destroy us, when our time has not yet come? Why do you wish to take away the power that was given us, when till now we have had reliance upon it? What have we to do with you, who has come to drive us out? **You have power over them that obey you, and we have power over them that are subject to us**. Why do you wish to use violence towards us before our time, when you enjoin others not to use violence towards any man? Why do you covet what is not yours? For your own does not suffice you. **Why are you like to God your Lord, who concealed his majesty and appeared in the flesh, and we thought regarding him that he was mortal, but he turned and did us violence?** For you, namely, are born of him. For when we thought that we could bring him under our power, he turned and hurled us down into the abyss; **for we did not know him, because he deceived us by his humble aspect, and by his need and his poverty; and we thought, when we saw him, that he was one of the children of men, and we did not know that he was the Giver of life to all mankind**. But he gave us power not to slacken our hold of our own, so long as our time lasts, and we occupy ourselves with our own. But you, lo, wish to acquire more than he has given to you and to afflict us".

Commentary. **What have we to do with you**, ܪܚ ܠ ܩܠܘ and Greek: τί ἡμῖν καὶ σοί, cf, Matth. 8,29: τί ἡμῖν καὶ σοί ... ἦλθες ὧδε πρὸ καιροῦ βασανίσαι ἡμᾶς, cf. "Why do you wish to destroy us, when our time has yet not come". This does not agree with the contents of ch. 33. **sharer in the holy mysteries**, ܒܪ ܐܝܗܘܡܐ̈, ܘ̈ܝ. Greek: "... of the holy Son of God." It seems that the Syriac version avoids a too close relationship between Thomas and God, cf ch. 39 in Syriac. This appears to disagree with Rom. 11,34. **You have power over them ... subject unto us**. Greek: "You have power over your own and we over ours". See ch. 32 and 76. Also here a too close relationship has been avoided. **Why are you like ... born of him**. The same idea as in John 1, 13; I John 2, 9; 3, 9; 4, 7; 5, 1.4.18. Cf. Barrett, *The Gospel according to St. John* 172: "It (*scil.* born of Christ) seems not to be present in the Apostolic Fathers, but in Justin it is firmly established in Christian usage, in unmistakable connection with baptism (*Apol.* I 6 if.)" the candidate for baptism is ὁ ἑλόμενος ἀναγεννηθῆναι. **for we did not know ... to all mankind**. The devil being deceived by Christ's incarnation is a common theme in early Christianity, cf. Acts of John, Syriac ed. Syriac Wright 45: "... master of ours, he fought with the Master of this (man), and the Master of this (man) overcame him ... who came down from Heaven; and our master did not perceive when he came down ... and our master imagined that he was a mere (man)"; History of Phillip, Syriac ed. Wright 78: "This Jesus has slain me by his death ... He has deceived me by his similitudes (likenesses); He has dazzled me with his humiliation; He has befooled me with his quietude"; Ephrem, *de parad.* XII 6, ed. Beck 47 (translation) and 51 (Syriac): "Es kam aber der Athlet ... und legte jene Rüstung an, mit der Adam besiegt worden war. Und es sah der Gegner die Rüstung des Gefallenen, und er freute sich, ohne zu bemerken, dass er getäuscht wurde. Das innere hätte ihn erschreckt, das Äussere ermutigte ihn. Der Böse kam um zu siegen; doch er wurde besiegt und hielt nicht stand", and see also *de fide* XXIV 2, ed. Beck 66 (translation) and 83 (Syriac). It is generally assumed that the devil was not able to perceive Christ's real nature, see Ignatius, *ad Eph.* 19. 1, and Bauer, *Handb. z. Neuen Testament*, Ergänzungsband II 216–218; Origen, *Comment. in Matth.* XIII 9 and XVI 8, see J. Daniélou, *Origène*, Paris 1948 267; Cyril of Jerusalem, *cat.* XII 15, ed. Rupp 18; *Pistis Sophia* 7. 28–29; Ginza R 153. 31–33; 154. 7–8; 274. 18–19; L 577. 15–18, and Mand. Liturg. 207. See also Bauer, *Leben Jesu* 311–312, and R. Bultmann, "Die Bedeutung der neuerschlossenen mandäischen und manichäischen Quellen für das Verständnis des Johannesevangeliums", in: *Zeitschr. f. d. neutestamentl. Wissensch.* 24 1925, 100–146, esp. 120–121.

46

And when the demon had said these things, he wept again and said: "**I quit you, O my fair wife, whom I found a long time ago and was at rest on you**. I quit you my sister and beloved, **on whom I hoped to abide**. What I shall do, I do not know, nor on whom I shall call for help, that he may aid me. I know what I shall do. I shall go to another country, where I shall not hear tell of this man; for you, my beloved, I shall find a substitute". And he lifted up his voice and said: "Fare you not well, who has taken **refuge** with one who is greater than I. I go to wander and seek for myself one like you; and if I find not (one) for me, **I will again return to you**; for I know that now, because this man is near to you, lo, you take refuge with him. I then depart from here, and you become as you were; but when night comes, and you forget him, I shall have an opportunity (of getting) at you, **for now the name of him whom this (man) proclaims has frightened me**". And when the demon had said these things, at that moment he was looked for and was not found, but **smoke and fire** were seen after him; and all those who were standing there were amazed.

Commentary. **I quit you, O my fair wife ... at rest on you**. Greek reads: τὴν καλλιστὴν μου σύζυγον, see ch. 27. In this chapter the same idea is met as in Luke 11, 23–26 about a demon looking for a place to rest, see Luke 11, 24: διέρχεται δι' ἀνύδρων τόπων ζητοῦν ἀνάπαυσιν. **in whom I hoped to abide**. Greek: "in whom I was well pleased", see Luke 3, 22 and also the Gospel of the Nazarenes in Hieronymus, *in Is.* 11, 1–3: *Fili mi, in omnibus prophetis expectabam te ut veniret et requiescerem in te. Tu enim es requies mea.* See A.F.J. Klijn, "Jewish-Christian Gospel Tradition", in: *Supplem. to Vigiliae Christianae* XVII. Leiden 1992. The contrast between Christ and the devil has been emphasized. **refuge**. See ch. 10. **I will again return to you**. Those who do not take refuge with Christ will be subjected to the devil, cf. Luke 11, 24–26. **For now the name ... frightened me**. The "name" is to be identified with Christ, see ch. 27. **smoke and fire**. See ch. 55–57.

47

And when the Apostle saw (this) he said to them: "**The accursed one has shown nothing strange, but the nature by which he has been consumed; for the fire consumes him, and the smoke**

ascends from him". And the Apostle began to say: "Jesus, **hidden mystery**, that has been revealed to me, **you have revealed your mysteries to me more than to all my fellows, and has spoken to me words with which, lo, I am burning, but which I am not able to utter. Jesus, born a man**, slain, dead; Jesus, God, Son of God, Life-giver and restorer of the dead to life; **Jesus, poor and catching fish for dinner and supper; Jesus satisfying many thousands with a little bread; Jesus resting from the fatigue of a journey like a man, and walking upon the waves of the sea like a God**;

Commentary. **The accursed ... ascends from him**. See for the word "strange" ch. 4 and for "nature" ch. 29. The devil dies in its own elements, see Rev. 20, 10. There exists a difference between Syriac reading "by which he has been consumed" and Greek: "wherein also he shall be consumed", see ch. 33. **hidden mystery**. Not only the revelation, see ch. 27, but also Christ is a mystery, see ch. 45. **you have revealed ... to utter**. Greek: "you are the one that has shown to us many mysteries; you called me apart from all my fellows and spoke to me three words wherewith I am inflamed, and I am not able to speak them to others". The Greek version is the original one. A striking parallel is met in the Gospel of Thomas *l.* 13: "And he took him, he withdrew, he spoke three words to him. Now when Thomas came to his companians they asked him: 'What did Jesus say to you?' Thomas said to them: 'If I tell you one of the words which he said to me, you will take up stones and throw them at me ...'" According to Ephrem, *de fide* XLVIII 1, ed. Beck 129 (translation) and 152 (Syriac), the three words have been spoken at baptism: "In den Gläubigen sind eingezeichnet die drei Namen, die niemals erörtert, niemals erfasst wurden". **Jesus, born a man**. Greek omits the words "born a man", which may have been added in Syriac, see ch. 10. **Jesus, poor ...** In ch. 10 a contrast was made between Jesus' manhood and godhead. This was illustrated with help of some episodes which have been ascribed to Jesus' manhood and other ones to his godhead. This is a well-known procedure in early Christian literature, cf. Ignatius, *ad Ephes.* VII 2: σαρκικός τε καὶ πνευματικός, γεννητός καὶ ἀγέννητος ... πρῶτον παθητὸς καὶ τότε ἀπαθής; Melito, *Passa-Hom.*, ed. Lohse 11. 5–12; Origen, *Comment. in Joh.* XX 11: ἄνθρωπος γὰρ ἐστιν ἀποθανὼν ἰησοῦς ... οὐκ ἀπεθανεν ὁ θεός λόγος and *c. Cels.* IV 15, see H. Koch, *Pronoia und Paideusis*, Berlin–Leipzig 1932, 70–71: "Alles Gott Unwürdige wird der

menschlichen Natur zugeschrieben, hierunter auch Leiden und Tod";
Eusebius *evang. demonstr.*, ed. Heikel 269. 17–19: ὡς μὲν ἄνθρωπος τὸ
σῶμα τῇ συνήθει παράχωρων ταφῇ, ἀναχωρῶν δὲ αὐτοῦ ὡς θεός, see
H. Berkhof, *Die Theologie des Eusebius von Caesarea*, Amsterdam 1939, 121:
"Auch bei Eusebius treffen wir neben der Beschränkung auf die Leib-
lichkeit, eine sehr scharfe Trennung des Logos und seines Instruments
an"; Aphraates, *demonstr.* VI 9, ed. Parisot 275–278, and especially in
Nestorian literature, cf. Diodorus of Tarsus, ed. Abramowski 23. 14;
39. 19 and 58. 46, and Badger, *Nestorians* II, 36–38. **poor ... supper**.
This may be an allusion to John 21, 3–6, cf. Ephrem, *adv. haer.*, ed.
Beck 109 (translation) and 120 (Syriac): "Er (*scil.* Gott) beeinträchtigte
sich nämlich selber (durch die Behauptung) er habe gegessen, obwohl
er nicht isst ..." **satisfying ... bread**. Cf. Mark 6, 35–44 and parallel
passages. **resting ... man**. Cf. John 4, 6 and the end of the present
chapter. **walking ... like a God**. Cf. Mark 6, 45–52 and parallel passages. This episode is often referred to in order to show Christ's godhead, cf. ch. 66; Ephrem, *de fide* VII 4, ed. Beck 24 (translation) and 32
(Syriac): "Da er im Schiffe sass, glaubten die Schiffer, er sei ein Mensch.
Er stieg heraus, trat auf die See. Die Seeleute staunten über ihn", and
Cyril of Jerusalem, *cat.* IV 9, ed. Reichl 100: καθεύδων εἰς τὸ πλοῖον
ἀληθῶς ὡς ἄνθρωπος, καὶ περιπατῶν ἐπὶ τῶν ὑδάτων ὡς θεός. In both
references Mark 4, 35–41 and parallel passages have been combined
with Mark 6, 45–52. It is possible that the words "resting ... like a
man" refers to Mark 4, 35–41.

48

Jesus, exalted Voice that arose from perfect mercy, Saviour of
all, and Liberator and Administrator of the world, and Strengthener
of the dead; **Jesus, right hand of the Father, who has hurled
down the evil one to the lowest limit, and collected his possessions into one blessed place of meeting**; Jesus, King over all
and subduing all; **Jesus, who is in the Father and the Father in
you, and you are one in power and in will and in glory and in
essence, and for our sake you were named with names, and
are the Son and put on the body**; Jesus, who became a Nazir,
and your grace provides for all like God; **Son of God Most High,
who became a man despised and humble**; Jesus, who did not
neglect us in anything which we ask of you, who is the cause of life to
all mankind. **Jesus, who was called a deceiver on our account,**

you who rescues from deceit your human beings; I entreat of you on behalf of these who are standing (here) and believing in you, and in need of your help, and expecting your gift, and taking **refuge** with your majesty, **and opening their ears to hear your words which are spoken by us**, -let your grace come, and your faith abide upon them **and make them new from their former deeds, and may they put off their old man with his deeds, and put on the new man which is proclaimed to them by me**".

Commentary. **exalted Voice**. See ch. 10. **that arose from perfect mercy**. See ch. 10. **Jesus, right hand of the Father**. Greek reads: "... of the light." The expression is not found in the New Testament, where it is said that Jesus sits at the right hand of the Father, see Matth. 26, 64 and other passages. Cf. Odes of Sol. 25. 2: "Because you are the right hand of salvat-ion ...", and *Epist. Apost.* 19, ed. Duensing 17: "Und die Rechte des Vaters bin ich ganz, ich bin in ihm, der vollendet". The expression in the Greek version is present in *Acta Archelai* V, ed. Beesson 5. 24–6. 1; Augustine, *c. Fel.* I 16, and *epist. fundam.* 13 (XI). See J.C. Thilo, *Acta S. Thomae Apostoli*, Lipsiae 1823, 105; Baur, *Manich. Religions- system* 21i, and Bornkamm, *Mythos* 107. **who hurled ... place of meeting**, ܪܟܣ ܗ ܪܟܣܘ݁ܡ ܠܣ cf. ch. 37: ܗܣܘܡ݁ ܠܣܕ, Greek: ἡ καταστρέφουσα τὸν πονηρὸν ἐν τῇ ἰδίᾳ φύσει καὶ πᾶσαν αὐτοῦ τὴν φύσιν συναθροίζων εἰς ἕνα τόπον, The Greek version is original. Christ assembles the incorruptible nature in the corruptible world. This agrees with the general opinion that the body is corruptible and the soul incorruptible, see, for example, Eusebius *evang. praep.* 332 b-c, ed. E.H. Gifford I 425: τὸ δὲ τούτῳ περιπεπλασμένον ἔζωθεν ἑτερογενὲς μὲν ὑπάρχειν τὴν οὐσίαν καὶ γηγενές ... τὸν δ'εἴσω δεσπότην, ὡς ἂν εὐγενῆ καὶ θεοῦ συγγενῆ τὴν φύσιν ... τιμᾶν ... This is different from Gnosticism according to Aphraates, *demonstr.* XXIII 3, ed. Parisot II 11–2: *Idque bonus (Deus) in sapientia sua restituit—ut nihilum recideret artificium filiorum maligni, duas radices ponentium, alteram bonam, alteram malam*, and Cyril of Jerusalem, *cat.* IV 20, ed. Reichl 110–112: οὐκ ἔστι τάγμα ψυχῶν κατὰ φύσιν ἁμαρτανουσῶν. In the present Acts the soul is supposed to return to its original nature. The word "assemble" which has been used is well known in the Old Testament, cf. Is. 40, 11; Jer. 23, 3; 29, 14, but see also John 11, 52 and Didache 9. 4. It is evident that the idea played an important part in Gnosticism, cf. Gospel of Philip, according to Epiphanius, *pan.* XXVI 13 2: συνέλεξα ἐμαυτήν, ἐκ πανταχόθεν ... καὶ συνέλεξα τὰ μελὴ τὰ διεσκορπισμένα. *Pistis Sophia*, ed. Schmidt–Till 127. 1–2: "... bis die

Zahl der Einsammlung der vollkommenen Seelen vollendet ist"; *Kephalaia* 44. 10–12 and Manich Ps. 115. 11–12. and 152. 10. **Jesus who is in the Father ... in you**. See John 10, 30. **one in power ... essence**. The word ܐܘܣܝܐ, "essence", is well known in Syriac literature, cf. I. Ortiz de Urbina, "Die Gottheit Christi bei Afrahat", in: *Orient. Christ.* XXXI 1, No. 87, Roma 1933, 90–93, and E. Beck, "Die Theologie des hl. Ephraem", in: *Stud. Anselm.* 21, Rome 1949, 5–7. **and for the sake ... names**. God cannot be named, see Justin Martyr, *apol.* II 6; Tatian, *Oratio ad Graecos* IV, and Aphraates, *demonstr.* III 9, ed. Parisot c. 115–116, about Valentinus: ... *dicitque Deum perfectum ore non appellari, neque mentem investigari* ... , and Philo, *somn.* I 67: ἀκατονομάστου καὶ ἀρρήτου καὶ κατὰ πάσας ἰδέας ἀκαταλήμπτου θεοῦ. Nevertheless God gave himself names to reveal himself, cf. Ephrem, *de fide* 44. 1, ed. Beck 118 (translation) and 141 (Syriac): "Seine Namen unterweisen dich, wie und als wen du ihn benennen sollst". Christ's incarnation can be identified with naming himself, cf. Ephrem, *de fide* 29. 2, ed. Beck 81 (translation) and 101 (Syriac): "Dem schwachen Körper nämlich, in den er herabsteigend sich kleidete, ihm gleichen seine Namen und seine Werke ... 3. Der gewaltige hat sich in dürftige Namen aus Liebe zu euch gekleidet, wegen des Körpers", and 31. 1, 85 (translation) and 105 (Syriac): "Last uns danken dem, der in die Namen von Gliedern sich kleidete". This adaptation explains the word πολύμορφος used in the Greek version, cf. *Acta Petri* XXI, ed. L.B. I 1, 69. 18–19: *quomodo alias et alias dominum viderint; Acta Johannis* 82, in: L.B. II 1, 191. 27–28: ὁ ἐμφυσήσας μοι ἑαυτὸν τῇ πολυμόρφῳ σου ὄφει. Ephrem, *adv. haer.* 36. 5, ed. Beck 130 (translation) and 144–5 (Syriac): "Gott ... hat sich in alle Bilder gekleidet", and Justin Martyr, *dial. c. Tr.* LVI and LVIII–LX. See also ch. 11; 34 and 153. **and are the Son ... body**. See ch. 10. **Jesus ... Nazir**. In the Syriac church the Naziraeans were living an ascetic life, see Bar Hebraeus, *Book of the Dove*, ed. Wensinck 33: "The Naziraeans abstain from eggs, milk, grease, cheese and fish". **Son of the Most High**. Greek: θεὲ ἐκ θεοῦ ὑψίστου also in *Symbolum Nicaenum*. **who became ... humble**. In the Greek version: ὁ ἄνθρωπος ὁ καταφρονούμενος ἕως ἄρτι. According to the Greek text the struggle is still going on, see ch. 33. F.C. Burkitt, "The original Language ...", in: *Journ. of Theol. Studies* 1 1900, p. 285, supposed that the word ܥܕܡܐ was read as ܥܕܡ = ἕως ἄρτι in Greek. In the Greek version "all mankind" has been added after the words. **that for us was judged and ... in bonds**. For Christ having been in prison see I Pet. 3, 19 and see ch. 10. **Jesus who was called ... human beings**. In the New Testament Jesus is called πλάνος in Matth. 27, 63 only. See also ch. 25. The Greek version reads τοὺς ἰδίους in place of "your human beings", see ch. 32. **refuge**. See ch. 10. **and opening their ears … spoken by us**. First of all man must be able to hear, see ch. 27, next is asked: "let your grace come", see ch. 27 and Didache 10. 6; Ignatius, *ad Smyrn.* IX 2; XI 1 and Irenaeus, *adv. haer.* XIII 2, about the Marcosians: ἵνα καὶ εἰς αὐτοὺς ἐπομβρήσῃ ἡ διὰ τοῦ μάγου τούτου κληιζομένη χάρις. In the Greek version it is said: ἐλθέτω ἡ εἰρήνη σου καὶ σκηνωσάτω ἐν αὐτοῖς, cf. Gal. 6, 16; II Thessal. 3, 16 and Eph. 6, 23. **and make them new … to them by me**. In Greek: καὶ ἀποδύσωνται τὸν παλαιὸν ἄνθρωπον οὑν ταῖς πράξεσιν. See ch. 58. The same words are found in Rom. 6, 6; Coloss. 3, 9 and Eph. 4, 22 and often in ancient Christian literature, see Odes of Sol. 11. 10–11; Ephrem, *On virginity*, ed. Mitchell II, LXXX and 171; Nestor. Taufliturgie, ed. Diettrich 19; *Kephalaia* 221. 15 and Manich. Ps. 25. 12–14. See K. Holl, "Urchristentum und Religionsgeschichte", in: *Stud. des Apol. Semin. in Wernigerode* 10 1925, 12; H.H. Schaeder, "Urform und Fortbildungen des manichäischen Systems", in: *Vortr. Bibl. Warburg* 1924–25, 65–157, esp. 93, n. 1, and H. Schlier, "Religionsgeschichtliche Untersuchungen zu den Ignatiusbriefen", in: *Beih. Zeitschr. f. d. neutestamentl. Wissensch.* 8 1929 88, n. 2.

49

And he laid his hand upon them and blessed them, and said to them: "May the grace of the Lord be upon you for ever and ever, Amen". And the woman begged of him and said to him: "**Apostle of the Most High, give me the seal of my Lord, that the enemy may not again come back on me". And he went to a river which was close by there, and he baptised her in the name of the Father and the Son and the Spirit of holiness, and many were baptised with her**. And the Apostle ordered his deacon to make ready the Eucharist; and he brought a bench thither, and spread over it a linen cloth; and he brought (and) placed upon it the **bread of the blessing**. And the Apostle came (and) stood beside it, and said: "Jesus, who has deemed us **worthy** to draw near to your holy body and to partake of your life-giving blood, and because of our **reliance on you we are bold** and draw near and invoke your **holy name**, which has been proclaimed by the prophets as your godhead willed; and you are preached by your apostles through the whole world according to your grace and are revealed by your mercy to the just: we beg of you that

you would come and communicate with us for help and for life and
for conversion of your servants to you, that they may go under your
pleasant yoke and under your victorious power, **and that it may be
to them, for the health of their souls and for the life of their
bodies in your living world**".

Commentary. **And laid his hand**. Greek: "… hands". In Syriac liturgical usage the singular is used, which agrees with the translation of
ἐπιτιθέναι τὰς χεῖρας in syr s in Mark 5, 23; 6, 5; Luke 4, 40; Mark 8,
23; Luke 13, 13 and Mark 16, 18. **Apostle … back upon me**. See
ch. 26; 118 and 152. Here the protecting meaning of the "seal" has
been emphasized, see bShabb 55a, ed. Goldschmidt 444: "Der Heilige,
gebenedeit sei er, sprach zu Gabriel: 'Gehe und zeichne mit Tinte ein
Tav auf dei Stirne des Gerechten, damit die Würgengel über sie keine
Gewalt haben …"; Ephrem, *hymni epiphan.* III 24, ed. Lamy I, c. 41–
42: *Venite, oves, accipite signum vestrum quo fugantur qui devorare quaerunt*, and
Cyril of Jerusalem, *cat.* XVII 35, ed. Rupp 294: καὶ δίδωσι σφραγίδα,
ἥν τρέμουσι δαίμονες. **And he went … baptised with her**. Baptism
in living water, see also ch. 121 (Greek); Didache VII 2; Justin Martyr,
apol. I 61; Ps.-Clement, *homil.* IX 19 4, ed. Rehm 138 and XI 36 2,
172. *Theologiches Wörterbuch z. N.T.* VI, 620–621, *s.v.* Ἰορδάνη (Rengstorf):
"Die Anhänger des fliessenden Wassers lassen erkennen, dass sie im
Zuge jüdischer Tauftradition stehen". The Greek version reads: "Then
he caused her to come near to him, and laid his hands upon her and
sealed her in the name …" Here it is not clear whether an anointing or
baptism with water is meant, but since also the Greek version mentions
the Trinity we assume that baptism with water is meant or possible
the entire baptismal rite. **deacon**, ܡܫܡܫܢܐ, which is the word used to
render διάκονος in the New Testament. **eucharist**. The word ܦܪܝܣܬܐ
has been used, which appears to be the bread before the consecration,
see also ch. 27 and 29. Greek reads: παραθεῖναι τράπεζαν. **bread of
the blessing**, ܠܚܡܐ ܕܒܘܪܟܬܐ and Greek: ἄρτον τῆς εὐλογίας, cf. I
Cor. 10, 16: τὸ ποτήριον τῆς εὐλογίας. **worthy**. See ch. 24 and Cyril of
Jerusalem, *procat.* 16: εὔχου … ἵνα θεός σε καταξιώσῃ τῶν ἐπουρανίων
καὶ ἀθανάτων μυστηρίων. **reliance … bold**, … ܗܟܢܐ ܡܪܚܝܢ and
Greek: τολμῶμεν, see ch. 25 about "boldness". **holy name**. See ch. 27.
and that … world. See ch. 29 and 50. For the relation between bodily
health and eucharist see ch. 51 and I Cor. 10, 30.

50

And he began to say: "Come, gift of the Exalted, come **perfect mercy**; come, **holy Spirit**; come, **revealer of the mysteries of the chosen among the prophets**; come, **proclaimer by his Apostles of the combats of our victorious Athlete**; come **treasure of majesty**; come **beloved of the mercy of the Most High**; come, **(you) silent (one), revealer of the mysteries of the Exalted**; come, **utterer of hidden things, and shewer of the works of our God**; come, **Giver of life in secret, and manifest in your deeds**; come, **giver of joy and rest to all who cleave to you**; come, **power of the Father and wisdom of the Son**, for you are one in all; come, **and communicate with us in this Eucharist which we celebrate and in the offering which we offer, and in the commemoration wich we make**". **And he made the sign of the cross on the bread**, and began to give (it). And he gave first to the woman, and said to her: "**Let it be to you for the remission of transgressions and sins and for the everlasting resurrection**". And after her he gave to the persons who were baptised with her. Then he gave to everyone, and said to them: "**Let this eucharist be to you for life and rest, and not for judgement and vengeance**"; and they said: "Amen".

Here ends the fifth Act

Commentary. A very interesting text of the contents of ch. 50 exists in an Irish sacramentary, see "Das Irische Palimpsestsakramentar im Clm 14 429 der Staatsbibliothek München" entziftert und herausgegeben von A. Dold u. L. Eisenhöfer mit einem Beitrag von D.H. Wright, in: *Texte und Arbeiten* 53/54 Beuron 1964, see 44–46, and M. McNamara, *The Apocrypha in the Irish Church*, Dublin 1975, 118–119. **perfect mercy**. See ch. 10. **holy Spirit**. Greek: ἡ κοινωνία τοῦ ἄρρενος, see ch. 27. **revealer ... prophets**. Greek: ἡ ἐπισταμένη τὰ μυστήρια τοῦ ἐκλέκτου. Christ being ἐκλεκτός, see Luke 23, 35 and John 1, 34 in some manuscripts and also in syr s c. The addition "among the prophets" is striking, although the name is met in the New Testament, see Luke 1, 76 and Matth. 21, 11 and O. Cullmann, *Die Christologie des Neuen Testaments*, Tübingen 1951, 11–49. **proclaimer ... Athlete**. Greek: ἡ κοινωνοῦσα ἐν πᾶσι τοῖς ἄθλοις τοῦ γενναίου ἀθλητοῦ. Christ being an "athlete", see ch. 39. The relation between Christ and the Spirit is not clear, cf. Hermas, *similit.* V VI, see M. Dibelius, "Hirt des Hermas", in: *Handb. z. Neuen Testament*, Erg. IV, Tübingen 1923, 571–576. **treasure of majesty**. The Spirit as "treasure", see II Cor 4, 7 and Coloss. 2, 3. **beloved ... Most High**. Cf. *Sap. Sal.* 8,3: "And the Sovereign Lord of all loved her (*scil.* Wisdom)". **(you) silent ... Exalted**. Greek: ἡ ἡσυχία ἡ ἀποκαλύπτουσα τὰ μεγαλεῖα τοῦ παντὸς μεγέθους. For the word "silent" see ch. 39. Both the Spirit and Christ break God's silence. The word μέγεθος for God is not found in the LXX or the New Testament, but the word μεγαλωσύνη is met in Hebr. 1,3 and cf. Ireneaus, *adv. haer.* I 13 3 about the Marcosians: ὁ δὲ τόπος τοῦ μεγέθους ἐν ὑμῖν ἐστί. **utterer ... works of our God**. See ch. 25. Greeks adds:ἡ ἱερὰ περιστερὰ ἡ τοὺς διδύμους νεοσσοὺς γεννῶσα. The influence of Eastern mythology has to be assumed. Parallels in *Acta Philippi*, in: L.B. II II 46. 2–7, and Ephrem, *adv. haer.* 55. 3, ed. Beck 187 (translation) and 207 (Syriac) do not explain the passage. See Bornkamm, *Mythos* 97. We might refer to Cyril of Jerusalem, *cat.* III 16, ed. Reichl 87: ... καὶ ἑξῆς αἱ πᾶσαι (*scil.* sheep in Song of Songs 4, 1) διδυμένουσαι διὰ τὴν διπλῆν χάριν, λέγω δὲ τὴν ἐξ ὕδατος καὶ πνεύματος τελουμένην. Greek adds also: **Come, the hidden mother**. See ch. 27. **Giver of life ... your deeds**. See for Giver of Life, ܡܘܗܒܬ ܚܝܐ, ch. 10. **giver of joy ... to you**. See for "joy" Hymn I, *l.* 41 and for "rest" cf. 35. **power of the Father**. See ch. 27 **wisdom of the Son**. See I Cor. 1, 24. **one in all**. The Spirit is supposed to be omnipresent. **communicate ... we make**. Here the word ܐܪܙܝܢܘܬܐ has been used. In both eucharist and baptism one receives the Spirit, see also ch. 27. In the Greek version it is said: "... communicate with us in this eucharist ... and in the lovefeast", where the word ἀγάπη has been used. Here is spoken of one meal but possibly consisting of two different parts. The idea "offering" is also found in ch. 169. **And he made the sign ... bread**. This is known from the Jacobite rite, see J.S. Assemani, *Bibliotheca Orientalis* II, Romae 1721, 181. See also F.J. Dölger, "Heidnische und Christliche Brotstempel", in: *Antike und Christentum* I, 1–46 and V 1936, 275–281. **Let it be to you ... resurrection**. See The Liturgy of the Nestorians, in: F.E. Brightman, *Liturgies Eastern and Western*, Oxford 1896, 295: "That they be to us, o my Lord, for the resurrection of our bodies and the salvation of our souls and life, world without end". See for similar formulas B. Botte, "L'Epiclèse dans les Liturgies syr. orient." in: *Sacris Erudiri*, VI 1954, 48–72, esp. 51–52. **Let this eucharist ... vengeance**. See ch. 29.

51

And there was there a young man, who had committed a very hateful deed; **and he came and took the Eucharist, and was going to put it into his mouth**, but both his hands dried up and did not come to his mouth. And when those who were with him saw him, they came (and) made known to the Apostle what had befallen him. And the Apostle called him, and said to him: "Tell me, my son, and be not ashamed before me. What have you done and come hither now? For lo, the gift of our Lord has convicted you, this (gift) which heals the many who draw near to it in love and in truth and in faith, but has utterly withered you away. These things have not befallen you without cause". And when the youth saw that he was convicted by the Eucharist of our Lord, he came (and) fell down before the feet of the Apostle and was begging of him, and interceeding before him, and saying to him: "An evil deed have I done. I loved a woman (who lived) at an inn without the city, and she too loved me; and because I heard from you the truth which you speak, and the faith of God whom you preach, and knew in truth that you are the Apostle of God, I too received the sign with those who received (it). And you said thus: "**Whoever indulges in filthy intercourse, especially in that of adultery**, has not life with this God whom I preach'. And because I loved her, **I begged of her and tried to persuade her to live with me a life clean and pure and tranquil and chaste and modest**, such as you teach, but she would not; and when I saw that she would not listen to me, **I slept with her and killed her**, because I could not bear to see her while she was having intercourse with other men".

Commentary. **and he came ... mouth**. See I Cor. 11, 30, but also ch. 49. The punishment is supposed by the words "... not for judg-ment" used in ch. 29 and 50. Cf. *Acta Petri* II, in: L.B. I I 46. 16–20: *Rufina, non tamquam digna accedens ad altarium dei, surgens a latere non mariti, sed moechi, et dei eucharistiam temptas accipere. Ecce enim satanas, contribulato corde tuo proiiet te ante oculos omnium credentium in domino*, and I Kings 13, 4. **Whoever ... adultery**. See ch. 13. **I begged ... modest**. The pas-

sage suggests that a spiritual marriage has been suggested, see H. Ache-
lis, *Virgines subintroductae*, Leipzig 1902; M. Viller and K. Rahner, *Aszese
und Mystik in der Väterzeit*, Freiburg 1939, 48, n. 32, and J. Duncan, "Baptism in the Demonstrations of Aphraates the Persian Sage", in: *Studies in
Christian Antiquity* 8, Washington 1945, 82. In this passage the following
words have been used: clean—ܪܟܝܐ, pure—ܘܕܟܝܐ, tranquil—ܫܠܝܐ,
chaste—ܢܟܦܐ and modest—ܚܫܝܢܐ. The first and the fourth word have
been used by the author often, see ch. 12. The third and the fifth word
have been added by the Syriac text and expresses the ascetic life. **I
slept with her ... killed her**. Greek reads: "I took a sword and killed
her". According to the Syriac version the boy committed sexual intercourse, but in the Greek version he is supposed to be acting righteously.
This also appears from the addition after "An evil deed have I done"
reading: "Yet I thought to do somewhat good". The Greek version may
be the original one, see ch. 52 in which it is said: "... since I thought
that I did well".

52

And when the Apostle heard these (things), he said: "**O corrupt love,
that has no shame, how it has incited this man to do these
things! O the companian of corruption, how this man has not
been able to bear up against it! O lascivious intercourse, how
it corrupts the minds of men (and turns them away) from the
purity of the Messiah! O work of deception, how it rears itself
up exceedingly in its own!**" And the Apostle ordered (them) to
bring him water in a basin for washing; and they brought him water
that he might pray over it. And he glorified (God), and blessed (it), and
said: "**Water that was given to us by the Living Water; Light
that was sent to us by the glorious Self-existent; Grace that
was sent to us by Grace; let your victorious power come, and
your healing and your mercy descend and abide upon this
water, over which I have proclaimed your name, Jesus our
Life-giver**". And he said: "**May the gift of the Spirit of holiness
be perfected in you**". And he said to the youth: "**Go wash your
hands in this water**". **And he went (and) washed his hands**,
and they became as they had been before they were dried up. And the
Apostle said to him: "Do you believe then in our Lord, that it is possible
for him to do everything?" The youth says to him: "I am not lacking in
faith; yes, because of this, that I believed in God, I did this deed, since

I thought that I did well; for I begged of her, as I have said before you, and she was not willing to listen to me (and) keep herself **in purity and chastity**; because of that I did thus".

Commentary. **O corrupt love ... exceedingly in its own**. Here the boy seems to be accused. The Greek version reads: "O insane union, how do you run to shamelessness. O unrestrained lust how have you stirred up this man to do this. O work of the serpent how are you enraged against thine own". This seems to be directed to the woman. **purity of the Messiah**. See ch. 12. **Water that ... perfected in you**. Greek reads: "Come, you waters from the living waters, that were sent to us, the true from the true, the rest that was sent to us from the rest, the power of salvation that comes from that power which conquers all things and subdues them to its own will; come and dwell in these waters, that the gift of the Holy Ghost may be perfectly consummated in them". This is an epiclesis over exorcistic water. See for living water ch. 25 and for light ch. 28. The word ܐܠܗܐ for God is not yet frequently used with Aphraates, see I. Ortiz de Urbina, "Die Gottheit Christi bei Afrahat", in: *Oriens Christiana* XXXI 1, No. 87, Roma 1933, 90–93, but is often met with Ephrem, see E. Beck, "Die Theologie des Hl. Ephraem", in: *Studia Anselm.* 21, Rome 1949, 7–13. The words "over which ... Life-giver" are not appropriate and seem to have been added because the name of Jesus is usually mentioned in an epiclesis. The Greek version appears to be original. This also applies to the words "May the gift ...". Here the youth is meant but originally the words were part of a prayer over the water. **Go wash ... his hands**. Exorcism with water is also found in the *Acta Petri* XIX, in: L.B. I I, 66. 7–10: *Accepit enim aquam et invocans nomen Iesu Christi sanctum cum ceteris servis ipsum pertinentibus ad eum, adspersi omnem domum meam et omnia triclinia et omnem porticationem usque foris ad ianuum ... .;* Tertullian, *de baptismo* 6: *ceterum villas, domos, templa, totasque urbes aspergine circumlatae aquae expiant passim;* Ps.-Clemens, *homiliae* XI 24, ed. Rehm 166; Epiphanius, *panarion* XXX 19 4, about the Ebionites: παραλαμβάνει νοῦν τοῦτον ἔνδον καὶ ἀποκλείσας τὴν θύραν ὕδωρ τε λαβὼν εἰς τὴν χεῖρα καὶ σφραγίσας, τὸ ὕδωρ ἐρράντισεν ἐστὶ τὸν ἐμμανῆ ἄνθρωπον φήσεις ἐν ὀνόματι ἰησοῦ and *Excerpta e Theodoto* 82. 2, ed. Sagnard 206: οὕτως καὶ τὸ ὕδωρ, καὶ τό ἐξορκιζόμενον καὶ τὸ βάπτισμα γινόμενον οὐ μόνον χωρ⟨ίζ⟩ει τὸ χεῖρον ἀλλὰ καὶ ἁγιασμὸν προσλαμβάνει. **in purity and chastity**, ܒܩܕܝܫܘܬܐ ܘܒܢܟܦܘܬܐ. See for the meaning of these words ch. 12. Cf. II Tim. 2, 15: ܘܒܩܕܝܫܘܬܐ ܒܢܟܦܘܬܐ, in Greek: καὶ ἁγιασμῷ μετὰ σωφροσύνης, but in

Homil. sur la Virginité I 7, ed. Amand–Moons 37: ἐὰν ... μείνωσιν ἐν ... ἁγιασμῷ καὶ σωφροσύνῃ.

53

Judas says to him: "Come, let us go to the inn where you did this deed". And he was going before the Apostle, and a great multitude were coming after him. And when they arrived at the inn, they went into it, and found the woman dead. And when the Apostle saw her, he was grieved for her, because she was **a girl**; and he said that they should take her up and bring her out into the midst of the inn. And when they had brought her and laid her on a couch, Judas Thomas laid his hand upon her, and began to say: "Jesus, our Life-giver, who never neglects us at any time when we came upon you; Jesus, who comes to us at all times when we seek you; you whose ear is inclined to this, that we should seek you, and you give to us; Jesus, who has not permitted us to ask, but has also taught us how to pray; **you who now is not seen by us with these bodily eyes of ours, but by means of these eyes of our understanding does not depart from us; you who is hidden from us in your aspect, and revealed to us in your grace and the administration of your works and your great deeds**; you whom we knew so far as we are able, according to our measure; but who has given us your gift beyond measure; you who has said: '**Ask and it shall be given to you, seek and you shall find, knock and it shall be opened to you**'; we ask therefore of you, our Lord, fearing because of our trespasses and because of our sins, that you would spread over us grace by your mercy. Not gold nor silver, nor riches, nor possessions, nor goods, nor clothes nor anything at all of these earthly things **that are of this world**, and come from it and return to it, do we seek; but we ask of you and beg of you benignity that you would raise up by your holy name this (woman) who is lying before you, to your great glory, and to the praise of your godhead and to the confirmation of your faith in these who are standing by".

Commentary. **a girl.** Greek: "a comely girl". The word "comely" has been omitted in Syriac because the girl acted wickedly. **you who now ... not depart from us.** In Greek is spoken of "the eyes of the soul". God is invisible, see ch. 27. See for the contrast between body and soul Eph. 1, 18; II Cor. 4, 6 and II Pet. 1, 10, where the word "heart" is used. This agrees with Jewish usage, see Nock–Festugière 82,

n. 5, cf. *Corpus Hermet.* IV 88 and VII 12, where the word νοῦς is used. In the present Acts we meet various equivalents, like "understanding", Greek: ψυχή, here; "faith", Greek: ἔννοια in ch. 145 and "heart" in both Syriac and Greek in ch. 166. This agrees with the usage in ancient Christian literature, cf. I Clem. 19. 3: ψυχή and 36. 2: καρδία and Justin, *dial.* III 7: ... ἀλλὰ μόνῳ νῷ ... ὥς φησι πλάτων καὶ ἐγὼ πείθυμαι αὐτῷ. We assume Hellenistic influence, see Plato, *republ.* XIV 533d: τὸ τῆς ψυχῆς ὄμμα; Ps.-Clemens, *recogn.* III 30 2, ed. Rehm 118: *Deus videtur mente non corpore, spiritu non carne;* Eusebius, *praepar. evang* 170a, ed. E.H. Gifford I 222: διάνοια; Theophilus, *ad Autol.* I 3: τὸ μὲν εἶδος τοῦ θεοῦ ... μὴ δυνάμενον ὀφθαλμοῖς σαρκίνοις ὁραθῆναι and Manich. Ps. 89. 6: "[Thou hast] opened the eyes of my heart". **you who is ... great deeds.** See ch. 10. **Ask and it ... opened to you.** See Matth. 7, 7. The text agrees with Syriac translation of the New Testament. **that are of this world.** The Syriac text uses the word ܪܘܒܢ thus better: "time", but the contrast between corruptible and incorruptible remains the same.

54

And he said to the youth: "**Stretch your mind toward our Lord**"; **and he signed him with the cross**, and said to him: "Go, take her by the hand, and say to her: 'I with my hand slew you with iron, but Jesus with his grace raises you up by my faith'". And the youth went (and) stood over her, and said: "I have in truth believed in you, my Lord Jesus the Messiah, the gift of your Father, that in you are all aids and in you all dispensations, and in you all healings, and in you life for the repentant, who in truth repent to you with all their heart. Yes, my Lord, I beg of your mercy, come to my help and to my conversion, and give life to this (woman) by my hands, since I dare to do this". And he was looking on Judas Thomas and saying to him: "Pray for me, Apostle of God, that my Lord may come to my aid, on whom I call". And he laid his hand on hers, and said: "Come, my Lord Jesus the Messiah, and give to this (woman) life and to me the pledge of your faith". And as soon as he took hold of her hand she sprang up (and) stood upright, and was looking on the great crowd who was standing by. And she saw the Apostle of our Lord, who was standing opposite to her, and ran and fell down at his feet and took hold of his skirts and said to him: "I pray you, sir, **where is the other** who was with you, who did not let me remain in that place which I saw, but gave me over to you, and said to you: 'Take this (woman) away to you, **that she may be made perfect in her love by faith, and then be gathered to my place'''**

Commentary. **Stretch your mind ... Lord.** See ch. 37 and 65, This passage is absent in the Greek version. **and he signed ... cross.** Greek uses the word σφραγίσας αὐτόν, see ch. 4 **where is the other.** Thomas is again at two places at the same time, see ch. 34. **That she may be made perfect ... faith.** Here Greek uses the words ἵνα τελειωθῇ see ch. 24. **and then be gathered ... place.** Greek reads καὶ μετὰ ταῦτα εἰς τὸν αἰτῆς χῶρον συναχθῇ, cf. ch. 48.

55

Judas says to her: "Tell me whither you went and what you saw?" She says to him: **"You, who was with me, and to whom he gave me over, do you ask to hear of me?"** And she began to tell him (saying): **"A man, whose aspect was hideous, and his body black, and his clothes filthy,** took me away and carried me to a place which was **full of pits,** and **a stinking smell** too was diffused in its midst. And he made me look down into each of the pits; and I saw the first pit, and as it were fire was blazing in its midst, and **wheels of fire** were revolving in its midst; **and he said to me:** 'Into this torment are destined to come those souls which transgress the law, **which change the union of intercourse that has been appointed by God;** and other (souls) are destined to come into this torment, which have not preserved their virginity, and have given themselves up to the **deed of shame,** and they shall come to this affliction, because they have transgressed the law of God, and shall be given over to evil spirits, and shall be for a mockery and a derision, and retribution shall be (exacted) from them, **and they shall go into another torment,** which is worse than this, and shall be tormented there'

Commentary. **You, who were ... hear of me?** See ch. 54. The same question as in ch. 152. **A man ... filthy.** Black as the colour of the evil, see ch. 31 and Schatzhöhle 3.7, ed. Riessler 945: "Von jenem Tag an bis heute sind sie, er und alle seine Heere, nackt, bloss und hässlich anzuschauen". **full of pits,** ܦܚ̈ܐ and Greek χάσματα. The same word in Luke 16, 26. The pits are places where the various sinners are tormented, cf. Hen. 53, 1 and 22, 2–3, see also Midr. Ps. XI 7, ed. Wünsche 103, saying that there are "sieben Wohnungen für die Frevler in der Hölle"; *Apocal. Pauli* 32 and *Pistis Sophia*, ed. Schmidt–Till 207, 9–10: "Und es sind viele Gerichtsörter". See J. Bonsirven, *Le Judaisme Palestinien* I, Paris 1935, 537, and Bornkamm, *Mythos* 49. **a stinking smell**. Cf. Ignatius, *ad Ephes.* 17. 1. See E. Lohmeyer, *Vom göttlichen Wohlgeruch* 7: "Wie man den Menschen gnädige Gottheit an ihrem Wohlgeruch erkennt, so die Menschen feindlichen göttliche Mächte an ihren widrigen Geruch". **wheels of fire**. Cf. Vergilius, *Aeneis* VI 616–617: *radiisque rotarum districti pendent*, see E. Norden, *P. Vergilius Maro, Aeneis Buch VI*, Berlin 1916, 86 and 290. See for fire in order to torture Eth. Hen. 10, 6; 18, 11 and 21, 7–11; Matth. 18, 8; 25, 41, Jud. 7; Rev. 19,20 and 20, 10. See also Bonsirven, *Le Judaisme* I, 536–537. From the words "and he said to me" the Greek version reads: "and souls were hanged upon those wheels, and were dashed against each other, and very great crying and howling was there, and there was none to deliver. And that man said to me: 'These souls are of your tribe and when the number of their days are accomplished, they are delivered unto torment and affliction, and then others brought in their stead, and likewise these unto another (place). These are they that have reversed the intercourse of male and female'. And I looked and saw infants heaped one upon another and struggling with each other as they lay on them. And he answered and said to me: 'These are the children of those (others), and therefore they sit here for testimony against them'". **which change ... God**. See Rom. 1, 26. This is also mentioned in *Apocal. Petri* 32. **deed of shame**. See ch. 14. In the Greek version the passage has been brought into agreement with the situation of the girl with the following words "These are the souls of your tribe" and is also spoken about the children. Also the *Apocal. Petri* speaks in 24 about the punishment for adultery and in 26 about "women with children over against them conceived in wedlock or caused by abortion", see also *Apocal. Petri* 40, and F.J. Dölger, "Das Lebensrecht des ungeborenen Kindes", in: *Antike u. Christentum* IV 1933, 1–11. **and they shall go into another torment**. See ch. 57.

56

And again he showed me another pit, and I looked down into it and saw dreadful things, to which are destined to come the souls that do evil; and I saw there many tortures which are prepared for men and women and youths and maidens. Those men who leave their own wives, and have intercourse with the wives of their fellows; and women who go beyond intercourse with their own husbands; and youths who do not keep their laws, but wantonly indulge themselves with harlots in their lust, and for whom it is not enough to transgress the law among harlots, but they lie in wait for virgins and wantonly indulge in sin; and maidens who have not kept their state of virginity, (but), because of their wanton lust, have brought shame upon their parents;—(these) shall come to the affliction and shall be recompensed, each according to his works.

Commentary. The chapter in Greek reads: "And he took me to another pit, and I stooped and looked and saw **mire and worms** welling up, and souls wallowing there, and a great gnashing of teeth was heard thence from them. And that man said to me: '**These are the souls of the women which forsook their husbands and committed adultery with others, and are brought into the torment**'. Another pit he showed me, whereinto I stooped and looked and saw souls hanging some by the tongue, some by the hair, some by the hands, and some head downward by the feet, and tormented with **smoke and brimstone**; concerning whom that man that was with me answered me: 'The souls which are hanged **by the tongue are slanderers**, that uttered lying and shameful words, and were not ashamed; and they that are hanged **by the hair are unblushing ones which had no modesty** and went about in the world bareheaded; and they that are hanged **by the hands, these are they that took away and stole other men's goods**, and never gave aught to the needy nor helped the afflicted, but did so, desiring to take all, and had no thought at all of justice, or the law; and they that hang upside down **by the feet, these are they that lightly and readily ran in evil ways** and disorderly paths, not visiting the sick nor escorting them that depart this life, and therefore each and every soul receives that which was done by it'". This means that Syriac does not go into the various punishments. In Greek is spoken of **mire and worms**. Cf. Judith 16, 17; Is. 66, 24; Mark 9, 44 and Revel. R. Josh b. Levi V 7, ed. Gaster 601: "men wallowing in the mire"; *Apoc. Petri.* 31: "boiling mire"; *Apoc. Pauli* 17; Akhmin Fragm. 25 IV, ed. Dieterich 6: ἐν τινι τόπῳ ... πεπληρωμένῳ ἑρπετῶν πονηρῶν **These are the souls ... this torment**. In Syriac is spoken of adultery in general, but the Greek version goes into details, see **by the tongue ... slanderer; by the hair ... no modesty; by the hands ... stole other man's goods; by the feet ... ran in evil ways**. Cf Revel. of R. Josh b. Levi V

7, ed. Gaster 600: "hanging by: hair—eyes—nose—tongues—hands—
sexual organs—feet—breasts" and in Gedulah Mosheh 35, ed. Gaster
581: "hanging by: eyelids—ears—hands—tongues—hairs -breasts". In
the *Apoc. Pauli* 39 we find hanging by eyebrows and hair; in Akhmin
Fragm. 22 I, ed. Dieterich 4–5, by the tongue in connection with slanderers and by the hair with adultery. **smoke and brimstone**. Cf.
R. Josh. b. Levi V 4: "… rivers of pitch and sulphur" and Rev. 21, 8.

57

**And he took me away again. and showed me a dark cave,
and a stinking smell was coming out of it. And he said to
me: 'Look down and see, for this is the prison of those souls
about which I said to you that, when the chastisement of each
of them is finished, another comes in its place; and there
are some of them which are utterly consumed, and there are
some of them which are handed over to other tortures'. The
guardians of those tortures say to the man who led me**: 'Give
us this (woman) that we may bind her in her place, until she goes to her
torture'. The man who led me says to them: '**I will not give her to
you because I am afraid of him who delivered her to me, and I
was not ordered to leave her here**; but I will take her up with me,
until I receive an order regarding her'. And he took me and brought
me out to the place where men were; **and he who was like to you**
took me and delivered me to you, and said to you: 'Take this (woman)
because she is one of the sheep that have gone astray'. And you took
me from him, and lo, I stand before you, and beg of you that I too may
believe through you, and may find grace because of your prayer, and
that I too may not go to those tortures which I have seen'.

Commentary. **And he took me again … say to the man who led
me**. In the Greek version: "Again he took me and showed me a cave
exceedingly dark, breathing out a great stench, and many souls were
looking out desiring to get somewhat of the air, but their keepers
suffered them not to look forth. And he that was with me said: 'This
is the prison of those souls which you saw, for when they have fulfilled
their torments for that which each did, thereafter do others succeed
them. And there be some that are wholly consumed and that are
delivered over to other torments. And they that kept the souls which
were in the dark cave said to the man that had taken me'". **dark cave**.

Also known from the Akhmin Fragm. 27 VI, ed. Dieterich 6, where is spoken of a dark place. **about which I said ... place**. See ch. 55: "and that shall go into another torment". Cf. Vergilius, *Aeneis* VI 612–614, ed. Norden 289–290: *quique arma secuti impia, nec veriti dominorum fallere dextras inclusi poenam expectant*. **and there are some ... other tortures**. Cf. Revel. R. Josh. b. Levi V 9, ed. Gaster 602: "some descend to hell forever"; 10: "others ascend"; 24, 605: "at the end the Almighty will have pity on all his creatures". In Judaism a difference is met between punishment during a certain time, total destruction and eternal punishment, see Bonsirven, *Le Judaisme* I, 538–441, with references. **and he who was like to you**. See ch. 54 and 55. **I will not give ... have her here**. The devil is only allowed to punish man, if God permits him, cf. Isaac of Antioch, "Gedicht über den Teufel", in: *BKV* 179: "Der Teufel ist nur ein Werkzeug zur Züchtigung; hierüber möge dich niemand täuschen. Denn ohne den Willen der Höheren Hand, welche ihn hält, kann er keinen Menschen beschädigen".

The Description of Hell (chs. 55–57). The description of hell in the Greek version of these Acts shows a striking agreement with that found in the Apocalypse of Peter.[1] The way in which hell has been described is based upon Orphic and Eastern traditions.[2] However, with this conclusion the problem of the descriptions in Judaism and Christianity has not yet been solved. It appears that the tradition in the *Apocalypse of Peter* is the oldest one and dates from the first half of the second century. For this reason it is generally supposed that the Acts of Thomas depend on the *Apocalypse of Peter*.[3]

A comparison of the contents of the *Apocalypse of Peter* and the *Acts of Thomas* shows that the agreement is limited to the way in which the var-

---

[1] See Bornkamm, *Mythos* 46. For the various fragments of the *Apocalypse of Peter* and their significance see M.R. James, "A new Text of the Apocalypse of Peter", in: *Journ. of Theol. Studies* 12 1911–12, 36–54; 157; 362–382 and 573–583, and M.R. James, "The Rainer Fragment of the Apocalypse of Peter", in: *Journ. of Theol. Studies* 32 1931, 270–279. See also Altaner, *Patrologie* 62, Quasten, *Patrology* I, 144–146, and especially J.K. Elliott, *The Apocryphal New Testament*, Oxford 1993, 593–612.

[2] See A. Dieterich, *Nekya*, Leipzig–Berlin 1913 (2. Aufl.), 212, but see also L. Rademacher, *Das Jenseits im Mythos der Hellenen*, Bonn 1903, 33, who assumes the influence from Eastern tradition only.

[3] See Bornkamm, *Mythos* 46: "Ja, man wird vielleicht behaupten, dass sie unmittelbar als Vorlage gedient hat"; H. Weinel, in: Hennecke, *Neutest. Apokryphen* 318, and James, *Apocr. New Testament* 390: "This description of hell torments is largely derived from the Apocalypse of Peter".

ious punishments have been described only. They also show an agreement with Jewish writings like Gadulah Mosheh and the Revelation of R. Joshua ben Levi.[4] Therefore we may conclude that the description of the punishments in the Acts of Thomas largely depend on Jewish sources.[5] This seems also to apply to the contents of the Acts of Thomas and this makes it difficult to assume a dependency on the *Apocalypse of Peter*.[6]

58

Judas says to them: "You have heard, my children, what this woman has said and there are not these tortures only, but also others, which are much worse than these. **You too, therefore, unless you are converted to this truth which I preach and restrain yourselves from evil deeds and from your actions which profit you not, and from your thoughts without knowledge, your end will come to these torments. But do you, therefore, believe in Jesus the Messiah**, and he will blot out your former actions, and will cleanse you from all your earthly thoughts that abide on the earth, and will purify you from your sins, which, unless you repent of them to God, will accompany you and go with you and be found before you. **Put off, therefore, each of you, his old man, and put on the new man, that is to say, (put off) your old courses and your fleshly works. Let those, then who stole of you, steal no more, but toil and work and live**; and let those of you who committed adultery, not commit adultery **and abandon themselves to the ease of the moment**, that they may not go to everlasting tor-

---

[4] See M. Gaster, "Hebrew Visions of Hell and Paradise", in: *Journal Royal Asiatic Soc.* 1893, 571–611, and A. Marmorstein, "Jüdische Parallelen zur Petrus-apokalypse", in: *Zeitschr. f. d. neutestamentl. Wissensch.* 10 1909, 207–300, who points to the difficulties with regard to the dating of the two writings and writes "dass die Parallelstellen in der mystischen Literatur nicht unbedingt der nachtalmudischen Zeit entstammen müssen". However, it seems improbable that Jewish sources depend on Christian traditions.

[5] See Gaster, *o.c.* 371: "All the Christian Revelations (St. Peter etc.)—are based directly upon Hebrew visions". See also Martha, Himmelfarb, *Tours of Hell: The Development and the Transmission of Apoclyptic Forms in Jewish and Christian Literature*, Diss. University of Pennsylvania 1981, esp. 25–31.

[6] The presence of the element of fire, water, smoke, darkness and wind, see Augustin, *epist. fundam.* 31 (XXVIII), *de hear.* XLVI and Mitchel, *Prose Refutations* II, p. CI and 214–215, was reason for Bornkamm, *Mythos* 48–52, to assume a relationship between the present Acts and Manicheism, but this seems not to be acceptable.

ment, for adultery is hateful before God more than all evil works; and put away from you **lying and oppression and drunkenness and slander**, and requite not any man evil for evil; for all these things are **odious** to this God whom I preach, and unclean to him, but walk in all **humility and temperancee** and purity, and hope in God, and you shall become **servants of him**, and shall receive from him the gifts which are given to some (only)".

Commentary. **You too therefore ... Messiah**. The first step to a new life consists of cleansing oneself from one's former deeds, see also ch. 37. The coming punishment as part of the preaching is also found in Philo, *immut.* 76, and Clemens of Alex., *paedag.* I 58 3: φόβῳ τῆς ἀπειλῆς τοῦ μὴ τὰ ὅμοια παθεῖν ἀποσχώμεθα τῶν ἴσων πλημμαλημάτων. See W. Völker, "Der wahre Gnostiker nach Clemens Alexandrinus", in: *Texte u. Unters.* 57 1952, 145–146. **Put off ... fleshly works**. See ch. 48. **Let those then who stole ... live**. Free rendering of Eph. 4, 28. **and abandon ... moment**. The words ܪ‍ܗ‍ܒ‍ܘ ܠܢܝܐ can also be translated by "and to be put to instantaneous rest". **lying ... slander**. See ch. 28. **odious**. Greek: ξένα ... ἀλλοτρία, see ch. 4. **humility ... temperance ... purity**, ܗ‍ܘ‍ܘ‍ܗ—ܗ‍ܘ‍ܘ‍ܗ—ܗ‍ܘ‍ܘ‍ܗ. These three virtues are very important in these Acts, see ch. 85. **servants of him**. Greek: "that you may become his own", see ch. 32. To become "his own" depends upon man's behaviour.

59

And these multitudes believed **and surrendered themselves** to the living God and to Jesus the Messiah and were enjoying the blessed works of the Most High and his holy service **and were each of them bringing much money for the relief of widows who were collected by the Apostle in each city** and to all of them whom he was sending by the hand of his deacons what was fitting for them for food and clothing. **And he never ceased to preach and to speak to them and to show them that it was Jesus the Messiah of whom the scriptures spoke and whose types and mysteries and likenesses the law and the prophets showed forth; who was given as a covenant to the people (of Israel) that they might be restrained for his sake from the worship of idols and as a light to the peoples (the Gentiles), by means of which the grace of God has dawned upon them and all those who**

keep his commandments shall find rest in his kingdom and be honoured in glory; and he came and was crucified and rose in three days. And he was narrating to them and expounding from Moses even to the end of the prophets, because they all preached concerning him and he came (and) fulfilled (all) in fact. And the report of him was heard among men in the cities and villages; and every man who had a sick (person) or one possessed by a spirit of a lunatic or paralytics,—some they brought on beds and placed them by the road-side, whithersoever they learned that he was going; and he was healing them all by the power of Jesus his Lord. And the sick who were ill of grievous diseases and in hideous torments were healed and the paralytics who were standing up quite sound; and they were all glorifying (God) with one mouth and saying: "To you be glory, Jesus the Messiah, who has given us healing by your servant and your Apostle Judas. For lo, being quite well and seeing, we pray of you that we too may become **children of your fold** and may be numbered among the number of your sheep. Receive us, our Lord, and reckon not against us our former sins which we committed in **ignorance**".

Commentary. **and surrendered themselves,** ܝܗ̈ܦܫܢ ܘܒ ܘܒܗ ܘܫܠܡܐܘ and Greek, καὶ τὰς ἑαυτῶν ψυχὰς πειθηνίους παρέσχον, obviously influenced by the Syriac version. **and were each ... in each city**. See ch. 26 The influence of II Cor. 8–9 and Rom. 15, 25, 25–26 is unmistakable. **And he never ceased ... spoke**. Cf, Acts 18, 28. **whose types,** ܝܗ̈ܣܦܛ and **mysteries,** ܝܗܙܐܪ and **likenesses,** ... ܝܗ̈ܣܡܕ **forth**. This passage is not present in the Greek version. Cf. *Hymni et Antiphonae, quae trib. S. Simoni bar Sabbae*, ed. Kmosko, in: *Patrol. Syr.* I 2, c. 1052–1053: *Oculis mentis et caritatis videamus omnes Christum per mysteria et typos,* ܐܬܩܛܡܘ ܐܙܐܪ ܒܕ *quae tradidit nobis,* and Ephrem, *de fide*, 49. 5, ed. Beck, 132 (translation) and 155 (Syriac): "Seine Symbole, ܝܗܙܐܪ finden sich in der Thora, und seine Typen, ܝܗ̈ܣܦܛ, in der Arche." **who was given ... fulfilled (all) in fact**. Greek: "who is come and crucifed and raised the third day from the dead. And next he showed them plainly, beginning from the prophets, the things concerning Christ, that is necessary that he should come, and that in him should be accomplished the things that were foretold of him". The Greek version and the end of this passage in Syriac were inspired by Luke 24, 17. The difference of opinion within Manichaeism is striking, cf. Manich. Hom. 8. 2–3: "Die Propheten haben über ihn gepredigt", and Augustine, *c. Faustum* XVI 3: ... *omnem Moseos scripturam scrutatus, nullas ibi de Christo prophetias inveni.* See for gnosticism R. Liechtenhan, *Die Offenbarung im Gnosticismus*, Göttingen 1901, 38–58. The Syriac text might show the influence of Is. 42, 6. **And the report ... Lord**. Cf. Acts 5, 15–16. **children of your fold**. See ch. 25. **ignorance**. See ch. 38.

60

Then, when Judas Thomas saw them, he lifted up his voice and said: "To you be glory, **Living (One) who is from the Living (One)**; to you be glory Live-giver of many; to you glory, **help and aider** of those who come to your place of **refuge**; to you be the glory (you that is) **wakeful from all eternity, and the awaker** of men, living and making alive. You are God, the Son of God, the Saviour and helper, and refuge and rest of all those who are weary in your work; **the giver of rest to those who for your name's sake, have borne the burden of the whole day at mid-day**. We praise you for your gift to us and for your aids to our feebleness and for your provision for our poverty.

Commentary. **Living (One) ... Living (One)**. Cf. John 5, 26; 11, 25 and 14, 6. Greek reads in place of "Living (One) ... many": "Glory be to the only-begotten of the Father. Glory be to the first-born of many brothers", which agrees with ch. 48. **help and aider**, ܘܣܝܥܬܐ ܐܝܟ, see ch. 39. **refuge**. See ch. 10. **wakeful ... awaker**. Also in ch. 66; 142 and 153 it is said that God does not sleep. Sleep belongs to the corruptible world, cf. Gen. R. 68. 11, ed. Freedman 624; Eph. 5,14; *Apost. Constit.* VII 45 3: δός μοι ... νοῦν ἐγρήγορον; Clemens Alex., *paedag*, II 78–81; Tertullian, *de orat.* 29; Irenaeus, *demonstr.* 13, ed. Froidevaux: "Dieu fit donc lui-même tomber une extase sur Adam et l'endormit ... comme le sommeil n'existait pas au paradis ..."; *Evangelium Veritatis* 29. 6–9: "... and (there were) empty fictions, as if they were sunk in sleep ..."; Huwidagman I 24, ed. Boyce 69: "Heavy sleep never overtakes their souls"; Ginza R. 112. 29: "Und weckte sein Herz aus dem Schlaf"; 214. 16: "Liebe keinen Schlaf"; Johannesbuch 225. 6–7: "Schlummere nicht, Adam. und schlafe nicht und vergiss nicht, was dein Herr dir aufgetragen", cf. 218. 13 and *Corp. Hermet.* I 27, see Nock—Festugière 26, n. 69; S. Pétrement, *Le Dualisme chez Platon, les*

Gnostiques et les Manichéens, Paris 1947, 88–93, and Jonas, *Gnosis* I 113–115 and 126–131. **the giver of rest ... at mid-day**. Cf. Matth. 20, 12.

61

Make perfect with us your grace and your mercy to the end and give us the boldness that is in you. Behold, Lord that you alone we love; and behold Lord that **we have left our homes and the homes of these our kindred** and for your sake are become **strangers** without compulsion. Behold, Lord, that we have left our possessions for your sake that we might gain you, the possession of life that cannot be taken away. Behold, our Lord that we have left all our kindred for your sake that we might be united in kinship to you. Behold, our Lord that we have left our fathers and our mothers and our fosterers that we might see **your exalted Father** and be filled with his **divine nourishment**. Behold, our Lord that we have left our fleshly wives and earthly fruits **that we might be united in true union with you and produce the heavenly fruits which (are) from above**, which men cannot take away from us, but which shall be with us and shall be with them".

Here ends the sixth Act

Commentary. **Make perfect ... to the end**. Greek: "Perfect, therefore, these things in us to the end", see ch. 25. **and give us ... in you**. See ch. 25. **We have left ... kindred**. Cf. Matth. 10, 28 and parallel passages. **strangers**. See ch. 4. **united in kinship to you**, ܢܬܚܠܛܝܢ and Greek: τῇ σῇ συγγενείᾳ, see ch. 34. Here it is clear that to be united with Christ depends upon one's way of life. **your exalted Father**. Cf. Hymn I *l.* *35–38*. **divine nourishment**. See ch. 36 and Hymn I *l. 48–51*. **that we have left ... from above**. This applies to the marriage of the soul with God, see ch. 12.

62

And whilst Judas was preaching throughout all India, the general of **a king** came to him and said to him: "I pray you, servant of God, and the more so that you see that I myself have come to you as to the Apostle of God, because you are sent for the healing of men who have need of the aid which is given them by your hands; and I have heard concerning you that you do not take fee from any man, but provide for the poor, for if you took a fee, I would have sent you a large sum of money, and I would not have come hither, because the king does nothing without me; for I have abundance and am rich, and am a great man throughout all India, and I have done no wrong to any man, **but this thing has happened to me contrary (to my deserts)**. I have a wife and by her I had a daughter; and I love her much, **as nature too teaches**, and I know no other wife along with her. Now there chanced to be a **banquet** in our city, and the givers of the entertainment were great friends of mine; and they came (and) asked of me, and prepared the feast for her and her daughter. And because they were friends of mine, I could not make any excuse, but I sent her, though against her will, and I sent with her also many of my servants, and I made a great display for her and her daughter.

Commentary. **a king**. Greek: τοῦ βασιλέως μισδαίου, see ch. 87. **but this king … (to my deserts)**, ܟ݁ܝܡ ܟܐܠܐ݂ ܐܕܪܝܠ ܐܘܪ̈ܝܒܘܡܐ, possibly better: "This reverse happened to me", cf. Greek: τὸ δὲ ἐναντίον μοι συνέβη. **as nature too teaches**. See ch. 29. **banquet**, ܐܠܘܐܟܣ and Greek: γάμον, but Syriac can have both meanings.

63

And when it was time to depart, I sent after her lanterns and lamps; and I too was standing in the street and was looking when she should come, that I might see her and receive her and her daughter with her. And whilst I was standing there, I heard a sound of lamentation and a sound of weeping: 'Alas for her, alas for her', was coming to my ears from all mouths. Then my servants came to me, rending their clothes, and made knnwn to me what had happemed, and say to me: 'We saw a man, and another, a boy was with him, who was like to him. And the man laid his hand upon your wife, and the boy upon your daughter; and they shrank with loathing from them, and we smote them with swords, but our swords sank to the ground; and at that moment the women fell down, and were gnashing their teeth, and dashing their heads on the ground; and we have come to inform you, of what has happened'. And when I had heard these things from my servants, I rent my clothes, and was beating my face with my hands, and running about in the street like a madman. And I came and found them lying in the street; and I took them and brought them to my house, and after a long time they came to themselves; and I restored (them and) made them sit up.

64

And I began to ask my wife: 'What has happened to you?' And she says to me: 'You do not know what you have done with me; for I asked of you that I might not go to the feast, because I was not well in body; and as I was going along the street, and had come to the pipe that throws up water, I saw **a black man** standing opposite to me and shaking his head, and another, a boy, who was like to him, standing beside him; and I said to my daughter: 'Look at these men, how **hideous** (they are)'; and my daughter said to me: "I saw a boy whose teeth were like milk and his lips like coals'. And we left them beside the water-pipe and went on. And when it was evening, and we quit the house where the entertainment was, and came away with the servants, and arrived at the water-pipe, my daughter saw them first, and came to me for refuge; and after her I too saw them coming towards us; and the servants who were with me fled; and they struck me and my daughter, and threw us down'. And whilst she was narrating (this) to me, they came upon them, and cast them down again; and from that hour they are unable to go out any more into the street, either to go to the bath, or to the house of feasting or the house of weeping, but they lie there night and day, the mother with her daughter, and are shut up by me in **a room within another**, because of the laughing-stock that I have become through them, and because, when they come upon them, they throw them down and **disgrace them** wherever they find them. I beg

therefore of you and entreat you, help me and have mercy upon me,
for, lo, for three years no table has been laid in my house, and my wife
and daughter have not sat at it; but specially for my poor daughter's
sake, who **has had no pleasure** (of her life)!"

Commentary. **black man.** See ch. 31. **hideous.** See ch. 55. **in a room
within another,** ܚܕܐ ܓܘ ܠܐܟ ܒܝܬܗ and Greek: ἐν ἑνὶ οἴκῳ ἢ δευτέρῳ,
which clearly shows Syriac influence. **disgrace them,** ܢܓܘܪܘܢ, which
means "to spread out" and Greek: ἀπογυμνοῦσιν **has had no pleasure,** ܚܝܐ, thus better "has seen …"

65

And when the Apostle had heard these things from the general, he
was very sorry for him, and said to him: "If you believe in my Lord
Jesus the Messiah that he can heal them, you shall see their recovery".
The general, when he had heard these things, says to him, because
he imagined that he was Jesus: "I believe that you can heal them".
The Apostle says to him: "**I am not Jesus, but his servant and
his Apostle**. Commit then yourself to him, and he will heal them
and help them". The general says to him: "Show me how I can ask
him and believe in him". The Apostle says to him: "As far as you are
able, **stretch your mind upward**, because **he is not visible now to
these bodily eyes, but by faith is recognized in his works and
glorified in his healings**". And the general lifted up his voice and
said: "I believe in you, Jesus the Messiah, God, that you are the Living,
the Son of the Living, and became man, and appeared (as) a Healer
and Life-giver and Saviour for all those who in truth repent to you.
Yes, Lord, I beg of you and intercede before you; **help my little faith**
and my fear, for with you I take refuge. And the Apostle commanded
his deacon **Xanthippus** to assemble all the brothers who were there.
And when he had assembled them, the Apostle came and stood in their
midst, and said to them:

Commentary. **I am not Jesus … Apostle.** Cf. Acts 14,15 and ch. 88.
stretch your mind upward. The same words as in ch. 54. **He is not
visible … healing.** We meet the idea of God seen in his works, cf.
ch. 10, and in faith, cf. ch. 28 and 53. **help my little faith,** Cf. Mark
9, 24. **deacon.** The word ܡܫܡܫܢܐ has been used to render διάκονος, in
the Syriac New Testament, but also the word λειτουργός, see Rom. 13,

6; 15, 16; Philipp. 2, 15; Hebr. 1,7 and 8,2. **Xanthippus**, ܘܐܟܣܢܬܘܣ and Greek: Ξενοφὼν

66

My sons and brothers and sisters in our Lord Jesus, abide in this faith, and trust in our Lord Jesus the Messiah, him, who I preach to you; and let your hope be in him, and he will keep you; and fall not away from him, because he will not forsake you. **And if it be that you sleep that sleep, which when a man sleeps, he is not, he will not sleep, but will be wakeful and preserve you. And if you sit in a ship and on the sea, where no man of you is able to help his fellow, he will walk upon the waves of the sea and support your ship**. Because I then am going away from you, and I do not know if I shall see you again in the body, be not you, therefore, like to the **children of Israel**, who stumbled, because Moses, their shepherd for a time, departed from them. But lo, I leave you in my stead the deacon Xanthipus, and he too will preach Jesus the Messiah like me. For I too am a man like one of you, and I have no wealth, which is found with some, the end of which is that it destroys him who possesses it, because there is no utility in it, since it leaves him in the earth, from which he came and the transgression and sins which he committed for its sake are with him; for there are (only) some who are rich and **charitable**. Neither have I any human comeliness, on which all those who place their reliance are quickly brought to shame; for if he who had **beauty** becomes deprived (of it), his beauty avails him nought, but those who loved him because of his beauty, they especially shun him with loathing; **for all things which are of the world are loved in their season** and hated in their season. But let your hope be in Jesus the Messiah, the Son of God, and be you holding fast by us and looking to us, as the servants of God, **since we too, if we bear not the burden that beseems this name, shall receive punishment, and shall be to us for judgement and vengeance**".

Commentary. **And if it be ... preserve you**. See ch. 60. **And if you sit ... your ship**. See ch. 47 and John 6, 19. **children of Israel**. See Ex. 32. **charitable**. Greek adds: οἱ δὲ ἐλεήμονες καὶ ταπεινοὶ τῇ καρδίᾳ αὐτοὶ κληρονομήσουσιν τὴν βασιλείαν τοῦ θεοῦ, inspired by Matth. 11, 29 and Matth 5, 4. **beauty**. See ch. 8. **for all things ... season**. See ch. 123 and Eccles. 3, 1 and 8. The text of Sinai is present from:

"since we too ..." until ch. 70: "And the general went, fearing greatly, because". **Since we too ... vengeance**. Greek reads: ἡμεῖς γὰρ αὐτοῖς ἐὰν μὴ τὸ τῶν ἐντολῶν φορτίον τελεσωμεν, οὐκ ἄξιοι ἐσμεν κήρυκες εἶναι τοῦ ὀνόματος τούτου καὶ ὕστερον τιμωρίαν ἀποτίσομεν τῆς ἐαυτῶν κεφαλῆς. See for τιμωρίαν ... κεφαλῆς ch. 5; for "burden" Matth. 23, 4 and Luke 11, 46 and for "judgement and vengeance" ch. 29.

<h1 style="text-align:center">67</h1>

And he prayed with them a long prayer, and committed them to our Lord, and said: "**Lord of all orders of creation, which await you, and God of all spirits, which hope in you,** (you) that delivers from **error your human beings, (and) frees from corruption and from slavery** those who obey you and come to your place of refuge; be you with the flock of Xanthippus, **and anoint his flock with your oil of life, and cleanse it of its disease and guard it from wolves and from robbers, that they may not snatch it out of his hands**'. And he laid his hand upon them and said to them: "**The peace of Jesus be with you, and go with us also**".

Commentary. **Lord ... hope in you,** ـܝܡܚܬܢ ܘܐܪܡ ܗܒ.ܕ ܘ̈ܚܡܣܩ and Greek: "O, Lord that rules over every soul that is in the body". Burkitt, *The Original Language* ... . 285, supposed that ـܝܡܚܣ must be read as ـܝܡܚܗܣ ܗܒ.ܕ. This is possible, although the soul is usually especially emphasized in the Greek version. **error**. See ch. 25. **your human beings**. Greek: "your own", see ch. 32. **frees ... slavery**. For "slavery" see ch. 2 and for "corruption" ch. 36. **and anoint ... disease**. Greek reads: "and anoint it with holy oil, and heal it of sores". The Syriac version refers to baptism in its usual Syriac order, see ch. 24. **and guard it ... hands**. See ch. 25. Greek reads: ἀπὸ τῶν λύκων τῶν διαρπαζόντων, cf. Matth. 7, 15. **The peace ... also**. See ch. 49.

68

And the Apostle set out to go on the way; and all of them were accompanying him with weeping, and were conjuring him by his Lord to be mindful of them in his prayers and not to forget them. And when the Apostle had mounted, he sat in the chariot of the general, and all the brothers remained behind. The general came and said to the driver: "**I am praying that I may be worthy to sit beneath the feet of the Son of God, Jesus, the Messiah, and to be his driver on this road, which many know, that he may be my guide on that road which some (only) shall go**".

Commentary. **I am praying ... shall go**. Instead of "the feet of the Son of God, Jesus the Messiah" the Greek version reads "his feet" and Sinai "the feet of the Apostle of our Lord". In this passage Christ and Thomas are identified again, see ch. 11. It appears that the chariot is ascending to heaven, cf. Odes of Sol. 38. 1–2: "I went up into the light of Truth as into a chariot ... And caused me to pass over chasms and gulfs, and saved me from cliffs and valleys", which again may be compared with ch. 71, where it is said that the chariot goes "gently and quietly". See Apocryphon of James 14. 34, ed. Robinson 35: "... for a chariot of spirit has borne me aloft ...", cf. H.-Ch. Puech et G. Quispel, "Les Écrits gnostiques du Codex Jung", in: *Vigiliae Christ.* 8 1954, 1–15, esp. 15–17, with references. The idea is also known from II Kings 2, 11, cf, Ps.-Clemens, *recognit.* II 22 4, ed. Rehm 65: *Non ergo nobis difficilis videatur huius itineris labor, quia in fine eius requies erit; nam et ipse verus propheta ab initio mundi per seculum currens festinat ad requiem*, and Cyril of Jerusalem, *procat.* 16, ed. Reischl 10: ... βάπτισμα ... ὄχημα πρὸς οὐρανόν.

69

And when he had gone about a mile, Judas Thomas begged of the general, and made him get up to sit beside him, and ordered the driver to sit in his place. And as they were going along the road, and Judas was conversing with the general, the cattle became tired from their having driven them so far, and stood still and would not stir. And the general was sorely vexed, and knew not what to do; and he thought of running on foot, and bringing other cattle, wherever he could get them, or horses, because his time was becoming short. And when the Apostle saw this, he said to him: "**Be not afraid and be not agitated, but only believe in Jesus, as I told you, and you shall see great wonders**". **The general says to him: "I believe in him, (and) that everything is possible for him to do who asks of him**". Now Judas saw a herd of wild asses feeding some distance off the highway, and he said to the general: "If you believe in Jesus, go to the herd and say to them: 'Judas, the Apostle of Jesus the Messiah, the Son of God, says, Let four of you come, for I require them'".

Commentary. **Be not afraid ... great wonders**. Cf. John 11, 40. **The general says ... of him**. This passage has been omitted by Sinai. **wild asses**, ܥܪ̈ܕܐ and Greek: ὄναγροι. This animal is known for his wildness, cf. Narsai, *Memra über die Seele* 142, ed. Allgeier 381: "Zu ihr (*scil.* die Natur des Leibes) (gehört) die Übermut der Wildesel, welcher sich gegen die Unterwerfung sträubt". In messianic time the wild beasts will be subjected to men, cf. Is. 11, 6–8; Apoc. Baruch 73. 6: "And wild beasts shall come from the forest and minister unto men"; *Orac. Sibyll.* III 788–795, ed. Kurfess–Gauger 108–109, and Papias in Irenaeus, *adv. haer.* V 33 3: *et omnia animalia iis cibis utentia, quae a terra accipiuntur, pacifica et consentanea invicem fieri, subiecta hominibus cum omni subiectione*. See W.A. Schulze, "Der Heilige und die wilden Tiere", in: *Zeitschr. f. d. neutestament. Wissensch.* 46 1955, 280–283, and R. Eisler, "Örphisch-Dionisische Mysteriengedanken", in: *Vortr. Bibliothek Warburg* II, Leipzig 1925, 11–32.

70

And the general went, fearing greatly, because they were many; and the more he went on, (the more) they came towards him. And when they were close to him, he said to them: "Judas Thomas, the Apostle of Jesus the Messiah says: 'Let four of you come to me, because I require them'". And when they heard this speech, all the asses came to him with a great rush; and when they came to him, **they bowed down to him** by the direction of our Lord. **And Judas Thomas, the Apostle of our Lord, lifted up his voice in praise, and said: "Glorious are you, God of truth and Lord of all natures,** for you wanted with your will and make all your works, and finish all your creatures and bring them to the rule of their nature, and lay upon them all your fear, that they might be subject to your command. And your will trod the path from your secrecy to manifestation, and was caring for every soul that you made, and was spoken of by the mouth of all the prophets, in all visions and sounds and voices; but Israel did not obey because of their evil inclination. And you, because you are Lord of all, have a care for the creatures, so that you spread over us your mercy in him who came by your will and put on the body, your creature, which you wanted and form according to your glorious wisdom. He whom you appointed in your secrecy and establish in your manifestation, to him you have given the name of Son, he who was your will, the power of your thought; so that you are by various names the Father and the Son and the Spirit for the sake of the government of your creatures, for the nourishing of all natures, and you are one in glory and power and will; and you are divided without being separated, and one though divided; and all subsists in you and is subject to you, because all is yours. And I rely upon you, Lord and by your command have subjected these dumb beasts, that you might show your ministering power upon us and upon them, because it is needful, and that your name might be glorified in us and in the beasts that cannot speak". And when he had said these things he said to the wild asses: "Peace be with you, because you have obeyed the Word, the sovereign of all. Let four of you come and be yoked in place of these cattle, which have stood still and are not able to go". And every one of the wild asses crowded round, (striving) which of them should be yoked. And there were some there, that were stronger than their fellows, and these were yoked; and the rest of them went along after and before the Apostle. And when they had proceeded a little way, he said to them: "To you I speak, you inhabitants of the desert; remain behind and go to your pasture; for if I had had occasion for you all, you would all have come. Now then go to the place in which you were". And the wild asses were going along gently, until they were out of sight.

Commentary. **they bowed down to him**. See Testtament Benjamin V 2, ed. Becker 153: "Wenn ihr Gutes tut, werden auch die unreinnen Tiere von euch fliehen, und selbst die wilden Tiere werden euch fürchten". **And Judas Thomas ... that cannot speak**. This passage is not present in Greek. **Lord of all natures**. Here the word "natures" stand for that which has been created. The same meaning in Aphraates, *demonstr.* XXIII 53, ed. Parisot II, c. 111–112 and 58, c. 117–118, see A.F.J.Klijn,, "The Word kejan in Aphraates", in: *Vig. Christ.* 12 1958, 57–60; Bardaisan, *Liber Legum Regionum*, ed. Nau, in: *P.S.* I, c. 680–611: *Et persuasi erunt stulti et defectus implebuntur et erunt pax et requies ex dono Domini omnium naturarum*, and Narsai, *Memra über die Seele* 163, ed, Allgeier 384: "Eine Quelle des Lebens hat der Herr der Naturen in ihre (*scil.* Seele) Natur gelegt. See also ch. 29. **was spoken ... prophets**. See ch. 39. **their evil inclination**, ܪܥܝܢܐ ܒܝܫܐ. See J. Bonsirven, *Le Judaisme Palestinien* II, Paris 1935, 18–23. Also in Aphraates, *demonstr.* III 1, ed Parisot c, 99–100: *Alius ieiuniat ab ira, et cupiditate (ܪܥܝܢ) calcat*, and *demonstr.* XV, c. 743–744: ܘܡܠܠ ܪܥܝܢ ܒܝܫܐ. **put on the body**. See ch. 10. **one in glory and power and will**. See John 17, 5; I Cor. 1, 24 and John 5, 30. **and you are divided ... divided**. ܘܐܬܦܪܫܬܘܢ ܦܠܝܠܬ ܚܕܐ ܡܣܝܡܐ ܘܗܝ ܚܕ ܚܕܥܝܢ. Cf. Ephrem, *de fide* LXXIII 2–8, ed. Beck 192–193 (translation) and 223–224 (Syriac): "Und obwohl nur eine, tritt (dennoch) eine Dreiheit in ihr in die Erscheinung ... Die eine ist eine Mehrheit, die eine ist drei und die drei (sind) die eine ... Gesondert (ܦܪܝܫ) ist die Sonne von ihren Strahl und doch mit ihm vereint ... (Sie sind) nicht abgetrennt (ܚܕܐ ܡܣܝܡܐ) und auch nicht wirr durcheinander; die Gesonderten, Vereinten (sind) verbunden und gelöst ...", see also XL 2, ed. Beck 107 and 130. **that you might be ... cannot speak**. Cf. Ginzberg, *Legends of the Jews* V, 61: "The conception that the animals and all created things chant praise to God is genuinely Jewish and is not only poetically expressed in the Bible (Ps. 65, 14 etc.), but occurs quite frequently in talmudic and midrashic literature".

71

And the Apostle was seated (in the chariot), and the general, and the driver, and the wild asses were going along gently and quickly and little by little, that the Apostle of God might not be shaken. And when they reached the gate of the city, they (*viz.* the asses) distinguished (the house), and went (and) stood before the gate of the court-yard of the general. Then the general was amazed and said: "I am not able to speak and tell what is happening; but let there be another wonder, and then I will tell". And the whole city was coming, because they saw the wild asses which had been yoked to the chariot, and because they heard the report of the Apostle's having gone thither. The Apostle says to the general: "Where is your house? And whither will you conduct us?" The general says to him: "You know that you are standing at the door of your servant, and these (beasts), which by your command are coming with you, know better than I". And when the general had spoken thus, he sprang down from the chariot.

72

And the Apostle began to say: "**Jesus, the knowledge of whom is denied in this country; Jesus, the report of whom is strange in this city; Jesus, a stranger among these men; Jesus, who sends** your Apostle on before to every country and every city, and is glorified in him and made known by him to all those who are **worthy** of it; **Jesus, who put on the body, and becomes man**, and appears to us all, that we might not part from your love; our Lord, **who gave yourself for us, and buy us with your blood and acquire us to yourself, a possession that was dearly bought;—for what have we that we can give to him for his life? For he gave his life for us**. It is not anything that belongs to each one (of us), nor does he ask of us anything save that we should ask of him and live".

Commentary. **Jesus, the knowledge ... stranger among these men**. Greek: "Jesus Christ, that is blasphemed by the ignorance of you in this country, Jesus the report of whom is strange in this city". The Greek version may be original. See for "strange" ch. 4 and for "knowledge" ch. 38. **Jesus, who sends**. Greek: ὁ παραλαμβάνων, which is not clear, see also ch. 1. **worthy**. See ch. 24 and Matth. 10, 13. **Jesus, who put ... man**. See ch. 10. Greek reads: Ἰησοῦ ὁ τύπον λαβὼν καὶ γενό-μενος ὡς ἄνθρωπος. The word τύπος must be the "visible appearance". **who gave ... dearly bought**. Cf. ch. 156 and 158. Influenced by passages like I Cor 6, 20; 7, 23 and Gal. 3,1. The idea that Christ bought with his blood in Rev. 5, 9 only, see R.H. Charles, "The Revelation of St. John" I, in: *Intern. Crit. Comm.*, Edinburgh 1920,147, who mentions the expression ἐν τῷ αἵματί του where the word ἐν refers to the price and shows the influence of Hebrew. It is generally said that this idea does not agree with the structure of Eastern Christianity, see H. Koch, *Pronoia and Paideusis*, Berlin–Leipzig 1932, 75: "In Origen's theology there is no room for "Erlösungs- und Versöhnungstheologie"; E. de Faye, *Origène, sa Vie, son Oeuvre, sa Pensée* III, Paris 1928, 230: "On peut la (*scil.* rédemption biblique) considérer comme une sorte d'annexe de sa (*scil.* Origène) doctrine générale du salut", and H. Berkhof, *Die Theologie des Eusebius von Caesarea*, Amsterdam 1939, 135: "Aber dieser biblisch-exegetische Gedankengang bleibt ein Fremdkörper im Rahmen dieser Theologie". Nevertheless the idea is often met, cf. Clemens, *paedag.* I 23 2 and 49 4; Eusebius, *theophania* IV XXV, ed. Gressmann 203–204, and *demomstr. evangel.*, ed. Heikel 104. 26–108. 27, who quotes Is. 53, 2b–3; *Liber Graduum*, ed. Kmosko c. 235–236: ... *et sanguine crucifixionis sane pacavit quae in terra et in caelo; Evangelium Veritatis* 20. 13–14 ed. Robinson 39: "... Jesus was patient in accepting sufferings ... since he knows, that his death is life for many"; Manich. Ps. 21. 12–13: "Thou put off (?) your glory and gave yourself up to death for souls, you gave yourself up to the enemy that your blood might be shed, in order that you might save us from the Darkness". **For what ... life?** Cf. Matth. 16, 26. **For he gave ... us**. Cf. John 10, 11.

73

And when he had said these things, many were coming from every place to see the Apostle of the new God, who had come thither. And Judas said: "**Why stand we here and are idle? Jesus, what do you want? Command the time, and let the deed be (done)**". Then the demons were sore upon the woman and her daughter, and the servants of the general did not think that they would last, for they did not suffer them to eat anything, but kept them constantly lying in bed, without being recognized by anyone, until the day whom the Apostle came thither. **And the Apostle said to one of the wild asses which were yoked on the right hand**: "Go into the court-yard, and, standing there, call those demons and say to them: 'Judas the Apostle, the disciple of Jesus the Messiah, says, Come out hither, because on your account I have been sent and against your kindred, that I might drive you to your own place, **ere the time** of the consummation comes and you go **to your pit**'".

Commentary. **Jesus, what ... be (done)**. Thomas cannot do anything without the direction of Christ, see ch. 9; 29 and 39. **And the Apostle ... right hand**. In the History of Phillip, Syriac ed. Wright 88, an ox is asked to raise a dead man. **ere the time**, ܐܡܬܐ and Greek: ἕως ὅτε. The Greek has to be translated by "until", which agrees with ch. 33, where it is said that the struggle between Christ and the devil is still going on. The Syriac text is ambiguous because ܥܕܡܐ can both mean "until" and "ere", but the second translation agrees with the contents of ch. 33. **in your pit**. Cf. ch. 55 in the Greek version: "to your own deep darkness".

74

And the wild ass went in, a crowd of people being with him, and said: "To you I speak, you enemies of mankind; to you I speak who close your eyes to the light that you may not see, **for the nature of evil cannot be with good**; to you I speak, offspring of Gehenna and **Abbadon**, children of him who has never been forced to keep quiet until to-day, of him who **produces afresh evil servants that suit his nature**; to you I speak, audacious wretches, who are to perish by your own hands. And what I should say concerning your end, I know not; and what I should tell, I am unable (to utter); for these things are too great for hearing and have no limit, for however great your bodies may be, **they are too small for your retribution**. To you I speak, demon, and to your son, who accompanies you, for now I am sent hither against you. Why do I go on speaking at great length of your **nature?** For you know (it) better than I, and are audacious. But now Judas Thomas, the disciple of Jesus the Messiah, this (man) who has been sent hither with mercy and grace, says: 'Come forth to this crowd, which, lo, is standing here, and tell me of what **race** you are'".

Commentary. **for the nature ... good**. See ch. 29. **Abbadon**, See Rev. 9, 11. **produces ... nature**. See ch. 29. **they are too small ... retribution**. The Greek version reads: "and greater are your doings than the torment that is reserved for you". **nature**. See ch. 29. Greek reads: τῆς ὑμῖν φύσεως τε καὶ ῥίζης. The word "root" has the same meaning as "race" or "origin", see *Acta Johannis* 98, in: L.B. II I 200. 14–16: σατανᾶς καὶ κάτωτικη ῥίζα ἄφες and 114, 214. 11–12: ὅλη ἡ ῥίζα αὐτοῦ ἀπορρηθήτω. This word is important in Gnosticism, cf. *Evangelium Veritatis* 41. 14–19, ed. Robinson 48: "Therefore, all the emanations of the Father are pleromas, and the root of all his emanations is in the one who makes them all grow up in himself ..."; Mand. Liturg. 506. 53–54: "Er heb mich zum Ort des Lebens empor, wo meine Wurzel vorher stand"; Johannesbuch 218. 10–11: "Meine Wurzel vom Leben ...", and Ginza R. 370. 24–25. See Jonas, *Gnosis* I, 232–233. **race**, ܓܢܣܐ and Greek: γένος see ch. 31 end.

75

And at that moment the woman and her daughter came out, like to the dead in appearance, and exposed, and disgraced. And when the Apostle saw them, he was grieved for them, and said: "**No pity has been shown to you; on this account you are scarcely conscious**. But in the name of Jesus the Messiah depart from them, and stand beside them". And when the Apostle had uttered this speech, the women **fell down and (to all appearance) died**, for there was no breath in them, nor did they utter any sound. And the demon cried with a loud voice and said: "You have come again, rebuker of our **nature! You have come here again, destroyer of our race!** You have come here again, effacer of our footsteps! And as I see, you do not wish to let us remain on earth; **but you are not able at this time to do this to us**".

Commentary. **No pity ... scarcely conscious**. Wright speaks about "mere guess-work". 211, n. b. Syriac reads: ܦܠܚ ܟܐܘ ܟܝܡܘ ܟܐܘ ܟܠ ܚܕܟܝ ܡܣܚܕܠ ܟܐܘܟ ܟܝܗ ܠܝ܂ and Greek: μὴ γένοιτο ἱλασμὸν γενέσθαι καὶ φειδὼ εἰς ὑμᾶς οὐδὲ γὰρ τὸ φείδεσθαι ἢ τὸ ἐλεεῖν ἐπίστασθε, which seems to be clear. If we read ܠܚܣܚܡ instead of ܠܚܣܚܡ which agrees with Sachau, we get: "no pity will be shown to you on this account that you do not know to spare". **Fell ... died**. Cf. Mark 9, 26. **nature ... race**. See ch. 29. **but you are ... to us**. This is contrary to the idea usually found in these Acts, see ch. 33.

76

And Judas percieved that it was the demon whom he had driven out of that (other) woman". And he said to him: "I beg of you, then, give me leave, (and) I will go whither you please (and) dwell (there); and I will **take orders** from you, and not be afraid of him who has authority over me; for as you have come to visit (and do good), so have I come to destroy; and as you, if you do not accomplish the will of him who sent you, are reproved, so I too, unless I do the will of him who sent me, go before the time to our **nature**; and as your Lord helps you in the things which you do, (so) too my father supports me in the things which I do; **and as he prepares for you vessels which are worthy for him to dwell in, so too he makes me aware of the vessels which obey him, that I may do in them his will**; and as he nourishes and provides for you and for those who obey you, so also does he torture me, and torment me and those in whom I dwell, and as to you he gives the reward of your work, that is to say life everlasting, (so) also to me he gives the recompense of my deeds, everlasting perdition; and as you take pleasure in your prayers and in your good works, and in the Eucharist, and in his chants of praise and psalms and hymns, so I too take pleasure in murder and adultery, and in sacrifices and **libations** of wine on the altars, and as you turn men to everlasting life, so I too turn men to me, to everlasting perdition and torment; and you receive your **reward, and I mine**".

Commentary. **take orders**. Cf. Mark 4, 10 and par. passages. **nature**. See ch. 29. **and as he prepares ... his will**. Like in ch. 43 and 44 Christ and the devil are opposites. For "worthy" see ch. 24. The word "vessel" can be compared with the use of "temple" in, for example, ch. 12, cf. *Acta Petri* VII, in: L.B. I I, 56. 11–13: *tenebrarum abyssus quae habes tenebras tuae tecum sint et cum vasis tuis quae possides*; IV Ezra 7. 80, where the "vessel of mortality" is the same as the body; Barnabas VII 3 and XII 9; Hermas, *mand.* V II 5, and Irenaeus, *adv. haer.* I 23 3, about Simon Magus: *ennoia ... veluti de vase in vas transmigraret in altera muliebra corpora*. One can be an instrument of God or the devil, see ch. 32; 45 and 46. **libations of wine**. Cf. Acts of John, Syriac ed. Wright, 4: "... it is necessary ... to teach all those who, in the worshipping of idols and with libations to devils, have kneeled before images ... (and) worshipped the accursed demons, the children of the left hand". In this way Christians are used to speak about heathen offerings, cf. Justin the Martyr, *apol.* I 66 4: ὅπερ καὶ ἐν τοῖς τοῦ μίθρα μυστηρίοις παρέδωκεν γίνεσθαι μιμησάμενοι οἱ πονηροὶ δαίμονες ὅτι γὰρ ἄρτος καὶ ποτήριον ὕδατος τίθεται ἐν ταῖς τοῦ μυουμένου τελεταῖς μετ' ἐπιλόγων τινῶν ἢ ἐπίστασθε ἢ μαθεῖν δύνασθε and Tertullian, *de praescriptione* 40: *celebrat (Mithras) panis oblationem*. **reward, and I mine**. Greek: "your own and I mine", see ch. 32.

77

And when the demon had said these things, the Apostle said: "To you and to your son Jesus says by me, that you shall not again enter the habitation of men, but go (and) dwell without the entire habitation of men". And the demons say to him: "Lo, we go, as you have commanded us; but what will you do to those who are hidden from you, and their vessels rejoice in them more than in you,—those whom many worship and do their will, sacrificing to them and pouring out to them wine as a libation, and offering to them offerings?" The Apostle says: "They too shall perish in the end with their worshippers". And the demons were sought and were not found, but the women were lying (there) as if dead, without a word.

Commentary. The idea that paganism really means the adoration of demons goes back to Jewish sources, cf. Eth. Hen. 19, 1, ed. Uhlig 551, and Deut. 32, 17 (LXX): ἔθυσαν δαιμονίοις καὶ οὐ θεῷ cf. also Jub. 11, 3f and 19, 28.

78

And the wild asses were standing one beside the other, and were not moving away from one another; but the one to whom speech was given by the power of our Lord, was standing in front of his fellows. And when all the people were silent and looking on him, that they might see what the Apostle would do, the wild ass looked on them all, and said to Judas: "Why do you stand (there) and are you idle, Apostle of the Most High? For, lo, the **Paraclete** is standing beside you and looking that you should ask him and he would give to you. Why do you delay, good disciple? For lo, your Master wishes to show great things through you. Why do you stand (there), preacher of the **Hidden?** For lo, your Master wishes **to disclose his hidden nature** through you to those who are **worthy** of him that they may hear these things. Why are you still, worker of miracles in the name of your Lord! **For lo, your Lord is standing by and encouraging you**. Fear not; **for he will not abandon you, and his godhead will not suffer your manhood to be grieved**. Begin, therefore, to call upon him, and he will answer you, as he is wont at all times. Why does amazement seize you at his manifold doings? For these are small things which he has shown through you; and if you were to tell of the number of his gifts, you would not be able to make an end of them. Why are you astonished concerning these **his bodily healings, (which are) ended by dissolution**, when you remember his healings of his possessions, which is not ended by dissolution? Why do you ponder on this temporal life, when, lo, you can reflect every day on the life everlasting?

Commentary. **Paraclete,** ܦܪܩܠܛܐ. The word is found in John 14, 16. 25; 15, 26; 16,7 and I John 2, 1, and often in *Liber Graduum*, ed. Kmosko, see Register p. 1077. **For lo, your Lord ... encouraging you.** In the Greek version: "For your Lord encourages you and engenders boldness in you". See for "boldness" ch. 25. **Hidden.** God is hidden, see ch. 39. **to disclose ... nature.** God is seen in his works, see ch. 10. **worthy.** See ch. 24. **for he will not ... grieved.** In the Greek version: "for he will not forsake the soul that belongs to you by race, κατὰ γένος". This means that the soul of the woman belongs to the same race as that of Thomas. The soul is the incorruptible part of man and can be saved, see ch. 30. **his bodily healings ... dissolutions.** The body is the corruptible part of man.

79

But to you, I say, you multitudes, who, lo, are standing by and waiting to see these arise who, lo, are lying here; believe in the **teacher of verity**, and believe in the **shewer of truths**; believe in the **revealer of secrets**; believe in the demonstrator of life; believe in the Apostle of the tried Son, Jesus the Messiah, who was **born**, that the born might live by his birth; and was reared that the perfect rearing might be seen in him; and **went to school that through him perfect wisdom might be known; he taught his teacher, because he was the teacher of verity and the master of the wise**; he went to the temple and offered an **offering**, that they might see that all offerings are sanctified in him. This is the Apostle of him; this is the Apostle of truth; this is the doer of the will of him that sent him. But there shall be a time when **false apostles** shall come, and **lying prophets**, whose end shall be like their works; who will say to you 'Beware of sins', whilst they at all times utter sins; who will put on the **clothing of lambs, whilst within they are ravening wolves**; who will not take one wife legally, but by their words and their deeds will corrupt many women; who will not beget children, but will corrupt many children, and pay the penalty for them; who will be distressed at the happiness of others, and will take pleasure in their distress; to whom what they possess will not suffice, but who will desire that all things should serve them, and will boast of them, and be esteemed as disciples of the Messiah; in whose mouth is one thing, and in their heart another; who teach that you should shun hateful things, but themselves do not even a single good thing; before whom **adultery is hateful and theft and**

oppression, and greed, but in themselves secretly these are all done, whilst they teach that a man should not do them".

Commentary. **teacher of verity**, ܪܕܐܘܢ ܪܘܠܕ. The word ܪܕܘܢ is used to render ἀλήθεια in Matth. 22, 16 and Luke 20, 23 in syr p, s and c and in John 1, 24 in syr p. **shewer of truths**, ܪܕܘܕ. Here the word ܪܘܕ has been used which renders ἀλήθεια in John 1, 14 in syr c and phil. See also ch. 2. **revealer of secrets**. See ch. 10. **born**. See ch. 143. **and went to school ... master of the wise**. The influence of Luke 1, 46 may be assumed, but cf. *Evangelium Veritatis* 19. 18–20, ed. Robinson 39: "He went into the midst of the school (and) he spoke the word as a teacher", and see also The Infancy Gospel of Thomas 6–7, ed. Elliott 76–77. **offering**. This might refer to Luke 2, 23–24. **false apostles**. Cf II Cor 11, 13. **lying prophets**. Cf. Acts 13, 6; I John 4, 1; Rev. 16, 13; 19, 20 and 20, 10. **clothing of lambs ... wolves**. See Matth. 7, 15. **adultery ... greed**. See ch. 28.

80

And when he spoke these things, all the wild asses were looking at him. And when he was silent, Judas said: "What am I to think of your servant, Jesus? **And how am I to call you, I know not**. O (you) **gentle** and **silent** and still and speaking! (You) **seer, that are in the heart, and searcher, that are in the mind!** Glory to you, (you) gracious (one)! Glory to you, **living word!** Glory to you, (you) **hidden (one), who has many forms!** Glory to your mercy, which has abounded to us. Glory to your grace which has been upon us! **Glory to your greatness**, which became small for us! Glory to your exaltation, which was humbled for us! Glory to your strength, which became feeble for us! Glory to your godhead, which for us put on manhood! Glory to your manhood, which was made new for us, and died for us to give life! Glory to your resurrection from the grave, that we might have a resurrection and a raising up! Glory to your ascension to heaven, by which **you did treat for us the road (leading) up on high!** And you promised and swore to us, that we should **sit on the right hand and on the left**, and should be **judges** with you. You are the word of heaven. You are the **hidden light of the understanding, and the study of the path of truth**, the **dispeller of darkness** and the **destroyer of error**".

Commentary. **And how am I ... I know not.** See ch. 48. **gentle,** ‏ܪܟܝܟܐ‎ see Matth. 11, 30. **silent,** ‏ܫܠܝܐ‎, see Matth. 22, 19 and 27, 12. **still,** ‏ܫܠܝܐ‎, see Matth. 11,30. **seer, that are ... mind.** Cf. Matth. 9, 4; 12, 25; Luke 6, 8; 11,17 and Hebr. 4,12. **living word.** Cf. John 1, 1ff. **hidden (one) who has many forms.** See ch. 48. **Glory to your greatness ...** In ch. 47 contrasts have been summed up between Jesus' godhead and manhood. Here his greatness and humiliation are emphasized. Cf. Ephrem, *sermo de Domino nostro,* ed. Lamy I, c. 252–256: *Non repulit ominus peccatricem, ut arbitrabatur pharisaeus, quia prorsus descendit ex altitudine illa ad quam homo attingere nequit, ut cum attingere possunt publicani pusilli, qualis fuit Zachaeus, quia natura quae attrectari nequit corpus induit, ut non peccatricis tantum sed omnium labia pedes eius osculari possunt.* The same is found in ch. 143. This adaptation of Christ to man is often found in ancient Christian literature cf. Barnabas V 10: εἰ γὰρ μὴ ἦλθεν ἐν σαρκί πῶς ἂν ἐσώθησαν οἱ ἄνθρωποι βλέποντες αὐτόν; Ignatius, *ad Polyc.* 3. 2: τὸν ὑπὲρ καιρὸν προσδόκα, τὸν ἄχρονον, τὸν ἀόρατον, τὸν δι᾽ ἡμᾶς ὁρατόν ... Clemens, *stromateis* VII 8 6: οὐ γὰρ ὃ ἦν τοῦτο ὤφθη τοῖς χωρῆσαι μὴ δυναμένοις διὰ τὴν ἀσθένειαν τῆς σαρκός, αἰσθητὴν δὲ ἀναλαβὼν σάρκα τὸ δυνατὸν ἀνθρώποις κατὰ τὴν ὑπακοὴν τῶν ἐντολῶν δείξων ἀφίκετο; Origen, *c. Celsum* II 64 and 67; *in Matth.* XIII 2: καὶ ἰησοῦς γοῦν φησί διὰ τοὺς ἀσθενοῦντας ἠσθένουν καὶ διὰ τοὺς πεινῶντας ἐπείνων, καὶ διὰ τοὺς διψῶντας ἐδίψων; Nest. Taufliturgie, ed. Diettrich 51: "Preis, Ehre ... bringen wir dar, du Höher, der herabstieg und den Leib unserer Erniedrigung anzog und uns Eins machte mit sich in allen Stücken seiner Gottheit", and Irenaeus, *adv. haer.* I 15 3, about the Marcosians: σάρκα περιβάλλετο ἵνα εἰς τὴν αἴσθησιν τοῦ ἀνθρώπου κατελθῇ **you did treat ... on high.** See ch. 10. **sit on the right ... left.** Greek omits "left hand". See for "left" and "right", Matth. 20, 21. **judges.** See Matth. 19, 28 and Barnabas VII 2. **hidden light of the understanding.** Cf Justin Martyr, *dial. c. Tr.* CXXI 2: ... ὁ τῆς ἀληθείας καὶ σοφίας λόγος ... εἰς τὰ βάθη τῆς καρδίας καὶ τοῦ νοῦ εἰσδύνων **study of the path of truth.** The word "study", ‏ܡܘܟܟܐ‎, has been rendered into ὑποδεικνύων in the Greek version. The word means "humility", see ch. 20. In ch. 48 Christ was called "Nazir", which is a similar idea. **dispeller of darkness.** See ch. 28, cf. Bardaisan, in: Moses bar Kepha (quoted in Nau, *Patr. Syr.* I II, 514–515): *Tunc ad vocem tumultus huius descendit verbum cogitationis Altissimi quod est Christus et praecidit tenebras illas a medio entium mundorum.* **destroyer of error.** See ch. 25.

81

And when the Apostle had said these things, he came and stood over those women who were lying (there), and said: "**My Lord and my God**, Jesus the Messiah, I doubt not regarding you, but I call upon you, as at all times you are aiding us and support us and encourage us. You **giver of freedom of speech and of joy to your servant and Apostle**, let these (women) be healed and arise, and let them be as they were before they were smitten by the demons". And when he had said these things, the women turned over, and sat up healed. And Judas commanded the general that his servants should take them and lead them in and **give them food**, for they had not eaten for many days. And when they had taken them and led them in, he said to the wild asses, "Follow me". And they went after him until he had brought them without the gate. And when they had gone out, he said to them: "Go in peace in your pasture". And the wild asses were going along gently, and the Apostle was standing and looking at them, lest perchance any man should hurt them, until they had got out of his sight and were no longer visible to him.

Here ends the eighth Act

Commentary. **My Lord and my God**. See ch. 10. **giver of freedom of speech**, ܪܚܘܬܐ and Greek: παρρησία, see ch. 24. **giver ... Apostle**. Greek reads: "who is breathing your own power into us and encourages us and gives confidence in love to your own servants". Cf. John 20, 22. **give them food**. Cf. Mark 5, 43.

82

And Judas returned from (accompanying) them, and went to the house of the general, and a great multitude with him. And it happened that a woman, (the wife) of a kinsman of the king, whose name was **Mygdonia**, had come to see the new sight of the new God who was preached, and the new Apostle, who had come to their country; **and she was sitting in a palanquin,** and her servants were carrying her. And because of the great press that there was, they were unable to bring her near to him; and she sent to her husband, and he sent his officers, and they were going before her, and pressing back the people. And the Apostle saw (this) and said to them: "Why do you ill-treat these (people), who are coming to hear the word? And (why are) you anxious that they should pass on, and you yourselves wish to come to me, being very far off? For our Lord said to these multitudes who were coming to him: '**Ears you have, and you hear not**, and eyes you have, and you see not', and (he also said): '**Come to me, all you that are weary and bearing burdens, and I will give you rest**'".

Commentary. **Mygdonia**, ܡܘܓܕܢܝܐ, and Greek: μυγδονία. She is mentioned in Manich. Ps. 193. 2–3 in a corrupt passage: "Mygdonia in the land (χώρα) of India." The name is known from that part of Mesopotamia in which Nisibis is situated. **and she was sitting … palanquin**. The Greek version omits this passage. In Syriac the word ܟܘܪܣܝܐ has been used. See also Krauss, *Talmud. Archäol.* II, 330–332. **Ears … see not**. A quotation taken from Mark 8, 18, which only slightly deviates in both the Syriac and Greek version from the accepted text. Greek adds a quotation taken from Matth. 11, 15 after "and he said to the multitudes". **Come … rest**. Taken from Matth. 11, 28, also in agreement with the accepted text in both Syriac and Greek.

83

And he looked upon those men, and said: "Now the blessing that was given to these falls to the share of you who are carrying; for you are bearing a **heavy burden**, and she directs you by her command. Though God has made you men, men make you carry a heavy load like beasts; and those who are borne on you, think in their minds that you are not men like to them, and do not know that all men are **equal before God, whether they be slaves or free**; and righteous is the judgment of God, which shall come on all souls that are on the earth, and no man shall escape from it, neither slaves nor free, nor rich nor poor. Those who have, shall not be profited aught thereby; and those who have not, shall not be delivered by their poverty from this judgment. For we are not commanded to do anything which we are unable to do, **nor to take up heavy burdens, nor to build buildings, which carpenters build for themselves with wisdom, nor (to practice) the art of hewing stones, which stonecutters know as their craft; but (we are commanded to do) something which we can do.**

Commentary. **heavy burden**, ܩܘܒܠܐ ܝܩܝܪܬܐ, see Luke 11, 46. **equal before God … free**. Cf. Gal. 3, 28. The manuscript Sinai is present from "build for themselves" until ch. 85: "who are nigh to it". **nor to take up heavy … we can do**. Greek reads: "nor has he laid on us burdens grievous to be borne which we are not able to carry, nor building which man build; nor to hew stones and prepare houses, as your craftsmen do by their own knowledge. But this commandment have we received of the Lord, that that which does not please us when it is done by another, this we should not do to any other man". Sinai reads: "… build for themselves, nor to practice the art of hewing stones, which stone-cutters know as their craft; but we are commanded (to do) something; that we should not do anything against anyone" (doubtful reading). This is also found with Bardaisan, *Liber Legum Regionum*, ed. Nau, in: *Patrol. Syr.* I II, c. 533: *Non enim jubemur sustinere magna onera lapidum aut lignorum aut aliquid huius modi, id quod tantum efficere possunt illi qui potentes sunt corpore; neque aedificare arces, neque condere urbes, id quod reges tantum efficere possunt,* and in *Liber Graduum*, ed. Kmosko, in: *Patrol. Syr.* I III, c. 851–852: *Non enim iubemur lapides caedere aut lateras formare aut aedificia aedificare, quae cras corruunt aut evanescunt, neque opes comparare et thesauros thesaurare in terra, quae brevi tempore durant, quoniam aut non morimur et opes nostrae manent in terra, aut ipsae intereunt et nos in terra reliquunt.* See for the negative Golden Rule in the Greek version G. Resch, "Das Aposteldekret nach seiner ausserkanonischen Textgestalt", in *Texte u. Unters.* 38 1905, and R.H. Connolly, "Negative Golden Rule in the

Syriac Acts of Thomas", in: *Journ. of Theol. Studies* 36 1935, 353–356.
Also in Aristides, *apol.* XV 5, ed. Goodspeed 20: ὅσα οὐ θέλουσιν αὐτοῖς
γίνεσθαι ἑτέρῳ οὐ πολοῦσι; Ginza R. 22. 42–43: "Alles, was euch selbst
verhasst ist, tue auch eurem Nächsten nicht"; Johannesbuch 175. 13–14
and Gospel of Thomas *l.* 6.

84

To refrain from **fornication, the head of all evils; and from
murder, by reason of which the curse came upon Cain**; and
from **theft, which brought Judas Iscariot to hanging**; and from
gluttony, which removed Esau from his birthright; and from
covetousness, to which when one is subject, he does not consider what
he does; and from vain-glory, and from destroying slander; and from
evil actions and from **deeds of shame**, and from hateful intercourse
and unclean connexion, in which there is eternal **condemnation**; and
this it is that seizes the uplifted by force, and casts them down to the
lowest depth, and brings them under its power, so that they cannot
discern what they do, and their works become hidden from them.

Commentary. See for the list starting with **fornication** ch. 28. **fornication ... evils**. See Test. of Simeon 5. 1: ἡ πορνεία μήτηρ ἐστὶ τῶν κακῶν
and Jubil. 33. 20: "And there is no greater sin than fornication which
they commit on earth". **murder ... Cain**. Sinai reads: "which brought
the curse upon Adam". This seems a mistake. Greek omits. In ch. 32
it was noticed that Adam has been omitted in this kind of summary.
gluttony ... birthright.. See Gen. 25, 31–34. **theft ... hanging**. See
ch. 32 and Acts 1, 18. **deeds of shame**. Sexual intercourse, see ch. 14.
condemnation. Sinai adds: "and this is the mother which still trem-
bles", ܐܝܟܐ ܠܒܬܐ ܐܡܟ ܗܘ ܗܝ. According to Smith Lewis 228, n. 1,
the reading is doubtful and must have been: ܐܟܠܠܒܐ ܐܡܟ ܗܘ ܗܝ cf.
the Greek version: ἔστιν γὰρ αὔτη ἡ μητρόπολις τῶν κακῶν ἁπάντων.

85

But hear me, and conduct yourselves with **purity**, which is chosen
before God more than all good things; and with **temperance**, for it
shows us intercourse with God, and gives eternal life. And also conduct
yourselves with **humility, for this is weighed with every (virtue),
and is heavy, and outweighs (them)**, and gains the crown; and

with **gentleness**, and stretching out of the hand to the poor, and supplying the wants of the needy; but especially it behoves you to conduct yourselves with purity, for this is chosen before God, and makes (us) enter into everlasting life, for it is the head of all the virtues, and **by it are done all good works**; for he who is not purified, is unable to do anything good, because all the virtues are after this of purity. For purity is seen of God, and destroys evil. Purity is pleasing to God; therefore it proceeds from him. Purity is the athlete who is not overcome. Purity is the truth that blenches not. Purity is the tower that falls not. Purity is worthy before God of being to him **a familiar handmaiden**. Purity is comeliness when it is found with many. Purity destroys corruption. Purity is the messenger of concord, which brings the tidings of peace. Temperance sets him who acquires it free from daily cares. Temperance cares for nothing but how it may be found pleasing to its Lord. Temperance holds on by hope, awaiting deliverance. Temperance sits at all times in tranquillity, because it does nothing that is odious. Temperance seeks a life of rest, and is a joy to all who acquire it, and exalts those who are nigh to it.

Commentary. In Greek the chapter reads: "But do you become well-pleasing to God in all good things, in meekness and quietness; for these God spares, and grants eternal life and sets death at nought. And in gentleness (which) follows on all good things, and overcomes all enemies and alone receives the crown of victory; with quietness and stretching out of the hand to the poor, and supplying the want of the needy, and distributing to them that are in necessity, especially them that walk in holiness. For this is chosen before God and leads to eternal life; for this is before God the chief city of all good; for they that strive not in the course of Christ shall not obtain holiness. And holiness did appear from God, doing away fornication, overthrowing the enemy, well-pleasing to God; for she is the invincible champion, having honour from God, glorified of many; she is an ambassador of peace, announcing peace; if any gain her he abides withour care, pleasing the Lord, expecting the time of redemption; for she does nothing amiss, but gives life and rest and joy all that gain her". **purity**, ܟܐܘܬܐ, **temperance**, ܢܟܦܘܬܐ, Greek: ἡσυχία **humility**, ܡܟܝܟܘܬܐ, Greek: πρᾳότης **gentleness**, ܒܣܝܡܘܬܐ, Greek: ἐπιείκεια. For a similar catalogue of virtues, cf. Midr. Song of Songs I I 19, ed. M. Simon 11: "R. Phinehas b. Jair used to say: 'Zeal leads to cleanliness; cleanliness leads to purity; purity leads to holiness; holiness leads to humility; humility leads to the fear of sin; the fear of sin leads to saintliness; saintliness leads to the Holy Spirit; the Holy Spirit leads to the resurrection of the dead; the resurrection of the dead leads to Elijah the prophet'" The word **purity** means sexual continence, see A. Vööbus, "Celibacy, a Requirement for Admission to baptism in the early Syrian Church". in: *Papers Est. Theol. Soc. in Exile*, Stockholm 1951, 22–23. According to P. Schwen, "Afrahat", in: *Neue Stud. z. Gesch. der Theol. u. Kirche* II 1907, 132, the word ܩܕܝܫܘܬܐ has to be taken in the sence of sexual abstinence of those married and the word virginity ܒܬܘܠܘܬܐ in the sense of sexual abstinence of the unmarried ones. See also J. v.d. Ploeg, *Oud-Syrisch Monniksleven*, Leiden 1942, and R. Asting, "Die Heiligkeit im Urchristentum", in: *Forsch. z. Rel. u. Lit. des A. u. N.T.* 46 1930. See also ch. 20. The word **temperance**, see also ch. 20 and 80, means an ascetic life, cf. ch. 86: "And temperance is the rest of God; for our Lord fasted …". In *Liber Graduum* X 9, ed. Kmosko, in: *Patrol. Syr.* I II, the word is found with *ieiunium*; in XX 6, c. 265–266, with *humilitas, renunciatio, caritas, sanctitas*, and in XX 6, c. 539–540, with *renunciatio, sanctitas, humilitas*. **humility … outweighs (them)**. Syriac reads: ܡܟܝܟܘܬܐ ܗܝ ܝܬܝܪ ܡܢ ܟܠܡܕܡ ܕܐܬܬܩܠ, ܟܕ which has probably to be translated by: "Humility is heavier than all that is weighed". The same in *Liber Graduum* XXI 12, ed. Kmosko, *Patrol. Syr.* I III, c. 617–620: ܚܟܝܡܘܬܐ ܡܢ ܟܠ ܕܐܬܬܩܠ ܡܗ, ܛܥܝܢ *humilitas omnibus pensitata praependit*, see also ch. 86. **gentleness**. The word is found in Col. 3, 12: χρη-στότητα—ταπεινοφροσύνην—πραΰτητα, in syr p: ܡܣܟܢܘܬܐ ܘܡܟܝܟܘܬܐ ܘܢܝܚܘܬܐ. **by it … all good works**. See *Liber Graduum* XXVIII 8, ed. Kmosko *Patrol. Syr.* I III, c. 831–832: *et humilitate fiunt omnia bona opera*. **a familiar handmaiden**. Sinai reads: ܩܕܝܫܘܬܐ ܠܐܠܗܐ ܫܘܝܐ ܕܬܗܘܐ, "Holiness is worthy to belong to God".

86

Humility has subdued death and brought him under its power. Humility has conquered enmity. Humility is the **pleasant yoke, and does not fatigue those who bear it**. Humility does not fear anything, for it is rude to none. Humility is concord and peace and joy and rest. Acquire purity, and take to you temperance and strive after humility; for by these **three cardinal virtues** is typified this Messiah, whom I preach. For purity is the **temple of God**, and every one who guards it, guards his temple and the Messiah dwells in him. And temperance is the rest of God; for our Lord fasted **forty days and forty nights**, and tasted nothing; and the Messiah dwells in him who observes it.

And humility is a mighty power; for our Lord said to Simon the Apostle: **'Return your sword back (to its sheath); if I am willing to ask strength of my Father, he will give me more than twelve legions of angels"**.

Commentary. **pleasant yoke ... bear it**. Cf. Matth. 11, 28–30. **three cardinal virtues**. These virtues are also mentioned in ch. 94; 126 and 130. In ancient Christian literature the words πραΰς and ἡσύχιος, πραΰτης and ἡσυχία are often used, cf. I Peter 3, 4; Hermas, *mand.* V 2 6, XI 8 1, *vis.* 5 2 3; 6 2 3; I Clem. 13. 4 and Barnabas 19. 4. The influence of Is. 66, 2 (LXX) can not be excluded: καὶ ἐπὶ τίνα ἐπιβλέψω ἀλλ' ἢ ἐπὶ τὸν ταπεινὸν καὶ ἡσύχιον τρέμοντα λόγους μου. The addition of the idea "purity" is characteristic for these Acts. One may compare Gal. 5, 23: πραΰτης, ἐγκράτεια, but the manuscripts D G and the Old Latin version add ἀγνεία See also Jonas, *Gnosis* II, 23–24: "Es sind (μετάνοια, ὑπακοή etc. and ταπεινοφροσύνη) nicht Tugenden, sondern ... praktische Ausserungen des Insuffizientsbewusstsein der Entweltlichungstendenz". **temple of God**. Cf. I Cor. 6, 18–19. **forty days and forty nights**. See Matth. 4, 2 **Return ... (to its sheath)**. Syriac reads: ܝܗܘܣܐ ܗܦܘܟ ܠܟܢܝܐ Syr p in Matth. 26, 52: ܠܕܘܟܬܗ ܣܝܦܐ ܗܦܘܟ which agrees with syr s, but reading ܣܝܦܐ. Greek reads: ἀπόστρεψεν τὴν μαχαιράν εἰς τὰ ὀπίσω, which deviates from the New Testament reading: ... εἰς τὸν τόπον αυτῆς. **if I am willing ... angels**. Syriac reads: ܐܢܐ ܨܒܐ ܐܢܐ ܐܢ ܕܐܫܐܠ ܚܝܠܐ ܡܢ ܐܒܝ ܗܐ ܡܢ ܥܣܪܝܢ ܘܬܪܝܢ ܠܓܝܘܢܝܢ ܕܡܠܐܟܐ ܝܗܒ ܠܝ and the Greek version: εἰ γὰρ ἤθελεν τοῦτο ποιῆσαι, μὴ οὐκ ἠδυνάμην πλέον ἢ δώδεκα λεγεῶνας παρὰ τοῦ πατρός μου παραστῆσαι ἀγγέλων which is a free rendering of Matth. 26, 53. It seems that the Greek text has been based upon the Syriac version, but has been adapted to the common Greek text.

87

And when Judas had said these things, all the multitudes were listening together, and trampling on one another. And the wife of **Karish**, the kinsman of king **Mazdai**, sprang up and came out of the palanquin, and fell down on the ground before the feet of the Apostle, and was begging of him and saying to him: "I beg of you, you Apostle of the new God, who has come to a desert place from the habitation of men—for we dwell in a desert, because we live like the beasts that have no speech, and now, lo, we are being tamed by your hands,—that you would turn to me too, and pray for me that I also may obtain grace from this God whom you preach, **and that I may become a handmaiden of him**, and that I too may be united with you in prayer and in hope and in thanksgiving, and that I too may become **a holy temple** and he may dwell in me".

Commentary. **Karish**, ܟܪܝܫ and Greek: χαϱισίος. See Pauly–Wissowa II 1899, c. 2146–2149. The name is well known. **Mazdai**. ܡܙܕܝ, Greek: μισδαῖος and Latin: *Mesdaeus.* The name is known from a Satrap in Western Cilicia during the reign of Artaxerxes III (from A.D. 362). See also Pauly–Wissowa XXIX 1931, 1–2, and Justi, *Iran. Namenbuch* 201. **palanquin**. Greek: δίφϱον, see ch. 62. **and that I may become a handmaiden of him**, ܐܘܬ ܗܘܐ ܠܗ ܒܝܬ ܡܥܡܪܐ and Greek: κἀγὼ γένωμαι αὐτοῦ οἰκτήϱιον which may be due to an error of the Greek translator. **sign**. See ch. 26. **a holy temple**. See ch. 12.

88

The Apostle says: "I pray and beg of you, my brothers in our Lord and my sisters in the Messiah, that **the word of the Messiah may dwell in you all** and abide in you, because **you are given power over your own souls**". And he began to say to the woman: "**Mygdonia, arise from the ground, and be mindful of yourself, and be not concerned about your ornaments, which pass away, nor about the beauty of your person, which perishes, nor about your dress, nor about this name and dignity in the world that passes away; and do not degrade yourself to this filthy intercourse, and be deprived of the true fellowship. For ornaments perish, and beauty becomes old and marred, and clothes decay, and power passes away, (accompanied) with punishment, according to how each person has conducted himself in it, and marriage passes away with much contempt. Jesus alone abides**, and those who hope in him and take **refuge** (with him), and deliver up themselves to him". And when he had said these things, he said to the woman: "Go in peace, and may our Lord make you **worthy of his divine mysteries**". She says to him: "I am afraid to go, lest you leave me and depart to **another place**". The Apostle says to her: "Jesus will not abandon you for his mercy's sake. And she bowed down and prostrated herself before him, because **she thought he was Jesus**; and she went home rejoicing.

Commentary. **the world of the ... in you**. Cf. Col. 3, 16: ὁ λόγος τοῦ Χριστοῦ ἐνοικείτω ἐν ὑμῖν, and Odes of Sol. 12. 12: "For the dwelling place of the Word is man ...". **you are given ... souls**. See ch. 34. **arise from the ground**. See ch. 37. **Mygdonia arise ... with much contempt**. See ch. 36. **ornaments**. Cf. Ps.-Clement, *homil.* VIII 21, ed Rehm 130, according to which ὁ χρυσὸς καὶ πᾶσα ἡ τρυφὴ τοῦ κόσμου τούτου belong to the kingdom of this aeon. **beauty**. Cf. Manich Ps. 148. 29–30: "I will [give] my body (σῶμα) to death for your body (σῶμα) and give my fair (?) beauty for your beauty"; Agnad Rosnan VII 10, ed. Boyce 147: "Come yet hearer, and be not fond of this beauty that perishes in all (its) varieties. 12: It falls and melts as snow in sunshine. There is no abiding for any fair form". **dignity of this world**. Greek reads: οὐδὲ ἡ ἐξουσία τοῦ κόσμου τούτου. Cf. *Acta Pauli*, ed. Schmidt 2. 18–20: γύναι ἡ τούτου τοῦ κόσμου ἄρχουσα ... ἡ τῆς τρυφῆς πολει[τ]ι[ς], see E. Peterson, "Einige Bemerkungen zum Hamburger Papyrus-Fragment der Acta Pauli". in: *Vig. Christ.* 3 1949, 142–162, esp. 143, n. 7: "Es erhält sich in diesen Formulierungen vielleicht die Erinnerung an die den Ps. Clementinen ausgesprochene Idee, dass der gegenwärtige Äon von der Frau bestimmt ist". See ch. 32; 103 and 127. **Jesus alone abides**. Cf. ch. 14 and 117. **refuge**. See ch. 10. **worthy ... mysteries**. See ch. 24. **another place**. See ch. 46: "because this man is never to you ..." **she thought ... Jesus**. The same as in ch. 65.

89

Now Karish, the kinsman of king Mazdai, had taken his bath and gone to supper; and he was asking for his wife, where she was, that she had not come to meet him from her chamber. And her maidens said to him: "She is not inclined (to come)". And he went into the chamber, and saw her lying on the bed with her face covered. And he kissed her, and said to her: "Why are you sad to-day and sorrowful?" She says to him: "I am very tired". He says to her: "Why did you not pay proper respect to your position as a free woman and stay at home, and do not go and hear vain words and (see) deeds of **witchcraft**? But get up, and come out, and sup with me, for I cannot sup without you". Mygdonia says to him: "To-day I must be excused from supping with you and from sleeping with you, for I am much agitated".

Commentary. **witchcraft**. See ch. 16.

90

And when Karish heard from Mygdonia that she spoke to him thus, he was unwilling to quit (the room) to sleep and to sup, but ordered his servants to bring (food) to him that he might sup in her presence. And when they had brought in (food, and) set it before him, he asked her to sup, but she would not; and since she would not sup, he supped alone. And Karish said to her: "On your account I excused myself to my lord, king Mazdai, from (staying to) supper, and you do not choose to sup with me!" Mygdonia says to him: "Because I am not inclined". And he stood up to go to bed and sleep as was his wont, and she said to him: "Did I not tell you that I must be excused to-day, that I may sleep alone?"

91

And when he had heard this speech, he went and slept in another bed. And when he awoke suddenly from his sleep, he said to her: "My lady and sister Mygdonia, listen to a dream which I saw this night. I saw myself reclining in the presence of my lord king Mazdai, and a table was laid before us. And I saw an **eagle** swoop down from heaven and carry off from before me and from before king Mazdai a brace of partridges; and he bore them up to his nest and placed them there, and came again and hovered over us. And king Mazdai bade them bring him a bow. And the eagle came again, and carried off again from before us a pigeon and a turtle-dove. And king Madai shot an arrow at him and it passed through him from side to side, and did not harm him; but he soared away to his nest. And I started (out of my sleep), being agitated, and being vexed on account of the partridges which I had tasted, and of which he did not let me put any more into my mouth, and lo, its taste was in my mouth." Mygdonia says to him: "Your dream is good; for you eat partridges every day, but perchance a partridge had never been tasted by that eagle until now".

Commentary. The story of the **eagle** may go back to a well known theme. This apears from Achilles Tatius II 12, ed. S. Gaselee, in: *Loeb Class. Library:* "My father was in the act of sacrificing (*scil.* for a marriage) and had just placed the victims upon the altar, when an eagle swooped down from above and carried off the offering. It was of no avail that those present tried to scare him away; he flew off carrying

away his prey". Bornkamm, *Mythos* 61–62, assumes that the eagle must
be identified with Christ, the two partridges with Tertia (the queen) and
Mygdonia, the pigeon with Vizan (the king's son) and the turtle dove
with Mnesara (Vizan's wife). They all will be converted. In addition to
this the soul is often showing the form of a bird, see Ginzberg, *The
Legends of the Jews* V 81, cf also Gregory the Great, *Dial.* II, c. 34,
in: *P.L.* 66, c. 186: *Cum ecce post triduum in cella consistens, elevatis in aera
oculis vidit (St. Benedict) eiusdam sororis suae animam de eius corpore egressam,
in columba specie coeli secreta penetrare.* The eagle can be identified with
God or Christ, cf. P. Fiebig, *Altjüdische Gleichnisse und die Gleichnisse Jesu,*
Tübingen–Leipzig 1904, 47, nr. 24: "und ich trug euch auf Adlersflügeln
(Ex. 19, 4) ... Aber gerade der Adler fürchtet sich nicht, ausser vor dem
Menschen allein, dass er nicht etwa auf ihn schiesse mit einem Pfeil.
[Deshalb sagte er]: es ist besser dass er (*scil.* der Pfeil) in mich (must be:
in ihn) eindringe und nicht in mein (must be: sein) Junges". Ginzberg,
The Legends of the Jews V 33: "The secret chamber of the Messiah in
paradise is called here (*scil.* Ma'asch de R. Joshua b. Levi 48–49) as in
Zohar II 8a by the peculiar name bird's nest". Cyrillonas, ed. *BKV*
36: "Der Adler Christus"; Manich. Ps. 188. 21: "Take me up upon
your wings, o eagle (ἀετὸς) fly with me to the skies", and Johannesbuch
129. 17–133. 13, where is spoken of birds who help those falling off the
tree.

92

And when it was morning, Karish, the kinsman of king Mazdai, arose
early (and) dressed and **put his left shoe on his right foot**, and said
to Mygdonia: "What is this action? Lo, the dream and the action!"
Mygdonia says to him: "This is not unlucky, but good; from an unlucky
thing something else good results". And he washed his hands, and went
to salute king Mazdai.

Commentary. **put his left shoe on his right foot**. The idea that left
means bad and right means good is widely assumed, cf. History of
Paul, Syriac ed. Wright 80: "Quit the destroying left hand, and the
unconquered right hand shall receive you", see R.H. Connolly, "The
original Language of the Syriac Acts of John", in: *Journ. of Theol. Studies*
8 1907, 249–261, esp. 250–251; *Acta Petri* XXXVIII, ed. L.B. II 94; Odes
of Sol. 19. 4: "And those who have received are in the perfection of the
right hand"; Matth. 25, 34 and 41; Ephrem, *adv. haer.* 22. 11, ed. Beck

79–80 (translation) and 81 (Syriac): "Und da er (*scil.* Judas) Anführer der Linken geworden war"; Irenaeus, *adv. haer.* I 6 1 and III 24 6; *Exc. e Theodoto* 18; 23.3; 43.1; 47.2; 71.2 and 73.1; *Pistis Sophia*, ed. Schmidt–Till 236. 14; Unbek. altgnost. Werk, ed. Schmidt–Till 360. 8–9: "Und nannte das [Gebiet] zur Rechten 'das Gebiet des Lebens', und das Gebiet zur Linken 'das Gebiet des Todes' ...", and Adamantius, *de recte in Deum fide*, ed. v.d. Sande Bakhuyzen 118: ... δεξίον ἐλεημονιχον ... ἀριστερόν ἀνηλεές

93

But Mygdonia, the wife of Karish, arose early too (and) went to salute Judas the Apostle. And she found him sitting and conversing with the general and with a great multitude, and he said to them: "My children, the woman who yesterday **received our Lord into her heart and soul**, whose wife is she?" The general says to him: "She is the wife of Karish, the kinsman of king Mazdai, and her husband is a hard man, and all that he bids the king (do), he humours him in; and he will not let her continue as she has promised, because, he tells many fine stories about her to the king, and has said that there is none like to her; and she too loves him much, and these things which you say to them are **alien** from them". Judas says: "If our Lord has really risen in her soul, and she has received the **seed which was sown in her**, she will neither make account of this life, nor be afraid of death; nor will Karish be able any more to do anything to her, nor to make her suffer, because he whom she has received into her soul is greater than he, if she has received (him) once for all with perfect love".

Commentary. **received ... into her heart and soul**. Greek omits "heart". This may be compared with ch. 12 about "the holy temples" and ch. 87 with "dwell in me". **alien**. See ch. 4. **seed which was sown in her**. See ch. 15.

94

And when Mygdonia heard these things, she says to Judas: "Of a truth, my lord, through your prayer I have received **the living seed of the Word**, and fruits which are like to the seed I shall yield in my Lord Jesus". Judas says: "**These our souls, which are yours, praise you, our Lord. These our spirits, which are your true pos-**

sessions, praise you, my Lord. These our bodies, which you have made worthy to be the dwelling-place of your Spirit, that is always to be glorified, praise you, my Lord". And the Apostle said to all those who were there: "Blessed are the pure, whose souls never upbraid them, because they have gained them and they are not in doubt regarding themselves. Blessed are the spirits of the pure, who have won the crown and gone up from the contest to what is given up to them. Blessed are the bodies of the pure, which are worthy to become clean temples in which the Messiah shall dwell. Blessed are you, pure, for to you it is allowed to ask and to receive. Blessed are you, pure, for you are called judges. Blessed are you, pure, for to you is granted power to forgive sins. Blessed are you, pure, for you have not destroyed what was delivered to you, but you take it up on high with you, rejoicing. Blessed are you, meek, for God has deemed you worthy to inherrit the kingdom. Blessed are you, meek, for it is you who have conquered the evil (one). Blessed are you, meek, for you are children of light. Blessed are you, meek, for you shall see the face of your Lord. Blessed are you, temperate, for you shall be contended and rejoice in these spiritual things, which pass not away and are not dissolved, and the eaters of which do not hunger. Blessed are you, temperate, for you are delivered from sin". And when the Apostle had said these things, whilst the whole multitude were listening to him, Mygdonia, the wife of Karish, the friend of king Mazdai, was greatly strengthened in purity and temperance and all meekness.

Commentary. the living seed of the word. See ch. 15. These our souls ... your. Also here the importance of the soul is emphasized. These our spirits ... my Lord. Generally speaking the idea "spirit" is not important in these Acts. Since the Greek version omits this passage we suppose that it has been added. The makarisms may go back to an existing source. These our bodies ... my Lord. See ch. 12. Blessed are the pure. Makarisms are found in Matthew 5, 2–12; *Acta Pauli et Theclae* 5, and see *Theol. Wörterbuch z. N.T.* IV, 365–375, *s.v.* μακάριος (Bertram/Hauck). Here they deal with three cardinal virtues, see ch. 86. Blessed are the spirits ... given up to them. Cf. I Cor 9, 25; Jam. 1, 12 and Rev. 1, 12 Blessed are the bodies ... shall dwell. Cf. ch. 12. ask and to receive. Cf. Matth. 7, 8. called judges. Cf. Matth. 12, 27; Luke 11, 19; Matth. 19, 28 and Luke 22, 30. forgive sins. Cf. Matth. 18: 18. for you have not

destroyed ... rejoicing. This has to be applied to the soul which man has to keep purely, but it is not to be excluded that the body is meant, see ch. 158. **meek ... kingdom**. Cf. ch. 86 and Matth. 5, 3 and 5, 5. **conquered the evil (one)**. Like in ch. 86. **children of light**. See ch. 28 and Luke 16, 8. **see the face of your Lord**. Cf. Matth. 5, 8 and 8, 10. **temperate**. In Greek: ἡσύχιος, see ch. 85. **not dissolved**. See for the contrast between corruptible and incorruptible ch. 36. **and the eaters ... do not hunger**. Cf. Matth. 5, 6. Greeks adds after the word "sin": καὶ τῆς ἀμοιβῆς τῶν ζώντων καθαρῶν καὶ τῶν ἀκαθάρτων ἀπαλλαγῆναι. This shows a Jewish background.

95

And whilst they were solacing themselves the whole day with the praises and the majesty of the Lord, Karish, the friend of king Mazdai, came to dinner, and did not find his wife at home; and he began to ask **all his servants** about her, (saying), "Wither is your mistress gone?" And one of them said to him: "She is gone to the **strange man**, and there she is". And when he heard these things from his servant, he was angry with his other servants that they had not informed him of what had happened. And he went (and) bathed and came back whilst it was still light and was sitting and waiting for Mygdonia till she should come. And when it was evening, she came, and he met her and said to her: "Where have you been till now?" And she said to him: "I went to the physician's house". He says: "That **strange** conjuror is the physician". She says to him: "Yes, he is the physician, and he is different from all (other) physicians, **for all (other) physicians heal these bodies which shall be dissolved, but this physician heals the bodies with the souls, which shall never more be dissolved**". And when Karish, the kinsman of king Mazdai, heard these things, he was angry in his mind with Mygdonia and with the **stranger**, but he said nothing to her,—because he was afraid of her, for she was far superior to him in wealth, and also in her understanding,—but he went, (and) entered into the dining-room, and sat down to supper; and she went again into her ante-chamber. And he told his servants to call her to come out (and) sup with him; but she did not wish (it).

Commentary. **his servants**. The Syriac text reads: ܥܒܕ ܒܝܬܗ, but the Greek: πάντες ἐν τῷ οἴκῳ αὐτοῦ, which may be influenced by the Syriac original. **strange man ... strange**. See ch. 4. **for all (other)**

physicians ... dissolved. Greek reads: "for most physicians do heal bodies that are dissolved, but he souls that are not dissolved". It is striking that the Greek version does not speak about the healing of the bodies.

96

And when he heard that she did not wish to come out, he went in to her and said to her: "Why do you not wish to come out to sup with me. And perhaps too you do not wish to sleep with me according to your wont? Of this I am sorely afraid, especially as I have heard that that **sorcerer** and deceiver is most anxious about this, that a man should not be with his wife; a thing that nature enjoins, and with which the gods too are pleased, he takes away (from us)". And when Karish had said these things to her, Mygdonia was silent, and he said again to her: "My sister and lady and beloved and wife, Mygdonia, be not led astray by idle and foolish words nor by deeds of witchcraft, which I have heard, he does in the name of his god; for from the day that the world came into being, it has never been heard that a man brought the dead to life; but this man, as I hear, makes as if he brought the dead to life. And as to his not eating or drinking, do not suppose that it is for righteousness' sake that he neither eats nor drinks, but because he has not got anything. For what shall he eat, who has not even bread for the day? And that he wears (only) one (garment) is because he has not another, and that he does not take pay from any man is because he knows that he does not in reality heal any man".

Commentary. **sorcerer**. See ch. 16.

97

And when Karish had said these things to Mygdonia, she was silent as a stone, and was praying, and asking when it would be morning, and when she could see the Apostle of God. And he left her and went (and) supped in sorrowful mood. And when he was thinking that, lo, he would sleep with her according to his wont,—but she, at the moment when he went out from her, kneeled down, and was praying and saying: **"My Lord, and my God**, and **my Life-giver, the Messiah**, do you give me strength to overcome the daring of Karish, and do you grant me that I may preserve the **purity** in which you take delight, and by which I shall find eternal life". And when she had prayed, she covered her face and lay down.

Commentary. **My Lord and my God**. See ch. 10. **my Life-giver, the Messiah**. Greek: Saviour Christ, see ch. 10. **purity**. See ch. 85.

98

Karish, as soon as he had supped, came and stood over her, and took off his clothes. And she perceived him, and says to him: "There is no place for you beside me, because my Lord Jesus, **with whom I am united**, is better than you, and he is always beside me". And Karish laughed and said to her: "You mock well that **sorcerer**, and laugh well at him for saying: 'You cannot live before God unless you be **pure**'". And when he had spoken thus, he dared to lie down beside her, but she did not endure (it), but cried out at him bitterly and said: "Help, you new God, who through a **strange** man have come to India! Help, Lord Jesus! Forsake me not, because I take **refuge** with you, **for as I have heard that you seek those who do not know you, lo, now that I am seeking you and have heard tell of you and have believed in you**, come to my help, and deliver me from the insolence of Karish, and let not his impurity prevail over me, and let him not have a place beside me". And she arose, and tied his hands, and fled from beside him, and laid hold of the curtain which covered the door of the chamber and wrapped herself (therein), and went out (and) went to her nurse, and slept beside her for that night.

Commentary. **with whom I am united**. See ch. 14. Greek reads: "who is with me and rests with me". See ch. 46 and Aphraates, *demonstr.* XXIII 59, ed. Parisot II, c. 121–122: *Apud placidos et rectos homines requiescis.* **sorcerer**. See ch. 16. **pure**. See ch. 85. **strange**. See ch. 4. **refuge**. See ch. 10. **for as I ... in you**. Greek: "for when I learned that you are the one that seeks out them that are veiled in ignorance and saves them that are held in error", see ch. 38.

99

But Karish was in sorrow all that night, and was beating his hands against one another, and was wishing to go during the night (and) inform king Mazdai of the violence that had been done him. And he was thinking and saying: "If I go in the great distress which I feel, who will give me admittance to king Mazdai? For I know that, if fate had not ruined me, and hurled me down from my pride and haughtiness and greatness into contempt and abasement, and separated my beloved Mygdonia from me, (even) to king Mazdai, had he been standing at this hour at my door, I would not have gone out and given an answer. But I will wait till morning; and I know that, whatever I say to king Mazdai, he will humour me therein. And I will tell him of the **sorcery** of the **stranger**, how he uses violence and casts down the exalted into an abyss; for I am not grieved at being cut off from intercourse with Mygdonia, but I am sorry for Mygdonia herself, that her greatness has been degraded, and her freedom brought low, and her high spirit humbled, and that a woman, whom none of her own servants ever saw in any evil tempers, runs naked out of the chamber, and perchance she has gone out into the street through the influence of the sorcery of the stranger; but I do not know whither she is gone, **for there was nothing to be seen with her**".

Commentary. **sorcery**. See ch. 16. **stranger**. See ch. 4. **for there is nothing ... with her**. Greek reads: "for there is nothing that appears to her loveable, except him and the things that are spoken by him". This might be original.

100

And when he had said these things, he began to weep and to say: "Woe to me for your sake, my true wife, of whom I am now deprived! Woe to me for your sake, my beloved and my lover, who was more to me than my whole kindred! And neither son nor daughter have I from you, with whom I might rest contented. A whole year you have not completed with me, and an (evil) eye has taken you from me. Would that the might of death had taken you by force from me,—and I should (still) have counted myself with kings and princes and nobles,—and not this **strange** man, who is perhaps a slave and a fugitive from his owners, and has come hither because of my ill luck! I shall never have rest, and never be stopped, until I destroy him **and chastise him and avenge myself on him**. To-night I will not appear before king Mazdai; but if he does not humour me, **and does not chastise that stranger**, I will tell him about the general Sifur too, that he has been the cause of destruction of this (woman); for, lo, he sits in his house, and many go in and out to him, and he teaches them the new doctrine of purity, and teaches and says that a man cannot live, unless he separates himself from all that belongs to him, and becomes **an ascetic and a wandering mendicant** like to himself, and lo, he wishes to make companions for himself".

Commentary. **strange**. See ch. 4. **and chastise him ... him**. Greek reads: "and avenge this night". **and does not ... stranger**. See ch. 5. **Sifur**, ܝܐܒܘܪ and Greek: Σιφῶϱ, a well known Persian name, see Justi, *Iran. Namenb.* 264–287, *s.v.* Sapor. **an ascetic and wandering mendicant**, ܐܝܘܬܐ ܟܠܝܐ and Greek: ἀποτεταγμένος, see ch. 107. The word ܟܠܝܐ has been derived from the verb ܢܠܐ, which means "to bereave" or "to deprive", cf. *Liber Graduum*, ed. Kmosko, in: *Patr. Syr.* I III, c. 261–262: *Fratres, respicite, peregrinos*, ܟܣܘܐܪ, *et egenos*, ܟܐܘܣܐ *et pusillos*, ܟܐܘܪܐ, *et orbatos*, ܟܐܝܠܐ, *et infirmos* ܟܘܪܐܒ. For the word ܟܝܘܬܐ, see ch. 107 and Ephrem, *Homil. ü. d. Pilgerleben*, ed. A. Haffner, in: *Sitzungsberichte der Kaiserl. Akadademie der Wissensch.*, Wien 135 1696, 12: "Der Eine nennt ihn (*scil.* Pilger) Bettler. Und der Andere Vagabund, ܟܝܘܬܐ.

101

And whilst Karish was meditating these things, it became morning. And he rose early (and) dressed and put on his shoes; but he put on sorry garments, and his countenance was gloomy, and he was very sad; and he went to salute king Mazdai. And when king Mazdai saw him, he said to him: "What is the matter, that you have come to me in this wretched plight? And why is your aspect sad, and your countenance changed?" Karish says to him: "King Mazdai, I have a new fact to tell you, and a new calamity, which Sifur has brought to India. A Hebrew, a conjuror, is sitting in his house and never goes out from beside him; and many go in to him, and he teaches them the new God and gives them new laws, which have never been heard of by us; and he says: 'You cannot be children of this everlasting life, which I teach, unless you sever yourselves, a man from his wife, and a woman from her husband'. Now it chanced that my wretched and miserable wife went to see him, and heard his words and believed them; and she arose by night and fled from beside me, she who could not bear to be away from me for a single hour and could not exist without me. But send (and) fetch Sifur and the conjuror who lays snares for him, **and chastise them**; and if not, all our countrymen will be destroyed by his words".

Commentary. **and chastise them.** See ch. 5.

102

And when Mazdai heard these things from his kinsman Karish, he said to him: "Be not grieved and vexed. I will send and fetch him, **and chastise him**, and then you shall get back your wife; **for if I avenge others who cannot avenge themselves, you, lo, especially (must I avenge).**" And he commanded that they should summon Sifur the general (to come) to him; and they went to his home and found him sitting on the right hand of Judas, the Apostle of God, and Mygdonia was sitting at his feet, with a great multitude, and they were listening to him. Those who went after Sifur the general answered and said to him: "Do you sit and listen to vain words, whilst king Mazdai in his wrath is seeking to destroy you, because of this sorcerer and seducer, whom you have brought into your house?" And when Sifur the general heard these things, he was grieved, not because the king was angered with him, but because the king had heard regarding him that he was acquainted with Judas the Apostle. And Sifur said to Judas: "I am grieved on your account, for I told you a day ago that that woman was the wife of Karish, the kinsman of king Mazdai, and that he would not let her do what she promised; and whatever he says to the king he humours him therein". Judas says to Sifur: "**Be not afraid, but believe in Jesus**, who pleads for both me and you, and for all those who take refuge with him and come to his **place of assembly**". And when Sifur the general heard these things, he put on his dress and went to king Mazdai.

Commentary. **and chastise him.** See ch. 5. **for if I avenge ... (must I avange),** ܐܠܟ ܐܢ̣ ܐܬܪ̈ܐ ܢܬܒܥ ܐܢܐ ܐܝ݀ܠܝܢ ܕܠܐ ܡܫܟܚܝܢ ܢܦܫܗܘܢ ܢܬܒܥܘܢ. Wright supposed that the word ܠܐ has to be deleted. But the translation may be: "... must I not (avenge) especially you?" **Be not ... Jesus.** ܠܐ ܬܕܚܠ ܐܠܐ ܗܝܡܢ ܒܝܫܘܥ. See Luke 8, 50 with minor deviations from syr p s and c and the Greek New Testament text. **refuge.** See ch. 10. **place of assembly,** ܠܒܝܬ ܟܢܘܫܗ, see ch. 37.

103

And Judas was asking Mygdonia, what was the reason that her husband was angry with her, and meditated these things against them. She says to him: "Because I did not give myself to **corruption** with him; for in the evening he wished to make me yield, and to subject me to that which he is wont to do; but he to whom I have committed myself delivered me from his hands, and I fled naked from beside him, and slept with my nurse, and I know not what has come to him that he plots these things against you". The Apostle says to her: "These things, my daughter, harm us not; but believe in Jesus, and he will restrain from you the lust of Karish, and he will deliver you from corruption and wantonness, and he will be to you a **guide** in the path of danger, and a **conductor** to his and his Father's kingdom, and he will bring you into everlatsing life, **and will give you a sovereignty that passes not away and changes not**".

Commentary. **corruption**. Sexual intercourse. **guide, conductor**. See ch. 10. **and will give ... changes not**. See ch. 88: "dignity in the world". Greek uses the word παρρησία here, see ch. 25.

104

And when Sifur stood before king Mazdai, Mazdai asked him and said to him: "What is his story, and whence is he, and what does he teach, the **sorcerer** who plots against you?" Sifur says to him: "Do you perchance not know, my lord, that I and all my friends were in great sorrow about my wife,—whom, as you know, many held in honour,— and about my daughter, in comparison with whom I counted as nought all that I possess? And what calamity and what trial came upon them? And how they became a laughing-stock and an imprecation through the whole country? And I heard tell of this man, and went to him, and asked of him, and fetched him, and we came hither; and I saw wonderful miracles whilst I was coming with him on the road, and here too many saw and heard what the wild ass said, and what the demon declared concerning him. And he healed my wife and my daughter, and lo, they are well, and he asked for no reward except belief and purity, that they might be participators in what he is doing; and he says, 'Fear one God, the Lord of all, and Jesus the Messiah, his Son, and you shall live for ever and ever'; and he eats nothing at all but **bread** and **salt** from evening to evening, and drinks **water**; and he prays much, and whatever he asks of God, he gives him; and he enjoins (us) too, (saying) that this his God is holy, and good and benign and gentle and a giver of life, and (that) therefore those who believe in him draw nigh to him in **cleanness** and **purity** and love".

Commentary. **sorcerer**. See ch. 16. **bread-salt-water**. See ch. 20.
cleanness, ܩܕܫܘܬܐ, **purity**, ܩܕܝܫܘܬܐ Greek reads: ἐν ἁγιωσύνῃ καὶ
ἁγνείᾳ, see ch. 85.

105

And when king Mazdai heard these things from Sifur, he sent a number
of soldiers from his presence to the house of Sifur, the general, to fetch
Judas Thomas and those whom they found with him. And when they
went in, they found him sitting and teaching a great many people, and
Mygdonia too was sitting at his feet. And they were afraid, when they
saw the great number of people that surrounded him; and they went
to tell king Mazdai (saying): "We did not dare to say anything to him,
because a great many people were with him, and Mygdonia too was
sitting at his feet and hearing his words". And when Mazdai and Karish
heard these things, Karish sprang up from before king Mazdai, and
took with him a number of soldiers, and said: "I will go and fetch him
and also Mygdonia, whose senses he has taken away". And he came
to the house of Sifur the general in haste, and came and found Judas
sitting and teaching. And when he went in, he saw Judas, but he did
not find Mygdonia there, for she had gone home, because she knew
that they would tell her husband about her that she was there.

106

And Karish said to Judas: "Get up, wretch and corruptor and enemy!
But what can your **witchcraft** do to me? For I will make **sorceries**
recoil upon your own head". And when he had spoken thus to him,
Judas looked upon him and said to him: "Your threats shall recoil upon
you, for me you can not hurt at all, because my Lord Jesus the Messiah,
with whom I take **refuge**, is greater than you and your king and all
your forces". And Karish took the **turban** of one of his servants, and
threw it round the Apostle's neck, and said: "**Drag him off**; let me see
if Jesus will deliver him from my hands". And they were dragging him
away until (they came) to king Mazdai. And when Judas stood before
king Madai, he said to him: "Tell me what is your story, by whose
power do you do these works?" **And Judas was silent and gave him
no reply**. And king Mazdai commanded the soldiers, and they struck
him a hundred and fifty lashes; and he gave orders that they should
convey him bound to prison; and they bound him and carried him off.

And when he was gone and had entered the prison, Mazdai and Karish were planning how they might kill him, because the whole poeple were worshipping him as God, and they took pains to say (everywhere), "He has reviled the king, and he is a conjuror".

Commentary. **witchcraft-sorceries.** See ch. 16. **refuge.** See ch. 19. **turban,** ܟܒܝܢܐ. Th. Nöldeke suggests the word "mantle" in his Review of Wright's edition in: *Zeitschr. f.d. Deutsch. Morgenl. Gesellschaft* 25 1871, 670–679, esp. 679. **dragging.** Cf. Gospel of Peter 6. **And Judas was silent and gave no reply.** Cf. Luke 12, 9.

107

But Judas, when he went to prison, **was glad and rejoicing** saying: "I thank you, my Lord Jesus the Messiah, that you have **deemed me worthy** not only to believe in you, but also to bear many things for your sake". And he said: "I thank you, my Lord, that you have deemed me worthy of these things. I thank you, my Lord, that your providence has been over me, and that you have deemed me worthy to bear many evils for your sake. I thank you, my Lord, that for your sake, I have been a **recluse** and an **ascetic** and a **pauper** and a **wandering mendicant. Let me then receive of the blessing of the poor, and of the rest of the weary, and of the blessing of those whom men hate and persecute and revile and say of them odious words. Lo, for your sake I am hated and shunned by many; for your sake they say of me I know not what**".

Commentary. **was glad and rejoicing.** Cf. Matth. 5, 12. **deemed me worthy.** Cf. Acts 5, 41. **recluse.** Wright supposed that the original word was ܚܒܝܫܐ, which means "prisoner" or "recluse" (?). In the text itself the word ܚܪܫܐ has been used, which means "sorcerer". This agrees with the Greek text: "That for your sake I am called a sorcerer and wizard". **ascetic,** ܣܝܡܐ derived from the verb ܣܡܝ which means "to torture", "to make in vain", "to make empty" or "to renounce". **pauper,** ܡܣܟܢܐ. This is the characteristic word for the ascetic, see A. Vööbus, "Einiges über die kariatative Tätigkeit des syrischen Mönchtums", in: *Contrib. of Baltic University* 51 1947, 11–12. **wandering mendicant,** ܫܐܝܢܐ, see ch. 100. The last word has been added by a Syriac rewriter in order to show that Thomas is the ideal christian. **Let me receive … odious works.** Cf. Matth. 5, 3; 11, 28 and 5, 11. **Lo, for your sake ... I know not what**. Greek: "... they call me such as one as I am not". Greek seems to be original and Syriac had to rewrite the text because the word "pauper" was added.

108

And whilst he was praying, all those who were in the prison saw that he was praying and begged of him to pray for them too. And when he had prayed and sat down, Judas began to chant this hymn.

The Hymn of Judas Thomas the Apostle in the country of the Indians.

1 "When I was a little child
   and dwelling in my kingdom, in my father's house,
2 and was content with the wealth and the luxuries
   of my nourishers,
3 from the East our home
   my parents equipped me (and) sent me forth;
4 and of the wealth of our treasury
   they took abundantly (and) tied up for me a load
5 large and (yet) light,
   which I myself could carry—
6 gold of Beth-'Ellaye
   and silver of Gazak the great,
7 and rubies of India,
   and agates from Beth-Kashan;
8 and they furnished me with adament
   which can crush iron.
9 And they took off from me the glittering robe,
   which in their affection they had made for me,
10 and the purple toga,
   which was measured (and) woven to my stature.
11 And they made a compact with me,
   and wrote it in my heart, that it might not be forgotten:
12 'If you go down unto Egypt,
   and bring the one pearl,
13 which is in the midst of the sea
   around the loud-breathing serpent,
14 you shall put on your glittering robe
   and your toga, with (which) you are contented,
15 and with your brother, who is next to us in authority,
   you shall be heir in our kingdom'.

109

16　I quit the East (and) went down,
　　there being with me two guardians.
17　for the way was dangerous and difficult,
　　and I was very young to travel it.
18　I passed through the borders of Maishan,
　　the meeting-place of the merchants of the East,
19　and I reached the land of Babel,
　　and I entered the walls of Sarbug.
20　I went down into Egypt
　　and my companians parted from me.
21　I went straight to the serpent,
　　I dwelt around his abode,
22　(waiting) till he should slumber and sleep,
　　and I could take my pearl from him.
23　And when I was single and was alone
　　(and) became strange to my family,
24　one of my race, a free-born man,
　　an Oriental, I saw there,
25　a youth fair and lovable,
　　the son of oil-sellers;
26　and he came and attached himself to me
　　and I made him my intimate friend,
27　an associate with whom I shared my merchandise
28　I warned him against the Egyptians,
　　and against consorting with the unclean,
29　and dressed in their dress,
　　that they might not hold me in abhorrence,
30　because I had come abroad in order to take the pearl,
　　and arouse the serpent against me.
31　But in some way or another
　　they found out that I was not their countryman,
32　and they dealt with me treacherously,
　　and gave me their food to eat.
33　I forgot that I was a son of kings,
　　and I served their king;
34　and I forgot the pearl,
　　for which my parents had sent me,
35　and because of the burden of their oppressions
　　I lay in a deep sleep.

110

36　But all these things that befell me
　　my parents perceived, and were grieved for me;

37 and a proclamation was made in our kingdom,
   that everyone should come to our gate,

38 kings and princes of Parthia,
   and all the nobles of the East.

39 And they wove a plan on my behalf,
   that I might not be left in Egypt;

40 and they wrote to me a letter,
   and every noble signed his name to it:

41 'From your Father, the king of kings,
   and your mother, the mistress of the East,

42 and from your brother, our second (in authority),
   to you, our son, who is in Egypt, greeting!

43 Up and arise from your sleep,
   and listen to the words of our letter!

44 Call to mind that you are a son of kings!
   See the slavery, whom you serve!

45 Remember the pearl
   for which you were sent to Egypt!

46 Think of your robe,
   and remember your splendid toga,

47 which you shall wear and (with which) you shall be adorned,
   when your name has been read out in the list of the valiant,

48 and with your brother, our viceroy,
   you shall be in our kingdom!'

III

49 My letter is a letter,
   which the king sealed with his own right hand,

50 (to keep it) from the wicked ones, the children of Babel,
   and from the savage demons of Sarbug.

51 It flew in the likeness of an eagle,
   the king of all birds;

52 it flew and alighted beside me,
   and became all speech.

53 At its voice and the sound of its rustling,
   I started and arose from my sleep.

54 I took it up and kissed it,
   and I began (and) read it;

55 and according to what was traced on my heart
   were the words of my letter written.

56 I remembered that I was a son of royal parents,
   and my noble birth asserted its nature.

57 I remembered the pearl,
   for which I had been sent to Egypt,

58 and I began to charm him,
   the terrible loud-breathing serpent.

59 I hushed him to sleep and lulled him into slumber,
   for my father's name I named over him,
60 and the name of our second (in power),
   and of my mother, the queen of the East;
61 and I snatched away the pearl,
   and turned to go back to my father's house.
62 And their filthy and unclean dress I stripped off,
   and left it in their country;
63 and took my way straight to come
   to the light of our home the East.
64 And my letter, my awakener,
   I found before me on the road;
65 and as with his voice it had awakened me,
   (so) too with its light it was leading me.
66 It, that dwelt in the palace
   gave light before me with its form,
67 and with its voice and with its guidance
   it also encouraged me to speed,
68 and with its love it drew me on.
69 I went forth (and) passed by Sarbug,
   I left Babel on my left hand;
70 and I came to the great Maishan,
   to the haven of the merchants,
71 which sits on the shore of the sea,
72 And my bright robe, which I had stripped off,
   and the toga that was wrapped with it,
73 from Ramtha and Reken
   my parents had sent thither
74 by the hand of their treasurers,
   who in their truth could be trusted therewith.

112

75 And because I did not remember its fashion,—
   for in my childhood I had left it in my father's house,—
76 on a sudden, when I received it,
   the garment seemed to me to become like a mirror of myself.
77 I saw it all in all,
   and I too received all in it,
78 for we were two in distinction
   and yet again one in one likeness.
79 And the treasurers too,
   who brought it to me, I saw in like manner
80 to be two (and yet) one likeness,
   for one sign of the king was written on them (both),
81 of the hands of him who restored to me through them
   my trust and my wealth,

82 my decorated robe, which
was adorned with glorious colours,

83 with gold and beryls
and rubies and agates,

84 and sardonyxes, varied in colour.
And was skilfully worked in its home on high,

85 and with diamond clasps
were all its seams fastened;

86 and the image of the king of kings
was embroidered and depicted in full all over it,

87 and like the stone of the sapphire too
its hues were varied.

113

88 And I saw also that all over it
the instincts of knowledge were working,

89 and I saw too that it was preparing to speak.

90 I heard the sound of its tones
which it uttered with its … :

91 'I am the active in deeds,
whom they reared for him before my father;

92 and I perceived myself,
that my stature grew according to his labours'.

93 And in its kingly movements
it poured itself entirely over me.

94 and on the hands of its givers
it hastened that I might take it.

95 And love urged me to run
to meet it and receive it;

96 and I stretched forth and took it.
With the beauty of its colours I adorned myself,

97 and I wrapped myself wholly in my toga
of brilliant hues.

98 I clothed myself with it, and went up to the gate
of salutation and prostration;

99 I bowed my head and worshipped the majesty
of my father who sent me,—

100 for I had done his commandments,
and he too had done what he promised,—

101 and at the gate of his … ,
I mingled with his princes,

102 for he rejoiced in me and received me,
and I was with him in his kingdom,

103 and with the voice of … all his servants praise him.

104 And he promised that to the gate too
of the king of kings with him I should go,

105 and with my offering and my pearl
with him should present myself to our king".

The hymn of Judas Thomas, the Apostle, which he spoke in the prison is ended.

Commentary. The text of Hymn II is found in Wright's Syriac edition on p. ܡܝ—ܠܝܕ and in the Greek manuscript U in *L.B.* II II on p. 219–224. The poem was rewritten by Nicetas of Thessalonica[1]. Contrary to the text of these Acts in general the Syriac text of this Hymn appears to be better than the Greek version. Since the text is often not quite clear a number of conjectures have been proposed. Some of them can be found in Wright's edition and other ones have been added by Bevan[2], Nöldeke[3], and Hoffmann[4]. Preuschen[5] published the text of the hymn in a separate edition following Hoffmann's corrections. Recently the text has been published and, if necessary emended, by J.E.Ménard[6], R. Köbert[7], J. Magne[8], H. Kruse[9], P.H. Poirier[10] and K. Beyer[11].

After the second world war the Hymn has been subjected to a number of studies in which it was supposed to be an example of pre-

---

[1] See M. Bonnet, "Actes de Saint Thomas, Apôtre. Le Poème de l'âme. Version grecque remaniée par Nicetas de Thessalonique", in: *Analecta Bollandiana* XX 1901, 159–164, text on 161–164, and P.-H. Poirier, "L'Hymne de la Perle des Actes de Thomas. Introduction, Texte—Traduction—Commentaire", in: *Homo Religiosus* 8, Louvain-la Neuve 1981, 285–295 and 363–375.

[2] A.A. Bevan, "The Hymn of the Soul",in: *Texts and Studies* V 1897.

[3] Th. Nöldeke, "Review of Wright's Apocryphal Acts", in: *Zeitschr. des Deutschen Morgenl. Gesellschaft* XXV 1871, 670–679, esp. 676–679.

[4] G. Hoffmann, "Zwei Hymnen der Thomasakten", in: *Zeitschr. f. d. neutestamentl. Wissensch.* IV 1903, 373–309, esp. 273–283.

[5] E. Preuschen, *Zwei gnostische Hymnen*, Gieszen 1904.

[6] J.E. Ménard, "Le Chant de la Perle", in: *Revue des sciences religieuses* 1968, 289–325.

[7] R. Köbert, "Das Perlenlied", in: *Orientalia* 38 1969, 447–456.

[8] J. Magne, "Le Chant de la Perle: à la lumière des écrits de Nag Hammâdi", in: *Cahiers du cercle Ernest-Renan* 100 1977.

[9] H. Kruse, "The Return of the Prodigal. Fortunes of a Parable on its Way to the Far East", in: *Orientalia* 47 1978, 163–214.

[10] P.-H. Poirier, "L'Hymne de la Perle des Actes de Thomas. Introduction, Texte-Traduction, Commentaire", in: *Homo Religiosus* 8, Louvain-la Neuve 1981.

[11] K. Beyer, "Das syrische Perlenlied. Ein Erlösungsmythos als Märchengedicht", in: *Zeitschr. des Deutschen Morgenländischen Gesellschaft* 140 1990, 234–259.

Christian gnosis.[12] This was questioned by A.F.J. Klijn[13] in the year 1960 and after that time a period has begun in which it was assumed that the Hymn has been subjected to more than one kind of influence which included even that of the New Testament.

Remarks on the Text

Since the Syriac text is not always clear it is necessary to give a number of remarks on the text as it is known to us in Syriac and Greek and a summary of the various conjectures.

2a. and was content, ܒܣܝܡ ܗܘܬ. Poirier: "je me reposais".

6a. ܒܝܬܐ ܕܠܥܠ, Nöldeke and Adam: "the house above", cf. Greek: Χρυσός ἔστιν ὁ φορτος τῶν ἄνω. Kruse: "the country of the Geleans"; Köbert: "vom Gelderland"; Ménard: 'de la maison des dieux" and Beyer: "aus dem Gebiet der Hochlandbewohner".

6b. ܓܐܙܐ, Adam: "der grossen Schatzkammer", cf. Greek: τῶν μεγάλων θησαυρῶν

7b. ܒܝܬ ܡܢ, Preuschen–Hoffmann: ܟܣܐ, cf. Greek: ἐκ κοσάνων

8b. These words have been omitted by the Greek version, but Nicetas reads: ᾧ πᾶς ἄλλος ὑπείκει καὶ διαπέφευγε σίδηρος.

14b. ܕܥܠܝܗ ܣܝܡ, "with (which) you are contented", see also 2a, but Poirier: "qui repose sur lui", cf. Greek: ἥν ἐπαναπαύεται, cf. Beyer: "die darüber getragen wird".

16b. ܦܘܢܩܣ, Preuschen–Hoffmann: "Postboten". Nöldeke refers to Persian "pawanak". Kruse: "messengers" and Poirier: "guides"

---

[12] See A. Adam, "Die Psalmen des Thomas und das Perlenlied als Zeugnisse vorchristlicher Gnosis", in: *Beih. Zeitschr. f. d. neutstaml. Wissensch.* 24, Berlin 1959, 49–54, and especially G. Widengren, "Der Iranische Hintergrund der Gnosis", in: *Zeitschr. f. Rel. und Geistesgeschichte* 4 1952, 97–114, esp. 112: "Reitzenstein (Das Iran. Erlösermyst. SS 70ff, 117) ist es gelungen aufzuzeigen, dass der junge Prinz das Symbol des erlösten Erlöser ist. Die Perle, die er rettet ist die Bezeichnung des aus der Materie erlösten Seelenkollektives, der Summe der zu errettenden Seelen".

[13] A.F.J. Klijn, "The so-called Hymn of the Pearl (Acts of Thomas ch. 108–111)", in: *Vigiliae Christianae* 14 1960, 154–164. See Kruse, *The Return* ... . 185, n. 29: "Two Dutch scholars have pioneered to oppose this tendency (*scil.* the "modern trend ... to consider the Hymn as 'gnostic'"): A.F.J. Klijn, *The so-called Hymn of the Pearl* ... , and G. Quispel, "das Thomas-evangelium und das Lied von der Perle", in: *Eranos-Jahrbuch* 34 1965, Zürich 1966, 9–32.

18a. ܡܣܢ, Greek: τὰ τῶν μοσάνων μεθόρια, a district between Basra and Wasit.

19b. ܣܘܪܒ. Wright suggests ܡܒܓ = Hierapolis. F.C. Burkitt, "Sarbog, Sabog, Shuruppak", in: *Journ. of Theol. Studies* 4 1903, 125–127, refers to the legendary Shruppak, and Nöldeke to ܣܝܪܒ = Borsippa.

21b. ܢܝܐܘܡ, ܕܐܟܣܢܝܐ ܒܝܬ, Preuschen–Hoffmann: "(und) liess mich um ihr Gasthaus nieder". ܐܟܣܢܝܐ is a house of entertainment for travellers.

23b. ܐܬܟܣܐ ܕܠܒܢܝ ܒܝܬ ܐܟܣܢܝ ܘܗܘܐ Preuschen–Hoffmann: "war ich den Mitbewohenrn meines Gasthauses fremd" and Poirier: "pour mes compagnons d'auberge, je devins un étranger", cf. Greek: καὶ τοῖς ἐμοις ἀλλότριος ἐφανόμην.

24a. ܒܪ ܚܐܪܝ, "a free-born man" may be translated by "noble", see Poirier: "un noble",

26b. The word ܒܪ ܡܫܚܐ has been rendered by "the son of oil-sellers". Preuschen–Hoffmann and Kruse: ܡܫܚܐ "Sohn Gesalbter"; Adam: "Sohn der Salbungen" in the sense of "wohlgesalbt" and Poirier: "un oint".

29b. ܕܢܬܟܪܗܘܢ, "that they might hold me in abhorrence", Greek: ἵνα μὴ ξενίζομαι, cf, Poirier: "de peur qu'ils ne me reprochent d'être venue du dehors".

35a. ܘܒܥܩܬܐ ܕܛܠܘܡܝܗܘܢ, "and because of the burden of their oppressions", but Nöldeke, Preuschen–Hoffmann, Adam and Poirier read: ܕܛܠܘܡܝܗܘܢ

50b. Greek reads: καὶ δαίμονες τυραννικοὺς Λαβυρίνθους Kruse proposes: "and (overwhelmed) by their heavy dishes".

51–52. has been omitted by the Greek version.

60. has been omitted by the Greek version

66. Wright reads: ܕܫܪܐ ܒܗܝܟܠܐ and renders: "It, that dwelt in the palace gave light before me with its form", but cf. Poirier: ܕܫܪܐ ܒܗܝܟܠܐ ܩܕܡܝ ܘܗܘ ܒܚܙܘܗ ܡܨܡܚ = "car la soie royale devant moi, par son aspect, replendissait", cf. Greek: ἔστι γὰρ ὅτε ἡ ἀπὸ σηρικῶν ἐσθῆς βασιλικῆ πρὸ τῶν ἐμῶν ὀφθαλμῶν, already suggested by Preuschen–Hoffmann.

69a. Greek reads: Λαβύρινθον, cf. 50b.

72–74. have been omitted by the Greek version.

73a. ܡܢ ܪܡܬ ܘܪܩܢ has been rendered by "from Ramtha and Reken", but already Bevan, Preuschen–Hoffmann, Adam and also Poirier and Kruse suppose an original: ܕܗܪܩܢ = "des hauteurs [de] Hyrcanie".

75a. Poirier reads "son arrangement" and Kruse "its rank (and dignity" in place of "its fashion".

84b. ܒܪܘܡܗ̇, "in its home on high", but Poirier: "dans sa grandeur".

90b. ܕܥܡ ܡܚܬܘܬܗ̇ ܡܪܢܢܐ is not clear. Preuschen–Hoffmann, read ܡܚܬܢܘܬܗ̇ instead of ܡܚܬܘܬܗ̇: "die es während seiner Herabkunft lispelte", cf. Kruse: "while it descended (on me). Poirier reads: ܡܚܬܘܬܗ̇ and renders: "alors qu'avec ceux qui le ⟨descendai⟩, il murmurait".

91a. ܕܗܘ̣ ܐܙܪܝܙܝܢ ܥܒ̈ܕܐ, "I am the active in deeds". Preuschen–Hoffmann rendered: "Ich gehörte den hurtigen Diener an". This has been rejected by F.C. Burkitt in his Review of Preuschen, *Zwei gnost. Hymnen*, in: *Theol. Tijdschrift* 39 1905, 270–282, esp. 278, who suggested: "He, the strenuous in action". Poirier reads: ܕܗܘ̣ [ܗܘܐ] ܙܪܝܙ ܥܒ̈ܕܐ = "C'est pour ⟨ce⟩ plus vaillant des serviteurs …".

101a. The word ܕܗܘܦܣ̈ܪܘܗܝ, Wright: ܕܦ݂ܣ̈ܪܘܗܝ is not clear. Poirier renders "de ses princes". and in 101b: "à ses grands" cf. Kruse: "… the court of his knights and grandees".

103a. ܕܕܪ̈ܘܣܐ is not clear. Preuschen–Hoffmann suggested ܕܗܕܪ̈ܘܠܐ, ἰδραυλεών; Bevan ܕܕܘܟܣܐ, δόξης and Poirier ܕܕܪ̈ܘܣܐ, "de louange (?)".

Contents

The Hymn can be divided into the following parts:

l. 1–15. The author (the hymn was written in the first person singular) is sent away from his father's house to fetch a pearl which is in the possession of a serpent. If he succeeds, he will be heir in his father's kingdom.

l. 16–35. Accompanied by two guardians he goes to Egypt. He associates himself with a noble-man and puts on the dress of the Egyptians. He falls asleep and he eats the food of the Egyptians and forgets his charge.

l. 36–50. In the house of his father a letter is written and sent to the author of the hymn.

l. 53–71. Awakened by the contents of the letter he charms the serpent and snatches away the pearl. The pearl leads him on his way home.

l. 72–105. This part is devoted to the robe which was promised to him. It is offered to him and he recognized himself in it.

The Hymn is often called the "Hymn of the Pearl" but the pearl is of minor importance. The main theme is the glittering robe which has been offered and finally been given to the principal person. The pearl is a way by which the robe can be received. When it is finally given to the King nothing is said about its value or its situation before it had been taken from the serpent.[14]

We assume that the real background of the significance of the pearl in this hymn has to be explained by a New Testament passage. In *l.* 12 it is said that the prince has to go down to Egypt in order "to bring the one pearl" (in Syriac: ܚܕܐ ܡܪܓܢܝܬܐ and Greek: τὸν ἕνα μαργαρίτην. It may be possible to render the expression "one pearl" by "some pearl", but on the other hand it agrees with Matth. 13, 46, where is spoken of ἕνα πολύτιμον μαργαρίτην and in syr s of ܚܕܐ ܡܪܓܢܝܬܐ, obviously in contrast with the other pearls mentioned in Matth. 13, 45. In both the New Testament parable and the Hymn we are dealing with the "one" or "unique pearl". Also in both sources the possession of this pearl opens up the way into the kingdom of God. It is not said for which the pearl is exactly standing. One may suggest various themes, like "belief in God", "an ascetic life" or even "finding one's own soul".[15] In the parable it is said: πάλιν ὁμοία ἐστὶν ἡ βασιλεία τῶν οὐρανῶν ἐμπόρῳ which agrees remarkably with the present hymn in which the principal person descends to Egypt along the Eastern trade routes and

---

[14] This does not say that the pearl is not supposed to be important in gnosticism, see *Kephalaia* 85, 24–25: "Er (der lebendige Geist) holte den Urmenschen aus dem Kampf (ἀγών) heraus wie eine Perle (μαργαρίτης), die aus dem Meere heraus[geholt] wird". Agnad Rosnan VI 51, ed. Boyce 147): "Thou art the buried treasure, the chief of my wealth, the pearl which (is) the beauty of all the gods" and Ginza L. 515,20: "Komm in Frieden, du Lichtspendende ... , 24: Komm in Frieden, du Perle, 25 die du aus dem Schatze des Lebens geholt wurdest".

[15] The pearl has been identified with many things, cf. Ephrem, *de fide* LXXXI–LXXXV, ed. Beck 211–223 (translation) and 248–262 (Syriac), but the following passage seems to be important: Ephrem, *de fide* LXXXV 12, ed. Beck 223 (translation) and 262 (Syriac): "Perlen habe ich gesammelt, um zu schaffen eine Krone für den Sohn. Statt der Makel an meinen Gliedern nimm (die) mein Opfer an". See also H. Usener, "Die Perle", in: *Theol. Abhandlungen C. von Weiszäcker*, Freiburg 1892, 203–213.

after having arrived in Egypt "he shared his merchandise" (*l.* 27).[16]

The principal person can be identified with the soul. It is originally a baby of royal descent (*l.* 1–15). Therefore, it does not remember its glittering robe. It puts on the dress of the corruptible world which has to be taken off again in order to receive its heavenly robe again. This means that the pre-existent soul has to fulfil a special task to return to its original life.[17]

Commentary on the Various Parts

l. 1–15. The hymn begins with a description of the soul living with his father. The idea of a pre-existent soul is known from Judaism.[18] The presence of a glittering robe reminds us of traditions about Adam and Eve in Paradise.[19] Heaven is described as a royal court in the East. This appears from *l.* 41 where is spoken of a mistress of the East, from

---

[16] See Adam, *Die Psalmen des Thomas* ... . 63: "Dass dieser Weg im Achämenidenreich und sicher auch später benutzt worden ist, dafür haben wir in dem Marchbefehl des persischen Satrapen Arsam an seinem Offizier Nehtihur aus dem Jahren 411/408 v. Chr. einen urkundlichen Beleg", but see also Ephrem, *hymni dispersi* V, in Lamy IV, c. 701–702: *Beatus es, o mercator, qui attulisti thesaurum in locum illo indigentem; tu es sapiens ille vir, qui, inventa una margarita pretiosa, vendidit omnia quae habuit ut acquireret eam ... Beata es, o civitas benedicta, quae margaritam accepisti; margarita pretiosa alia in India non est inventa nisi haec*, and Ephrem, *on virginity*, ed. C.W. Mitchell, A.A. Bevan, F.C. Burkitt, in: S. Ephraim's Prose Refutations of Masi, Marcion and Bardaisan, vol. II, London/Oxford 1921, LXXXVIII–XLIV: "Thy pearl is a pearl that from two thieves flies away to be lost, for, it is Merchants who are single that can get it, and if they have become unclean both of them lose it ..."

[17] The idea that the principal person has to be identified with the soul can be found with Nöldeke, *Rev. of Wright's edition* 677; Lipsius, *Apokr. Aostelgesch.* I, 296–297; Hoffmann, *Zwei Hymnen* ... 283; F.C. Burkitt, "Review of Preuschen, Zwei gnost. Hymnen", in: *Theol. Tijdschrift* XXXIX 1905, 207–282; F.C. Burkitt, *Urchristentum im Orient*, Tübigen 1907, 151–152. The idea that we are dealing with a redeemer is found with: Preuschen, *Zwei gnost. Hymnen* ... . 46 (Christ); W. Bousset, *Hauptprobleme* ... . 353; Haasse, *Zur bardes. Gnosis* ... 57–59 (originally Christ and later Thomas); R. Reitzenstein, "Himmelswanderung und Drachenkampf", in: *Festschrift F.C. Andreas*, Leipzig 1916, 33–50, esp. 44–50 (pre-Christian redeemer); W. Bousset, "Manichäisches in den Thomasakten", in: *Zeitschr. f. d. neutestamentl. Wissensch.* 18 1918/19, 1–39 (Mani); Bornkamm, *Mythos* ... . 115 (Mani); A. Hilgenfeld, "Review of Bevan The Hymn of the Soul", in: *Berl. Phil. Wochenschr.* LXIII 1890, 389–395 (Mani), and Adam, *Thomaspsalmen* ... . 56: "... die Gesamtseele, die als zweite Ausströmung des Lichgottes gedacht ist".

[18] See J. Bonsirven, *Le Judaïsme Palestinien* II, Paris 1935, 7; Strack–Billerbeck II, 340–347, and R. Meyer, "Hellenistisches in der rabbinischen Anthropologie", in: *Beiträge z. Wissensch. des A. u. N.T.* 74, Stuttgart 1937, 88–114, esp. 91–93.

[19] See E. Preuschen, *Die apokryphen gnostischen Adamschriften*, Giessen 1900, 13 and 27–29, and W. Staerk, *Die Erlösererwartung in den östlichen Religionen*, Stuttgart/Berlin 1938, 11–12.

l. 73 about ܢܘܠܐ ܐܡܙܢ and *l.* 38 dealing with the kings and princes from Parthia. Burkitt concluded that the hymn has to go back to a time before the fall of the Parthian dynasty.[20] However, it is acceptable that all this belongs to the mythological setting of this hymn. Nevertheless a great number of Parthian words and names are met.[21] Although a relation between Mani and Parthia is undeniable, it is not acceptable that Mani has to be related with the principal person.[22] The load taken with the prince on his journey has been supposed to be a treasure in order to pay the guardians between heaven and earth[23] or to be compared with the Mandaean "Reisezehrung".[24] In the first place the soul is accompanied by two guardian angels on his way and in the second place "Reisezehrung" is meant to be used on the way back to heaven.[25] In lines 4 and 5 it is said that the load, ܢܘܒܣܐ, was "large" but "light", ܩܠܝܠܐ. These are qualifications which can also be found in Matth. 11, 30. We assume that the soul has been given the "light load" of Christ in order to fulfil its task.[26] The soul descends to Egypt, the place of darkness and imprisonment.[27] The prince has to take away a pearl which is in the possession of a serpent lying in the middle of the sea. Here we are dealing with a fairy tale which can, for example, also be found in the Prayer of Cyriakus.[28] Above we dealt with the pearl. It appears that after having fulfilled his task the prince is allowed to put on his glitterring robe (see under) and that he will live with his brother who is next in authority to the Father. This brother plays an important part

---

[20] Burkitt, *Urchristentum* 152, and Nöldeke, *Rev. of Wright* 26.

[21] See Bevan, *The Hymn* ... , and Widengren, *Der Iran. Hintergrund* ... .

[22] See Schaeder, *Urform* ... . 68, n. 4.

[23] See Preuschen, in: Hennecke, *Handbuch* ... . 587.

[24] See Reitzenstein, *Iran. Erlösungsmysterium* ... . 71, cf. Jonas, *Gnosis* I, 322.

[25] Cf. Ginza R 273, 13: "Meine Reisezehrung kommt von dem fremden Manne, den das Leben wünschte und geplanzt hat. Ich werde unter die Guten kommen, die jener fremde Mann geliebt hat".

[26] See already Preuschen, *Zwei gnostische Hymnen* ... . 49. In ch. 66 it is said: "... since we too, if we bear not the burden that beseems this name, shall rceive punishment".

[27] See Jonas, *Gnosis* I, 322, n. 4, and Preuschen, *Zwei gnost. Hymnen* ... 40–50.

[28] See H. Gressmann, "Das Gebet des Kyriakos", in: *Zeitschr. f. d. neutestamentl. Wissensch.* 20 1921, 23–35. In this prayer it is said that the mother of Cyriakus gives a robe to her son adorned with pearls. He is sent to a dark city with a letter. In this city are living many beasts and a serpent. The serpent is supposed to be the same that deceived Adam, Cain and the people of Israel. Cyriakus puts the letter into the mouth of the serpent. At the end he is able to gather the power of Israel. See also R. Reitzenstein, "Zwei hellenistische Hymnen", in: *Archiv f. Religionswissensch.* VIII 1925, 167–190, and Reitzenstein, *Himmelswanderung* ... . 44–46, and cf. also Bousset, *Manichäisches* ... . 26.

in the hymn. The background of his presence has been discovered by
E. Peterson[29] who referred to Tatian, *Oratio ad Graecos* XIII 2: συζυγίαν
δὲ κεκτημένη τὴν τοῦ θείου πνεύματος οὐκ ἔστιν ἀβοήθητος, ἀνέρχεται
δὲ πρὸς ἄπερ αὐτὴν ὁδηνεῖ χωρία τὸ πνεῦμα. Here is spoken about the
relation between the soul and the spirit in a way which can be found in
the present Hymn.[30]

l. 16–35. On his way to Egypt the soul passes a number of places
accompanied by his guardian angels. In general it is not easy to localise
these cities. The author possibly only knew them by name. During his
journey it is said that he associates himself with one of his race. It is
not clear what is meant. It might be that the story of Thomas and
Abbanes influenced the author (see ch. 2). However, this event does
not influence the contents of the hymn. The principal person clothes
himself in the dress of the Egyptians. The reason is that "they might
not hold (him) in abhorrence". This agrees with what we read about
Christ who deceived the devil because he appeared in the form of
a man, and with the contents of ch. 44 where the devil reproaches
Thomas because he is dressed like a human being. It appears that the
prince tries to struggle with the serpent without being recognized. Next
we read that the prince falls asleep, a well known theme in Eastern
theology.[31]

l. 36–52. A letter is sent to the prince which reminds him of his noble
birth. The idea of a letter from heaven is known from Jewish sources.[32]

---

[29] See E. Peterson, "Einige Bemerkungen zum Hamburger Papyrus-Fragment der
Acta Pauli", in: *Vigiliae Christ.* 3 1949, 142–162.

[30] Peterson, *Einige Bemerkungen* ... . 160: "Das bedeutet doch dass das πνεῦμα als
σύζυγον der Seele mit dieser (im πνευματικοῖς) wie ein Bruder oder ein Zwilling
verbunden ist". The opinion of H. Leisegang, "Der Bruder des Erlösers", in: *ΑΓΓΕΛΟΣ*
I 1925, 24–33, see also A.Marmorstein, "Ein Wort über den Bruders des Erlösers in der
Pistis Sophia", in: *idem* 2 1926, 1, who refer to the κόσμος νοητός and κόσμος αἰσθητός
has to be rejected. Reitzenstein, *Iran. Erlösungsmysterium* ... . 72, referred to Mandaean
sources, but cf. Leisegang on p. 25, n. 1, and Bornkamm, *Mythos* ... . 114.

[31] See F.C. Conybeare, "The Idea of Sleep in the 'Hymn of the Soul", in: *Journ. of
Theol. Studies* 6 1905, 19–5, 609–610.

[32] See M. Dibelius, "Der Hirt des Hermas", in: *Handb. z. N.T.*, Erg.b. IV, Tübingen
1923, 443, about "Himmelsbriefe" on Hermas, *vis.* II 1 3, but cf. also *Kephalaia* 182. 2:
"Siehe an den Ruf, der vom Lebendigen Geist im Anfang ausgesandt worden ist. Er
hat ihm [zum Ur]menschen geschickt. Ein Friedens- und Grussbrief (εἰρηνη, ἀσπασμός,
ἐπιστολή) ist er, den er an seinen Bruder geschrieben und geschickt hat in dem alle
Botschaften (ἀγγελία) niedergeschrieben sind und alle Dingen, die geschehen werden
um die zu erichten durch jenen Ruf", and Ginza L 552. 34–554. 4.

The contents of the letter show a close relationship with Eph. 5, 14.[33] The presence of a "book of the valiant" goes back to Parthian influence.[34]

l. 53–71. The prince remembers his birth and charms the serpent with help of the name of the Father. He returns to heaven. On his way home his letter awakens and leads him. We might suppose the influence of Ps. 119, 105.

l. 72–105. The last part of this hymn consists entirely of a description of the robe. It is brought to him by treasurers and presented to him.[35] It becomes a mirror in which the prince recognizes himself. This means that man's real likeness is in heaven only and that the soul has found its destination.[36]

We may conclude that a number of ideas has been used in order to compose this hymn. The main theme, however, is the pre-existent soul on its way from the Father to this world and its return. All this has been rendered in the form of a fairy-tale and with help of generally known Eastern and especially Parthian motives.

In the Syriac manuscript published and edited by Wright follows a hymn entitled: "The Song of Praise of Thomas the Apostle". In this hymn we meet christological themes known from these Acts. Here the text has been printed without commentary. It does not belong to the original Acts.

> To be glorified are you, Lord of all, self-existent, unutterable, who is hidden in the brightness of your glory from all created things.

---

[33] Adam, *Die Psalmen* ... , 50, assumes, "dass das Zitat in Eph. 5, 14 auf eine Vorlage deutet, die ihrerseits vom Seelenliede abhängig ist". This seems to be far-fetched. Cf. also Johannesbuch 225. 6–7: "Schlummere nicht, Adam, und schlafe nicht und vergiss nicht, was der Herr der aufgetragen hat".

[34] See Widengren, *Der Iran. Hintergrund* ... . 110.

[35] See R. Kuntzmann, *Le Symbolisme des jumeaux au Proche-Orient ancien*, Paris 1983, 183–212: "Le Symbolisme Gémellaire au Service d'une Reognaissance soi-même".

[36] See Odes of Sol. 13. 1: "Behold, the Lord is our mirror ..."; Ginza L 559. 29–32: "Ich gehe mein Abbild entgegen, und mein Abbild geht mir entgegen. Es kost mich und umarmt mich, als käme ich aus der Gefangenschaft zurück". See also W. Schmithals, "Die Gnosis in Korinth", in: *Forsch. z. Religion u. Literatur des A. u. N.T.* 66 1956, 93–94: "Dieser Gedanke, dass Abbild oder auch Kleid der Seele im Himmel ist, ist offenbar vor allem im weiteren Umkreis des Judentums verbreitet und hat sich in der Kabbala bis in die Neuzeit erhalten". See also Bultmann, *Das Evangelium des Johannes* ... . p. 108, n. 4 and Jonas, *Gnosis* I, 325–326.

To be praised are you, the Son, the first-born of life, who are from the exalted Father and the Word of life.

To be glorified are you, the one Father, who portrayed yourself with wisdom in all creatures and in all worlds.

To be praised are you, the Son of light, the Wisdom and the power and the knowledge, who are in all worlds.

To be glorified are you, the Father exalted, who rose (like the sun) from your secrecy into manifestation by means of all your prophets.

To be praised are you, Son of mercy, by whom all things were fulfilled in wisdom and in silence.

To be glorified are you, the Father supreme, born of your First-born in the silence and tranquillity of meditation.

To be praised are you, the Son adored, who rose (as the sun) from the Father, with his aspect, in peace and in glory.

To be glorified are you, the good Father, who revealed the mystery of your First-born to the prophets by the Spirit of holiness.

To be praised are you, the proved Son, who revealed the glory of the Father in your Apostles in all nations.

To be glorified are you, the Father serene, who hallowed your majesty for ever in your First-born, the giver of life in your creation.

To be praised are you, the comely Son, who rose (like the sun) from the splendour of the Father, and delivered our souls by your innocent blood.

To be glorified are you, Father omnipotent, who dwells in your glorious light, and is shrouded in your glory, and manifested in all your grace.

To be praised are you, the perfect Son, who is sown in the living earth, and was before the world with your holy Father.

To be glorified are you, the Feeder of all, who is in all worlds, on high and in the deep, and there is no place that is void of you.

To be praised are you, the Son, the adored fruit, who rose (like the sun) upon all in mercy, and put on humanity, and whom our adversary slew.

To be glorified are you, the infinite Father, who made the angels of the overflowings of your Spirit and your ministers your flaming fire.

To be praised are you, the Son of light, who is borne on the Spirit, and shrouded in the light of the Father, on holy clouds.

To be glorified are you, the Father giving life to all, who assembled the worlds for your glory by the hand of your dear (Son), that they might make praise to ascend to you.

To be praised are you, Son of life, of whose gift the Father gives in abundance to the holy, and through it they set out and arrive in the path of peace.

To be glorified are you, the Father giving life to all who have revealed the mysteries of your Son by the Spirit to his saints, in tranquillity and rest.

To be praised are you, the Son, the fruit of the Father, who hides your chosen ones under your wings, and have fulfilled the will of your Father, and redeemed your dear ones.

To be glorified are you, the good Father, giving life to all creatures by the hand of your dear (Son), in mercy and in grace, through his death by crucifixion

To be praised are you, the first-born Son, feeding created beings with your body, and blotting out our sins with the sign of your wounds and with the sprinkling of your blood upon us.

To be glorified are you, the good Father, who dwells in the pure heart, in the mind of your worshippers, and are hidden from all in our aspect, and revealed to us in your Messiah.

To be praised are you, the Son, the word, proclaiming your coming in stillness, who put on our humanity and deliver us by your living and innocent blood.

To be glorified are you, the living Father, who gave (new) life to our deadness, for we had erred from your way and were dead and perished, but your mercy was upon us.

To be praised are you, the beloved Son, who gave (new) life to our deadness, and turned back our going astray and was to us a medicine of life by your life-giving body and by the sprinkling of your living blood.

To be glorified are you, the Father exalted by all mouths and by all tongues, who have been reconciled to us by your Messiah, and whom we have tasted through your fruit and have become children of your place.

To be praised are you, the Son, the peace-maker, who have healed our wounds and persuaded our hardness (of heart), and collected our wandering, and trained us in your truth and we have known through you your Father.

To be glorified are you, the Father omnipotent, who have sent to us your living and life-giving fruit; and he reconciled by the blood of his cross your mercy with your creatures.

To be praised are you, the Son, the word of light who rose (like the sun) from on high and satisfy us with the knowledge of you, and cleansed our impurity and gave (new) life to our deadness by your sign, the cross of light.

To be glorified are you, the Father of all praises and to be exalted is your great name in all worlds, for you have not reckoned against us our sins, but have given us life through your Messiah, who is the life of your will.

To be praised are you, the voice conceived of knowledge, our holy priest, who have made atonement for us by your pure and holy offering, and have poured out your living blood on behalf of sinners.

To be glorified are you, the Father exalted, who are hidden from all worlds, and are revealed according to your will to all your worshippers.

To be praised are you, the Son of life, accomplishing the will of your Father; who has reconciled your creatures, so that they worship in you him who sent you and are become partakers of your mysteries.

To be glorified are you, the Father exalted, by every knee which shall bow to you, both in heaven and on earth, through your dear (Son).

To be praised are you, the adorned Son of perfect mercy, through whom there has come peace and hope for the creatures, that they may know the Creator.

To be glorified are you, the Father giving like to all, the riches of whose mercy are never exhausted by the abundance of your gifts, but at all times you have a need of giving to us.

To be praised are you, the Son, the fruit, for you are the gate of light and the way of truth, and you have made us run in your footsteps, that we may arrive at the house of your exalted Father.

To be glorified are you, the Father benign, who has given us peace by the hand of our Life-giver and has revealed to us your glorious and holy mysteries by the hearing of your doctrine.

To be praised are you, the only(-begotten) Son of the Father, whose mercy has been upon us, and you have signed us with your living and life-giving Cross.

All mouths and all tongues glorify the Father and worship the Son and praise your Holy Spirit, the worlds and the creatures which are hidden and which are manifest.

Your angels glorify you on high through your Messiah, who became in Sheol peace and hope to the dead, who came to life and were raised.

We beg of you, our Lord and our Life-giver (the accomplishment) of all that you have said and promised. Fulfill with us your grace, and raise us up to the place of your peace; for you are our Life-giver, you are our Paraclete, you are the medicine of our life, you are our sign of victory.

Blessed are we, Lord, who have known you. Blessed are we, who have believed in you. Blessed are we through your wounds and your blood, (suffered and shed) on our behalf. Blessed are we, for you are our great hope. Blessed are we, for you are our God, and for ever and ever. Amen

114

And Karish, the husband of Mygdonia, went to his house, rejoicing greatly, because he thought in his mind that henceforth his wife would be with him as formerly, before she heard the words of Judas and believed in our Lord Jesus the Messiah, the Son of God. And when Karish went, he found his wife sitting and her looks were downcast, and her clothes rent, and she was like a mad woman, because of Judas. He says to her: "My lady and sister Mygdonia, what is the wicked folly that has taken possession of you? And why have you done these things? I am Karish, the husband of your youth, and I am he who from the gods and by the law has power of you. Why have you now acted like a mad woman? And why have you become a laughing-stock through this whole country? But from this moment dismiss the thought of that **wizard** from your mind, for I am about to take away the sight of him from before your eyes, that you may see him no more.

Commentary. The contents of the chapters 114–116 show some agreement with those in Hellenistic "love-romances", especially those of Achilles Tatius, see edition S. Gaselee, V 25–26. **wizard**. See ch. 16

115

And when she heard these things from Karish her husband, she was again sorely grieved and afflicted. And he said again to her: "What crime, pray, **have you committed** against the gods, that they have let you come to this great misery? And what sin **have you brought** before them that they have brought you to this degradation and ridicule? I beg of you, Mygdonia, torture not my soul by the sight of you, and pain not my heart by your care. I am Karish, the husband of your youth, and I am your true husband, whom the whole country honours and whom they fear. What I shall do henceforth, I do not know, nor how I shall conduct myself, nor what plan I shall devise. Shall I remember in my heart your beauty and be silent? Or shall I think of your chaste conduct, and say nothing? Who is there, from whom they (try to) take away a goodly and fair treasure, and he lets go his hold of it? Am I able to bear (the loss of) your winsome beauties, which are with me at all times? Your sweet fragrance, lo, is in my nostrils; and our fair colour, lo, is before my eyes; my soul, which they (are trying to) take away from me; my bright eyes, with which I saw and which they are plucking out and taking away from me; my fair body, of which I was proud and which they are ill-using and taking away from me; my right arm, which they are cutting off from me; my beauty, which is destroyed; my comfort, through which they are distressing me; my joy, which is turned into sorrow; my rest, which has become an affliction to me; my life which is changed into death; my light, which is dyed with darkness. The members of my great house shall not see me (again), for in this affliction I have had no help (from them). My noble friends shall not see me (again), who have not saved me from affliction. I will no longer worship the gods of the East, who have brought me to these miseries, nor will I pray before them, nor sacrifice to them again nor offer to them an offering, because I am deprived of this my true union. For what (prayer) should I again pray to them? Or what should I beg of them, or ask of them to give me, who have deprived me of that which was dearer to me than everything which I possessed in the world, and with which I was contented? For I have more wealth than I can use, and possessions, the amount of which I cannot reckon. A prince too I have been made, and I have been named the king's deputy; and many fear me, and many are under my hand. Would that someone would take away from me all these glories and my great wealth, and give me one hour of your past years, Mygdonia! Would that someone would blind one of my eyes, and that your eyes would look upon me as they were wont! Would that someone would cut off my right arm, and that I might embrace you with my left arm!"

Commentary. **have you committed** and **have you wrought**. See Geiger, "Sprachliche Bemerkungen zu Wright's Apocr. Acts", in: *Zeitschr. d. Deutschen Morgenl. Gesellschaft* 26 1870, 798–804, esp. 804.

116

Whilst Karish was saying these things and weeping, Mygdonia was sitting like one stone-deaf, and looked not at him, but upon the ground, and was silent. And he came near to her again, and said to her: "My daughter and my beloved, Mygdonia, remember that you please me above all the women of India, and that I chose you when I might have taken many who were of higher rank than you. But indeed, I lie not, Mygdonia; no, by God, there is not for me another (woman) in all India like to you. What beauty, and what ornament, and what elegance, and what noble qualities am I losing! Woe to me and to the world, for I shall never hear you speak again! Although he has reviled (me), I beg of you, lift your eyes and look on me, for I am far better than that **wizard**, and am handsomer than he, and I have wealth and honour, and every one knows that no one has a lineage like mine. And you are more to me than my kindred and than all that I have; and lo, they are taking you away from me!"

Commentary. **wizard**. See ch. 16.

II7

And when Karish had said these things, Mygdonia said to him: "Karish, he whom I love is more than all that you possess and all that you have; for all that you have is of the earth and remains on the earth; but he whom I love is in heaven, and he will take me up to heaven to himself. For your **wealth** passes away, and your **beauty** becomes marred, and your robes become old and decay and perish, **and you (are) left alone with your trespasses and your sins**. If you are not delivered from them, they will cleave to you. Remind me not of your former doings with me, which I pray and beg of my Lord to blot out for me. Remind me not of your filthy pleasures and your fleshly deeds, from which I pray that I may be rescued by the love of my Lord. I have forgotten all your practices and your familiarities and your doings are at an end with yourself; but my Lord and my Saviour, **Jesus, abides** alone for ever, with those souls which have taken **refuge** with him. He with whom I have taken refuge and in whom I have believed will save me and deliver me from all your deeds, which I used to do with you, when I did not believe." And when Karish heard these things, he went and lay down to sleep, being grieved. And he said to her: "Reflect and consider (this) in your mind to-day, the whole night. If you will be with me as you were, before you saw this **wizard**, I will humour you in all that you wish. And if you wish, because of the love that you have had for him, I will lead him forth (and) convey him away, and he shall go to another country, and I will not cause you any distress, for I know that you **cleave to him**. And this did not begin with you, but the like of this thing has befallen many women; but at last they have bethought themselves, and discerned what has befallen them, and come to themselves, and have been saved from insult and mockery. Let not, then, these things which I have said to you, seem to you as nothing, and let them not pass away as external to you; and make me not a mockery and a laughing-stock and a proverb in India".

Commentary. **wealth ... beauty ... robes**. See ch. 36. **Jesus abides**. See for similar contrasts ch. 88. **and you (are left) alone ... sins**. The words ܘ̈ܢܝ ܚ̈ܛܗܝܟ ܘܒ̈ܣܟܠܘܬܟ are the same as in the Lord's Prayer, see ch. 144. Greek: μόνος δὲ σύ μετὰ τῶν πλημμαλημματῶν σου γυμνός. For the word γυμνός, see Apocalypse of Moses 20, ed. von Tischhendorf 11, see ed. Riessler 145: "Zur selben Stunde werden mir die Augen aufgetan, und ich (Adam) erkannte: Ich bin entblösst von der Gerechtigkeit, womit ich war bekleidet". Ginzberg, *The Legends of the Jews* V, 121–122: "The haggadic interpretation (of Gen. 3, 7 and 10) is: And they became aware that they were bare of good deeds". See also *Theologisches Wörterbuch z. N.T.* I, 773–775, *s.v.* γυμνός (Oepke). **refuge**. See ch. 10. **wizard**. See ch. 16. **cleave to him**. Greek: σφόδρα τοῦ ξένου ἀποποιῇ. See ch. 4.

118

And when he had said these things to her, he went (and) slept. But Maydonia took **twenty zuze** and went, without any one perceiving her, to the prison, to give it to **the keepers of the prisoners**, that they might let her in to Judas. And as she was going, **Judas met her**, coming to her; and she saw him and was afraid, for she thought that it was **one of the nobles**, because of the **great light** which was shining before him; and she said: "**Woe to you, feeble soul that is perishing! I shall never again see Judas, the Apostle of Jesus, the living God, because I have not yet received the sign of baptism from him**". And she fled, and went into another street, and says: "It is better for me that others, (who are poor), should take me, for I can persuade them (to let me go), and that this **great man** should not take me, who will not accept a bribe from me".

Commentary. **twenty zuze**, ܐܪ̈ܝ ܙܘܙܐ, which apparently means: ten zuze. **the keepers of the prisoners**. The passage has a deeper meaning and deals with the guardians between earth and heaven, see also ch. 148. Cf. Ginza R 405. 31–32: "Was werdet ihr den Wachthäuslern und den Gefangenenaufseher sagen, die dort wohnen", and Ginza L 547. 25. The world being a prison, see Ephrem, *adv. haer.*, ed. Beck 97 (translation) and 106 (Syriac): "In einem Kerker gebar uns Eva … Der Gefangene betet, dass man ihn (von den Fesseln) löse; der Eingekerkerte fleht, (dem Körper) zu entkommen". **Judas met her**. See ch. 34. **one of the nobles**, ܪܘܪ̈ܒܢܐ and Greek: ἕνα τῶν ἀρχόντων obviously the leader of the keepers of the prisoners, cf. Origen, *c. Cels.* VI 30, ed. Chadwick 345, n. 6 and 334, n. 2, and *Pistis Sophia*, ed Schmidt–Till 129. 37–130. 3: "… denn meine Brüder predigen (κηρύσσειν) es unter dem Menschengeschlecht (-γένος) damit sie hören und Reue empfinden (μετανοιεῖν) und for den gewaltigen Gerichten (κρίσις) der bösen (πονηρός) Archonten (ἄρχοντες) gerettet werden und zur Höhe gehen und das Lichtreich ererben (κληρονομεῖν)". **great light**.

See ch. 27. Here Thomas himself shines with a great light, cf. *Acta Pauli*, ed. Schmidt 3. 10–4. 5, where Paul leaves the prison to baptise Artemilla, and 3. 28–30: καὶ νεανίσκ[ος ὅ]μοι[ος] ... [... σῶ]μα παύλου φαίν[ων] ... προῆγεν αὐτούς. **Woe to you ... baptism from him**. Baptism has protective value, see ch. 49. Here it protects during the journey to heaven, cf. *Acta Philippi* 144, in: L.B. II II, 86. 5–8: ἀλλ᾽ ἔνδυσον με τὴν ἔνδοξον σου στολήν, τὴν φωτεινήν σου σφραγῖδα τὴν πάντοτε λάμπουσαν, ἕως ἄν παρέλθω πάντας τοὺς κοσμοκράτορας καὶ τον πονηρὸν δράκοντα τὸν ἀντικείμενον ἡμῖν. Very often in gnostic literature, cf. Irenaeus, *adv. haer.* I 21 5, about the Marcosians: *Alii sunt, qui mortuos redimunt ... mittentes eorum capitibus oleum et aquam ... ut incomprehensibiles et invisibiles principibus et potestatibus fiant;* Origen, *c. Celsum* VI 27 about the Ophites; Hippolytus, *refut.* V 10 about the Naasenes: σφραγῖδας ἔχων καιαβήσομαι; Book of Jeu I, ed. Schmidt–Till 294. 38–295. 4: "... so saget ... ihre Siegel (σφραγῖδας) ... so ziehen sich die Wächter (φύλακες) ... zurück, bis ihr zu dem Orte (τόπος) ihres Vaters gelangt. **great man**, ܪ̈ܒܐ ܗܘ ܓܒܪܐ and Greek: ἄρχων. See above.

119

And whilst Mygdonia was meditating these things, Judas came and entered in behind her. And she was afraid, and fell down from terror; and he stood over her, and said to her: "Be not afraid, Mygdonia; Jesus the Messiah will not forsake you, and your Lord will not forsake you, to whom you have committed your soul; the Gracious will not forsake you, whose mercy is great; the Benign will not forsake you for his kindness' sake; the Good will not forsake you for his goodness' sake; the Great will not forsake you for his greatness' sake. **Rise from the ground, above which you once were (raised)**. Look upon the **light of your Lord, for he will not let those that love him walk in darkness**. Behold the **Companion** of his servants, to whom he is a light in darkness. Behold the Help of his servants to whom he is a helper in afflictions". And Mygdonia arose and was looking at him and saying to him: "Whither were you going, my Lord? And who let you out of prison to see the sun?" Judas says to her: "Our Lord Jesus the Messiah is **stronger than all powers and kings and rulers; he opened the doors and lulled the keepers to sleep**".

Commentary. **Rise from the ground.** See ch. 37. **above which you once were (raised)**, ܠܗ ,ܗܘܡ ܡܢ ܠܥܠ ܘܗ ܐ ,ܗ. Greek: ὑπεράνω ταύτης ἅπασα γενομένη. The translator probably read ܠܗ in place of ܠܗ. **light ... darkness.** See ch. 28. **Companion.** See ch. 10. **Help.** See ch. 30. Greek: σύμμαχος ἐν κινδύνοις see also ch. 39. **stronger than all powers,** ܚܝܠܐ, **kings,** ܡܠܟܐ, **rulers,** ܫܘܠܛܢܐ. Cf. Col. 2, 10, where it is said that Christ is: ἡ κεφαλὴ πάσης ἀρχῆς καὶ ἐξουσίας cf. syr p: ܫܘܠܛܢܐ, and Eph. 1, 21: ἀρχὴ ... ἐξουσία (syr p: ܫܘܠܛܢܐ)—δύναμις (syr p: ܚܝܠܐ) **he opened the doors ... sleep.**, Cf. ch. 153.

120

Mygdonia says to him: "Give me the sign of Jesus the Messiah, and let me receive his gift from your hands, before you depart from the world". And she took him, and went and entered into her house, and awakened her nurse and says to her: "My mother and nurse **Narkia**, all your deeds of help to me, and your kindnesses from my childhood until now, you have done to me in vain, and my fleeting favour I bestow to you for them; but do me this favour which (lasts) for ever, and you shall be rewarded by him who gives everything to his, and fortune cannot deprive them (thereof)". Narkia says to her: "What do you want, my daughter Mygdonia? And what comfort can you have? For all the former humours, (which) you promised to do to me, the **strange** man does not let you (do), and you have made me a reproach in this country. Now, I pray, what do you want to do anew to me?" She says to her: "Be with me a sharer in the everlasting life, and let me receive from you the **perfect education**. Fetch secretly for me a loaf of bread, and bring out for me a **mingled draught of wine, and have pity on me a freeborn woman**". Narkia says to her: "I will fetch you bread in plenty and many flagons of wine, and I will do your pleasure (for you)". Mygdonia says to her nurse Narkia: "Many flagons are of no use to me, but a mingled draught in a cup, and one whole loaf, and a little oil, even if (it be) in a lamp, bring to me".

Commentary. **Narkia**, ܢܰܪܩܺܝ and Greek: μαρκία. **strange**. See ch. 4. **perfect education**, ܪܰܒܽܘܬܳܐ ܓܡܺܝܪܬܳܐ. She apparently asks for a christian education in contrast to what she received from her during her childhood. Greek reads: τροφὴν, which refers to oil, bread and wine. **mingled draught of wine**. See also ch. 158. For water mingled with wine see Justin, *apol.* I 65; Irenaeus, *adv. haer.* V 2 3; Clemens of Alex., *paed.* II 20 1, and *Test. Domini nostri* II X, ed. Rahmani 131–132. **and have pity on me, a freeborn woman**, ܘܚܳܣ ܥܰܠ ܚܺܐܪܽܘܬܝ and Greek: τῆς ἐλευθερίας μου φειδομένη. It seems that Narkia is supposed to prepare the means by which Mygdonia is going to become free. Baptism making free, see ch. 121: "… and heal her with this freedom" (in Greek), cf. Ephrem, *hymni in festum epiphaniae* IV 7, ed. Lamy I 45–46: *Servus enim qui omnis libertatis largitorem in aquis induit, in terra quidem servus remanet ad in coelo liber fit, quia ipsa libertate cooperitur*, and *Exc. e Theodoto* 78. 2, ed. Sagnard 202: ἔστιν δὲ οὐ τὸ λουτρὸν μόνον τὸ ἐλευθεροῦν ἀλλὰ καὶ ἡ γνῶσις. See also Rom. 6, 1–23 and *Theol. Wörterbuch z. N.T.* II 492–500, *s.v.* ἐλεύθερος (Schlier).

And when Narkia had brought (them), Mygdonia uncovered her head, and was standing before the holy Apostle. And he took the oil, and cast (it) on her head, and said: "**Holy oil, which was given to us for unction, and hidden mystery of the cross, which is seen through it—you the straightener of crooked limbs, you our Lord Jesus, life and health and remission of sins,—let your power come and abide upon this oil, and let your holiness dwell in it**". **And he cast (it) upon the head of Mygdonia, and said: "Heal her old wounds, and wash away from her sores, and strengthen her weakness**". And when he had cast the oil on her head, **he told her nurse to anoint her**, and to put a cloth round her loins; and he fetched the **basin of their conduit**. And Judas went up (and) stood over it, and baptized Mygdonia in the name of the Father and the Son and the Spirit of holiness. And when she had come out and put on her clothes, **he fetched and broke the Eucharist** and (filled) the cup, and let Mygdonia partake of the table of the Messiah and of the cup of the Son of God. And he said to her: "Now then you have received the sign and gained to yourself your life for ever and ever". And a voice was heard from heaven which said: "Yes, amen and amen". And when Narkia heard this voice, she was amazed, and she too begged of the Apostle that she also might receive the sign; and he gave (it) to her and said: "May the great Jesus be with you as with the rest of your companions". And he went to be shut up in prison, and found the doors open and the watchmen asleep.

Commentary. **Holy oil ... seen through it**. The first act of baptism is the anointing. In Greek the word εἰς ἁγιασμὸν is used in stead of "unction", cf II Thess. 2, 13: εἵλατο ὑμᾶς ὁ θεός ... εἰς σωτηρίαν ἐν ἁγιασμῷ πνεύματος and I Peter 1, 2. In ch. 157 is spoken of a relation between oil and the cross which can be understood if we know that in paradise an olive tree was supposed to be present, see Slav. Hen. 8, 5 and cf. 22, 8, see H. Troje, ΑΓΑΜ ΖΩΗ, in: *Sitzungsber. der Heidelb. Ak. der Wissensch.* phil.-hist. Kl. VII 1916, 82–89; Widengren, *Mesopotamian Elements* ... . 125; G.P. Wetter, "Altchristliche Liturgien", in: *Forsch. z. Rel. u. Lit. des A. u. N.T*, n.F. 13 1922, 93 and H. Bergema, *De Boom des Levens in Schrift en Historie*, Hilversum 1938, 151–152. In addition to this the cross was identified with the tree of life, see *Theol. Wörterbuch z. N.T.* V, 40, *s.v.* ξύλον, (Schneider) and Origen, *c. Cels.* VI 27: κέχρισμαι χρίσματι λευκῷ ἐκ ξύλου ζωῆς; The Sacr. of Serapion, ed. Brightman 265, about the conformation: ἐπικαλούμεθα σε, ὥστε διὰ τῆς θείας καὶ ἀοράτου σου δυνάμεως τοῦ κυρίου καὶ σωτῆρος ἡμῶν ἰησοῦ χριστοῦ ἐνεργῆσαι ἐν τῷ χρίσματι τούτῳ ἐνέργειαν θείαν καὶ οὐράνιον, ἵνα οἱ βαπτισθέντες καὶ χριόμενοι ἐν αὐτῷ τὸ ἐκτύπωμα τοῦ σημείου τοῦ σωτηριώδους σταυροῦ τοῦ μονογενοῦς δι’ οὗ σταυροῦ διετράπη καὶ ἐθριαρβεύθη σατανᾶς καὶ πᾶσα δύναμις ἀντικειμένη; Ps.-Clement *recognit.* I 45, ed. Gersdorf 26: *nunc (Christum) primum pater oleo perunxit, quod ex ligno vitae fuerat sumtum,* and Ephrem, *de Thoma apostolo,* ed. Lamy IV c. 701–702: *tu es lucerna magna (Thomas), una e duodecim plena oleo crucis quas profundas filiae Indiae tenebras luce profundisti.* See for an identification of the tree and the Holy Spirit *Liber Graduum,* ed. Kmosko, in: *Patrol. Syr* I III, c. 855–858: *Hoc enim est vitae arbor horti Eden, per quam reviviscunt homines a morte, quae arbor est Spiritus vivificans.* **you, the straightener of the crooked limbs** and **Heal her of her old wounds … weakness.** Cf. Hebr. 12, 13–14. Baptism means the healing of man, cf. ch. 10 and 157. The Greek version adds after the word "limbs": "you are the humbler (ταπεινωτῆς) of hard things (τῶν σάληρῶν ἔργων), you are the one that shows the hidden mysteries, cf. ch. 27, you are the sprout of goodness. Let the power … Mygdonia and heal her by this freedom", see ch. 120. **let your power … dwell in it.** Greek: "let your power come, let it be established (ἱδρυνθήτω) upon your servant Mygdonia". In the Syriac version the epiclesis is on the oil and in the Syriac version on the one who is going to be baptized. **he told her nurse to anoint her.** Greek omits this passage. Anointing by women, see Tertullian, *de praescr. haer.* 41. 5; *Didascalia* III 12 2; *Testam. Domini nostri* II 8, ed. Rahmani 129–130. See also ch. 157 and A. Kalsbach, *Die altkirchliche Einrichtung der Diakonissen bis zu ihrem Erlöschen,* Freiburg 1926, 26–27. **basin of their conduit.** Greek: "there was there a fountain of water", which means that the use of "living water" has been emphasized, see ch. 49. **he fetched and broke the Eucharist.** Greek: "he broke bread and took a cup of water and made her partaker (κοινωνὸν ἐποίησεν) in the body of Christ and the cup of the Son of God". This has been influenced by I Cor 10, 15. **voice.** See ch. 27.

122

And Judas said: "Who is like unto you, o God, who does not withhold your love and mercy from man? Who is like unto you in mercy and grace, save your Father, who has delivered his universe from misery and **error**? Love that has conquered desire; truth that has destroyed falsehood; you **fair** (one) in whom nothing odious is seen; you **humble** (one), who has cast down pride; you living (one), who has destroyed death; you **tranquil** (one), who has put an end to toil;—glory to the Only(-begotten), who (is) of the Father! Glory to the **mercy** which was sent by **mercy!** Glory to your mercy which is upon us!" And when he had said these things, the watchmen awoke, and found all the doors open, but the prisoners asleep; and they said: "**We forgot these doors and did not close them; had this been (done) by an adversary, not a man would have remained here**".

Commentary. **error**. See ch. 25. **fair**. See ch. 8. **humble**. See Matth. 11, 39. **tranquil**. ܢܝܚܐ and Greek: ἡ ἄνεσις see Math. 11, 29. **mercy ... mercy**. See ch. 10. **We forget ... here**. Cf. Acts 16, 27–28.

123

And Karish went early in the morning to Mygdonia and to her nurse, and found her and her nurse praying and saying: "New God who has come hither through a **strange** man; holy God, who is hidden from the whole race of the Indians; God who has shown us your glory through your apostle Thomas; God of whom we have heard tell and have believed in you; God, to whom, because we perceived that there was life in you, we have run that you might give us life; God, who, because of your mercy and your grace, **reached down to our littleness**; God, who sought us when we did not know you; God who sits on high, and nothing that is in the depth is concealed from you;—you, Lord, keep off from us the hot anger of Karish; stop his lying mouth; and cast him beneath the feet of your believers". And when Karish heard these hings, he says to Mygdoia: "Well have you called me evil and hot and odious and bitter, for had I not humoured you, this wretchedness and bitterness would not have come about me, and you would not be invoking against me the **witchcraft** of that (man). But what thought have you then conceived, Mygdonia? And what do you wish me do for you? Believe me, Mygdonia, there is no good in that wizard and he cannot do anything that he promises to anyone. But I will show you before your eyes all that I say to you, if you will be persuaded by me and listen to my words, and be with me as you were with me".

Commentary. **strange**. See ch. 4. **reached … littleness**. See ch. 15 and 80. **witchcraft**. See ch. 16.

124

And he drew near again to her, and was begging of her and saying to her: "I shall feel no distress, if you will be persuaded by me. Remember, my sister, your wedding-day, and the first day on which you accepted me (as your husband), and tell me now in truth, who is dearer to you, I at that time or Jesus at this time". Mygdonia says to him: "Karish **that time required its due and is gone; and this time required its due**. That was the time of the beginning, this is the time of the end. That was the time of the temporal life which passes away, this is the time of the life everlasting. That was the time of transitory joy; this is the time of the eternal joy which does not pass away. That was the time of day and night; this is the time of day without night. That marriage-feast you see how it has passed away and is gone; but this marriage-feast shall never pass away. That was a marriage-feast of corruption; this is a marriage-feast of life everlasting. Those were the groomsmen and bridesmaids who pass away; these are the groomsmen and bridesmaids who abide for ever. That (union) was founded upon the earth were there is an unceasing press; this was founded **upon the bridge of fire, upon which is sprinkled grace**. That was a bridal-chamber which was taken down; this is a bridal-chamber which remains for ever. That was a bed which was covered with goodly clothes that decay; this is a bed which is covered with love and faith and truth. You are a bridegroom who passes away and is changed; Jesus is the true bridegroom who endures for ever, and never dies, and is never subject to corruption. That marriage-gift was money and clothes which decay and pass away, this marriage is living words which never pass away."

Commentary. **That time … due**. See also ch. 66. The contrasts are characteristic for these Acts, see ch. 12 and 36. Cf. Aphraates, *dem.* VI 6, ed. Parisot, c. 269–270: *Pro gentibus filiarum Hevae, cantica Sponsi proferunt. Convivia filiarum Hevae septem dierum spatio [celebrantur]; illarum vero Sponsus non descendet in aeternum. Habent Hevae filiae ornamenta lanea, marcida et corruptibilia; illarum autem vestimenta non veterascent. Venustas filiorum terra immutantur senecta; illarum pulchritudo tempore se resurrectionis innovabitur.* **upon the bridge of fire**, ܐܢܘܪܐ ܕܡܒܥܪܐ ܥܠ, **upon which is sprinkled grace**. Greek is corrupt: ἐκεῖνος ὁ γάμος ἐπὶ γῆς ἵστησιν φιλανθρωπίαν δροσίζων. Cf. Bar Hebr., *Book of the Dove*, ed. Wensinck, 77: "Every clear soul seeks its original country, and directs itself towards it on the straight way, which is nearest. The righteous pass as it were a bridge of fire, because fire burns upward in a straight line, without impediment." See also Lipsius, *Apokr. Apostelgesch.* I, p. 304, n. 1 and 321, n. 1. Sinai is present from: "never pass away" until ch. 127: "that is worse than you".

125

And whem Karish had heard these things, he went (and) told them to king Mazdai. And king Mazdai said: "Let us fetch (and) destroy him." Karish his friend says to him: "Have patience with him a little, and bring him out (of prison) and speak to him, and frighten him; perhaps he will go and persuade Mygdonia to be with me as she was."

126

And king Mazdai sent and fetched Judas Thomas, the Apostle of the Most High. And all the prisoners were grieved because Judas the Apostle had departed from them, and were looking for him and saying: "The pleasure which we had they have taken away from us." And king Mazdai said to Judas: "Why do you teach a doctrine which gods and men abhor, and in which there is nothing pleasing?" Judas says to him: "What do I teach that is bad?" Mazdai says to him: "What you say, that men cannot live with God, unless they keep themselves **purely** for the God whom you preach." Judas says to him: "Verily this I say and I do not lie in what I say. Pray, can your servants stand before you in mean garb or when soiled and dirty? You, therefore, who are an earthly king and perish with the earth, require of your servants things fair and clean; as to my King, how do you say that I speak ill (in saying) that his servants should serve him with **holiness** and **purity** and **temperance** and should be without care and without concern and should be free from the **heavy burden of sons and daughters** and from the great care of wealth and from the trouble and empty pride of riches? For you have wanted that those who serve you and obey you should conduct themselves as you do; and if one of them transgresses one of your commandments, he receives chastisement from you. How much more does it behove us who believe in the name of this God of mine to serve him in **purity** and in **holiness** and in temperance and in **chastity** and in **modesty**, and that all these fleshly (lusts) should be strange to us, **adultery and theft and drunkenness and lavishness and the service of the belly and deeds of shame and odious actions?**"

Commentary. **purity**, ܙܟܘܬܐ, see ch. 12. **holiness-purity-temperance**, ܩܕܝܫܘܬܐ - ܕܟܝܘܬܐ - ܡܟܝܟܘܬܐ, see ch. 86. **heavy burden of sons and daughters**, see ch. 12. **purity**, ܕܟܝܘܬܐ, **holiness**, ܩܕܝܫܘܬܐ, **temperance**, ܡܟܝܟܘܬܐ, **chastity**, ܢܟܦܘܬܐ, which actually means "splendour", "glow" or "honour", in Greek: ἀσφαλεία cf. syr phil in Luke 1, 4 rendering ἀσφαλεία by ܢܟܦܘܬܐ **modesty**, ܟܢܝܟܘܬܐ, see ch. 12 and 52. **adultery ... odious actions**, see ch. 28.

127

And when king Mazdai had heard these things, he said to Judas: "See, I let you free; (and) persuade Mygdonia, the wife of Karish, not to part from him." Judas say to him: "If you wish to do anything to me, delay not; for, if she has really received what she has heard, neither iron nor fire, nor anything else that is worse than these, will do anything to her or sever him who has taken possession of her soul." King Mazdai says to Judas: "I have heard that **wizards** can dissolve charms and **that the sting of a viper can be healed by an antidote which is got from another creature that is worse than a viper**. Now, therefore, if you choose, you are able to dissolve these former charms of you and to make peace and concord between the husband and his wife; and (in so doing) you will have pity upon yourself, for you are not yet sated of your life. And know that, if you do not persuade her, I will destroy you out of this life which is dear to all men." Judas says to him: "This life is but a loan and this time passes away and is changed, but the life which I teach never passes away and is never changed. This beauty and youth which is now apparent (in me), will not be mine after a little." King Mazdai says to him: "I advised you that which was to your advantage but you know better than I."

Commentary. **wizard**. See ch. 16. **that the sting of a viper ... viper**. For the word "antidote", ܬܪܝܩܐ Greek: ϑηριακή, see Krauss, *Talmud. Archäol.* I, p. 257. **beauty**. See ch. 88.

128

And when Judas Thomas had gone out from before king Mazdai, Karish came to him and said to him: "I ask of you—I have never done any wrong to you nor to any (other man) nor the the gods— why did you bring this calamity upon me? And why have you brought this desolation to my house? And what profit accrues to you from this? Ask me and I will supply it to you without labour. And why do you do mischief to me, when you cannot escape from my hands? For know that if you do not persuade her (to return to me), I will destroy you, and her too I will destroy out of this life and finally I will destroy myself out of the world. And if, as you say, there be life and death and condemnation and acquittal and judgment and recompense, there I will stand with you in judgment; and if your God who teaches you, be just and takes vengeance justly, I shall be recompensed as I have done you no wrong, but you have afflicted me and I have not aimed against you, but you have sinned against me. But even here I can take revenge on you and do to you all that you have done to me. Listen to me therefore and come with me to my house and speak to Mygdonia and persuade her to be with me as she was before she saw your face."

And Judas went with him laughing and said to him: "If men loved God as they love their fellows, all that they asked of him he would give them and there would be nothing which would not obey them."

Commentary. Sinai is present from "I will supply" until ch. 136 "gives life to all those".

129

And when he had said these things, Judas entered the house of Karish and found Mygdonia sitting and Narkia standing before her. And her hands were placed on her cheeks and she was saying to her nurse: "Would that the days passed swiftly over me, my mother, and that all the hours were one that I might go forth from this world and go (and) see that **Beautiful** (One) of whom I have heard tell, that Living (One) and Giver of Life to those who believe in him where there is **neither night nor day and no darkness but light** and neither good nor bad, nor **rich nor poor, nor male nor female, nor slaves nor freemen** nor any who are proud and uplifted over those who are humble."

And while she was saying these things, Judas came in; and she sprang upright (and) prostrated herself to him. Karish says to him: "See, she fears you and loves you and whatever you say to her she will gratify you (therein)."

Commentary. **Beautiful**. See ch. 8. **neither night ... light**. Cf. Apoc. 21, 25 and 25, 5. **rich ... freemen**. Cf. Gal. 3, 28.

130

Judas says to her: "My daughter Mygdonia, consent to what your brother Karish says to you." Mygdonia says to him: "You are unable to name the deed and how can you persuade me to do it? For I have heard you say: 'This temporal life is (but) a loan, and this rest is (but) temporary and these possessions do not abide'. And again you said: '**Whoever hates this life, shall go (and) receive life everlasting**; and whoever hates this light of day and night shall go (and) receive the light in which there is no night.' And again you said: 'Whoever forsakes these earthly possessions shall go (and) find possessions that abide for ever, and other things (similar to these). Because you are afraid, you say these things to me (now). Who is there that is doing a thing and exults in it and turns round (and) renounces it? And who is there that is building a tower and overturns (and) roots it up from its foundations? And who is there that is digging a well in a parched place and throws in stones and fills it up? And who is there that is finding a goodly treasure and does not make use of it?" And when Karish, the kinsman of king Mazdai, heard these things, he said: "I am not like to you and I will not be in haste to destroy you, but you I will bind, because I have power over you and I will not let you go to this **wizard** and converse with him. And if you yield, (good and well), and if not, I know what I will do."

Commentary. **whoever hates ... everlasting**. Cf John 12, 25. **light of day**. Cf. *Corp. Hermet*. I 28: ἀπαλλάγητε τοῦ σκοτεινοῦ φωτός, μεταλάβετε τῆς ἀθανασίας καταλείψαντες την φθοράν. **wizard**. See ch. 16.

131

And Judas went out from the house of Karish and went to the house of Sifur the general and was dwelling there. And Sifur said to Judas to **prepare for himself** an **apartment** and be teaching in it. And he did as he said to him. And Sifur the general said to him: "I and my daughter and my wife will henceforth live **purely** in one mind and in one love and we beg **that we may receive the sign (of baptism) from your hands and may become true servants to our Lord and may be reckoned among the number of his flock and his sheep**." Judas says: "I am meditating what to say and am afraid **and I know what I know, (but) I am not able to utter it**."

Commentary. **prepare for yourself.** Geiger, "Sprachl. Bemerkungen zu Wright's Apocr. Acts", in: *Zeitschr. d. Deutschen Morgenl. Gesellschaft* 26 1872, p. 798–804, p. 804: "I will prepare for you". **apartment**, ܪܟܠܘܝ, Greek: τρίκλινον. A similar idea in Acts 19, 9. **purely**. See ch. 85. **that we may receive ... his sheep**. See ch. 25. **and I know ... utter it**. Cf. ch. 3.

132

And he began to speak about baptism and said: "This is the baptism of the **remission of sins**; this is the bringer forth of **new men**; this is the **restorer of understandings**, and the **mingler of soul and body**, and the establisher of new man **in the Trinity** and which becomes a participation in the remission of sins. Glory to you, (you) **hidden power** of baptism! Glory to you, (you) hidden power, that communicates with us in baptism! Glory to you, (you) power that are visible in baptism! Glory to you, (you) new cratures who are renewed through baptism who draw near to it in love!" And when he had said these things, he cast oil upon their heads and said: "Glory to you, (you) beloved Fruit! Glory to you, (you) name of the Messiah! Glory to you, (you) hidden power that dwells in the Messiah!" And he was speaking and they brought a large vat and he baptised them in the **name of the Father and the Son and the Spirit of holiness**.

Commentary. After **remission of sins**, cf. Acts 2, 38, the ms U reads in Greek: τοῦτο ἀναγεννᾷ φῶς περιεκχυνόμενου· τοῦτο ἀναγεννᾷ τὸν νέον ἄνθρωπον, τοὺς ἀνθρώπους μειγνύον πνεῦμα καινοῦν ψυχήν, ἀνιστῶν τρισσῶς καινὸν ἄνθρωπον, καὶ ἐστιν κοινωνὸν τῶν ἁμαρτιῶν ἀφέσεως· σοὶ δόξα τῷ ἀπορρήτῳ τῷ βαπτίσματι κοινωνούμενον· σοὶ δόξα ἡ ἐν τῷ βαπτισματι ἀόρατος δύναμις· σοὶ δόξα ἀνακαινισμὸς δι' οὗ ἀνακαινίζον-ται οἱ βαπτιζόμενοι οἱ μετὰ διαθέσεως σοῦ ἁπτόμενοι, and ms P: τοῦτο ἀναγεννᾷ καὶ νεόν ἄνθρωπον τὸν τοῦτο κτώμενον ἀπεργάζετο. ψυχὴν τρισσῶς ἀνιστᾷ καὶ πνεύματος ἁγίοι γίνεται κοινωνός. καὶ λεγει· Δοξα τῃ ἀπορρήτῳ σου δυναμει· δόξα ὁ τὸ λουτρὸν τοῦ βαπτίσματος ἐνδυόμενος· σοὶ δόξα τῷ ἐκ τῆς πλάνης τοὺς ἀνθρώπους λυτρομένῳ καὶ τῇ σῇ κοινωνοὺς ποιούμενος κοινωνίᾳ. **new man.** In Greek and Syriac, cf. John 3, 4; I Peter 1, 3. 23; Tit. 3, 5; Justin, *apol.* I 61. 3; *dial. c. Tr.* 138. 2 This idea is especially emphasized in Theodor of Mopsuestia, ed. Mingana 50–57. **restorer of understandings,** ܪ‍ meaning that one is freed from ἄγνοια, cf. ch. 38. **mingler of soul and body,** ܡ‍ ܘܥ‍ ܢ‍, cf. U: τοὺς ἀνθρώπους ... καινοῦν ψυχήν and P: ψυχήν τρισσῶς ... κοινωνός. The meaning of this expression is not clear. The best reading seems to be present in P, where we meet an idea that can be compared with Tatian, *Or. ad Graecos* XIII 2: συζωγίαν δὲ κεκτημένη (ψυχὴ) τὴν τοῦ θείου πνεύματος οὐκ ἔστιν ἀβοήθητος, ἀνέρχεται δὲ πρὸς ἅπερ αὐτὴν ὁδογεῖ χωρία τὸ πνεῦμα. The soul has been united with the Spirit. **in the Trinity,** ܬܠܝܬܝܘܬܐ. Not in Greek where we read "in threefold wise". The word "Trinity" is usually given as ܬܠܝܬܐ in Ephrem, see *de Fide,* ed. Beck 112 (translation) and 133 (Syriac)) XLI 10, but the word is found in *Liber Graduum,* ed. Kmosko, in: *Patrol. Syr.* I III c. 408) XVI 10: *ut vivant et glorificent Patrem et Filium et Spiritum Sanctum, perfectam Trinitatem,* ܬܠܝܬܝܘܬܐ. **Glory to you, (you) hidden power ... in the Messiah.** Sinai reads: "may you have remission, who looses the hidden power which is in the Christ!". This means that the anointment has been omitted. **hidden power.** Cf. ch. 27. **name ... holiness.** See ch. 27. Sinai is defective and not quite clear.

133

And when they were baptised and had put on their clothes, he brought **bread and wine** and placed it on the table and began to bless it and said: "Living bread, the eaters of which **do not die!** Bread, that fills hungry souls with your blessing! You are worthy to receive the gift and to be for the remission of sins, that those who eat you may not die! We name the name of the Father over you; **we name the name of the Son over you; we name the name of the Spirit over you, the exalted name that is hidden from all.**" And he said: "In your name, Jesus, may the power of the blessing and the understanding come and abide upon this bread that all the souls which take of it may be renewed and **their sins may be forgiven them.**" And he broke and gave to Sifur and to his wife and to his daughter.

Commentary. **bread and wine**. Sinai and Greek omit "wine". The word was added but a celebration with wine has not to be excluded. **do not die**. Cf. Ignatius, *ad Eph.* 20. 2; Clemens, *paed.* II 19 4; Eusebius, *de solemn. pas.* 12, in: *P.G.* 24, c. 705; Chrysostomus, *in I Cor. Hom.* 24. 2, in: *P.G.* 61, c. 200; *Constit. Apost.* VIII 13 9; Firmicus Maternus, *de err. prof. rel.* 18. 2, ed. Ziegler p. 62. **we name ... hidden from all**. God's real name can not be expressed, see ch. 48. Greek: ἐπιφημίζομενα σε τὸ τῆς μητρὸς ὄνομα (cf. ch. 27) ἀπορρήτου μυστηρίου ἀρχῶν τε καὶ ἐξουσιῶν. Striking is the use of "powers and authorities" with a positive meaning which may be due to Jewish influence, see Test. of Levi 3. 8; Slav. Henoch 20. 1, see *Theol. Wörterb. z. N.T.* II 559–571, *s.v.* ἐξουσία (Foerster). **their sins may be forgiven them**. See ch. 50.

134

And king Mazdai, when he had dismissed Judas Thomas, went to his house to sup. And he was telling his wife what had happened to his kinsman Karish and said to her: "See, my sister, what has befallen that afflicted (man). You know, my sister **Tertia**, that a man has no one like his wife, on whom he relies. Now it happened that Mygdonia went to see the **sorcerer** of whom she had heard tell and of what he was doing and he bewitched her and has parted her from her husband, I do not know (how). And he does not know what to do. And I wished to destroy him but he would not let me. But do you go and advise her to listen to her husband and do not listen to the vain words of that (man)."

Commentary. **Tertia**, ܬܪܬܝܐ, Greek: τερτία, a well-known name, see Pauly–Wissowa IX 1934, p. 821–822. **sorcerer**. See ch. 16. **do not listen**. Geiger, "Sprachl. Bemerkungen zu Wright's Apocr. Acts", in: *Zeitschr. Deutsch. Morgenl. Gesellsch.* 26 1872, 804, proposes: "that she does not listen".

135

And in the morning Tertia arose and went to the house of Karish, her husband's kinsman, and found Mygdonia sitting on the ground with sackcloth on and ashes cast upon her and begging of the Lord that he would forgive her former sins and that she might be delivered from this world speedily. And when Tertia came in to her, she said to Mygdonia: "My sister and my beloved and close friend, what is this folly that has taken possession of you? And why are you becoming like to a mad woman? Be mindful of yourself, be mindful of your family; and bestow a thought on your numerous kindred and have pity on your true husband Karish and do not do anything which does not befit your free birth."

Mygdonia says to Tertia: "You have not heard the tidings of the new life **and have not tasted the words of the preacher of life** and are not freed from the **troubles of corruption**. You have not seen the everlasting life and, see, you are standing in the temporal life. You have not become sensible of the true wedlock and you are afflicted by the **wedlock of corruption**. You are clothed with **garments that decay** and you do not long for the garments of eternity. You are proud of this **beauty of yours that is corruptible** and you do not care about the loathsomeness of your soul. See, you are proud of a number of slaves and your own soul from **slavery** you have not set free. You are proud of the pomp of many (attendants) and you are not delivered from the judgement of death."

Commentary. **and have not tasted ... of life**. Greek: οὐδέπω ἐγεύσω τοῦ τῆς ζωῆς φαρμάκου, cf. ch. 133. **troubles of corruption—wedlock of corruption—garments that decay—beauty of yours that is corruptible**, see ch. 36. **slavery**, see ch. 2.

136

And when Karish had heard these things from Mygdonia, she went in haste to the house of Sifur the general that she might see the new Apostle who had come thither. And when she came to him, he began to say to her: "**What have you come to see? A wanderer, despised and wretched above all men, without possessions or wealth?** But he has a possession which kings and princes cannot take away from him and which is incorruptible and cannot be plundered,—Jesus the Messiah, the **Life-giver** of all mankind, the Son of the Living God who gives life to all those who believe and come to his refuge and become of the **number of his sheep**."

And when Tertia heard these things from him, she says to him: "I too would become a sharer and a handmaiden in this life which you teach and I too would become a servant of this God whom you preach and I would receive from him this life which you promise which he gives to those who come to his **place of assembly**."

Judas says to her: "The treasury of the heavenly King is open and every one **who is worthy takes and finds rest and when he has found rest he becomes a king**. But at first a man **cannot come near him, when he is unclean and when his works are evil** for he knows what is in the heart and in the imagination and no man can deceive him. You too, therefore, if you really believe in him, he will **make worthy of his holy mysteries** and he will exalt you and enrich you and renew your mind and make you an heiress in his kingdom."

Commentary. **What have you come ... wealth**. Cf. Matth. 11, 7. **A wanderer**, ⲣⲓⲃⲣ̄ ⲟⲃ̄ⲃ̄ⲃ ⲣⲃⲃⲗ, Sinai: ⲣⲩⲟⲙⲃⲣ̄, cf. Greek: ξένος, see ch. 4. **Life-giver**. Greek: Saviour, see ch. 10. **number of his sheep**. See ch. 25 **place of assembly**. See ch. 37. **who is worthy ... king**. Also in the Gospel of Hebrews, see Clemens of Alex., *strom*. II IX 45 5 and V XIV 96 3, and the Gospel of Thomas *l*. 2, related with Apoc. 1, 6; 5, 10 and Rom. 5, 17. See also A.F.J.Klijn, "Jewish-Christian Gospel Tradition", in: *Supplem. to Vigiliae Christianae* XVII, Leiden 1992, 47–51. **cannot come ... evil**. See ch. 24 and 26. **worthy of his holy mysteries**. See ch. 24.

<h2 style="text-align:center">137</h2>

And when Tertia had heard these things, she went home rejoicing and found Mazdai her husband expecting her and he had not dined. And he said to her: "Why does our coming in from the street seem more pleasing to me to-day than on any other day? And why do you come on foot,—a thing that is not proper for women like you to do?" Tertia says to Mazdai: "I owe you a debt of thanks that you sent me to Mygdonia. I went and I have heard of the new life and have seen the Apostle of the new God and I believe that he is the Apostle of God who gives life to every one who believes in him and does his will. It is my duty that I too should recompense you for the kindness which you have done me; and I will give you a good counsel so that you too shall become **a king and a prince** in heaven if you will be persuaded by me and do what I say to you. I beseech you to fear the God who has come hither by means of this **stranger** and to keep yourself **purely** to God, because this royalty of yours will pass away and this rest of yours will be changed into trouble. But come, go to that man and believe in him and you shall live forever."

And when he had heard these things from his wife Tertia, he smote his face with his hands and rent his clothes and said: "**May the soul of Karish have no rest who has brought this sorrow upon my soul!** May he have no hope who has cut off my hope!" And he went out sore troubled.

Commentary. Sinai is present from "I went and have heard" until ch. 139: "he will kill you. Now tell". **a king and a prince**. See ch. 136. **stranger**. See ch. 4. **purely**, ⲃⲩⲣⲃⲃ.ⲃ, Greek: ἅγιος. See ch. 12 and 52. **May the soul ... upon my soul**. Sinai omits.

138

And he found his kinsman Karish in the street and said to him: "Why have you taken me as your companian into Sheol? Why have you defrauded me, not profiting yourself? Why have you injured me doing yourself no good? Why have you killed me, not coming yourself to life? Why have you done a wickedness to me, when you were not in equity? Why did not you let me destroy that wizard before he could corrupt my wife by his **sorceries**?" And he was upbraiding Karish. Karish says to Mazdai: "What is this that has happened?" Mazdai says to Karish: "He has bewitched Tertia also."

And they two went to the house of Sifur the general and found Judas sitting and teaching. And all the people sprang up and stood, but Judas did not stand up before them. And king Mazdai knew that it was he who was sitting and he seized a seat and turned it over and took it **by the two legs** and beat him on the head and smote him. And he seized him and delivered him to the attendants and said to them: "Drag (him) off that I may sit and hear him publicly." And they were dragging Judas and going to the place where Mazdai used to give judgment.

And when he came to the place, he was standing, while the attendants of Mazdai held him.

Commentary. **sorceries**, See ch. 16. **by the two legs**, ܩܢܝܟܐ ܐܝܘܗܝ. Greek: ἀμφοτέραις ταῖς χερσίν.

139

And **Vizan**, the son of king Mazdai, came and said to the attendants: "Give him to me that I may talk with him until the king comes." And they gave him to him. And he took Judas and went within to (the place) where the king used to sit and judge. Vizan says to him: "You know that I am the son of king Mazdai and that I have liberty to say to the king all that I wish and that if I tell the king he will let you live and if I tell him he will kill you. Now tell me, who is your God? And by whose power do you hold fast and glory (in it)? And if it be **witchcraft**, teach it to me and I will speak to the king and he will let you go."

Judas says to Vizan: "You are the son of Mazdai, this king who **passes away and I am the servant of Jesus, the king who abides for ever**. You have power to speak to your father and to preserve alive those whom you please in this short life in which men do not abide, even when you have given it to them and both you and your father are mortal. And I beg of my Lord and beseech of him on behalf of men and he gives them the new life which lasts for ever. You glory in men and in slaves and in riches and garments and attendants and in concubines and in meats which pass away and in the bed of uncleanness and I glory in poverty and **ascetism** and contempt and in fasting and prayer and great thanksgiving and in the communion of the brothers and of the Spirit of holiness and in the intercourse of the brothers who are **worthy** before God to live in everlasting life. You take **refuge** with a man like unto you who cannot even deliver his own soul from **judgment** and from death and I take refuge with him who is the Condemner and the Absolver and the Great and who is Judge of all men. You and he with whom you take refuge are to-day and to-morrow and after a time you are not. And I take refuge with him who is for ever and who knows all times and seasons. You too, therefore, my son, if you wish to become the servant of this God whom I serve can become his quickly. And you are seen to be his servant by these things which I mention to you,—by **purity**, the chief of all good qualities and the great beginning and the returning to a better state and the communion of this God whom I preach and by **cleanness** and by **temperance** and by love and by faith and by hope in Him and **by simplicity of pure life**."

Commentary. **Vizan**, ‎ܩܙܘ‎, Greek: οὐαζάνης and ἰουζάνης Latin: *Zuzanes*. See Justi, *Iran. Namenbuch*, p. 367, *s.v.* Wezan. **witchcraft**. See ch. 16 **passes away ... abides for ever**. See ch. 36. **asceticism**, ‎ܪܚܘܩܘܚ‎. See ch. 20 and 85. **worthy**. See ch. 24. **refuge**. See ch. 10. **judgment**. See ch. 30. **purity**, ‎ܪܚܩܙܘܩ‎. See ch. 20 and 85. **cleanness**, ‎ܪܚܩܘܚܙ‎, see ch. 30 and 52. **temperance**, ‎ܪܚܩܘܩܘܚ‎, see ch. 20 and 85. In Greek: ἁγιωσύνη φιλοσοφία. Cf. Infancy Gospel of Thomas, Greek, see J.K. Elliott, *The Apocr. New Testament* 75: "The Account of Thomas the Israelite, the Philosopher ...". **by simplicity of pure life**, ‎ܪܚܩܘܙܘܚܙܘ‎ ‎ܪܚܙܙܙ ܪܚܙܩܘܚܙ‎ Greek: ἑνότητι καθαρᾶς τροφῆς, which may be original, see ch. 20.

140

And the youth Vizan was persuaded through our Lord and was seeking some way by which he might rescue Judas.

   And whilst he was considering, the king came. And the attendants came and took Judas and led him out. And Vizan too went out with him and was standing beside him. And the king took his seat and sent (and) had Judas brought in, with his hands bound behind him. And when he stood before him, the king said to him: "Tell me, who you are and by whose power do you do these things?" Judas says to him: "I am a man like to you, and I do these things by the power of Jesus the Messiah, the Son of God." Mazdai says to him: "Speak truly, before I destroy you." Judas says to him: "**You have no power over me** as you think and you cannot make me suffer." And when Judas had said these things, king Mazdai was enraged and gave orders to heat two plates of iron and to make him stand upon them barefoot. And when they had made him sit down, they drew off and took away his shoes and he was laughing and saying: "Far better is your wisdom Jesus than all the wisdoms of all men. Do you take counsel against them and let your loving-kindness make preparation against the anger of these (men)." And they brought the plates (glowing) like fire, and laid hold of Judas to make him step upon them. And suddenly much water rose out of the earth and the plates were immersed in it and the men let him go and fled.

Commentary. **You have no power over me ...** Cf. John 19, 11. Sinai is present from "was enraged" until ch. 152 "Mazdai he cut off from me".

141

And when the king saw the abundance of water, he said to Judas: "Ask of your God and he will deliver us from this death by the flood and we shall not die thus." And Judas prayed and said: "Our Lord Jesus, I ask of you, bind this **nature** and confine it to one place. You have distributed it to various places and have given many wondrous signs through your servant and your Apostle Judas. You that make my soul long that I too may receive your **splendour**; Giver of the reward of all my labours. **You that let my soul be at rest with its own nature**, without any intercourse of the harmful one. You that are the cause of my life at all times. Do you make this flood cease that it may not rear itself proudly and destroy for here are (some) of these who are standing by who shall believe in you and live." And when Judas had prayed there was quiet and little by little those waters were swallowed up and disappeared but the place became as if it had been dried up.

And when king Mazdai saw (this), he said: "Drag (him) off to prison till we can consider what we shall do with him."

Commentary. **nature**. See ch. 29 and 43. **You that let ... nature**. Greek: "restoring it into its own nature", cf. ch. 43. Greek adds after **places**: "that brought disorder into order", cf. Gen. 1. Bardaisan's cosmology was based on the principle of disorder being made into order. See H.J.W. Drijvers, *Bardaisan of Edessa*, Assen 1966, 94: "... God created the world, or more exactly set it in order, to restrict the hateful influence of its mingling ..." and *passim*. **splendour**, ܢܘܗܪܐ Greek: φέγγος, cf. Hymn I *l*. 1.

142

And Judas went to be imprisoned and the whole people were coming after him. And Vizan, the son of king Mazdai, was coming at the right hand of Judas and Sifur the general at his left hand. And when Judas had entered the prison, he permitted Sifur and Vizan and the wife of Sifur and his daughter to sit down, because they too had gone in with him that they might hear the word of life, for they knew that king Mazdai would destroy him because of his great anger.

And Thomas began to say: "**You deliverer of my soul from the slavery of many because I gave myself to be sold to one**, now, see, I am glad and rejoice because I know that the **times and the seasons** and the years and the months and the days are at an end and I shall come and receive you, **my giver of rest**. See, **I shall be delivered from (the things) of to-day and of to-morrow and it is for to-day that I care**. See, I shall give up hope and receive truth. See, I shall escape from the sorrow and **the gladness of every day and put on joy alone**. See, I shall be without care and without sorrow and without distress and shall dwell in rest for ever. See, I shall be **set free from slavery and shall go to the liberty** to which I am called. See, I have waited upon times and seasons and (now) I am raised above times and seasons. See, I shall receive my pay from a **Paymaster** who does not enter into a reckoning but gives (freely), because his wealth suffices for all his gifts. Lo, **I shall take off and I shall put on** and not take off any more. See, I shall lie down in sleep and **I shall arise and not lie down to sleep any more**. See, I shall die and I shall live and not die any more. **See, they shall rejoice and look on me because I shall go and be united with their joy and they shall place flowers in their garlands**. See, I shall be made **king** in your kingdom, Jesus, for from hence have I hoped for it. (See), the wicked shall be put to shame who thought to subdue me by their powers. See, the rebellious shall be destroyed before me for I have risen above them. See. I shall have the peace to which **the great** shall be assembled."

Commentary. **You deliverer of my soul ... to one**. A contrast between the "many" and the "one", cf. Christ being "one", ch. 165 and the "many" being the powers Ps.-Clement, *Recogn.* V 13.4, ed. Rehm 171: *Expedit enim vobis huic uni domino servire, ut per ipsum cognoscentes unum deum, a multis quos inutiliter timebatis liberemini. Evang. Veritatis* 25. 12–15, ed. Robinson 41: "... within knowledge he will purify himself from multiplicity into Unity ..." **slavery ... sold** and **set free from slavery ... liberty**. See ch. 2. **my giver of rest**. See ch. 35. **I shall be delivered ... I care**. Cf. Matth. 6, 34. **times and seasons**, ܙܒ̈ܢܐ ܘܥ̈ܕܢܐ Greek: Χρόνοι καὶ καιροι, cf. Acts 1, 7. **the gladness of every day ... alone**. See I. Sinai omits. **Paymaster**, ܐܓܪܐ ܒܥܠ, Greek: μισθαποδότος, cf. Hebr. 11, 6: μισθαποδότης, where the Syriac versions renders ܦܪܘܥܐ cf. also Did. VI 7: τίς ἐστιν ὁ τοῦ μισθοῦ καλὸς ἀνταποδότης. **I shall take off ... put on**. The passage deals with the taking

off of the body and the putting on of the heavenly clothes, cf. II Cor. 5,
4 and also Odes of Sal. 25. 8: "And I was covered with the covering
of your Spirit and I removed from me my garments of skin"; Gregory
of Nyssa, *Orat. Cat.* VIII 5: οὐκοῦν ἐκ τῆς τῶν ἀλόγων φύσεως ἡ νεκρό-
της οἰκονομικῶς περιέθη τῇ εἰς ἀθανασίαν κτισθείσῃ φύσει, τὸ ἔξωθεν
αὐτῆς περικαλύπτουσι, οὐ τὸ ἔσωθεν, τὸ αἰσθητὸν τοῦ ἀνθρώπου μέρος
διαλαμβάνουσα, αὐτῆς δὲ τῆς θείας εἰκόνος οὐ προσαπτομένη; Ginza L
515. 12–14: "Die Seele löste die Kette, sie sprengte die Bande. Sie legte
den körperlichen Rock ab" and Ginza R. 193. 26–29; *Corp. Hermet.* VII
2: πρῶτον δὲ δεῖ σε περιρρήξασθαι ὃν φορεῖς χιτῶνα, τὸ τῆς ἀγνωσίας
ὕφασμα, τὸ τῆς κακίας στήριγμά, τὸν τῆς φθορᾶς δεσμόν, see ed. Nock–
Festugière 82–83, n. 9. **I shall arise … any more**. See ch. 60. **See,
they shall rejoice … garlands**. Greek: ἰδοὺ χαίροντες προσδοκῶσιν
ἵνα ἐλθὼν συγγένωμαι τοῖς αὐτῶν συγγενέσιν καὶ τεθῶ ἄνθος ἐν τῷ στε-
φάνα αὐτῶν. Syriac is secondary. For the word "kindred" see ch. 34. It
is not clear what is meant with "be set … crown" but the Syriac version
might be better, cf. Hymn I *l.* 5–6. **king**. See ch. 136. **the great**. See
Hymn 1 *l.* 40 in Greek.

143

And whilst Judas was saying these things, all those who were there were
listening and were thinking that his departure from the world would be
at that moment.

And again Judas said: "**Believe in the Healer of all pains, hidden and manifest** and the **Giver of life to those souls** which
ask help of him. This, the freeborn and King's son who became **a
slave and poor**, this the healer of his creation and the sick because
of his servants, this, the purifier of those who believe in him and the
despised and insulted by those who did not hear him; this (who) sets
free his possessions from slavery and from corruption and from subjec-
tion and from loss and is made subject to and insulted by his slaves;
**this, the Father of (heaven) above, and the Lord of all crea-
tures and the Judge of the world; this who came from on high
and became visible through the virgin Mary and was called
the son of Joseph the carpenter; this the littleness of whose
body we have seen with our eyes and whose majesty we have
received through faith; this whose holy body we have felt with
our hands** and whose **sad aspect** we have seen with our eyes **and
whose divine form on the mountain we were not able to see**

by ourselves alone; this who was called an **imposter** and who is the True one that does not deceive **and the payer of the tax and the head-money for us and for himself; this of whom the enemy when he saw him was afraid and trembled and asked him who he was and what was said of him and he did not make known to him the truth because there is no truth in him, this (who) though he was the Lord of the world and of its pleasures and of its wealth and of all its delights put them away from him and admonished those who hear him and believe in him not to make use of these (things)."**

Commentary. **Believe in the Healer … manifest**. For Christ being physician see ch. 10. The expression "hidden-manifest", cf. *Acta Andreae* ch. 9, in L.B. II I 42. 5–6: ἴδε ἅς αὐτὸς ὁρῶ, καὶ ἅς ὁρᾶς πηρώσεις· ἴδε ἃ δεῖ, καὶ ἃ μὴ δεῖ οὐκ ὄψει; Liturg. Hom. of Narsai, ed. Connoly, 42 and 64: "… and the open and hidden [diseases] he heals by the divine power"; Severus of Antioch 29 IV VI, *Patrol. Orient.* 70: "… and before whom everything is open and exposed, deed word and motions of mind". **Giver of life to those souls**. Greek: Saviour, see ch. 10. **a slave and poor**. Cf. Philipp. 2, 7 and ch. 2. **this, the Father … world**. Sinai: "this the Father of nature, ܟܝܢܐ and Lord of the heights, and the supreme judge" and Greek: "this the Father of the height, ὕψους, and the Lord of nature and the judge". See for "Father of nature" ch. 29. "Lord of heights" may go back to passages like Is. 57, 15; 33, 5 and Ps. 93, 4. **this who came from on high … Mary**. Sinai: "this, who (came) forth from the Father … Son … and became visible through the virgin Mary" (the text is corrupt)" and Greek: "he came of the greatest, παρὰ τοῦ μεγίστου the only-begotten son of the deep, βάθους, and was called Son of Mary the virgin", see *Theol. Wörterb. z. N.T.* I 515–516, *s.v.* βάθος (Schlier). In ch. 32 Jesus is called the Son of Mary. **and was called … carpenter**, ܢܓܪܐ ܒܪ ܝܘܣܦ. This agrees with Luke 3, 23 in syr s: ܝܘܣܦ ܗܘ ܒܪܗ ܢܓܪܐ cf. syr p: ܡܣܬܒܪ ܗܘܐ ܒܪ ܝܘܣܦ. In Greek: ἠκούσθη υἱὸς τέκτονος ἰωσήφ cf. Luke 3, 23: ὢν υἱὸς ὡς ἐνομίζετο ἰωσήφ. It is not clear whether there is a difference between "become visible" in Syriac and "was called" in Greek. In both versions Mary is responsible for the body of the heavenly Christ, cf. ch. 10. This differs from Bardaisan in *S. Ephraem Syri Commentarii in Epistolas D. Pauli a Patribus Mekitharistis translati, Venetiis* 1893, 118: *Neque, inquiunt, terrestri corpore venit Dominus noster, sed coelesti corpore. Neque ex Maria Virgine volunt ipsum natum esse. Etenim transeundo transiit, inquiunt, per eam,* *tamquam si nihil assumpserit ex ea*, and Adamantius, *dial.* V, ed. W.H. v.d. Sande Bakhuyzen 190. 25: … ὥσπερ γὰρ ὕδωρ διὰ σωλῆνος διέρχεται and from the Manichaeans, see *Acta Archel.* V, ed. Beesson 80. 15–20: *Archelaus dixit: Ergo non putas eum ex Maria virgine esse? Manes dixit: Absit ut Dominum nostrum Iesum Christum per naturalia pudenda muliebris descendisse confitear; ipse enim testimonium dat quia de sinibus patris descendit* and Valentinus in Tertullian, *adv. Valent.* 27. **this, the littleness … faith**. For the contrast between Christ's body and the heavenly Lord, see ch. 80. For faith that is able to see things that are invisible, see Hebr. 11, 27. Greek: "and saw it in his works", cf. ch. 10. **this, whose body … hands**. See I John 1, 1. **sad aspect**, ܪܚܝܩܘܬ from ܪܚܩ = to despise, cf. Is. 53, 3. **and whose divine form … alone**. Greek: "and his aspect we saw transfigured, ἐνηλλοιωμένην, with our eyes, but his heavenly semblance on the mount we were not able to see". Syriac reads: ܘܩܝܡܬܗ ܐܠܗܝܬܗ ܟܕ ܒܛܘܪܐ ܒܠܚܘܕ ܐܝܬܝܢ ܠܐ ܐܫܟܚܢ ܠܡܚܙܐ which may be rendered: "And his heavenly semblance, when we were on the mountain alone, we were not able to see". The transfiguration is often mentioned in ancient Christian literature, cf. *Acta Petri* XX, ed. L.B. II 67. 11–20, where it is said that Peter was not able to see the glory; *Acta Johannis* XC, ed. L.B. II I 105. 8–11, where it is said that the light can not be described; Origen, *c. Celsum* II 64 and 67; IV 16 and VI 68 and 77, and *Comment. on Matth.* XII 36, 37 and 41, where it is said that only the true gnostics were allowed to be with Jesus on the mountain. See Bauer, *Leben Jesus* 149–150. **imposter**. See Matth. 27, 63. **and the prayer … himself**. This refers to Matth. 17, 27. It means that Jesus by giving his life, see ch. 72, was paying the tax-collectors, see ch. 147, and thus opened the way to heaven, see ch. 148. **this, of whom the enemy … truth**. See about the *descensus ad inferos* ch. 10. **this, (who) though … these (things)**. Cf. ch. 48 about "Nazir".

144

And when he had finished saying these things, he stood up to pray and spoke thus: "**Our Father who (is) in heaven, hallowed by your name; your kingdom come; and your will be (done) on earth as in heaven; and give us the constant bread of the day; and forgive us our debts and our sins that we may too forgive our debtors; and bring us not into temptation but deliver us from the evil (one).** My Lord and my God and my **hope** and my **confidence** and my teacher and my **comforter**, you taught us to pray thus. See, your prayer I am praying and your will I am accomplishing. Be you with me until the end. You who from my youth **have sown life in me** and has guarded me from corruption. You, who have brought me to the **poverty** of the world and has prepared me for your true wealth. You, who have made me know that **I am yours** and **I have not come near to women that what is desired by you might not be found with stain**.

Commentary. **And when he had finished ... things**. Cf. Matth. 7, 28 and 26, 1. Contrary to the Greek manuscript U the manuscripts P and three, partly four, other manuscripts add the prayer given in ch. 144–148 after ch. 167. **The Lord's Prayer reads:** ܐܒܘܢ ܕܒܫܡܝܐ ܢܬܩܕܫ ܫܡܟ. ܬܐܬܐ ܡܠܟܘܬܟ. ܢܗܘܐ ܨܒܝܢܟ ܐܝܟ ܕܒܫܡܝܐ ܐܦ ܒܐܪܥܐ. ܗܒ ܠܢ ܠܚܡܐ ܕܣܘܢܩܢܢ ܝܘܡܢܐ. ܘܫܒܘܩ ܠܢ ܚܘܒܝܢ ܐܝܟ ܕܐܦ ܚܢܢ ܫܒܩܢ ܠܚܝܒܝܢ ܘܠܐ ܬܥܠܢ ܠܢܣܝܘܢܐ ܐܠܐ ܦܨܢ ܡܢ ܒܝܫܐ. This means that, generally speaking, the text agrees with the Old Syriac version. Noteworthy is the plural ܚܘܒܝܢ which is also found in Theodore of Mopsuestia, ed. Mingana p. 9 and 134 (Syriac) and the addition ܘܦܨܝܢ which is also found in the Liturg. Homilies of Narsai, ed. Connolly p. 25 and Theodore of Mopsuestia, ed. Mingana p. 11 and 136 (Syriac). See also ch. 117. The deviations of the Greek text according to Nestle 26th ed. are: ἐπὶ τῆς γῆς *l.* ἐπὶ γῆς with K D Θ and many other witnesses; addition of τὸν ὕρτον ... σήμερον and τὰς ὀφειλὰς *l.* τὰ ὀφειλήματα **hope**. See ch. 10. **confidence**, ܬܘܟܠܢ, Greek: πεποιθήσις See Ps. 65,6. **comforter**, ܡܒܝܐܢܐ from ܠܒܐ = to encourage. **has sown life in me**. See ch. 15. **poverty,** ܡܣܟܢܘܬܐ, which is the translation of צנוה in the Peshitto version of the Old Testament. Also in ch. 145, see Matth. 5, 3 and Luke 6, 20. See also Ps. Clem., *Hom.* XV 10 and Gospel of Thomas *l.* 54; Manich. Ps. 117. 5–6: "... and let us love poverty and be poor in the body (σῶμα), but rich in the Spirit". See also M. von Dmitrewski, *Die christliche freiwillige Armut vom Ursprung der Kirche bis zum 12 Jahrhundert*, Berlin 1923. **I am yours**. See ch. 32. **I have not come ... woman**. See ch. 12. The greatest sin which can be conmitted by a "stranger" is marrying a woman, see Ephrem, *Über das Pilgerleben*, ed. Haffner 14: "Wenn er *(scil.* Pilger) aber an ein Weib sich wegwirft, so ist er fertig mit dem Streit. In dem Fall hat ihn der Satan erniedrigt ..." **that what is desired ... stain**. This refer to the soul.

145

My mouth does not suffice to praise you nor my understanding to glorify your goodness which (is) on me. You who when I was wishing to acquire and become rich was showing me by your vision that harm comes to many from wealth and from possessions and I believed your vision and was abiding in lasting **poverty** until you, the true wealth manifested yourself to me and was filling with your true wealth those who are **worthy of you** and was delivering them from need and from care and from avarice. See, then, I have fulfilled your will and accomplished your work. **I have been poor and needy and a stranger and a slave and despised and a prisoner and hungry and thirsty and naked and barefoot and weary for your sake**. Let not my trust fail nor my hope which (is) in you be put to shame. Let not my labours be in vain and let not my toils be found fruitless. Let not my fastings and my urgent prayers perish and let not my works which (are) in you be changed. **Let not the enemy snatch away your wheat-seed from your hand and let not his tars be found in it**. For your land cannot receive his tares and they cannot fall into the garners of your husbandman."

Commentary. See for ch. 145 until 149 in the various manuscripts and versions p. 3. **poverty**. See ch. 144. **worthy of you**. See ch. 24. **I have been poor ... your sake**. The passage shows some resemblance with Manich. Ps. 175. 2–30. **stranger**. See ch. 4. **slave**. See ch. 2. **barefoot**. History of John, ed. Wright 8: "He (*scil.* John) was walking barefooted". **Let not the enemy ... found in it**. Cf. Matth. 13, 25.

146

And again he was saying: "**I have planted your vine in the land**. May it cast out roots downwards and may its tendrils twine upwards and may its fruits be seen in the land and may those who are **worthy of you** and whom you have acquired delight in them. **Your silver which you gave me I have cast down on your table. Try it and give it to me with usury as you have promised. With your talent I have gained ten. Let them be added to what was mine** as you have promised. **To my debtors I have remitted the talent; let not that which I have remitted be demanded at my hand. To the supper I have been invited and have come quickly and**

have excused myself from the field and the plough and the wife. Let me not be cast out from it and let me not eat of it by reason of adjurations. **To the wedding-feast I have been invited and I have put on white garments. May I be worthy of it and may my hands and feet not be bound nor I be put out into outer darkness. My lamp is bright with his light. Let its Lord keep it until he leaves the banquet-room and I receive it (and) may I not see it sputter by reason of its oil**. Let my eyes receive you and let my heart rejoice that I have fulfilled your will and accomplished your commandments. Let me be like to the wise and God-fearing servant who with prudent diligence neglects nothing. **I have wearied myself with watching the whole night to protect my house from robbers that it might not be broken into**.

Commentary. **I have planted ... land**. The vine-tree has to be identified with the "people of God", see Justin, *dial. c. Tr.* CX 4: ἡ γὰρ φυτευθεῖσα ὑπὸ τοῦ θεοῦ ἄμπελος καὶ χριστοῦ ὁ λαὸς αὐτοῦ ἐστι; Manich. Ps. 13. 21–22: "... the vine-trees have filled (?) every place" and 76. 6–7: "The vine tree is the Church, we are the ... (corrupt) ... laden (?) with fruit". **worthy of you**. See ch. 24. **Your silver ... promised**. A summing up of parables for paranetical puposes is also found in Aphraates, *dem.* VI 1, ed. Parisot c. 239–254. The passage refers to ch. 3 and the background may be Luke 19, 23. **With your talent**, ⲕⲩⲙⲥⲟ Greek: ἐν τῇ σῇ μνᾷ, **... mine**. See Luke 19, 16. Cf. Liturg. Homilies of Narsai, ed. Connolly 65: "A spiritual talent he has received from His Lord to trade withal, and he was to cast the silver of (his) words upon the table of the soul"; Ginza R 68. 24–25: "Deine Söhne sollen den Ruf des Lebens vernehmen lassen und Kaufleute sein, die Handel treiben und ihren Handel erfolgreich durchführen". **To my debtors ... hand**. Cf. Luke 7, 41–42. **To the supper ... wife**. Cf. Luke 14, 14–24. The word ⲣⲁⲟⲍⲣⲱⲣ has been used which agrees with syr p s and c. **To the wedding-feast ... darkness**. Cf. Matth. 22, 1–14. The word ⲣⲁⲟⲇⲣⲍⲟ = supper has been used which agrees with syr p s and c. The two parables of Luke 14 and Matth. 22 were used separately. According to Burkitt, *Evang. da-Meph.* II, 102–103, this is proof that the author of these Acts used the separate Gospels. However, in the Sinai manuscript we find instead of "field-plough-wife" the words "field-merchandise-plough" and instead of "wedding-feast" the word "supper" which shows according to M.J. Lagrange, *Critique Textuelle*, Paris 1935, 206, that the original author used the Diatessaron. **My**

lamp ... its oil. Cf. Matth. 25, 1–13. The passage also refers to Luke 12, 26 using the words ܫܟ ܘܟܝ, "until he leaves" which agrees with syr s and c. In syr p the words ܕܐܟܣܟ, ܢܒܐܝ, πότε ἀναλύσῃ have been used. In Manich. Ps. 25. 15–17: "Hail, day of joy, the blessed bridegroom; lo, our lamps (λαμπάς) are ready; lo, our vessels (ἀγγεῖον) are full of oil", see also 191. 18–30. **I have wearied ... broken into**. Cf. Luke 12, 39 and Matth. 24, 43. The word "robbers", ܓܝܣܐ Greek: ἀπὸ τῶν λῃστῶν is used. In the Syriac translations of the New Testament the word ܓܢܒܐ has been chosen, but cf. Gospel of Thomas l. 103.

147

My loins are girded with truth and my sandals are bound on my feet. Their thongs may I not see loosened. **I have put my hand to my ploughshare and have not looked behind me that my furrows might not be crooked. My fields are white and are already fit for reaping**. May I receive my reward. **The garment that wears out I have worn out** and the work that brings to rest I have accomplished. **I have kept my first watch and my second and third**. May I receive your face and worship before your holy **beauty. I have pulled down my barns and destroyed them on earth**. May I take of your treasures that do not fail. I have dried up the running spring that was in me. May I lie down by your living spring and rest beside it. The bound whom you delivered to me I have slain. The unbound who is in me you set free** and let not my soul be kept back from its **trust. The internal I have made external and the external internal**. Let your will be fulfilled in all my members. **I have not turned back and I have not stretched forward. Let me not be a wonder and a sign. The dead I have not brought to life and the living I have not brought to death**. And the deficient I have (not) filled up. **Let us receive the Crown of victory**, the Ruler of both worlds. **Scorn have I received on earth; a recompense do you make me in heaven**.

Commentary. **My loins ... feet**. Cf, Eph. 6, 14–15. **I have put ... crooked**. Cf. Luke 9, 62. For ploughshare the word ܚܪܒܐ ܦܕܢܐ has been used, in Greek: τῷ ἀρότρῳ τῷ ζευκτῷ. This reading was caused by ܦܕܢܐ being ζευκτός, see F.C. Burkitt, "The Original Language ...", in: *Journ. of Theol. Studies* I 1900, 280–290, esp. 285. **My fields ... reaping**.

Cf. John 4, 35. **The garment ... worn out**, Obviously referring to the body, cf. Sinai: "May I receive a garment for the one that wears out." **I have kept ... third**. In Luke 12, 38 the first watch is not mentioned. The present Acts agree with the reading in syr c, cf. also the manuscripts D fam. 1 and some Old Latin ones. **beauty**, ܢܝܘ, Greek: ἀπαύγασμα, cf. Hymn I *l.* 1. **I have pulled down ... does not fail**. Cf. Luke 12, 18 and Matth. 6, 20. **I have dried up ... rest beside it**. The passage seems to deal with man's own strength. **The bound ... free**. The contrast between the "bound", ܐܣܝܪ, Greek: τὸ δέσμιον, and the "unbound", ܫܪܐ Greek: λελυμένος refers to the contrast between body and soul. The unbound nature belongs to God, cf. Ephrem, *de Fide*, ed. Beck 221 (translation) and 260 (Syriac)) 84. 14: "Es stieg herab aus der Höhe eine gelöste Natur, ܟܝܢܐ ܫܪܐ". See also ch. 30 and 34. **trust**, ܬܘܟܠܢܐ Greek: πεποιθήσας, cf. Eph. 3, 12. **The internal ... internal**. Also known from II Clement XII 2: ὅταν ἔσται τὰ δύο ἕν, καὶ τὸ ἔξω ὡς τὸ ἔσω. According to Clement, *strom.* III 92, found in the Gospel of the Egyptians, but cf. also Gospel of Thomas *l.* 22. **I have not turned ... not stretched forward**, ܘܠܐܟܕܝ ܠܐ, ܐܬܬ ܘܐܬܡܬܚܬ thus "... altogether stretched forward ...'. Cf. Philipp. 3, 14 ܘܠܐܟܕܝ ܡܬܡܬܚ ܐܝܟ. **Let me be ... sign**. Cf. Ps. 71, 7. **The dead ... death**. Greek is secondary: τὸν νεκρὸν ἐζωοποίησα, cf. ch. 41. **Let us receive ... victory**. Cf. Apoc. 2, 10. **Scorn ... heaven**. The afflictions in this life are a reconciliation for the punishment in the life to come, cf. ch. 6.

148

The powers shall not perceive me, nor the rulers take counsel against me. The tax-gatherers shall not see me, nor the collectors of tribute oppress me. The low shall not mock at me and the wicked at the brave and the humble. Nor shall the slave and the mean and the great who exalts himself dare to stand before me because of your victorious strength, o Jesus, which surrounds me. For they flee and hide themselves from it, because they are not able to behold it. For with treachery and in silence they fall upon those who obey them. The portion of my children, behold, cries out and shines and no man is hidden from them because it is the fragrance of their **nature**. Wicked men are separated (from them). **Their fruit-tree is bitterness. I will make it pass away to their place in silence and I will come to you. Let joy and peace support me and I**

shall stand before your glory and let not the slanderer look upon me but let his eyes be blinded by your light in which I dwell and let his lying mouth be closed for he has nothing against me."

Commentary. **The powers ... take counsel against me,** ܐܠ ܢܒܠܥܐ ... ܠܚܕܐ ܡܩܠܝܠܐ ܠܟ ܚܣ. ܬܫܝܠ ܠܟ ܐܢܫܡܩܐ. Cf. Acts 4, 25–26: ... ܐܠܚܕܐ ܕܢܬܐ ܚܒܝܬܐ. Thus better: "stir against me". See F.C. Burkitt, "Another Indication of the Syriac Origin of the Acts of Thomas", in: *Journ. of Theol. Studies* 3 1902, 94–95. The passage speaks about the guardians of heaven, see also ch. 118. The same idea in Clement, *strom.* VII 82 5: καὶ διελθὼν τὰς πνευματικάς οὐσίας καὶ πᾶσαν ἀρχὴν καὶ ἐξουσίαν ἄπτεται των θρόνων τῶν ἀκρων; Origen, *c. Celsum* VII 31, see Chadwick 334, n. 2, with literature; Philoxenus of Mabug, ed. Lemoine 289, XI 322: "Arme-toi de courage pour traverser ce lieu dedoutable qui est placé entre les deux (*scil.* la vie et la condamnation mortuelle). Car il est profond et plein d'animaux méchants et de serpents malfaisants et meurtriers". Very often in Gnostic literature, cf. Geschichte Jos. d. Zimmermanns, ed. Morenz 6, XIII 7: "Lasse nicht zu, dass die deren Angesicht verschieden ist, mir beschwerlich fallen auf dem Wanderwege, wenn ich zu dir komme, 8 Lasse nicht zu, dass 'die auf den Toren', meine Seele anhalten und beschäme mich nicht auf deinem furchtbaren Richterstuhl"; *Pistis Sophia*, ed Schmidt–Till 7. 38–39: "... und nicht haben mich die Archonten (ἄρχοντες) der Äonen (αἰῶνες) erkannt; Flügel, *Mani*, Fihrist 100: "Auch erscheint ihm der Teufel der Habgier und der Sinnenlust mit anderen Teufeln. Sobald der Wahrhaftige diese erblickt, ruft er die Göttin, welche die Gestalt der Weisen angenommen hat und die andere Götter zu Hilfe, und diese nähern sich ihm. Sobald der Teufel sie gewahr werden, wenden sie sich fliehend um". See A. Dieterich, *Eine Mithrasliturgie*, Leipzig 1903, 179–212; W. Bousset, "Die Himmelsreise der Seele", in: *Archiv f. Religionswissensch.* IV 19–1, 136–169 and 229–373; G.G. Scholem, *Major Trends in Jewish Mysticism*, London 1955, 50; W. Anz, "Zur Frage nach dem Ursprung des Gnostizismus", in: *Texte und Unters.* 15 1897; E. Schweizer, "Erniedrigung und Erhöhung bei Jesus und seinen Nachfolgern", in: *Abh. Theol. A. u. N.T.* 28 1955, and J. Quasten, "Der gute Hirte in frühchristlicher Totenliturgie und Grabeskunst", in: *Studi e Testi* 121 1956, 373–406. **taxcollectors,** ܡܟܣܐ, **... collectors of tribute,** ܓܒܝܐ **oppress me.** The word ܡܟܣܐ is used to translate the word τελώνης in Matth. 5, 46; 16, 17 etc., the word ܓܒܝܐ is used to translate the word ὑπηρέτης in Matth. 5, 25 in syr p s and the word πράκτωρ in Luke 12, 38 in syr s c phil. The guardians take from the souls passing the heavens that which belongs to them, see ch. 32 and Ephrem, *On Virginity*, ed. Mitchell II LXXXIII and 175: "The signature is on every tax-collector's bond, ܒܠ ܟܪܣܡܐ ܝܠܕ, for him who owes money; so by the same illustration regret is a tax-collector, ܟܪܣܡ, in its silence for him that is in debt of sins"; Book of the Bee, ed. E.A. Wallis Budge, 131: "When the soul goes forth from the body, as Abba Isaiah says, the angel goes with it; then the hosts of darkness go forth to meet it, seek to seize it and examine it, if there is anything of theirs in it", Very often in Mandaean literature, cf. Ginza R 21. 17–18: "Sie (*scil.* Dämonen) eilen den Seelen auf dem Wege voraus und bedrängen sie im Zöllnerhause"; Ginza L 509. 18–19: "O Seele, nimm dich mit deiner Rede in acht, dass sie dich nicht im Hause der Zöllner fesseln. Der Weg, den wir zu gehen haben ist weit und endlos". **The low, ܬܚܬܝܐ, ... humble**. It is not clear what is meant. The same applies to the Greek: μη μου καιαβοήσωσιν οἱ ἥττονες καὶ πονηροὶ καὶ ἀνδρείου καὶ ἐπιεικοῦς. Obviously the passage points to some evil powers. **nature**. See ch. 29. **Their fruit-tree is bitterness**. See ch. 44. **I will make it pass ... light**. See Decease of John, Syriac, ed. Wright, 67: "let the angels accompany, let the demons be afraid, let the princes be cast down, let the powers of darkness fall, let the place of the right hand stand, but those on the left hand not stand ... But my path to you render for me free from insult."

149

And again he began to say to those who were with him in prison: "Believe, my children, in this God whom I proclaim. Believe in Jesus the Messiah, whom I preach. Believe in the **Life-giver** and Helper of his servants. Believe in the **Giver of life** to those who toil at his work; in Him, in whom, behold, my soul now rejoices. For the time is come that I may go and receive him. Believe in this fair (one), whose beauty incites me to say concerning him what he is, though I am unable to say it fully. For you, my Lord, are the Feeder of my poverty and the supplier of my want and the dispenser of my need. Be you with me to the end that I may come and receive you.

Commentary. **Giver of life**. Greek: "Saviour", see ch. 10. **fair**. See ch. 8.

150

And the youth Vizan, the son of king Mazdai, was asking of him and saying to him: "I beg of you, holy man, Apostle of God, permit me to go and I will entreat the keepers of the prisoners and they will grant me that you may go with me to my house and you shall give me the **sign of life** and I too shall become a servant of this new God whom you preach because in all these things which you say I was walking in my youth until my father Mazdai constrained me and gave me **Manashar** (as) a wife. For I am twenty-one years old to-day, and see, it is seven years since I was united in marriage to a woman. For before I took a wife I knew no other woman and by my father I was counted as good for nothing. And I have not yet had son or daughter by the woman whom he gave to me. And my wife has lived with me in **chastity** during these years. And to-day, if she were well and had seen you or heard your word I should be at rest and she would live and would receive everlasting life for she is in great affliction, see, for a long time through disease. I will therefore entreat the keepers of the prisoners if you will promise me to go with me to my house for I live alone in a home by myself and will heal the feeble and the sick." And when Judas, the Apostle of the Most High, heard these things, the Apostle says to Vizan: "**My son, if you believe you shall see the wonders of our God**, how he **brings to life** and has compassion upon his servants."

Commentary. **sign of life**. See ch. 26. The expression is also found in Aphraates, *dem.* XXIII 63, ed. Parisot II, c. 133–134: ܗܕ ܡܠܒ ܝ‍ܘ‍ܪ‍ܙ‍ܐ ‍ܝ‍ܐ‍ܘ‍‍ܘܕ‍.‍, see E.J. Duncan, "Baptism in the Demonstrations of Aphrates the Persian Sage", in: *Cath. Univ. of Am. St. in Chr. Ant* 8, Washington 1945, 27–31. **Manashar**, ܡ‍ܝ‍ܒ‍ܐ, Greek: ἀνισάρα but in ch. 154: μνησάρα and Ms U: μνασάρα, and in Latin: *manazar*. See Justi, *Iran. Namenbuch* 189, *s.v.* Manasar. **chastity**, ‍ܝ‍ܘ‍ܣ‍ܐ‍ܝ. See ch. 20 and 52. **My son ... our God**. Cf. John 1, 51. **brings to life**. Greek: "he saves", see ch. 10.

151

And whilst they were speaking, Tertia and Mygdonia and Narkia her nurse were standing at the door of the prison. And they gave **360 silver zuze** to the keepers of the prisoners and they let them in to Judas. And they entered and saw Judas and Sifur and Vizan and the wife and daughter of Sifur and all the prisoners sitting and listening to Judas. And they three stood before him and he said to them: "Who let you come to us? And who opened to you the gate that was closed in your faces?" Tertia says to him: "**Did not you open the door for us** and say to us: 'Come to the prison that we may go and take our brothers who are there and then our Lord will show his glory (in dealing) with us?' And when we came to the door (of the prison) you disappeared from us and we heard the sound of the door which was shut in our faces. And we gave (money) to their keepers and they let us in. And see, we stand (here) and beg of you that you would do what we wish that we might let you escape until the wrath of king Mazdai cool to you." Judas says to Tertia: "Tell us first how you were shut up."

Commentary. **360 silver zuze**. Greek: τραχοσίους ἑξήχοντα τρεῖς στατῆρας ἀργυρίου. Sinai: 368. See ch. 118. In the *Acta Pauli*, in L.B. II 147. 8–14, it is said that Thecla gives her bracelets to the doorkeepers to let her in. The number 360 might correspond with the number of heavens, cf. Michael Syrus, ed. J.B. Chabot T. I, fasc. II, 1842 about Bardaisan: "… et les mondes qui sont au nombre de 360". **Did you open … for us**. The same idea as in ch. 34.

152

Tertia says to him: "**You yourself have never quit us, save for a moment and do you not know how we were shut up? But if you wish to hear, hear**. King Mazdai sent and had me Tertia brought to him and he said to me: 'That conjuror has not yet got power over you, because I have heard that he **bewitches** with oil and water and bread **and wine** and he has not yet bewitched you. But listen to me, then, (and hear) what I say to you that I will not torture you until I destroy you. For I know that as long as he has not given to you water and oil and bread and wine he has not yet got full power over you.' And I said to him: 'Whatever you will, do to me. **Over my body you have power to do all that you will, but my soul I will not destroy**

with you.' And when he heard these things from me, he shut me up in dark room under his dining-room. And his kinsman Karish too brought both Mygdonia and Narkia and shut them up with me. And light did not depart from us and you yourself brought us out and see, we stand before you. But give us the **sign** and let the hope of Mazdai be cut off from me who is plotting these things against me."

Commentary. **You yourself ... hear**. The same as in ch. 55. **bewitches**. See ch. 16. **and wine**. Greek omits. **over my body ... with you**. Cf Luke 12, 4–5. **sign**. See ch. 26.

153

And when Judas the Apostle of our Lord had heard these things which she said, he says: "To you be glory, Jesus, **manifold in form!** To you be glory **who shows yourself like to our poor humanity!** To you be glory, our **Strengthener and Encourager and Reprover and Gladdener who stands by us in all our afflictions and strengthened our weakness and encourages our fear!**" And when he had said these things the prisoners were encouraged and the keepers said: "Blow out the lamps that they may not slanderously accuse us before king Mazdai." And they blew out all the lamps and went (and) slept. But Judas said to our Lord: "Yours now is the speed (to help us), **Jesus our Illuminator, for behold, the children of darkness have made us sit in their darkness, but you, our Lord, enlighten us with the light of your nature.**" And instantly the whole prison was bright as by day. And all those who were shut up there were **asleep and only those who believed in our Lord were awake.**

Commentary. **manifold in form**, ܣܓܝ ܒܕܡܘܬܗ. See ch. 48. **who shows ... humanity**. See ch. 143. **Strengthener ... our fear**. The idea that Jesus is supposed to help is emphasized. **Jesus, our Illuminator ... your nature**. See for the contrast between light and darkness ch. 28 and for "nature" ch. 29. Christ shines with his light in the prison of this world, cf. Irenaeus, *dem.* 38, ed. Froidevaux 92: "Et sa lumière apparut et fit disparaître les ténèbres de la prison et sanctifia notre naissance et abolit la mort en défaisant ces mêmes liens dans lesqels nous avions été enchaînés"; Severus of Antioch, in: *Patrol. Orient.* ed. E.W. Brooks VI 123: "Christ ... shone in the chambers of Sheol"; Ginza

R 349. 6–8: "Am Tore der Gefangenen bin ich vorbeigegangen, mein Glanz ging über ihrem Gefängnisse auf. Über ihrem Gefängnisse ging mein Glanz auf", and *Pistis Sophia*, ed. Schmidt–Till 73. 9–10: "Und möge grosse Finsternis sie bedecken und finsteres Dunkel ihnen kommen". **asleep ... awake**. See ch. 60.

154

And Judas said to Vizan: "Go before us and prepare for us what is needful for our service." Vizan says to him: "Who will open for us the doors of the prison? For, see, they have closed them all and the keepers are asleep." Judas says to him: "Believe in Jesus and doubt not and you shall go and find the doors open and turned on their hinges." And when he had gone out, he went before them and all (the rest) of them were coming after Judas. And when they had gone half-way, Manashar, the wife of Vizan met them, coming to the prison. And she knew him and says to him: "My brother Vizan?" And she says to her: "Yes and you my sister Manashar?" She says to him: "Yes". He says to her: "Where do you go at this time alone? And how were you able to arise from the bed?" She says to him: "**This youth laid his hand on me and I was healed**. And I say in my dream that I should go to the **stranger** where he is imprisoned that I might be quite healed." Vizan says to her: "Where is the youth who was with you?" And he says to him: "Do you not see him?" For, see, he is holding my right hand and supporting me."

Commentary. Sinai is present from "half-way" until ch. 158: "voice was heard, saying". **This youth ... healed**. Jesus appears in the likeness of a youth, see ch. 27 and *Acta Pauli*, ed. Schmidt 3. 10–4. 5, where it is said that Paul and Artemilla are led out of prison by a child. **stranger**. See ch. 4. **is holding ... supporting me**. Cf. Ps. 44, 4 and 110, 5.

155

And while they were talking, Judas came with Sifur and his wife and daughter and with Mygdonia and Tertia and Narkia and they came and entered into the house of Vizan. And when Manashar the wife of Vizan saw him she bowed down and worshipped him and says to him: "Have you come, my **healer from sore disease? You are he whom I saw in my dream** who gave me this youth that he might bring me to you to the prison. And your kindness did not suffer you (to permit) that I should become weary but you yourself have come to me." And when she had said these things she turned round (to look) behind her and the youth was not (there). And she says to Thomas: "I am not able to walk alone and the youth whom you gave to me is not (here)." Judas says to her: "Jesus then will be a Supporter to you." And she was running and coming before them. And when they entered into the house of Vizan, the son of king Mazdai, the time was night **and our Lord was giving them light in abundance.**

Commentary. **healer from sore disease**. See ch. 10. **You are he ... dream**. For Thomas' omnipresence, see ch. 34. **and our Lord ... abundance**. See ch. 153.

156

And Judas began to pray and to speak thus: "**Companion** and **Help** of the feeble; **Hope and Confidence** of the poor; Refuge and Rest of the weary; **Voice** that came from on high, **comforting the hearts of your believers; Resort and Haven** of those that go forth into the **region of darkness; Physician without fee, (who) was crucified among men for many** and for whom no man was crucified; **you descended into Sheol with mighty power and the dead saw you and became alive and the lord of death was not able to bear (it); and you ascended with great glory and took up with you all who were seeking refuge with you and trod for them the path (leading) up on high and in your footsteps all your redeemed followed. And you brought them into your fold and mingle them with your sheep. Son of perfect mercy** who was sent to us with power by the Father whom his servants praise. Son, who was sent by the supreme and perfect Fatherhood. Lord of possessions that cannot be defiled, wealthy (one) who has filled your creation with the treasure of your wealth. **Needy (one) who bore poverty and fasted forty days**. Satisfier of our thirsty souls with your blessing, be you, Lord, with Vizan and with Tertia and with Manashar and **gather them into your fold and mingle them with your number** and be to them a **guide** (when they are) in the **path of error**. Be to them a healer in the **place of sickness**. Be to them a strengthener in the **weary place**. Make them **pure** in the **unclean place; and make them clean of corruption in the place of the enemy**. Be

a physician for their bodies and give life to their souls and make them
holy shrines and temples and may the holy Spirit dwell in them."

Commentary. **Companion**. See ch. 10. **Help**. See ch. 30. **Hope and
Confidence**. See ch. 10. **Voice**. See ch. 10. **comforting ... believers**. Greek: ὁ παρήγορος ὁ ἐν μέσῳ κατοικῶν. The expression "in the
middle" stands for "earth", see Odes of Solomon 22. 1–2: "He who
caused me to descend from on high and to ascend from the regions
below and he who gathers what is in the Middle ... , ܪܒܝܢܬܐ" The
same in Irenaeus, *adv. haer.* I VII 1 and 5. **Resort, ܒܝܬ ܡܥܘܢܐ, and
Haven**. See ch. 37. **region of darkness**. This may be the world,
cf. ch. 153, but probably hell is meant. **Physician**. See ch. 10. **without fee**. See ch. 96. **(who) was crucified ... many**. Cf. ch. 72. **you
descended ... followed**. See also ch. 10. **You brought ... sheep**.
See ch. 25. **Son of perfect mercy**. See ch. 10. **Needy (one) ... forty
days**. See Luke 4, 2 and Matth. 4, 2. **gather them ... number**.
See ch. 25. **guide**. See ch. 10. **path of error**. See ch. 25. The world
is described as a **place of sickness-weary place-unclean place-
place of the enemy**. Thomas asks for **purity**, see ch. 37, **cleanness-
healing and life. holy shrines and temples**. See ch. 12

157

And when he had prayed thus, he said to Mygdonia: "My daughter,
strip your sisters". And she stripped them and put girdles on them
and brought them near to him. And Vizan came near first. And Judas
took oil **and glorified (God) over it and said: "Fair Fruit, that
is worthy to be glowing with the word of holiness that men
may put you on and conquer through you their enemies, when
they have been cleansed from their former works,—yes, Lord,
come abide on this oil, as you abode on the tree and they
who crucified you were not able to bear your word. Let your
gift come which you breathed on your enemies and they went
backward and fell upon their faces and let it abide upon this
oil over wich we name your name**." And he cast it upon the head
of Vizan and then upon the heads of these (others) and said: "In your
name Jesus the Messiah, let it be to these persons for the remission
of offences and sins and for the destruction of the enemy and for the
healing of their souls and bodies." **And he commanded Mygdonia
to anoint them and he himself anointed Vizan**. And after he had

anointed them, he made them go down into the water in the name of the Father and the Son and the Spirit of holiness.

Commentary. **strip your sisters**. See ch. 121. **and glorified ... your name**. In Greek: "in a cup of silver and spoke thus over it: 'Fruit more beautiful than (all) other fruits, to which none other whatsoever may be compared, altogether merciful; fervent with force of the word; **power of the tree** which men putting upon them overcome their adversaries; crowner of the conquerers; help and **joy of the sick**; that announced to men their salvation that has shown light to them that are in darkness; whose leaf is bitter, but in your most sweet fruit you are fair; that is rough to the sight but soft to the taste; seeming to be weak but in the greatness of your strength able to bear the power that beholds all things. Having thus said, περιωχεί μας (?), Jesu: let his victorious might come and be established in this oil, like it was established in the tree that was its kin, even his might at that time, **whereof they that crucified you could not endure the word**; let the gift also come whereby breathing upon (your) enemies you caused them to go backward and fall headlong and let it rest on this oil, whereupon we invoke your holy name.'" **that men may ... enemies**. For the protecting value of baptism see also ch. 49. **when they ... works**. Before obtaining life man has to cleanse himself. See ch. 26. **as you abode ... crucified you**. For the relation between the cross and oil see ch. 121. Here it is asked whether Christ may be on the oil as he was on the cross. **your gift ... faces**. Cf. John 18, 6. **name your name**. See ch. 27. In Greek is spoken of the **power of the tree**. See ch. 121. Here the relation between the tree and the oil is present in the power which Christ has given to them both. Later is spoken of the oil which is "kin" of the tree. The same is found in ch. 121. **whereof they that ... word**, ἧς τὸν λόγον οὐκ ἤνεγκεν ἁ σταυρώζαντες, which is not clear but may be an allusion to I Cor. 1, 18. **joy of the sick**. As in ch. 121 the healing power of baptism is emphasized. Baptism is followed by forgiveness of sins, destruction of the enemy and healing of the body. See also ch. 37. **And he commanded ... Vizan**. It seems as if the anointing took place twice, *viz.* the first time upon the head and a second time upon the whole body. Women are anointed by women. See ch. 121. After the anointing a baptism with water takes place, see ch. 27.

158

And after they had been baptised and had come up he brought bread and the **mingled cup** and spoke a blessing over it and said: "**Your holy body which was crucified for our sake, we eat and your life-giving blood which was shed for our sake we drink**. Let your body be to us for **life** and your blood for the remission of sins. For the **gall** which you drank for us, let the bitterness of our enemy be taken away from us. And for your drinking **vinegar** for our sake, let our weakness be strengthened. And (for) the **spit** which you received for us, let us receive your perfect life. And because you received the crown of thorns for us, let us receive **your perfect life**. And because you received the **crown of thorns** for us, let us receive from you the crown that does not wither. And because you were wrapped in a **linen cloth** for us let us be girt with your mighty strength which cannot be overcome. And because you were buried in a **new sepulchre** for our mortality, **let us too receive intercourse with you in heaven**. And as you **arose** let us be raised and let us stand before you at the judgment of truth." **And he broke the Eucharist and gave to Vizan and Tertia and to Manashar and Sifur and Mygdonia and to the wife and daughter of Sifur and said: "Let this Eucharist be to you for life and rest and joy and health and for the healing of your souls and of your bodies**." And they said: "Amen", and **a voice was heard** saying to them: "Yes and Amen." And when they heard this voice they fell on their faces. And again the voice was heard saying: "**Be not afraid, but only believe**."

Commentary. **mingled cup**. See ch. 120. Sinai and Greek omit "mingled". **Your holy body ... drink**. See ch. 72. **life**. Greek: "salvation", see ch. 10. **gall ... vinegar**. In Matth. 27, 34 is spoken of οἶνον (or ὄξος, in many manuscripts) μετὰ χολῆς μεμιγμένον. This was rejected by Jesus. In vs. 48 it is said that Jesus is drinking ὄξος, see, however, Saint Ephrem, "Commentaire de l'Évangile concordant", ed. L. Leloir, in: *Corp. Script. Or.* vol. 145 (translation) and 137 (Armenian), Louvain 1954 and 1953, 214: *Et quod dederunt ei bibere acetum et fel.* In this commentary we notice contrasts similar to those in the present chapters, see, for example, 214: *Et quod dederunt ei bibere acetum et fel, pro eo quod laetificaverunt eos dulci vino suo, porrexerunt isti accetum, et pro felle dulcem fecit virtus miserationis eius,* and 216: *Et dum mors unum in cruce hac ligat multi qui ligati stabant in inferis, per unius vincula liberabuntur.* See also Acts of John, Syriac ed. Wright, 16: "and gave him vinegar and gall", cf. Ps. 68, 22 (LXX): καὶ ἔδωκεν εἰς τὸ βρῶμα μου χολήν καὶ εἰς τὴν δίψαν μου ἐπότισαν με ὄξος. **spit**. Cf. Matth. 26, 67 and 27, 30. In Greek in place of **let us receive ... life**: "let us receive the dew of your goodness". The "dew of God" is a special gift, see Is. 26, 19 and Odes of Solomon 11. 14 and 35. 1; Liturg. Hom. of Narsai, ed. Connolly 46: "and he sprinkled his gift of dew and watered our soul" and 64: "He (priest) sprinkles the dew of mercy on men's clay", and Manich. Ps. 203. 17–18: "He woke clouds of brightness dropping dew (?) and life". **crown of thorns**. Cf. Matth. 27, 30. **linen cloth**. Cf Matth. 27, 59. **new sepulchre**. Cf. Matth. 27, 60. **let us too ... heaven**. Greek: "Let us receive renewing of soul and body". It is striking that the Greek is speaking here of the resurrection of the body. **arose**. Cf. Matth. 28, 6. **And he broke the Eucharist**. See ch. 17. **Let this Eucharist ... bodies**. See ch. 39. For the healing of the bodies, see ch. 37. **a voice was heard**. See ch. 27. **Be not afraid ... believe**. See Luke 8, 50.

159

And Judas went (back) to be imprisoned and likewise Tertia and Mygdonia and Narkia, these too went (back) to be imprisoned. And Judas
said to them: "My daughters and sisters in our Lord and my companians and handmaidens of Jesus the Messiah, listen to me on this last
day that I shall deliver my word to you, for I shall never speak with you
again in this world. For I shall be lifted up to our Lord Jesus the Messiah; **to him who sold me; to him who humbled his lofty soul
to my littleness** and has brought me to his greatness which does not
pass away and has deemed me worthy of being a servant of him in verity and in truth. And see, I rejoice that the time is fulfilled and the day
has come that I may go and receive my reward from my Lord. For my
Pay-master is just and he knows how I ought to be recompensed. For
he is not wicked **nor envious** but his gifts abound. And he does not
count and give for he is confident that his wealth will not fail. Listen,
my daughters.

Commentary. **to him who sold me**. See ch. 2. **to him … littleness**.
See ch. 15 and 80. **worthy**. See ch. 24. **my Pay-master, ܡܦܪܥ ܐܓܪܐ**.
Greek: μισθαποδότης, see ch. 142. **not envious**. Contrary to the devil,
see ch. 44.

160

I am not Jesus but I am the servant of Jesus. I am not the Messiah
but I am one who ministers before him. I am not the Son of God
but I pray and beg that I may be deemed **worthy** of God. But do
you, my daughters, abide in the **faith** of Jesus the Messiah and look
for the **hope** of the Son of God. And be not weary, my daughters, in
persecution and be not in doubt because you are seeing me treated
ignominiously and imprisoned too and dying because I am fulfilling the
will of my Lord. For if I were to pray that I should not die, you know
that I am able (to do so). But this which is seen (by us) is not death
but a release from the world. For this reason I receive it gladly and

for this reason I am delivered that I may go and receive him who is **comely**, him whom I love, who is beloved. For much have I toiled in his service and I have completed (my task) because of his **grace which has supported me** and has not forsaken me. Let not, therefore, the enemy enter into you by treachery and let him not agitate your minds with doubt. Let not that perfidious disturber find an opportunity (of assailing you) because he, whom you have received and in whom you have believed is stronger than he. Look for his coming for he will come and receive you that is (to say), **you shall go and see him**."

Commentary. **I am not Jesus**. See ch. 65. **worthy**. See ch. 24. **faith ... hope**. Cf. I Cor. 13, 13. **but a release from the world**. Greek: "freed from the body", see ch. 21. **comely**. See ch. 8. **grace which has supported me**. Cf. ch. 2. **you shall go and see him**. See Hymn I *l.* 35-38.

161

And when Judas had finished speaking to them, they entered into the dark house. And Judas said: "**Our Life-giver** and bearer of many things for our sake, let these doors be as they were and let them be sealed with their seals." And he left them and went himself too to be imprisoned. And they were grieved and were weeping because they knew that king Mazdai would kill him.

Commentary. **Our Life-giver**. Greek: "Saviour", see ch. 10.

The Consummation of Judas Thomas

162

And when he had gone to be imprisoned, he found the keepers quarrelling saying: "What wrong have we done to this **sorcerer** that he has opened the doors by the art of his charms and has wished to let all these prisoners escape? But let us go and make (it) known to king Mazdai and let us tell him also about his wife and his son who come to him." And while the chief (keeper) of the prisoners was saying these things, Judas was silently listening. And they rose early in the morning and went to king Mazdai and said to him: "Our lord the king either let this sorcerer go or imprison him in another place for we are unable to guard him because twice your good fortune has guarded the prisoners otherwise they would all have escaped for we shut the doors and we find them open. And both your wife and your son with the rest of the people never leave him." And when king Mazdai heard these things he went to look at the seals which he had placed upon the doors and he found the seals as they were. And he said to the keepers: "Why do you tell lies for see, the seals of the houses are as they were sealed? And how do you say (that) Tertia and Mygdonia come to him, to the prison?" The keepers say: "We have told you the truth."

Commentary. **sorcerer**. See ch. 16.

163

And king Mazdai went (and) sat in (the hall of) judgment and sent and fetched Judas and stripped him and put a girdle round his loins and they made him stand before Mazdai. And Mazdai said to him: "Are you a slave or a free man?" Judas says to him: "**I am a slave** but you have no power whatever over me." Mazdai says to him: "And how did you run away (and) has come to this country?" Judas says to him: "I came hither that I might **give life** to many by the word and by your hands I shall quit the world." Mazdai says to him: "Who is your master? And what is his name? And of what country are you?" Judas says to him: "My Master is your Master and (the Master) of the whole world and the Lord of heaven and earth." Mazdai says to him: "What is his name?" Judas says to him: "**You are not able to hear his true name now at this time but the name that is given to him is Jesus the Messiah**." Mazdai says to him: "I have not been in haste to destroy you but I have had patience with you and you have added to your deeds and your sorceries are spoken of through the whole country. But I will do to you (so) that they shall accompany you and go along with you and that our country shall be relieved of you." Judas says to him: "These sorceries which you say shall accompany me, shall never fail from this place."

Commentary. **I am a slave**. See ch. 2. **give life**. Greek: "save", see ch. 10. **You are not able ... Messiah**. See ch. 48. **sorceries**. See ch. 16.

164

And when he had said these things, Mazdai was considering how he should give orders concerning him that he might die because he was **afraid of the great multitude** which was there. For many believed in our Lord, even (some) of the king's nobles. And Mazdai took Judas and went outside the city and there came with him a few soldiers with weapons. And people were thinking that Mazdai was wishing to learn (something) from him and they were standing and looking at him. And when they had gone about half a mile he delivered him **to (some)** of the soldiers who were with him and to one of the princes and said to them: "Go up on this mountain (and) stab him." And he turned to come (back) to the city.

Commentary. **afraid ... multitude**. Cf. Luke 20, 19; 22, 2 and Acts 5, 26 **to (some)**. Greek: "to four".

165

And people were running after Judas to rescue him but **the soldiers** were going on his right and **on his left** and were holding spears and that one of the princes was holding him by his hand and supporting him. And Judas said: "O the hidden mysteries which even to the (hour of) departure (from this world) are fulfilled in me! O the riches of the grace of him who does not let us feel the sufferings of the body! How they surround me with weapons and fight with me even to death! **But to One I am given up, for behold, one chief leads me and holds me by my hand in order that he may deliver me to One** whom I look for that I may receive him. And our Lord, because he is One, suffered (blows) at the hand of one."

Commentary. **the soldiers**. Greek: "two (soldiers)". **on his left**. Greek: "two ons his left." **But the One ... One**. Greek: "Four are they that cast me down for of four am I made and one is he that draws me for of one I am and to him I go. And this I now understand that my Lord and God Jesus Christ, being of one was pierced by four." In the Greek version the "hidden mysteries" are clear: Thomas was made out of four elements and he knows to belong to One. This corresponds with the four soldiers and the chief. The idea that man was formed out of four elements is well known in Jewish and christian literature, cf. Slav. Hen. 30, 13; Sibylline Oracles III 24–26, ed. Gauger–Kurfess 66–67: "... Gott ist's, der gebildet den vierbuchstabligen Adam"; Philo, *de somn.* I 15, see R. Meyer, "Hellenistisches in der rabbinischen Anthropologie", in: *Beitr. z. Wissensch. des A. u. N.T.* 22 1937, 122–128, see also Justin, *dial. c. Tr.* LXII 2; Firmicus Maternus, *de errore prof. rel.*, ed Ziegler 41; *Constitut. Apost.* VII XXXIV 6; *Apocr. Joh.* 55. 4–11. See F.C. Burkitt, *The Religion of the Manichees*, Cambridge 1925, 76, and H.H. Schaeder, "Bardesanes von Edessa in der Überlieferung der griech. u. syr. Kirche", in: *Zeitsch. f.d. Kirchengesch.* LI 1932, 21–74. The passion was also known to Manich. Ps. 142. 27–30: "The same thing also did Thomas endure on his cross (σταυρός). Four soldiers at once pierced him with the point of the lance (λόγχη). They surrounded him on four sides and made his blood flow ... How many mysteries did he perform. Many a sign did he fulfil." For Christ being "one", see Odes of Solomon 41. 15: "The Messiah in truth is one"; Ignatius, *ad Magn.* VII 2, see H.-W. Bartsch, "Gnostisches Gut und Gemeindetradition bei Ignatius von Antiochien", in: *Beitr. z. Förd. der Theol.* 44 1940, 9–23, and *Evang. Veritatis* 25. 10–15, ed. Robinson 47: "It is within Unity that each one will attain himself."

166

And when he had ascended the mountain, the place where they were about to stab Judas he said to those who were holding him: "Listen to me now at least when I am on the point of departing from the world and let not the **eyes of your hearts** be blinded nor your ears be deafened that you too should not hear. Believe in this God whom I preach and do not walk in your hardness of heart but walk in all the virtues that beseem the **freedom** and the glory of men and the life that is with God."

Commentary. **eyes of your heart**. See ch. 53. **freedom**. See ch. 120 and 121.

167

Judas says to Vizan: "Son of the earthly king Mazdai and servant of Jesus the Messiah permit the attendants to do the will of their king Mazdai. I will go (and) pray." And Vizan spoke to the soldiers and they let Judas go. And Judas went and was praying and saying thus: "**My**

Lord and my God and my **Hope** and my Saviour and my **Guide** and **Conductor** in all the lands which I have traversed in your name, be you with all your servants and guide me too that I may come to you. For to you I have committed my soul **and no man shall take it from your hands. Let not my sins hinder me. See, Lord, I fulfilled your will and became a slave for the sake of this freedom which I am receiving to-day. Do you, Lord Jesus, give (it) to me and fulfil it with me for I am in no doubt whatever regarding your truth and your love but for the sake of these who are standing (by) that they may hear, I speak before you.**"

Commentary. **My Lord and my God**. See ch. 19. **Hope**. See ch. 10. **Guide**. See ch. 10. **Conductor**. See ch. 10. **and became a slave ... freedom**. See ch. 2. **and no man ... speak before you**. Greek: "let not the publicans, οἱ τελῶναι, see me and let not the exactors, οἱ ἀπαιτηταῖ, accuse me falsely, συκοφαυτείτωσας. Let not the serpent, ὁ ὄφις, see me and let not the children of the dragon hiss at me, καὶ οἱ τοῦ δράκοντος παῖδες μη συριττέτωσαν. See ch. 148.

168

And when Judas had prayed thus he said to the soldiers: "Come, fulfil the will of him who sent you." **And the soldiers** came (and) struck him all together and he fell down and died. And the brothers were weeping all together. And they brought goodly garments and many **linen cloths** and buried Judas in the **sepulchre in which the ancient kings were buried**.

Commentary. **And the soldiers**. Greek: "and the four soldiers". **linen cloths**, ܟܬܢܐ, Greek: ὀθόνιας. The Syriac word is used for ὀθόνιον in the New Testament in syr p c s phil in Luke 24, 12; in syr p s phil in John 19, 40 and 20, 5; for σινδών in syr p s in Matth. 27, 59 and in syr p in Mark 15, 46 and for λίνον in syr phil in Matth. 12,20. **sepulchre ... buried**. Cf. Is. 53, 9.

169

And Sifur and Vizan would not go down to the city but were sitting there the whole day and they passed the night there also. And Judas appeared to them and said to them: "**I am not here**. Why are you sitting and watching me? I have ascended to my Lord and I have received what I was looking for and hoping for. But rise and go down hence, for yet a little while and you too shall be gathered to me." And Mazdai and his kinsman Karish brought Mygdonia and Tertia and afflicted them much but they would not yield to their wish. And Judas appeared to them and said to them: "Forget not, my daughters, Jesus our Lord, the Holy and the Living (One) and he will soon prepare for you your **rest** and your help." And when king Mazdai and his kinsman Karish saw that they would not be persuaded by them, they left them alone to walk according to their own will. And all the brothers who were there were assembling together and praying and **offering the (Eucharist) offering and breaking (bread)** because Judas had made Sifur a **priest** and Vizan a deacon on the mountain when he was going to die. And our Lord was helping them with his love and was increasing his faith by their means.

Commentary. **I am not here**. See Luke 24, 6. **rest**. See ch. 35. **offering ... (bread)**, ܟܚܡܐ ܡܚ ܩܝܒܐ ܡܚܢ, Greek: "and rejoiced in the grace of the Holy Spirit". See for "offering" ch. 50. **priest**, ܩܝܫܐ, Greek: πρεσβύτερος Cf. I Clem. 42, 4: κατὰ χώρας σῦν καὶ πόλεις κηρύσσοντες καθίστανον τὰς ἀπαρχὰς αὐτῶν δοκιμάταντες τῷ πνεύματι εἰς ἐπισκόπους καὶ διακόνους τῶν μελλόντων πιστέυειν. See J. Munck, "Discourse d'adieu dans le Nouveau Testament", in: *Mélanges ... Goguel* 155–170, esp. 165.

170

And it happened after a long time that one of the sons of king Mazdai had a devil and no man was able to bind him because he was very violent. And king Mazdai thought in his mind and said: "I will go (and) open the grave of Judas and take one of the bones of the apostle of God and will hang it upon my son and he will be healed." And Judas appeared to him in a vision and said to him: "You did not believe in one living, will you believe in one who, behold is dead? But do not fear. My Lord the Messiah will have mercy on you because of his clemency." And he did not find his bones for one of the brothers had taken them away secretly and conveyed them **to the West**. And king Mazdai took (some) of the **dust** of that spot where the bones of the apostle had lain and hung it on his son and said: "I believe in you my Lord Jesus now that he has left me who always troubles men that they may not see the light." And when he had hung (it) upon his son and had believed, he was healed. And he was united with the brothers. And king Mazdai was bowing his head beneath the hand of the priest Sifur and was entreating and begging of all the brothers that they should pray for him that he might find mercy with them before our Lord Jesus the Messiah in his kingdom which is for ever and ever. Amen

Here end the Acts of Judas Thomas the apostle of our Lord Jesus the Messiah who suffered martyrdom in the land of India by the hands of king Mazdai. Glory to the Father and the Son and to the Spirit of holiness, now and all times and for ever and ever. Amen.

Commentary. **to the West**. Greek: "to Mesopotamia, but manuscripts A K R U V: εἰς τὰ τῆς δύσεως μέρη. The legend is well known, cf. Ephrem, *Hymni dispersi*, in Lamy IV c. 703–704: *O Thoma, quaenam est prosopia tua adeo illustris evadas? Mercator attulit ossa tua, et pontifex solemnitatem tibi instituit atque rex templum aedificavit.* In *Chron. Edess.*, ed Hallier 103, XXXVIII is said: "Am 22 Abi des Jahres 705 (*scil.* 394) brachte man den Sarkophag (γλωσσόκομον) des Apostels Mari Thomas in seinen grossen Tempel, in den Tagen des Bischofs Mari Kune" (which means the 22nd of August 394). See also Michael Syrus, ed. Chabot T. I, fasc. II, Paris 1900, 147: "Thomas de la tribu de Juda, prêcha aux Parthes et aux Mèdes et fut couronné [du martyre] à Calamina, ville de l'Inde. Son corps fut rapporté à Edesse". Also in Socrates, *hist. eccles.* IV 18 and Sozomenus, *hist. eccles.* VI 18. See for other traditions P. Devos, "Le miracle posthume de Saint Thomas l'apôtre", in: *Anal. Bolland.* LXVI 1948, 231–275, and U. Monneret der Villard, "La Fiera di Batne et la Traslazione di S. Thomaso a Edessa", in: *Rendic. dell' Academ. naz. dei Lincei*, ser. VIII, vol. VI 1951, 77–104. **dust**. Cf. Ephrem, *hymni dispersi* VI, Lamy c. 703–704: *In vita tua fecisti signa quae post obitun tuum continuasti; cum labore in una regione sanitatem reddebas, nunc sine labore ubique sanas.*

INDEX

Biblical Passages

Euch   215 Ch 133